Ovillers Military Cemetery then and now

The Thiepval Memorial to the Missing of the Somme   *J Kerr*

WHERE ARE THE BOYS?

The First Day of the Battle of the Somme

including ten walks and drives

Front cover: Thiepval Memorial   J Kerr
Back cover: Martinsart British Cemetery

Where are the Boys? is dedicated to all those who died
on 1st July 1916 in the Somme

Published by Dene House Publishing
Dene House, Walton, Warwick, CV35 9HX
www.meetatdawnunarmed.co.uk

Designed by Ruth Smith, Damson Creative Ltd.
www.damsoncreative.co.uk

Printed and bound in Slovenia on behalf of Latitude Press Ltd.
www.latitudepress.co.uk

ISBN 978-0-9561820-4-3

Opposite page:
Row of soldiers of the Manchester Regiment in Dantzig Alley British Cemetery

WHERE ARE THE BOYS?

The First Day of the Battle of the Somme

including ten walks and drives

by

Andrew Hamilton
and
Alan Reed

*Colour photographs by
Andrew Hamilton unless
otherwise acknowledged*

The Authors

Andrew Hamilton (left) at the unveiling of the 'Football' Memorial at Plugstreet Wood in Belgium, December 2014

Andrew Hamilton retired in 1989 from teaching History at schools in Hereford and Worcester. He was responsible for the restoration of a watermill to full working order in Warwickshire and managed it as a popular tourist attraction. He started Dene House Publishing in 2009 with the publication of the well-received *Meet at Dawn, Unarmed*, a commentary on his grandfather Robert Hamilton's diary of his experiences with the Royal Warwicks in 1914 and his part in the Christmas Truce at St. Yvon in Belgium. There was much TV, radio and newspaper interest for the centenary in 2014 and the diary was used for the Royal Shakespeare's production of 'The Christmas Truce'.

Alan Reed with Rifleman William McFadzean's VC medal

Alan Reed retired from full-time teaching in Cheshire in 1996 to concentrate on guiding school and adult groups on the Western Front. He gives numerous talks on various aspects of the Great War. His interest was inspired by his father who worked for the Commonwealth War Graves Commission in northern France. A fluent French speaker, his vast knowledge of the battlefield sites of France and Belgium has been invaluable in the research and planning for the four publications. He has been a consultant for and appeared in several BBC's 'Songs of Praise' programmes.

REVIEWS *of publications by Andrew Hamilton and Alan Reed:*

Meet at Dawn, Unarmed: Captain Robert Hamilton's account of trench warfare and the Christmas Truce in 1914

It is quite magnificent, all the more so because of the many illustrations synthesised into the text. It is more than usually interesting for a variety of reasons, amongst them the occasional appearances of both B.L. Montgomery and Bruce Bairnsfather, and, of course, for another view of the Christmas Truce… It is a really stupendous effort.
Professor Richard Holmes

Stolen Lives: Individual Tragedies of the Great War

They have raised the standard, for it is a product that puts most recent Great War titles to shame in terms of quality of materials and production ... Each story is deeply researched, not only in terms of the individual's biography but the historical context in which they died. They make for absorbing and sobering reading. It is a great effort that had taken several years in the compilation and a very good read. Recommended.
Chris Baker 'Long, Long Trail' website

The authors' previous work, *Meet at Dawn, Unarmed* may be known to members of the WFA. I therefore expected another high quality volume and I was not disappointed… I can recommend this book to those having a casual interest in the period but also to more serious students of the conflict.
Stand To! No. 101 September 2014   Western Front Association

We Good, We No Shoot: The Christmas Truce at Plugstreet Wood in 1914
This book is a joy to read and its very fascination hides the fact that this is also a serious academic study of an extraordinary event.   *Major Tonie and Mrs Valmai Holt*

Contents

Maps

All maps by George Sayell except 'The Somme 1916' by Alan Reed

FOREWORD

A few years ago, when in the Somme, I visited New Munich Trench British Cemetery, just above Beaumont, for the first time. It is one of the smaller Somme cemeteries, with less than 150 graves. Looking in the visitors' book before leaving, I noticed that there were nine filled pages before the half-filled one I was about to sign. These pages recorded visits spanning the previous nineteen years. Not every visitor would have signed the register, but in 1985 no one at all signed it and in 1986, the 70th anniversary of the Somme battles, only one visit was recorded. It was a lonely place, as was much of the Somme in those days.

Things are different now and in many ways, I think they are better. The increase in the number of companies providing guided battlefield tours has brought a corresponding increase in the number of visitors to these important sites, leading to improved roads, access, information and accommodation. These improvements have made life easier also for those making their own way to the Somme to drive or walk around the battlefield sites at their own pace. The Somme is full of rewarding sites to visit for those who have the time and their own transport and they illustrate so many aspects of what happened here in 1916, especially on the first day - 1st July. They illustrate tragedy, bravery, suffering, endurance, fear, errors, sacrifice and the truly noble behaviour of ordinary people caught up in extraordinary times.

So many wonderful places to visit. The problem - especially if you are travelling without a guide is knowing where they all are and learning what happened at each one. This is where *Where are the Boys?* comes in.

There are many excellent books on the terrible first day of the battle. Some cover what happened, some what went wrong, some how to get from place to place, some aimed at the car driver and some at the walker. Some consider the events of 1st July from the viewpoints of specific units, some from the experiences of individuals while yet others concentrate on particular parts of the attack. The authors of *Where are the Boys?* set themselves the task of encompassing all these aspects, doing so for the whole of the 1st July attack line from Montauban in the south to Serre in the north and also the diversionary attack at Gommecourt further north.

So in this one book, the reader will find an informative account of the planning of the battle, the physical preparations which had to be made, and, for those who were about to take part, the mental preparations, too, given in their own words, generals and privates alike. To illustrate how events unfolded in the assaults of the key objectives on the day, 13 men have been chosen as focal points for the consideration of their parts of the attack - some well-known and some newly-researched, casualties and survivors. The later sections of the book provide details, down to Division and Battalion level, of where each assaulting unit was, what the objectives were and what happened on the day in terms of successes, failures and casualties - the statistic for which 1st July 1916 is mostly remembered. For those tracing the actions of relatives, therefore, the authors have done most of the work for you already.

Finally, thanks to the very well-researched walks and driving tours, visitors can see for themselves the topography of each sector, identify where the trench-lines were and in many places, literally walk in the footsteps of the soldiers who set off across No-Man's Land on 1st July 1916.

I have been reading about the Somme for most of my life, visiting the area for something like twenty-five years, and guiding people around the battlefields for nearly twenty, but *Where are the Boys?* has introduced me to people, ideas, places and events which were new to me. I think it will become an important and valuable addition to the "battlefield library" for new and established visitors alike.

Tom Morgan   Hellfire Corner Great War Web-Pages www.hellfirecorner.co.uk
(Tom Morgan was one of the first to dedicate a website to the Great War)

View from the Thiepval Memorial - the 16/ Northumberland Fusiliers (Newcastle Commercials)
attacked uphill from behind the trees   J. Kerr

I

'That Awful Day'

The first day of the Battle of the Somme, 1st July 1916, was described by Major Alfred Plackett of the 12/ York and Lancaster (Sheffield City Battalion) as 'that awful day'. Captain James Jack served on the Somme with the 2/ Cameronians and recalled that it was 'one of the worst days I have experienced' and Lance-Corporal Thomas Higgins, 1/ 5 North Staffs, was adamant that 'I shall never forget that day if I live to be a hundred.' For a 'soldier journalist' writing in the Sheffield Telegraph a year after the event, 'the date is too full of tragedy ever to be forgotten.'

Many of the inscriptions on 1st July graves in the Somme express the reasons for enlisting- this is in Lonsdale Cemetery

It was the first day of a series of 12 battles in the Somme region that lasted until 18th November 1916. It was known at the time as the Battle of Albert - the main town behind the British front line. A Royal Flying Corps pilot, Cecil Lewis, flew over the battlefield during the day, hoping to report positive news of progress by British troops along the 18 mile front. He expressed gratitude in his memoirs that he had been spared the 'murder' that took place several thousand feet below during an offensive that he considered 'senseless, brutal and ignoble'.

1st July 1916 was the worst catastrophe in British military history; most of the 58,000 casualties were sustained in the first minutes after Zero Hour at 7.30 a.m. The death toll was impossible for the participants to comprehend in the immediate aftermath of the Battle when darkness fell. The Sheffield 'Pals' started their assault with 750 men. Later that evening their CO, Major Plackett, reported that 'only four officers and 31 men remained of our splendid battalion.'

As news of the sheer weight of numbers of dead and wounded reached the Home Front, there was incredulity at what had happened and unsurprisingly, a number of inscriptions on graves in the Somme articulated the hope that 'one day we may understand'. To many it was incongruous that so many men had been slaughtered after volunteering willingly and patriotically to serve their King and Country. University lecturer Captain Alfred Bland, 22/ Manchesters (7th Manchester Pals), had enlisted because of a fiercely patriotic desire to serve his King and Country: 'Think of the cause, the cause, It is England … Hardship be damned! It's a long blaze of glory.' He was killed on 1st July and is buried in Dantzig Alley Military Cemetery. (Dantzig is the IWGC incorrect spelling.)

King George V visited a number of the British cemeteries after the War in 1922. He was struck by the mind numbing, serried ranks of graves and was moved to comment:

King George V on a tour of the British Cemeteries with Rudyard Kipling NPG X36220

The grave of 2nd Lieutenant Francis Hicking in Fricourt New Military Cemetery

'In the course of my pilgrimage, I have many times asked myself whether there can be more potent advocates of peace on earth, through the years to come than this massed multitude of silent witnesses to the desolation of war.'

During one of our visits to the Somme in the autumn of 2015, we stumbled on one such 'silent witness' in Fricourt New Military Cemetery where, on 1st July, 134 soldiers of the 10/ West Yorks were mown down by machine-gun fire. They were buried virtually where they fell, in four mass graves. Only later were they allocated individual graves. There is so much to look for and see in such a cemetery: battalion badges, the ages and ranks of those who fell, inscriptions on their graves - many of them heart-rendingly sad, the Cross of Sacrifice and the beauty of the seasonal array of flowers and roses, and the beautifully tended grass lawns and pathways. As we wandered round, our attention was caught by something different - a photograph, propped up against the gravestone of 2nd Lieutenant Francis Hicking, of a junior school cricket team outside a small Victorian wooden pavilion. Serious and unsmiling, the 12 and 13 year old boys looked out at us, immaculately attired in their 'uniform' of long sleeved shirts, trousers, boots and hooped caps. Which boy, we wondered, was Francis Joseph Hicking of the 10/ West Yorks, a mere 19 years old when he was killed? Which school were they representing and how many other boys caught on camera would die in the service of their country?

Those in group photographs are often encouraged to smile and make, at least, a token effort at looking happy - but not here. There is something rather eerie and portentous about the photograph - in a few years' time the small cricketers' white uniform would be exchanged for khaki and the cricket ball replaced by the grenade.

We found that Francis Hicking was one of six of the boys in the photograph who later died in the Great War. He was born on 20th May 1897 - his parents Joseph and Kate were grocers and wine merchants, firstly at Ruddington in Nottinghamshire and later in prosperous Cheltenham. They sent Francis away to board at Bramcote School in Scarborough, Yorkshire where he loved playing cricket and football despite being cruelly castigated by a critical schoolmaster: 'Kicking jolly bad: no dash: turning his back and funking …' He left Bramcote at 13 to attend Uppingham School and within a year of leaving there had volunteered to join the war effort.

It is extraordinary to think of a mere 19 year old, with scarcely any experience of life, arriving on the Somme, in charge of a platoon of about 50 men, many considerably older than himself and then at 7.30 a.m. on 1st July leading them into a hail of machine-gun fire

Photograph of Bramcote School Cricket XI in 1907, Francis Hicking is back row far left. Six of the boys in the photograph died in the Great War

without, one suspects, any outward signs of 'funk', as he strove to set an example to his men. His brother George, three years his senior, was a lieutenant in 8/ York and Lancaster and he too died on the same day, not far from where Francis fell.

The Hickings' parents received the news of George's death fairly soon but they did not learn of Francis's fate for an agonising two weeks. It is impossible to imagine the suffering, faced for the rest of their lives, by the parents of Francis and George Hicking and those of the other five boys in the photograph.

At least Joseph and Kate Hicking had Francis's grave to help the grieving process. But for families of over 12,000 soldiers killed on 1st July 1916, there was no such tangible memorial to their loved ones, just an inscribed name on the panels of the Thiepval Memorial to the 'Missing of the Somme'. On its panels are 72,255 names of British soldiers who died on the Somme with no known grave, one of which is that of George Hicking.

The 12,398 names on the Thiepval Memorial of those who fell on 1st July emphasise the brutality and destructiveness of the fighting and the nature of the strategy employed. It is a statistic that begs questions about the tactics utilised by the main architects of the offensive - Commander-in-Chief of the British Army, General Sir Douglas Haig and General Sir Henry Rawlinson of the Fourth Army which was involved in all the assaults apart from the attack at Gommecourt in the north by General Allenby's Third Army.

We examine the Generals' tactics in Chapter VI and attempt to determine the extent to which they and their staff were culpable for the massive losses and whether the criticism aimed at them in the ensuing years was justified. On the eve of the Battle, troops were told by their superiors that 'it would be a walkover' and that they would cross No Man's Land 'as if on parade'. Within minutes that confidence had been shattered as bodies lay in heaps on the battlefield. We attempt to establish why 1st July 1916 should have ended in such woeful tragedy.

British Mills Bomb still live one hundred years on at Hawthorn Ridge Cemetery No.1

The Somme battlefield has, after 100 years, reverted to its pre-1914 pastoral idyll. The villages and church spires that nestle on the gently rolling hills were once in the bitterly fought-over front line. Agricultural life continues slowly in time-honoured fashion; farming villages are still surrounded in summer by wheat and sugar beet fields and visible hints of the countryside's dark past are the beautifully kept cemeteries, and unexploded shells and grenades left on the side of roads and tracks, awaiting removal by relevant experts. The chalky soil is very different from the clay in Flanders where in 1917 after torrential rain soldiers drowned in the Passchendaele mud. No one enjoyed digging trenches but given the choice most preferred doing so in the Somme, except at Gommecourt where, just before 1st July, some soldiers were knee deep in cloying mud.

John Buchan, author and historian of the War, described the river Ancre, a tributary of the Somme, before the fighting as it meandered through the battlefield, as the kind of stream 'that may be found in Wiltshire with good trout in its pools.' On either side of the river 'on a hot midsummer day the slopes are ablaze with yellow mustard, red poppies and blue sunflowers.' He could indeed have been describing the gentle, undulating landscape typical of Sussex or Warwickshire.

Another celebrated author, John Masefield, visited the Somme before the end of the offensive in November and the picture he paints of the area offers a stark contrast. He describes Thiepval Wood as 'shattered, burnt, dead, and desolate' and the slope up to the strongest of the German fortifications, the Schwaben Redoubt, as being scarred by 'the usual black enemy wire, much tossed and bunched by our shells, covering a tumbled, chalky and filthy parapet … near the road and up the slope to the enemy the ground is littered with the relics of our charges, mouldy packs, old shattered scabbards,

Gordon Cemetery

rifles, bayonets, helmets curled, torn, rolled and starred, clips of cartridges.' Most of the bodies had by then been removed from the battlefield but he commented on the 'very many graves' with wooden crosses dotted around No Man's Land, many of which might have been demolished by shells at a later date.

Cemetery 'Crosses of Sacrifice' now punctuate the Somme landscape. Bodies were recovered and when the War ended, the Imperial War Graves Commission, founded in

1917, organised burials in specially created cemeteries designed mainly by Sir Herbert Baker, Sir Reginald Blomfield and Sir Edwin Lutyens. The cross of the Gordon Cemetery can be seen from the site of the German front line; the cemetery was started by the 2/ Gordon Highlanders who buried some of their 1st July dead after their successful attack on Mametz, in what had been a support trench.

A few hundred yards away, the final resting place for soldiers of the 8 and 9/ Devons was in a section of their front line trench on the edge of Mansel Copse. Both cemeteries are moving reminders of the losses that befell three battalions as they attacked south of the fortified village of Mametz. Other ranks and officers were buried together in the Devonshire Cemetery regardless of rank: the poet Lieutenant William Hodgson was buried near his batman. Not far from their graves, is that of Captain D.L. Martin who had tried to convince his superiors, with the aid of a plasticine model he had created when on leave, that when 'going over the top' his men would be at the mercy of a machine-gun positioned at 'The Shrine' in Mametz Civilian Cemetery. His prediction proved depressingly accurate.

Grave of Captain D.L. Martin in Devonshire Cemetery

Few of the soldiers buried in the Somme cemeteries or whose names are to be found on the Thiepval Memorial were the 'regular' professionals who had played their part in the opening campaigns of 1914 at Mons, in the Marne, the Aisne and in 1915 at Neuve Chapelle. The first day of the Somme was fought in the main by men raised by Lord Kitchener's New Army of more than 1,100,000 volunteers; the Minister for War had recognised that the British Expeditionary Force, witheringly described by Kaiser Wilhelm as a 'contemptible little army' would have to be augmented - even he was taken aback by the alacrity with which men joined up for an outfit that he intended should not play its part in a major offensive until 1917.

'Duty' and patriotism were important motivating factors. In January 1915 the Co-operative Society in Lincoln was grateful that all sectors of society were playing their part in bringing the War to a close: 'England's call has been met with a magnificent response from all classes and conditions of people: "cooks' sons", and "dukes' sons", are comrades in arms fighting the common foe … as a society we are immensely proud of them, we know they will do their duty, and play their part well, and thus do something to bring this terrible war to an end.'

At Zero Hour on 1st July, 7.30 a.m., 63 battalions attacked the German first and second lines; 15 were of 'Regulars', 9 were 'Territorial' Battalions of trained volunteers, and more than their combined total were the 39 New Army 'Service' Battalions. Hundreds of thousands had flocked to recruiting stations throughout the country in a wave of patriotic fervour to fight for their King and Country inspired by the campaign master-minded by Lord Kitchener. Men from all walks of life joined up together - many 'Pals' Battalions were formed in Britain's industrial heartlands: Accrington, Barnsley, Birmingham, Durham, Glasgow, Leeds, Manchester and Sheffield to name but a few.

Private William Millar

2nd Liverpool Pals - a clerk, a cabinet maker and a broker, buried in Dantzig Alley British Cemetery

Private Harry Zodickson

Captain Charles Brockbank

In many Kitchener New Army Battalions there was an interesting social mix. The 18/ King's (2nd Liverpool Pals) included Private William Millar, a clerk at a Liverpool shipping company, Private Harry Zodickson, a cabinet maker and one of nine children from a family of Jewish immigrants who fled Russian pogroms and Captain Charles Brockbank, educated at Malvern College, was a partner in his father's firm of West African produce brokers. They are all buried in Dantzig Alley British Cemetery.

New Army Battalions contained a variety of volunteers: the 16/ Middlesex, consisted of mostly former public school boys and was dubbed the 'Public Schools Battalion'; the 10/ Lincolns known as the Grimsby Chums, were predominantly former pupils of the town's Wintringham Grammar School and the 17 and 23/ Middlesex attracted large numbers of professional football players and were described as the 'Football Battalions'; the 16/ Royal Scots Battalion included players, directors and supporters of Edinburgh's Heart of Midlothian Football Club. Four battalions of the 92nd Brigade in the 31st Division were raised in Hull and comprised 'Commercials', 'Tradesmen', 'Sportsmen' and endearingly, 'T'Others'.

The grave of Harold Goodwin, 16/ Middlesex (Public Schools) in Hawthorn Ridge Cemetery No. 1

It took nearly two years to train men from all walks of life to a basic level of military competence; the 'Big Push' on the Somme was the first time, after many practice sessions against 'dummy' trenches, that officers and men would go into battle against a real enemy. It was understandable that General Rawlinson, in particular, should have been concerned by their inexperience and his battle plans took their 'rawness' into account. For the young officers, fresh from public schools and universities, with limited military experience and in many cases without a hunger for war, huge responsibilities were thrust on their shoulders.

Eton College lost 1,157 old boys during the Great War, Charterhouse School in Surrey 695, 10 of whom died on 1st July including 25 year old Harold Goodwin, son of Albert Goodwin, a well-known and prolific water colour artist. Harold was a 2nd lieutenant in the 16/ Middlesex and was killed during the attack on Hawthorn Ridge. His father wrote wearily in 1915 that 'we have become accustomed to being under this great shadow' and despite having had 'little fears' about his son's future, in 1916 his bleak diary entry was that 'Harold is at rest'. He is buried in the Hawthorn Ridge Cemetery No.1.

Ex Charterhouse pupil Captain G.H. Scott (Queen's Royal West Surreys) buried in Dantzig Alley British Cemetery

Three 'Grimsby Chums', old boys from Wintringham Grammar School, Grimsby - Lieutenant Eason, Sergeant Oldroyd (both in Gordon Dump Cemetery) and Private Hall (Ovillers Military Cemetery)

A different type of school, Wintringham Grammar in Grimsby, provided the backbone of the 10/ Lincolns, the only volunteer battalion to be known as 'Chums'. The school's headmaster encouraged a number of old boys to join the Battalion which would be severely affected on 1st July, sustaining 502 casualties – 15 officers and 487 other ranks. 14 Wintringham old boys were killed on the day.

In the early months of recruitment, hundreds of boys under the legal age of 18 joined up. So great was the need to bolster numbers that a collective blind-eye was turned towards the problem- providing the youngsters were fit and strong enough they remained in the Army. After two years of war, there were still under age soldiers taking part who had lied initially about their age - none more so than Reginald St. John Beardsworth Battersby, who received his commission as a 2nd Lieutenant in May 1915 at the extraordinary age of 15 years and 2 months. He led a platoon of 11/ East Lancs (Accrington Pals) on 1st July aged 16 and 4 months and was wounded in the attack on Serre. In 1917 he lost a leg in the Somme but continued his war efforts in the RE record office in London. After the War he became a vicar. Not so fortunate to survive was Private Henry (Harry) Woodward, the only son of Mrs. Florence Woodward, who volunteered in Birmingham for the Royal Warwickshire Regiment and was killed during the 1/ 6 Royal Warwicks' attack on the Redan Ridge. He was likely to have been the youngest to fall on that day - a mere 15 years old. According to Richard van Emden in *Boy Soldiers of the Great War* at least 118 boys aged 17 or under died on 1st July 1916.

When Martin Middlebrook wrote his ground-breaking 1st July 1916 *The First Day on the Somme* in 1971, he noted that there were few visitors to the Somme battlefields. That has changed dramatically – thousands now visit the Thiepval Memorial, the Ulster Tower Memorial to the 36th (Ulster) Division, the massive Lochnagar crater and the cemeteries at Serre. For those interested in a thorough exploration of the 18 mile front on 1st July 1916, we have devised ten walks in Chapter IX that guide you backwards and forwards across No Man's Land and enable you to follow the action of 13 full Divisional attacks on the Germans' main fortified positions from Montauban in the south to Gommecourt in the north. We guide you to cemeteries to visit the graves of those we mention in the book. You will see the variance in width of No Man's

No Man's Land in places was only 80 yards wide, here between photographer and author at Bois Français

Land, at its greatest 800 yards and at its most narrow, a mere 50 yards. We take you to the mine craters at Hawthorn Ridge, the Tambour near Fricourt, and the breath-taking Lochnagar crater at La Boisselle. The tour includes visits to villages fortified by the Germans, fortresses like the Schwaben and Leipzig Redoubts, and the sites where flame projectors were fired, footballs kicked and VCs won.

G/8673 PRIVATE
C. D. DAVIS
MIDDLESEX REGIMENT
1ST JULY 1916 AGE 16

11173 PRIVATE
J. MAYHEW
THE QUEEN'S
1ST JULY 1916

3288 PRIVATE
R. O. CONMY
WEST YORKSHIRE REGIMENT
4TH JULY 1916 AGE 16

8763 PRIVATE
R. POWER
ROYAL IRISH RIFLES
1ST JULY 1916 AGE 16

1784 PRIVATE
HORACE ILES
WEST YORKSHIRE REGIMENT
1ST JULY 1916 AGE 16

18452 PRIVATE
J. HASTON
K.O. SCOTTISH BORDERERS
1ST JULY 1916 AGE 16

68157 GUNNER
LIONEL REGINALD WILLS
ROYAL GARRISON ARTILLERY
1ST JULY 1916

19773 PRIVATE
A. BARKER
EAST YORKSHIRE REGIMENT
1ST JULY 1916 AGE 16

4748 PRIVATE
J. J. PERKINS
ROYAL WARWICKSHIRE REGT
1ST JULY 1916 AGE 16

23433 PRIVATE
C. P. TEMPEST
YORKSHIRE REGIMENT
1ST JULY 1916 AGE 16

MOONEY. J.
MOORES. J.
MORGAN. W.
MORRIS. E. A.
MORRIS. K.
MORRIS. W.

You can walk in the trench systems at the Newfoundland Memorial Park, visit Sheffield Memorial Park and the nearby cemeteries and discover the many memorials to battalions and divisions, dotted round the Somme. Let us not forget the Germans who fell and their cemetery at Fricourt is well worth a visit; it is moving and very different from a typical British cemetery.

If you do not wish to walk, you can pick and choose locations to visit from the car itineraries using the satellite navigation coordinates.

In Chapter III the events of 'that awful day' are seen from the perspective of ten soldiers who took part in the divisional attacks, as well as a chaplain who played a vital role in helping with the wounded and identifying bodies and organising their burial. We examine how the day unfolded for two Generals, one responsible for the 46th (North Midland) Division's attack on Gommecourt and the General who masterminded the Fourth Army's attack between Serre and Montauban.

The detail of what happened to each battalion, division and corps on 1st July can be found in Chapter VIII where you can explore how each of the 172 battalions were involved - if and when they went into No Man's Land, how far they reached, the problems they faced and the casualties suffered. It is virtually impossible to be accurate with any degree of confidence over casualty numbers as few figures tally. We feel, however, that the numbers of deaths taken from the Commonwealth War Graves Commission's records are reasonably accurate so for each battalion we have given the number of deaths of officers, other ranks and the numbers of soldiers with no known grave recorded on the Thiepval Memorial for 1st July. Where there is sufficient evidence we include the numbers of casualties. We hope you will find interesting snippets in this chapter about, among other things, the heroics of VCs, individual stories of bravery, personal recollections of interest and examples of successes, admittedly limited and blunders which were not.

In *Where are the Boys?* the build up to 'Z' Day and the events of 1st July are seen through the eyes of those from many ranks who were involved: diaries, letters and military reports tell their stories of the most extraordinary day in Britain's military history and one that has provoked intense debate about how such a catastrophe could have happened and whether the numbers of casualties could have been reduced by the pursuit of different tactics.

Opposite page 16 year olds who died on 1st July 1916

A. Barker, Fricourt New Military **R. Conmy**, Daours Communal Extension (died 4th July of wounds) **C. Davis**, Ovillers Military **J. Haston**, Knightsbridge **H. Iles**, Serre Road No.1 **J. Mayhew**, Péronne Road **W. Morgan**, Beaumont Hamel Memorial **J. Perkins**, Sucrerie Military **R. Power**, Ovillers Military **C. Tempest**, Dantzig Alley British **R. Wills**, Bertrancourt Military

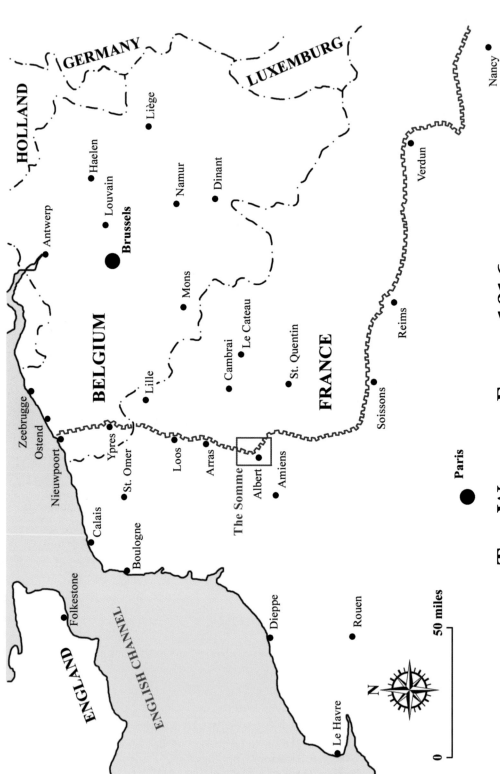

THE WESTERN FRONT 1916

© George Sayell

12

II

1st July and the Build-up...in brief

- General Sir Douglas Haig replaced Sir John French as Commander-in-Chief of the British Expeditionary Force on 19th December 1915
- Haig appointed Sir Henry Rawlinson as Fourth Army Commander on 24th January 1916
- Lord Kitchener's New Army of over one million Pals volunteers received training in 1914 and 1915 and most sailed to France in January 1916
- The pivotal moment was 21st February 1916 when German General Erich von Falkenhayn attacked Verdun, drawing French divisions away from the Somme
- The British became the major player on the Somme supported by only five rather than the originally intended 40 French Divisions. Haig worked with Generals Joffre, Foch and Fayolle
- By June 1916, the British Expeditionary Force was one million strong - the force in the Somme was 660,000 with 400,000 ear-marked for the 'Big Push'
- Preparations for the 'Big Push' on the German front took place throughout June - training and practice on 'dummy' trenches were held behind the lines
- The British attack was to take place along an 18 mile front from Montauban in the south east to Gommecourt in the north
- The British were faced by five German Divisions of General Fritz von Below's Second Army
- Intense bombardment of German lines started on 24th June with a view to 'Z' Day being on 29th June. It is estimated that the Germans sustained 10,000 casualties caused by British shelling prior to 1st July
- Thundery rain resulted in the postponement of the assault for two days. 'Z' Day would now be 1st July
- The final bombardment was watched by General Rawlinson from 'The Grandstand' near Dernancourt, south west of Albert which commanded a view of much of the front
- 19 mines were laid - the biggest explosions were at Hawthorn Ridge and La Boisselle (the Lochnagar Crater)
- Zero Hour was 7.30 a.m. In the first wave 66,000 men went over the top
- The German held villages under attack- Montauban, Mametz, Fricourt, La Boisselle, Ovillers, Thiepval, Beaumont, Serre and Gommecourt were the main objectives
- Units taking part: Third and Fourth Armies:

Corps:	6
Divisions:	13 fully used and 3 partially
Brigades:	39 fully used and 4 partially
Battalions:	New Army (Kitchener volunteers): 94 (55%)
	Regulars (professional soldiers): 47 (27%)
	Territorials (trained volunteers): 31 (18%)

Some of the 39,000 wounded - at Mametz   *IWM   Q000815*

A number of the British do not look too unhappy at having been captured

German prisoners some being used as stretcher-bearers

- The regiments with the most battalions were: Northumberland Fusiliers - 14, West Yorkshire and Royal Irish Rifles 10 each and Manchester and London 9 each

- British casualties - approximately 19,000 were killed or died of wounds, 39,000 wounded and over 600 taken prisoner. The number of German prisoners captured on the day by the British and the French was over 4,000. Numbers of German casualties are estimated at between 10 - 12,000

- 39 battalions had losses of over 500. The 10/ West Yorks at Fricourt sustained the highest number with 772

- 3 out of 4 officers were casualties

- Along the 1st July front line, there is one German cemetery and 49 British cemeteries

- The main memorial is at Thiepval on which there are 72,000 names of those with no known grave

- 14 German Regiments defended their lines – a regiment comprised 3 battalions of 1,000 men each

THE SOMME 1916

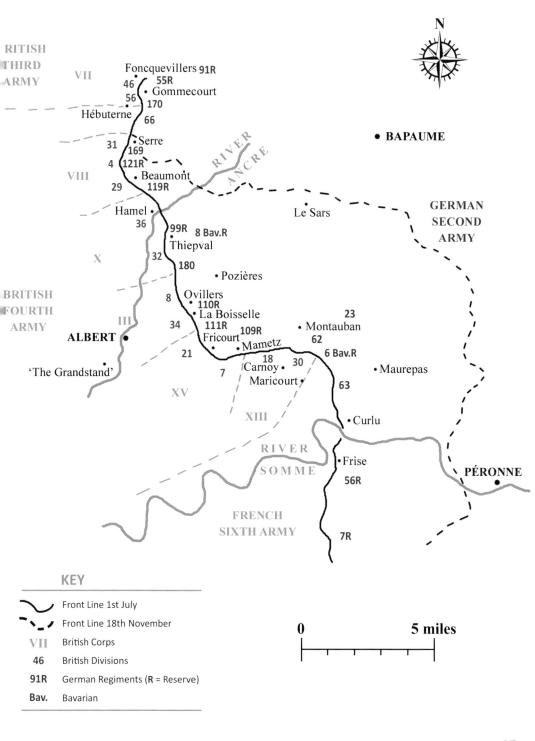

N

RITISH
THIRD
ARMY

VII

Foncquevillers **91R**
46 **55R**
• Gommecourt
56 **170**
Hébuterne 66

• Serre
31 **169**
4 **121R**
29 • Beaumont
119R

VIII

Hamel •
36

X

32 **99R**
Thiepval **8 Bav.R**

180

• Pozières

8 Ovillers
• **110R**
• La Boisselle
34 **111R**
Fricourt **109R**
21 • Mametz
7 **18** **30**
Carnoy •
Maricourt •

III

ALBERT •

'The Grandstand'

XV

XIII

RIVER
SOMME

FRENCH
SIXTH ARMY

• BAPAUME

• Le Sars

GERMAN
SECOND
ARMY

23
• Montauban
62
6 Bav.R

• Maurepas
63

• Curlu

• Frise
56R

PÉRONNE •

7R

BRITISH
FOURTH
ARMY

RIVER
ANCRE

KEY

〜 Front Line 1st July

‑ ‑ ‑ Front Line 18th November

VII British Corps

46 British Divisions

91R German Regiments (**R** = Reserve)

Bav. Bavarian

0   **5 miles**

'Zero Hour'
Individual Experiences of
1st July

1. General Sir Henry Rawlinson
2. Private Arthur Seanor
3. Captain 'Billie' Nevill
4. Lieutenant Roy Mellor
5. Lieutenant Robert Gilson
6. Lieutenant-Colonel Edwin Sandys
7. Sergeant James Turnbull VC
8. Lieutenant-Colonel Frank Crozier
9. Private 'Jim' Stacey
10. Sergeant Arthur Cook
11. 2nd Lieutenant Kenneth Perkin
12. The Rev. Julian Bickersteth
13. Major-General Edward Stuart-Wortley

Gommecourt

Serre

Beaumont

RIVER ANCRE

KEY

〜 Front Line 1st July 1916

Thiepval

Ovillers

La Boisselle

Montauban

ALBERT

Fricourt

Mametz

'The Grandstand'

0   5 miles

General Sir Henry Rawlinson Bt. GCB, GCSI, GCVO, KCMG

Commander of the Fourth Army

'We have done all that we can, and the rest is in the hands of the Bon Dieu'

General Rawlinson recorded in his diary that on the morning of 1st July 1916 'I was at my observation post at 6.30.' He had travelled by car from his headquarters at Querrieu to a location he described as the 'Grandstand', south west of Albert. John Buchan, wrote that it offered 'a singular view'- it was indeed a panoramic vista of most of the front line manned by Rawlinson's Fourth Army; Serre to the north would have been out of sight but he hoped to catch the action from Thiepval in the north to Montauban in the east. He was in position to witness an

General Sir Henry Rawlinson at his Querrieu HQ
IWM Q 004031

assault that he hoped would result in a major breakthrough in the war effort, the culmination of months of planning and organisation. His view would have been limited; most of the front line was shrouded by an early morning mist and viewing was hampered by the smoke and debris from the British bombardment which had intensified at 6.25 a.m. According to Sir James Edmonds, the Official War Historian, Rawlinson was back in his office at Querrieu château (which in his diary he insisted on spelling Querrieux) by 8.00 a.m. where 'he remained the whole day … in direct and private telephone communication with his Corps commanders.' It is likely that he had stayed on at the 'Grandstand' to see and hear the Hawthorn Ridge mine explode at 7.20 a.m. and eight minutes later subsequent explosions, the most notable of which was the Lochnagar mine at La Boisselle. Influenced perhaps by the monstrous crescendo of noise, his initial feeling was that soon after 7.30 a.m. 'all the front line trenches had been captured easily.' It would not be long before the reality of what had, or more to the point, what had not happened, would begin to dawn - that most of the German artillery and machine-guns had survived the intense week-long bombardment and had responded with a vengeance.

General Sir Henry Rawlinson was appointed to the command of Fourth Army on 24th January 1916 by Commander-in-Chief of the British Army, General Sir Douglas Haig who had replaced Sir John French on 19th December 1915. It was, Rawlinson believed, a privilege as 'it is not the lot of many men to command an army of over half a million men.' His was a conventional path to one of the top military posts. He was educated at Eton College, after which he attended the Royal Military College at Sandhurst and he came to notice as a soldier of ability and vision in the Sudan in 1898 when he served under Lord Kitchener; he benefited greatly from the experience of fighting the Boers alongside Lord Roberts in 1899 and was promoted to lieutenant-colonel of the Coldstream Guards. He became a full colonel in 1903 and by 1910 had taken command of the 3rd Division. At the outbreak of war in 1914 he was commanding 4th Division and on 4th October was promoted to temporary lieutenant-general in charge of IV Corps which was sent out to help the Belgians' defence of Antwerp. During 1915 he led the Corps in the major battles - at Neuve Chapelle, 2nd Battle of Ypres, Aubers Ridge, Festubert and Loos. They were, apart from 2nd Ypres, mini versions of what would take place in the Somme in 1916.

The early months of 1916 were spent by politicians and military commanders debating how best to defeat the Germans and formulating a timetable for a 'Big Push.' For the British and French, 1915 had been marked by a series of costly battles which defined the increasingly horrific and futile nature of the fighting: little territorial gains and high casualty figures. The main British offensive was at Loos in September, at a disastrous cost of more than 50,000 men. Coupled with the calamitous campaign in the Dardanelles, it was imperative that the British and French re-vamped their strategy and in Britain's case, introduce new faces for its implementation. At a conference at Chantilly near Paris from 6th to 8th December 1915, the Allies' agenda was set by General Joseph Joffre, commander-in-chief of the French Army, who argued for concerted action on the Italian, Eastern and Western Fronts. In France he proposed an Anglo-French offensive on a 60 mile front driven by the French.

The French President Poincaré and Joffre, were pressing throughout for haste but British politicians like the Foreign Secretary A.J. Balfour and former First Lord of the Admiralty, Winston Churchill, cautioned against precipitate action. Balfour believed it was vital that artillery provision was increased at least to match the Germans' and the opinion that mattered most was that of the Minister of Munitions, David Lloyd-George

Foreign Secretary A.J. Balfour with four times Wimbledon Singles Champion Tony Wilding who was killed in 1915

who insisted that he needed time to provide adequate supplies. Since his self-imposed exile from government after his Dardanelles disaster in 1915, Churchill had joined the war effort at Ploegsteert in Belgium where he commanded the 6/ Royal Scots Fusiliers - his experience of trench warfare was such that he could at least advise that German defences were 'undoubtedly the strongest and most perfectly defended positions in the world.'

Haig found himself playing a subordinate role to the French who, on home territory, understandably took the lead in military planning. Their Army had suffered 1,900,000 casualties from August 1914 to January 1916 and they were desperate to drive the Germans from their country. He had to bow to their desire for a concerted effort in the Somme - his favoured option of an offensive in Belgium, in the main to destroy German railway communications, failed to pass muster.

By February plans and strategies were in a state of flux. On 14th February 1916, Joffre and Haig agreed a joint offensive in the Somme where their lines met. At this stage the plan was for the French to attack along a 25 mile front and the British, the junior partners, a 14 mile front.

Allied minds were concentrated, however, after 21st February when the German General Erich von Falkenhayn attacked Verdun, a fortress in eastern France of great strategic and symbolic importance to the French. His aim was to 'bleed the French Army white'; it was a battle that lasted until mid-December at a cost of more than 800,000 French and German soldiers - the highest density of dead per square yard on the Western Front. It had the desired effect of drawing French troops away from the relatively quiet 'live and let live' Somme sector; it was clear to Haig, Rawlinson and the CIGC - General Sir William Robertson that the British Army would now have to take on the lion's share of the offensive; Robertson wrote to Haig on 6th March: 'I am more convinced than ever it is we who will have to finish this war.'

German General Erich von Falkenhayn

The French became increasingly frantic for an increase in British support; Haig's preference, however, was to prevaricate on account of the 'rawness' of the Kitchener Pals Battalions, evidenced by his diary comment for 29th March: 'I have not got an army in France really, but a collection of divisions untrained for the field … The actual fighting army will be evolved from them.'

Preparations for the offensive were compromised by Haig and Rawlinson's disagreements on two key issues; the latter had predicted early in their working relationship that 'I shall tussle with him…' and he did - over the extent of the attack and the length of a pre-attack bombardment. Haig wanted to force a breakthrough facilitated by short, sharp and intensive bombardments, undertake a rapid advance to the Pozières Ridge and then capture territory beyond. Unlike Rawlinson, Haig was by training and nature a cavalryman who believed that once a breakthrough had been achieved, the cavalry could be utilised to break out with speed into the open country.

Rawlinson was more cautious; true to his family motto of 'Festina Lente' (make haste slowly) he believed in limited objectives, to advance in deliberate stages, to 'bite and hold', a strategy he first envisaged after the Battle of Neuve Chapelle in March 1915, and to consolidate territorial gains made. Much of his strategy was influenced by anxiety over the inexperience of the New Army 'Service' battalions that made up 55% of the manpower dedicated to the assault. His policy was supported by his Corps commanders; for example, Lieutenant-General Sir Aylmer Hunter-Weston commander of VIII Corps, who was 'strongly opposed to a wild rush for an objective 4,000 yards away.'

Rawlinson pressed Haig for a five day pre-attack bombardment to destroy, in effect, everything along the first two German lines. The Somme was, he believed, 'a capital country in which to undertake an offensive' but only 'when we get a sufficiency of artillery … with plenty of ammunition we ought to be able to override heavy losses which the infantry have always suffered on previous occasions.' The performance of the artillery would be crucial if victory was to be achieved and heavy losses averted.

He had appreciated ever since he first reconnoitred the Somme in February 1916 that 'acres and acres' of extensive German barbed wire entanglements would have to be 'cut' if the assaulting infantry were to have any chance of making progress. Hence his belief in the need for a five day bombardment which would provide the added advantage of weakening enemy morale: 'Bearing in mind the existence of numerous dug-outs and cellars in the enemy lines, I do not think the moral (sic) effect of six hours intensive bombardment will be so great as that over several days.'

It is interesting that he acknowledges the existence of dug-outs and cellars at this early stage but it is uncertain as to what extent he understood how well they were constructed. He pinned his hopes on the intensive bombardment destroying them and everything else - trenches, their occupants, barbed wire, artillery, machine-guns and ammunition. Rawlinson was taking a massive gamble.

The sparring between the two British generals was settled with a *quid pro quo* whereby Haig agreed to a five day bombardment and Rawlinson, against his better judgement, yielded to Haig's broader objectives and the bombardment of targets up to 5,000 yards behind the German front line. At an early stage of the War, during the 1st Battle of Ypres in October and November 1914, experience had shown that with the improvements in weaponry, the halcyon days and usefulness of the cavalry were on the wane. He was lukewarm about its use and foresaw that '... I shall have to make a vitally important decision when to send the cavalry through but I shall not be rash' - a case of 'Festina Lente' but in reality he would do his utmost not to embrace Haig's wish for it to swing into action at the appropriate moment.

General Sir Douglas Haig by William Orpen 1917   IWM Art 324

From the spring of 1916, the French Army on the Somme was reduced dramatically as divisions were redirected to Verdun - on 20th May the number was cut from 39 to 20 and at 7.30 a.m. on 1st July the British Army could count on the support of only five French divisions to the east of Maricourt. The British Army's line of attack stretched about 18 miles from Montauban in the south east to Gommecourt in the north with no offensive planned between Serre and Gommecourt. It was more than originally anticipated and in conjunction with Haig's extended objectives, there would be huge pressure to produce a sufficient supply of munitions.

Haig was leant on constantly by Joffre to attack as soon as possible - his preference was for a date in August or September to leave time to build up munitions and deliver more training and practice to the New Army Battalions. He and Joffre met at Château Beaurepaire, his HQ near Montreuil-sur-Mer, 70 miles from the front line, at the end of May; the French supremo warned that 'there would be no French Army left' if the British Army was unable to commit to an attack until August: Haig displayed in his diary the strategic imperative that 'VERDUN MUST ON NO ACCOUNT BE ALLOWED TO FALL INTO THE ENEMY'S HANDS' and in so doing would also wear down German manpower and in his diary Rawlinson emphasises the importance of 'killing Germans'.

There was much vacillation over deciding on a precise date for the offensive. On 4th June Haig promised the French that the British would be ready for an attack on 1st July. Rawlinson was led to believe on 11th June that 'the French are in difficulties at Verdun and both from a military and political point of view they want us to go into the attack earlier on 25th June.' Interestingly, he wrote that if the date was brought forward to the 25th he was 'much inclined to omit Montauban, particularly as we may be short of guns' as XIII Corps (i.e. Maxse and Shea's 18th and 30th Divisions respectively) would not be ready until 1st July. It was ironic that these two Divisions would achieve the only lasting successes on 1st July.

Haig returned to England on 6th June; he met King George V and they discussed among other things the importance and role of the cavalry. Two days later he and his wife Doris lunched at Sunningdale Golf Club and played a post prandial round but as the caddies were on military duty, they had to carry their own clubs: a sign of the times! In his diary entry for 10th June, Haig emphasised the need for an attack to be made in 'full strength' if German reserves were to be drawn away from Verdun. He was strongly of the opinion that 'a hastily prepared attack without an adequate supply of ammunition' would unquestionably fail in its objective. He was concerned about too early a date for the assault - Joffre was, apparently, anxious on 13th June that the British assault should take place on 25th June. Haig was unwavering in his view that 'it would be a very short-sighted policy for the French to ask us to start our attack before all is quite ready.' At least he could escape from the trials of working with the French with more games of golf in Deal and Sandwich!

Rawlinson was informed on 17th June that Joffre had requested by phone that the attack be postponed to 29th June or even 1st July. Haig's irritation was palpable - 'we had arranged to be ready on 25th to please him and 29th should be the latest date.' He feared that a further postponement would mean running the risk of the Germans 'discerning our area of concentration'. The Germans, of course, knew only too well what was being planned and where. He was concerned about the effect of postponement on his troops who had been gearing up for and expecting to attack, and he agreed, that 29th June would be the date for the assault only to find that General Foch wished to postpone the attack by a further two days: Rawlinson phoned Haig and they insisted on keeping to the agreed date.

The ultimate decision, however, rested with the vagaries of the weather - thundery downpours on the 27th and 28th meant that the attack could not proceed and was postponed … to Haig's original date of 1st July. Foch was delighted and made a special visit to Querrieu to thank Rawlinson for the delay.

The prolongation of the bombardment suited Rawlinson as he believed the Germans would be further demoralised. He was prepared to put trust in prisoners' claims that their front line troops were starving, having had no rations for 48 hours. Pipelines had been cut by the shelling and water was in short supply: 'If this is true and I see no reason to disbelieve it, we ought not to have much serious trouble in gaining the green line'- a clear case of, at best, wishful thinking.

The attention to detail in the planning of the attack is hard to fault - commanders at all levels were bombarded with paperwork, much of it based on Rawlinson's *Fourth Army Tactical Notes*. Captain Charles May of the 22/ Manchesters wrote that 'the mass of detail we have waded through to reach this point has been enormous but at least we have mastered it and the army is ready to strike.'

Captain Jack of the 2/ Cameronians, when based in Authuille Wood, wrote that 'while the battle storm blows up in front we have to ride out a gale of paper at our backs. There are sheaves of orders, amendments, counter-orders, returns and reports to be dealt with … If writing can win a campaign our foes may soon be at our mercy'!

Attention to written detail does not guarantee success and Rawlinson's diary entries for June highlight growing concern. He wrote on 5th June: 'Hunter-Weston says the 29th Division trench raid found deep dug-outs between the German front and support line with exits into both.' Rawlinson accepted the potential problem: 'This may be difficult to deal with' but how seriously did he confront the issue in the ensuing weeks?

The supply of guns and ammunition was a constant worry. Rawlinson conceded on 11th June that there might be insufficient numbers of guns and ammunition: 'There is a shortage which may be serious.' Six days later he expressed pleasure at the way things were going but next day suspected that 'trench mortars and flares are behindhand and we may get neither in time.'

On 21st June he received a letter from Haig's Chief of the General Staff, Lieutenant-General Sir Launcelot Kiggell, reporting that the Commander-in-Chief wanted 'one day of the bombardment to be cancelled as he was afraid of a shortage of guns and ammunition.' This chimed with Rawlinson's often expressed view that a reduction in German defences could not be achieved without a satisfactory state of ammunition supply. Just days before the bombardment was due to start, the main two men responsible for it were evidently apprehensive about an adequate supply of ordnance and, even after it had started, Rawlinson was, on 25th June, 'anxious about 9.2 ammunition and our heavy trench mortars.'

It would appear that High Command was aware that the Germans sheltered in deep dug-outs and seemingly they had chosen to ignore their potential impregnability. Raiding parties were the main source of information about them - a dug-out opposite 31st Division was reported to be deep with about 18 steps and able to accommodate about eight men. Those who saw it stated that 'there was a notice up with the following in English characters "M.G. No 1 Post"… The dug out was not damaged by our fire.' The warning from the raiding party could not have been much clearer.

R.F.C. pilots and kite balloons provided useful information about trench systems, barbed wire entanglements and enemy troop movements but nothing of use about underground dug-outs. Rawlinson could never be sure of how successful a bombardment had been - on 27th he noted 'the wire seems to have been well cut on most of the front' but on the day before Zero Hour, privately in his diary, he accepted that he was 'not satisfied that all the wire has been thoroughly well cut and in places the front trenches are not knocked about as I should like to see. The bit in front of 34th Division has been rather let off.'

The time of the assault was another matter for on-going negotiation between the Allies. Rawlinson met Generals Foch, Commander of French Northern Army Group and Fayolle, Commander-in-Chief of Sixth Army on 16th June: 'I tried 7 a.m. But had to agree to 7.30. Fayolle would have preferred 9 a.m.' Rawlinson dug his heels in arguing that such a late start would entail keeping the infantry waiting in the assembly trenches for six hours and more. On 20th June Foch tried again for a 9 a.m. start but 7.30 was the agreed compromise but one that would receive criticism by those tasked with 'going over the top.'

French Generals Joffre, Foch and Fayolle

It is important to acknowledge that Haig, Rawlinson and General Sir Edmund Allenby, commander of the Third Army, were dealing on the Somme with over 90 battalions of soldiers who were driven by enthusiasm and patriotism but lacking in experience of trench warfare. If they had been working with the fitter and more experienced 'regulars' who crossed the Channel in August 1914, their tactics might have been less simplistic and cautious. Discipline is a crucial cornerstone for any military activity and Rawlinson stressed its importance at a conference at Flixecourt on 1st June for commanding officers: 'Little things indicate discipline. You cannot hold on to a position gained without discipline. Discipline counteracts fear. Fear is the most important thing to overcome.' Hence the recommendation, not necessarily followed, that assaulting battalions walk in lines to maintain control and order. At a briefing of Corps Commanders on 22nd June, Rawlinson concentrated again on the need for 'discipline, determination and tenacity' amongst the New Army troops. When faced by machine-guns and shells, narrow exits to leave their front line, battered terrain and uncut barbed wire in front of the German trenches, the discipline in attack that Rawlinson exhorted and the Fourth Army practised in the weeks beforehand, disintegrated in minutes.

Without the Pals Battalions that Kitchener raised, the British Army might not have contributed as successfully to the eventual victory in 1918. Rawlinson's diary reflects his great sadness at the news of Lord Kitchener's death by drowning on 5th June when *HMS Hampshire* was sunk by a German mine west of the islands of Orkney. He received the news on 7th June, 'a heavy shock to me and a serious loss to the Army and the Nation but it is well that it happened when Kitchener had completed his great work of raising the New Armies.' A Memorial Service was held at the Front: 'It made me feel very sad when I recollected the many interesting hours that I have spent with him during the 18 years I have been privileged to know him intimately … the Sudan War where he taught me more about active service than I could otherwise have learned. He has been a great friend and a great example to me and I shall miss him more than I care to think. I wish he could have lived to see his New Army Divisions fight in the coming battle. He was a much kinder man than he ever dared to admit even to himself.' The 'kind' Kitchener, the popular hero of 19th century British campaigns, had he lived, might have been moved to tears on hearing how his army of volunteers fared on 1st July 1916.

In the period from 1st to 17th June, Rawlinson visited all the Divisions due to take part in the assault. He rode out on 1st June to cast his eye over a practice attack by the 32nd and 8th Divisions and the men appeared 'healthy and their spirit excellent.' On the following day he was unimpressed with an attack by two brigades of the 4th Division 'which I criticised to both Billy Lambton (4th Division) and Hunter-Weston (VIII Corps). The troops are getting on but are by no means perfect yet.' He visited 34th Division on 6th June and found they were not as far forward in their preparations as he would have wished. Hudson's 8th Division was better prepared. Two days later he was most unimpressed with his visit to Major-General Oliver Nugent's 36th Division's training: 'I was not wholly satisfied with them and I told Nugent so. There is too much doubt and not enough precision and determination. The men are a fine looking lot but it is in the upper ranks that doubt exists.' His opinion of a brigade in the 31st 'Pals' Division was damning: '... the worst I have seen - their methods were bad, things had not been thought out and the whole thing was disappointing. I told them I was much displeased.' He deemed the schemes of VIII Corps (Hunter-Weston) and XV Corps (Lieutenant-General Horne) as 'all right'- hardly a ringing endorsement. At least he was happy that there was a good spirit in the 21st and 7th Divisions.

Rawlinson mentioned in his diary on several occasions, the positive spirit he found amongst the other ranks and junior officers. He lacked confidence, however, in some of his commanders, Nugent of 36th (Ulster) Division being singled out for particularly trenchant criticism: 'He has too many fads and objections and finds difficulty in making up his mind. He sees too many difficulties and has fads which are not sound. Now is too late to make a change unless he goes sick. His flaws as a whole are the worst I have yet seen but his men are good fighters and his brigadiers are good so they may pull him through.' Nor was Rawlinson a great fan of Hunter-Weston.

Haig visited Rawlinson on 28th June who told him he was not satisfied with VIII Corps (Hunter-Weston) 'who have not been doing their counter battery work well.' For his part Haig expressed concern that raids had been made and not one had managed to enter enemy lines, merely reporting that the wire had not been cut. 'Let it be cut at once' he cried out in his diary and complained that VIII Corps' counter battery work was unsatisfactory. At least the delay, he believed, would be advantageous but he was unhappy with de Lisle's 29th Division and O'Gowan's 31st which 'seem poor'. A mere two days before the attack was due Commander-in-Chief General Sir Douglas Haig's diary account underlines a lack of confidence in those commanding the attack: 'The conclusion I come to is that the majority are amateurs.' At least he could console himself that at the southernmost part of the front, XIII Corps and the French XX Corps were working well together and were indulging in a 'mutual admiration society.'

The success of the offensive for Haig and Rawlinson was dependent on the effectiveness of the bombardment. They had cause for optimism on 24th June, Rawlinson recording that 'we have been busy wire cutting all day with little hostile reply ... the Bosch is ...very quiet ... Hardly any reply when 3 German balloons were brought down ... the hostile reply was again feeble.' The 'feebleness' of the German response to the bombardment was tactical and during the week leading up to Zero Hour, Rawlinson was, it can be argued, taken in by it.

He took a trip up to the 'Grandstand' on 26th June at 9.a.m. to see the artillery in action considering that 'it was good.' The following day Haig dropped in for tea and was taken there to have a look around. It was Foch's turn two days later when he saw the 4 o'clock bombardment and admitted he was 'delighted with what he saw.'

How confident was Rawlinson on the eve of battle on 30th June? He spent the evening reviewing the preparations: 'All the units are up to strength and the spirit of all ranks is splendid.' Despite admitting that there were 'a few weak spots' amongst his Corps and Division commanders, most were 'the best we have got.' He expressed satisfaction with the state of the trenches and the roads, and approaches had been 'carefully prepared and improved … Many mines are ready' and he noted that 'shallow galleries (i.e. Russian saps) have been dug to make communications across No Man's Land easy.' He had ridden around the cavalry divisions which were 'in the best of form and dying to get at the Bosch but I shall not let them go unless there is a really good chance for them.' He took heart from more intelligence gleaned from German prisoners about shattered morale.

Whatever Haig's reservations, he was heartened by the quiet confidence conveyed to him by Morland, Pulteney, Horne, Congreve and Rawlinson who 'one and all are full of confidence.' He signed off his diary on the eve of one of the greatest military operations in British history: 'With God's help, I feel hopeful tomorrow. The men are in splendid spirits: several have said that they have never been so instructed and informed of the nature of the opposition before them. The wire has never been as well cut nor the artillery preparation so thorough'.

There are though, signs of unease - Rawlinson admitted that the artillery work during the bombardment and the wire cutting was 'behindhand' in the VIII Corps. He may have expressed his satisfaction with the spirit of all ranks but his diary entries during the build-up to the great attack were dominated by his dissatisfaction with much of the training and practice being undertaken. He makes little mention of it after 17th June. It is doubtful that matters would have improved much and it is questionable how useful it would have been attacking unmanned trenches without the reality of rifles, machine-guns and shells. The training sessions must have resembled a football team playing without an opposition.

He concluded: 'What the actual results of the battle will be no one can foretell, but I feel pretty confident of success myself, though we shall only get it after heavy fighting', an admission that was at odds with the copious messages transmitted to the men that 'it would be a walkover' or a 'cake-walk'.

He had recognised since at least 14th June that there would be 'heavy fighting' and with it heavy casualties, shown by an order he sent to the Quartermaster-General on 14th June in which he demanded that enough trains be provided 'for at least 10,000 wounded per day.'

The day appeared to start well for General Haig - reports up to 8 a.m. were 'most satisfactory' as troops had everywhere apparently crossed the enemy's front trenches. By 9 a.m. the news was less hopeful - 29th Division had been held up and he had to concede on two occasions that positive reports 'proved not to be the case'. It appears incongruous that while the great assault was proceeding disastrously in most sectors, General Haig was assessing proposals brought to him by a young naval officer from Admiral Bacon about action on the Ostend coast. As negative reports of the attack flowed into his office, his wrath was concentrated on Hunter-Weston's VIII Corps: 'I am inclined to think that few of VIII Corps left their trenches!!' He was mindful of the advantageous diversionary work of VII Corps' 56th and 46th Divisions at Gommecourt in assisting VIII Corps but damningly conceded that 'in spite of this, the VIII Corps achieved very little.'

To improve chances of success in the morning of 1st July, Rawlinson like Haig put in a request for divine intervention: 'We have done all that we can, and the rest is in the hands of the Bon Dieu.'

General Rawlinson's HQ at Querrieu

General Rawlinson was driven back to Querrieu and from 8.00 a.m. news began to filter through about how the advance was progressing. Initially everything was positive - the 7th Division were over the enemy 3rd line, 21st Division had passed the front line, the whole of III Corps were over the German second line. The optimism and detail of the first reports were soon superseded by comments that exuded negativity and confusion. At 9.00 a.m. 'there are a large number of Germans in deep dug-outs who are giving trouble'… Communications from forward troops were sketchy. Divisions were 'believed to be' in a certain location, or reports were considered 'not reliable', there were 'no further reports' and advances by corps were 'nil'. Fourth Army Summary of Operations contains much about numbers of prisoners taken but nothing on British casualties. A message was sent to all Corps: 'Could you give us any indication from reports of wounded or otherwise of the extent of enemy casualties today. Brief reply on telephone will suffice'- the lack of communication at all levels would prove to be just one of many problems faced during the day. Typifying the confusion was the report at 2.33 p.m. that 'all quiet at Thiepval which appears to be in our hands' which it certainly was not. It took some time for the enormity of the casualties to percolate through to Querrieu. For General Rawlinson and his staff, 1st July would prove to be deeply depressing and disappointing.

Private Arthur Seanor
18/ King's (2nd Liverpool Pals), 21st Brigade, 30th Division

'Proud to die a soldier'

It was Private Arthur Seanor's 28th birthday. Waiting in a front line trench before 'entering the greatest battle the world has ever known' was not his chosen way of celebrating it. He had written a letter a week earlier to be forwarded, in the event of his death, to his fiancée of ten months, Florrie Ledson: 'You have been a dear friend to me Florrie and ever since we became such close friends, I have lived and longed for the day when we would become man and wife.' He thanked her for supporting him during the 'hard and trying times on active service.'

His final letters to her were pessimistic and downbeat. He grumbled that his Battalion, the 18/ King's (Liverpool), had not been granted as much leave as others; he admitted to being 'very pessimistic about things' and yearned to see her again after their nine month separation, thanking her for sending him a much treasured photograph of her: '… it is simply splendid, how it has made me long for home … I could just kiss it for ever.' He penned a touching poem in his missive of Sunday 25th June - of which an extract:

> *I often think of the homeland*
> *And the future that's in store …*
>
> *How sweet will sound the music*
> *Of that old song 'Home Sweet Home'*

He told her that he had attended communion early that morning when 'I asked God to forgive me all my sins… so I am not afraid to die, in fact I am proud to die a soldier.'

Prior to the outbreak of hostilities in August 1914, Arthur Seanor was not a soldier but a clerk in a timber-merchants in Liverpool. Lord Kitchener's recruitment campaign was particularly successful in the Liverpool area where the baton was enthusiastically taken up by Lord Derby whose appeal encouraged 2,865 men to sign up between 31st August and 4th September, enough for nearly three battalions. His first request for volunteers had resulted in the formation of the Pioneer 11th Service Battalion, the first of its kind and composed mostly of working men from Liverpool who would be involved in manual work at the Front.

Lord Derby turned his attention to raising a battalion from the commercial classes - 'clerks and others engaged in commercial business who wish to serve their country and would be willing to enlist in the battalions of Lord Kitchener's New Army if they felt assured that they would be able to serve with their friends. Lord Kitchener has sanctioned my endeavouring to raise a battalion that would be composed of the classes mentioned, and in which a man could be certain that he would be amongst friends.' Thus was born the idea of 'Pals' Battalions which, in theory, seemed an appealing concept and endorsed by Rawlinson at the time. Little did he think that within 20 months, he would be commanding an army mostly composed of these volunteers.

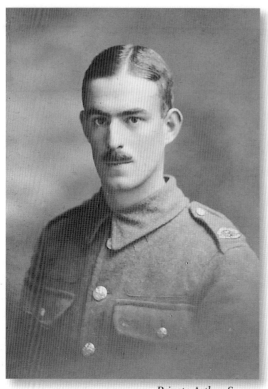

On Monday 2nd September, Arthur Seanor, with his employers' blessing, queued at St. George's Hall in Liverpool to enlist with fellow 'pals', brothers Alfred and John Kirkwood; he passed a cursory medical and was assigned to the 18th Battalion of the King's (Liverpool) Regiment - the 2nd Liverpool 'Pals' Battalion as it would soon be commonly known.

He and the Kirkwoods received military training at a number of centres during 1914 and 1915, finishing at Larkhill Camp on Salisbury Plain in November. The Battalion sailed from Folkestone to Boulogne on 7th November 1915.

Arthur had played regularly for his home town cricket club in Bootle, which may explain why he was selected to be a battalion 'bomber' or grenade thrower and was enrolled at the 30th Division Grenade School from 22nd April to 6th May 1916.

Private Arthur Seanor

The Battalion left billets at Bray-sur-Somme on 29th June and moved to Trigger Wood near Méaulte where they bivouacked for the night. The following day was spent 'resting'; at 6.30 p.m. the Pals marched about five miles from Trigger Wood; by midnight they had reached the assembly trenches to the right of Talus Boisé opposite the village of Montauban, at the southernmost end of the line of attack. Sleep in the

trench was virtually out of the question. When dawn broke, the gentle slope towards Montauban was shrouded in mist. The men were quietly nervous and excited at the prospect of playing a part in what they hoped would bring the War to a speedy conclusion.

At 6.25 a.m. the skylarks' chorus high above the trenches was rudely drowned out by a furious bombardment of the German first and second lines by the British Artillery.

'Furious British bombardment' Le Miroir July 1916

Arthur could scarcely hear himself think; his equipment was ready for the impending action - rifle, bayonet, 50 rounds of S.A.A., waterproof sheet, rations, water bottle and ten Mills bombs: a heavy load for a small man only 5 foot 5 inches high and 120 lbs in weight. He would have liked to have taken the photograph of Florrie with him but men had been ordered not to take with them souvenirs or anything that might provide useful information to the Germans.

His CO, Lieutenant-Colonel Trotter, went down the line offering encouragement to his men ten minutes before Zero Hour. The bombardment lifted at 7.28 and two minutes later, the wait was over - Arthur and his friend, Company Sergeant Major John Kirkwood, shook hands and wished each other luck. Whistles blew - the signal for the 2nd Liverpool Pals to scale ladders, jump off the parapet, circumspectly make their way through specially cut gaps in the barbed wire, and cross No Man's Land in 'extended order' and at walking pace.

Private Arthur Seanor's body was never identified. It is unlikely that he reached the Battalion's objective of the German trench west of the Glatz Redoubt. He and his friend Alfred were probably mown down by a machine-gun that had escaped the early morning bombardment and their bodies were likely to have been obliterated by shell fire in No Man's Land.

John Kirkwood wrote to the vicar of St. Paul's, Kirkdale, a district near Bootle, about the loss of his brother and Arthur, of whom he wrote: 'I could never hope to have a better soldier. Cheerful at all times he was perfectly happy when I shook hands with him about three minutes before we passed on the top of the parapet, and he had not gone more than 200 yards (about the same distance as my brother Alf) where he was fatally wounded.' Kirkwood claimed to have seen Arthur's body on the battlefield the following day and that he, like Alfred, 'lay with his face to the foe', and not in retreat.

John himself was mentioned by Lieutenant Cotter in the Battalion War Diary for having distinguished himself 'with gallantry and devotion to duty' on 1st July. It was ironic that having survived the slaughter and scarcely signed off his letter,

Liverpool Pals' Memorial at Montauban

John Kirkwood was killed on 8th July. The three Pals from Bootle who had shared communion on Sunday 25th June, did not receive a Christian burial. Their bodies were never identified and with no known grave, they are three of over 12,000 names of soldiers commemorated on the Thiepval Memorial who died on 1st July 1916.

Arthur and the Kirkwoods were robbed of the opportunity to celebrate the capture of Montauban, one of very few successes on that fateful day. Communities in and near Liverpool had fervently answered Lord Kitchener and Lord Derby's calls-to-arms but facing such massive losses, deep psychological scars were suffered for many years. It was meagre consolation for them that 'Liverpool has every right to be proud of this Battalion. They went forward as on the parade ground, not hesitating in the hail of lead, and although our losses were rather heavy, our objective was attained to a scheduled time.'

Florrie Ledson received the letter Arthur had written in the event of his death - the love between the two was clear to see in their letters. Not surprisingly she was heart-broken and one wonders whether she found any solace in a letter from a colleague of her fiancé at the timber-merchants in Liverpool: 'You have the consolation of knowing that he has given his life in one of the noblest causes.' She married several years after the War - her family, however, maintained contact for many years with Arthur's mother, four brothers and three sisters.

A message in the *Liverpool Echo* on 14th July reflects the torment suffered by loved ones throughout the country: 'SEANOR- July 1, on his 28th birthday, Private Arthur Seanor, "Pals". "Thy will be done". Deeply mourned by the sorrowing fiancée Florrie.'

*Private Arthur Seanor may be buried in an
unidentified grave*

Captain Wilfred ('Billie') Nevill
8/ East Surreys, 55th Brigade, 18th (Eastern) Division

'A brave man, he was a good man. He made us better for having known him'

Captain Wilfred Nevill, or 'Billie' as he was known by most, strolled along the 8/ East Surreys' front line trench. It was opposite German trenches which were located in front of the fortified village of Montauban at the southern end of the Front. The epitome of calmness, he shared a last joke with Lieutenant Alcock of 'B' Company before Zero Hour.

When on leave in May 1916, he had dreamed up an interesting but not necessarily novel way of counteracting any potential anxieties and fears his men may have faced before and during the planned assault. One football had been kicked by men of the 1/18 London (London Irish Rifles) at the Battle of Loos in the autumn of 1915. Nevill returned to France with two footballs. On one was inscribed:

Captain 'Billie' Nevill

'The Great European Cup-Tie Final East Surreys v Bavarians. Kick off at Zero'

The message on the other ball was simple - the Germans were not to be treated too leniently… there would be: 'NO REFEREE'

Nevill's plan was that the footballs would be kicked over No Man's Land and into the Germans' trenches. Major Irwin, the CO of the 8/ East Surreys, gave the go-ahead to the idea on condition that Nevill and his officers kept command of their units and did not allow the scheme to degenerate into a rush after the ball - if a man saw a ball, he could kick it but not break rank and rush after it. Irwin felt that it would 'help them enormously' and take 'their minds off it.'

'Billie' Nevill was the archetypal public school-educated young officer recruited by Lord Kitchener's campaign in August and September 1914. He was bright, energetic and a talented sportsman. He was born on 14th July 1894, one of seven children. His father Thomas ran a coal business successful enough to buy houses in Twickenham and Westgate-on-Sea in Kent. When he died in 1903, his widow Elizabeth and the children moved to Dorking in Surrey.

Nevill's grave in Carnoy Military Cemetery

Captain Nevill in trench   *Surrey History Centre*

'Billie' was sent away to board at Dover College where he excelled at many sports including cricket, hockey, fives and athletics. He was Head Boy and a member of the OTC both of which would guarantee him officer status in 1914. There are few records of his academic achievements which nonetheless must have been significant as he took up a place at Jesus College, Cambridge, in 1913 to read Classics, a degree which he intended to complete after the hostilities with Germany ended.

He relished life as a soldier; he was trained at the Staff College at Camberley, received a temporary commission as a 2nd lieutenant with the East Yorkshire Regiment on 27th November 1914, was promoted to lieutenant with the 8/ East Surreys in May 1915 and by July 1915, when the Battalion departed for the Front, he had been elevated to the rank of captain in Kitchener's New Volunteer Army.

The 8/ East Surreys were one of four Battalions in the 55th Brigade of Major-General Ivor Maxse's 18th (Eastern) Division. The Brigade trained at Picquigny, north of Amiens during May in preparation for the impending 'Big Push' and at different times was inspected by General Sir Douglas Haig and General Sir Henry Rawlinson. In June the 8/ East Surreys were sent to trenches near the village of Carnoy where Nevill wrote that it was 'a wee bit wet and muddy' but 'quite nice to be in a trench again', a view that may not have been shared by many of his men.

He was impressed by the British bombardment that started on 24th June: 'It is a wonderful sight' and in a letter to his sister Elsie, he recorded that 'as I write the shells are fairly hairing (sic) over; you know one gets sort of bemused after a few million, still it will be a great experience to tell one's children about. So long old thing, don't worry if you don't hear for a bit. I'm happy as ever.'

Overall the mood in the Battalion was optimistic. Major Irwin was confident that the barbed wire entanglements in front of the German trenches had been cut by the bombardment; the 'Bosches' would be 'massacred' and the objectives of Breslau Trench and houses in Montauban would be achieved - Nevill, however, may not have been as sanguine; in a letter to Elsie he expressed concern that the enemy's machine-guns had not been destroyed.

The 8 / East Surreys were more fortunate than some - theirs was a short march from billets and bivouacs in Billon Valley, south of Carnoy, to their assembly trenches but on arrival they were welcomed by a period of sustained German shelling which flattened some of their front line trenches; it had been confidently predicted that the British bombardment would destroy the German guns - something had gone seriously wrong …

Exits in the barbed wire defences were cut, and ammunition, bombs, flares, tools and enough food to survive for 48 hours were issued. Breakfast was served at 4.30 a.m. with tea and generous tots of rum. 'Billie' visited Major Irwin in the Battalion's H.Q. dug-out before dawn broke and ushered his Company into position by 5.30 a.m. The low lying mist had burnt off by 6.30 a.m. when the British bombardment of the German front line increased in intensity.

At 7.27 a.m. Captain 'Billie' Nevill and Lieutenant Bobby Soames jumped off the parapet; Nevill strolled quietly ahead giving an occasional order 'to the dressing square on to the line of advance' and then both officers punted their footballs in the direction of the German trenches. It was not a case of 'kick and rush'- the Generals' 'think tank' had ordained that men were to walk, not run, across No Man's Land.

'B' Company were caught in a hail of machine-gun fire. The two officers reached the German barbed wire but no further. Bomb in hand, 'Billie' Nevill was shot through the head and Bobby Soames fell near his friend.

The footballing venture was witnessed by Private L.S. Price of the 18th (Eastern) Division's Pioneer Battalion, 8/ Royal Sussex, who saw 'an infantryman climb onto the parapet into No Man's Land beckoning others to follow. As he did so he kicked off a football; a good kick, the ball rose and travelled well towards the German line.'

'Billie' Nevill's footballing venture was a gift to the newspapers. He and his Company displayed heroism and courage as they 'played the game'. Touchstone of *The Daily Mail* articulated national sentiments of patriotism:

> *On through the hail of slaughter*
> *Where gallant comrades fall,*
> *Where blood is poured like water,*
> *They drive the trickling ball.*
> *The fear of death before them,*
> *Is but an empty name;*
> *True to the land that bore them,*
> *The Surreys played the game.*

The Daily Telegraph of 12th July 1916 told of 'a dribbling competition all the way over the mile and a quarter of ground they had to traverse … platoon commanders kicked off and the match against Death commenced. Captain Nevill was killed … still the footballs were booted onwards.' *The Thames Valley Times* reported that the East Surreys were 'playing football under fire.' The story was, of course, embellished- No Man's Land in the East Surreys sector was nearer 700 yards than one and a half miles, and the men were too busy with self-preservation to be engaged in a focused 'dribbling competition'. The German press, sensing a propaganda opportunity scoffed at the stupidity of such a stunt and for treating war as a sport. The British press used the incident to heighten a sense of patriotism and fair play- one headline trumpeted 'The Surreys Play the Game.'

Controversy has surrounded the number of footballs that were actually kicked. The Battalion's War Diary recorded that Nevill's Company 'took four footballs out with them which they were seen to dribble forward into the smoke of our intense bombardment on the Hun front line.' One football for each of the four platoons offers a comfortable symmetry but it would appear that 'Billie' and his brother Howard bought three balls but only two were taken to France. After Zero Hour they were kicked first by Nevill and Soames although a letter of condolence sent by a Captain Thorne of 'C' Company to the mother of Private A.A. Fursey may have been a case of softening the blow of bad news with a surfeit of the truth: two footballs were kicked and '… it was actually your son who kicked off the other one.' As Thorne was in a different Company, the letter should not be given too much credence.

'Billie' Nevill was one of 177 Dover College old boys who lost their lives in the Great War; 50 DSOs, 76 MCs were awarded and there were 155 Mentions in Despatches. It was ironic that Nevill did not receive a posthumous award. Jesus College, Cambridge lost 153 alumni, seven on 1st July 1916.

Major Irwin was distraught at the loss of so many officers: 'All my best chaps had gone - we buried eight young officers in one grave before we left. It was a terrible massacre. The attack should have been called off until the wire was cut. They ought to have known the condition of the wire before we ever got to July 1st.'

Nevill's football being held aloft in the regimental barracks in Kingston-on-Thames Surrey History Centre

There is little doubt that 'Billie' Nevill was a first class officer and that his letters home were not unduly overstated. A sergeant who had served with 'Billie' for seven months comforted Elizabeth Nevill with his belief that there was not a man in the Battalion who would not have followed her son anywhere. Another sergeant told her that her son was 'a brave man, he was a good man. He made us better for having known him.' For one of his fellow officers he was his 'ideal hero, a perfect pattern of the British officer and the British gentleman' and he felt his loss 'personally more than any other.'

'Billie's loss was hard for the family to come to terms with- Howard wrote to his mother on 20th September '… I too cried for most of the first afternoon that I heard the news, as I have not since I was a child.'

The two footballs were recovered from the German front line on the Monday thanks to the successful offensive by the 18th and 30th Divisions. According to the Battalion War Diary the capture of Montauban was celebrated by 'all the East Surrey officers engaged in the attack who had not been killed or wounded' with a bottle of 1906

Heidsieck champagne which had been especially assigned 'to be drunk in Montauban ON DER TAG' and brought up by Lance-Corporal Brain. One imagines that a glass or two must have been raised to their missing friend.

The footballs were sent back to England and one was held aloft at a special parade at the Battalion's barracks in Kingston-on-Thames. One is now to be found at the Dover Castle museum and sadly, the other was destroyed when a fire broke out at the regimental museum in the National Trust's Clandon Park House in Surrey.

Captain 'Billie' Nevill's deeds of derring-do were of a Boys Own Paper type heroism that appealed to the nation's patriotism. He and his friend Lieutenant Bobby Soames were buried virtually next to each other in the cemetery at Carnoy.

The Surreys Play the Game' by R.Caton Woodville, originally published in black and white in the Illustrated London News, 27th July 1916 (Incorrectly captioned as occurring at Contalmaison)
Surrey History Centre

Lieutenant Roy Mellor
22/ Manchesters (7th City Pals), 91st Brigade, 7th Division

'If anything should ever happen to me, I hope you will write to Dagny'

A cartoon appeared in the *Macclesfield Courier* in September 1914 calling for volunteers 'to fight for England, Home and Duty'. In a subsequent edition a photo was published of six of the first nine old boys to enlist from the King's School in Macclesfield. They were typical of educated young men at the time who considered it their duty to fight for their country. Four had been school football captains, two had just graduated from the University of Manchester, three would become officers, one of whom won the MC and two were killed: Arthur Simpson, a 21 year old architect, in the Somme on 20th July 1916 and Roy Mellor on 1st July 1916.

Six old boys of King's School, Macclesfield who enlisted first - Roy Mellor is far right and Arthur Simpson next to him

Roy was born in January 1895, the only son of Harriet and Richard Mellor, owner of a silk dyeing mill in Macclesfield and captain of the local cricket club. Over six feet tall and well built, Roy excelled in sport at school - he was captain of football, vice-captain of cricket and won the Sports Challenge Cup in 1913, the year he was also school captain.

His academic ability was rewarded with a Science Scholarship to study Chemistry at the University of Manchester. The school magazine commented that despite 'a certain reserve and an almost excessive diffidence, his personal charm, his quiet dignity, and his fine sense of humour made him a great force in school life.' When at Manchester, he joined the OTC which would guarantee him a commission in due course.

He and the other boys in the school photograph enlisted in the Public Schools Battalion of the Royal Fusiliers which would provide many officers for other units. Roy was commissioned in March 1915 into the 22/ Manchesters (7th City Pals).

Roy Mellor in uniform - he is wearing what soldiers described as a 'Gor Blimey' cap

Roy had two sisters, Hilda a year younger and Marjorie, three years his senior, who kept the letters he wrote to her from his training camps and the Front. The 27 letters that survive from her 'loving brother' offer an interesting insight into the mind of a young man not cut out to be a professional soldier but prepared to fulfil the promise he gave in September 1914 to fight for his King and

Country. His early letters reflect a wariness of censorship with little mention of life at the Front. Most of the content is about family matters, requests for certain items to be sent, news of friends and his hopes for some leave.

Roy and the 22/ Manchesters were sent to Belton Park near Grantham for training in April 1915. In June he was laid up with a lacerated wound to his left leg following a motor cycle accident but life took a turn for the better when he confided to Marjorie that 'a most awful thing has happened. I have fallen deeply in love with a girl named Ethel who isn't really good looking, but very charming … There doesn't seem to be any chance of it wearing off. What must I do please?' Whatever the nature of his older sister's advice, Ethel never features again in his letters!

The Battalion moved to Larkhill on Salisbury Plain for further training. In a letter from there, he refers to having

Roy and sisters- Marjorie (on the right) and Hilda

had lunch with 19 year old Dagny Pogson and her family in Birmingham. After the meal 'the rest of the family melted away miraculously' so that he was left alone with Dagny, a doctor's daughter, who 'was nicer and more beautiful than ever.'

Their relationship became serious: '… Dagny gave me (or I took, whichever you like) a ring which she has had rather a long time' Roy then sent his sister a cheque for £5 asking her to find 'a suitable substitute … something of a delicate and unobtrusive nature.'

Roy became the Battalion's musketry and intelligence officer. After a long wait, the 22/ Manchesters were at last sent to France in November 1915. His letters paint a detailed picture of the bleakness of life at the Front, the highs and lows, the discomforts, dangers, the homesickness and the missing of loved ones. In his first letter home, he described France 'as this miserable country' and asked Marjorie if she had 'been able to find a decent ring' and touchingly he drew a circle to signify the size of the ring. He was finding life in France unappealing and his mood was increasingly negative. When describing some filthy billets, he confessed that 'I was nearer dropping out than I have ever been before.'

Life in the trenches was harsh: '… they are everywhere a foot deep in mud … every blessed thing is wet through'. In fact the conditions were 'so awful' and German shells so numerous that 'one or two of the men would be glad if one dropped on them.' Marjorie must have been troubled by the fatalism of one of Roy's letters when he wrote: 'If anything should ever happen to me, I hope you will write to Dagny.'

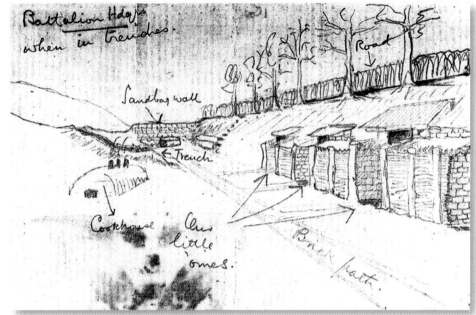

A drawing by Roy Mellor of his Battalion's HQ 'when in trenches'

His letters from December 1915 reflect his depressed state. He referred in one to a man in 'C' Company who was shot in the middle of his hand and added 'lucky beggar'. Most officers found censoring their men's letters a mind numbingly dull chore - Roy was no different complaining that 'They are always the same and get a bit dull after the first lot … They do write awful rot!'

He wrote at length in one letter about learning to throw Mills bombs: 'Once they start, they go off in five seconds so you can tell it is a pretty ticklish job … One way of winning the VC is to pick up a live bomb thrown by the Germans and hurl it back. I think bombs are the things with which the Germans are going to be driven back into Berlin.'

Roy had at least made an impression on his superiors for when the adjutant fell ill, 'I had to do his job. It had the disadvantage of more responsibility but the advantage of a dug-out of my own'!

Life in new billets improved for Mellor and 'D' Company who now 'stayed at a large ironmongers shop with jolly nice people' who included four daughters whose names all began with M and with whom they sang English songs around their piano; it was a great treat when 'Papa produced a bottle of Benedictine.'

His mention of Captain Townsend's impending marriage during his leave is particularly poignant: 'I think I shall wait till after the war. By the way the war will be over this year.' In another letter he mentions 'Bairnsfather's latest in the *Bystander*.' Bruce Bairnsfather's cartoons or as he called them 'sketches' of 'Old Bill' and 'Alfs and Berts' were popular amongst the men who enjoyed their gently mocking tone of life at the Front. The cartoon to which he was referring, makes the serious point that Tommies were on occasions hit by 'friendly fire'.

The 22/ Manchesters manned trenches south of Mametz on the 7th Division's right. By May 1916 the strain was showing: 'I am fed up with France.' Life in the trenches was 'awfully boring' and he was missing shops, cafés and the theatre. He told of a man shot through the head when peering over a parapet, an officer hit by shrapnel and the death of three officers during a 2nd June raid on a listening post at Bulgar Point which provoked a bitter reaction: 'I am sick of war.' To overcome his disaffection with his present circumstances he was obviously thinking of the future - he asked Marjorie if their sister Hilda had told her that 'Dagny and I were more or less engaged?' He was not alone in musing over the possibility of catching a 'blighty'- a wound serious enough to send him home, hopefully for ever.

As 'Z' Day approached, his letters became briefer and less informative: 'I can't tell you anything as there are stricter orders than usual' and he advised that for a general idea of what was happening it were best that events be followed in the newspapers. Cunningly, however, he dropped into one of his letters the fact that the day of the offensive had been postponed for two days: 'Imagine being put off two days at the last minute.'

A Matter of Moment

" What was that, Bill ? "
" Trench mortar "
" Ours or theirs ? "

Bruce Bairnsfather's sketch about the danger of 'friendly fire'

At Zero Hour, the 22/ Manchesters went over the top as part of the first wave. Their objective was to capture the head of the Mametz spur and the eastern part of the village - it entailed crossing No Man's Land which varied in width from 100 to 200 yards.

Captain Charles May was the CO of 'B' Company. He had written to his wife Maude on 17th June that 'I do not want to die. Not that I mind for myself. If it be that I am to go, I am ready.' The final entry in his diary mirrors the feelings of many officers about to lead their men into No Man's Land who realised that the week-long bombardment had failed in destroying the enemy trenches, dug-outs, guns and barbed wire. He and his men were to attack through 'a tangled desert'. He expressed the fear that 'we do not yet seem to have stopped his machine-guns … I trust they do not claim too many of our lads before the day is over.'

Lieutenant Roy Mellor went into battle with his old school pal Frank Harrison, also featured in the photograph over the page on the far left and another old boy, Frank Earles, son of John Earles, a correspondent for the *Macclesfield Courier*.

One of Roy's fellow officers, Captain Alfred ('Bill') Bland, is unlikely to have allayed the fears of his wife Violet who was looking after their two sons: 'I can't bear you to be unhappy.' His last words were touchingly brief: 'My darling. All my love for ever' and with the letter he enclosed a pressed forget-me-not.

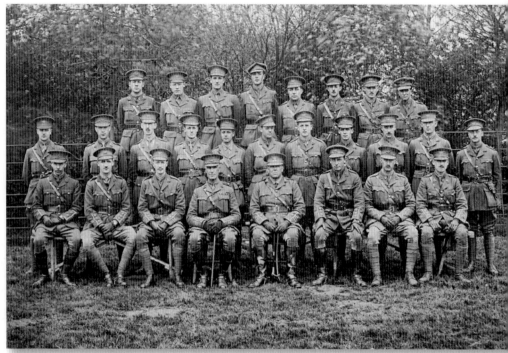

Officers of the 22/ Manchesters before they left for France: Frank Harrison and Roy Mellor are 2nd and 3rd from the left in the back row, Charles May is sitting second from left with Captain Townsend on his left and Frank Earles is third from the right. Alfred Bland is standing middle row far right

'B' and 'D' Companies left their trench at Zero Hour and made good progress, advancing 700 yards quickly. They reached their first objective, Bucket Trench by 8 a.m. and were in touch with Danzig Alley at 8.15. The supporting Companies 'A' and 'C' pushed on towards Fritz Trench, the final objective, but were halted in their tracks by large numbers of Germans who had emerged unscathed from Danzig Alley dug-outs which had not been 'mopped up' by bombing parties.

The advance was achieved at a cost. The 22/ Manchesters sustained 472 casualties on 1st July - 202 were killed, 235 wounded and 35 were missing. Roy, Bland and May were among seven officers killed - Bland and May are buried in Dantzig Alley British Cemetery and Roy Mellor's name is to be found on the Thiepval Memorial. Roy's parents received a letter from the wife of his commanding officer, Lieutenant-Colonel Paul Whetham who personally knew their son. She confirmed that Roy had been killed by shrapnel and that his body had been recovered and buried. The grave was subsequently destroyed probably during the fighting in 1918. It is possible that his is one of the unidentified graves in Dantzig Alley British Cemetery.

A description of the actions of Roy's unit by Frank Harrison appeared in the *Macclesfield Courier*: 'Mellor was in front of all … he must have been slightly hit the first time, because I was only about 150 yards behind him … he got a lot of shrapnel and was killed.' More details were provided by a wounded soldier visited by Roy's father in Stockport. The soldier had seen Roy wounded in the leg when re-loading his revolver and urging his men forward. On his return half an hour later, he could find no trace of Roy and assumed he had been rescued and taken to a Dressing Station.

A tablet to the 70 fallen of King's School Macclesfield was unveiled in May 1929 and the names include a member of staff and 35 officers from the rank of brigadier-general to private. It was a high cost for a small school that numbered only 190 pupils in 1914. Roy was one of 14 of the fallen who were the only sons of their respective families. The tablet was updated in 2015 by the addition of a new plaque to list 15 extra names including six officers.

The six young men in the photograph taken in September 1914 who enlisted, did so through a deep sense of patriotic duty. Little did they know how the War would develop - propaganda had encouraged the thought that it would be 'over by Christmas', but theirs was a selfless sacrifice during the type of warfare that few considered possible in the balmy days of August 1914 which left thousands of families and loved ones to grieve and find ways to understand how and why such tragedies had befallen them.

We shall never know the extent to which Roy Mellor's parents would accept their loss. The fact that Dagny Pogson died unmarried in 1981 suggests that she never did come to terms with the death of her fiancé, Roy.

Captain Charles May's grave in Dantzig Alley British Cemetery

Dagny Pogson, Roy's sweetheart who never married

41

Lieutenant Robert Gilson

11/ Suffolks (Cambridgeshire), 101st Brigade, 34th Division

'...line after line of dead men were lying where they had fallen'

Lieutenant Gilson

Lieutenant Robert Gilson and the 11/ Suffolks were served an early breakfast in the yard of a small château in Bécourt Wood. Their tea was laced with rum: 'the goods, real thick treacly stuff' as one private recalled. At 5.00 a.m. they marched half a mile to assembly trenches. They were about to take part in the 34th Division's attack on German strongpoints at La Boisselle, following the 10/ Lincolns (Grimsby Chums), a 'Pals' Battalion. They were to attack over a wide area of No Man's Land, about 500 yards, up Sausage Valley to take Sausage (Heligoland) and Scots Redoubts and ultimately Contalmaison village. Sausage Valley was so called by British troops because Germans flew sausage-shaped kite balloons to observe below British activity during the build up to the July offensive. In typical 'Tommy' humour the other side of the village was inevitably dubbed 'Mash Valley'.

For a brief time light rain fell: '... we got our dixies out and let the rain run into them from our tin hats ... enough to quench our thirst.' Stress levels amongst the 11/ Suffolks were high - not all troops had been convinced that German opposition would be snuffed out after the seven day bombardment and that the assault would be a 'walk over'. 'A shot went off ... a fellow had shot himself right through the knee ... It was a strange sight, seeing him being carried away on a stretcher under arrest.' Another man went berserk, having to be restrained, and a youngster was crying inconsolably.

The 11/ Suffolks were composed of volunteers from Cambridgeshire - the university, the town and the rural areas of the county. Gilson's 'dear, stupid, agricultural platoon' hailed from Ely in the Fens and working with them was a novel experience for the Cambridge-educated high flying Classicist.

He was born on 25 October 1893 at Harrow-on-the-Hill where his father was teaching; the family moved to the Midlands when Robert Cary Gilson became the Chief Master of King Edward's School, Birmingham. The young Robert excelled academically and was a member of a self-styled intellectual group that called

A German sausage-shaped observation balloon

themselves the Tea Club and Barrovian Society after the school shop. Gilson, Geoffrey Bache Smith and J.R.R. Tolkien, future author of *Lord of the Rings*, enjoyed scholarly debate and went on to study at Oxford or Cambridge. They enlisted in 1914 and after training, fought on the Somme. Bache Smith fought on 1st July in the 19/Lancashire Fusiliers (3rd Salford Pals) but died of wounds in December 1916 aged 22 and is buried at Warlincourt Halte British Cemetery.

When at King Edward's, Gilson developed an interest in painting and debating. He professed to a loathing of militarism and in a school debate in 1910 argued that an international court of arbitration should be established to bring an end to wars. It was ironic that he should have chosen to enlist in 1914 out of duty rather than a deep-seated desire to fight. When War broke out, he had successfully completed the third year of a Classics degree with First Class Honours. His father cautioned against joining up - he should complete his degree and continue in the University's OTC. However, peer group pressure was so great that he decided to enlist on 28th November 1914 and was immediately gazetted as a second lieutenant in the 11/ Suffolks. His performance,

which included the writing of a military manual for use in schools, merited promotion to the rank of full lieutenant by the time the TCBS met for the last time in September 1915. On 8th January 1916 Robert Gilson sailed to France, armed with Greek versions of the *New Testament* and *The Odyssey*.

It was planned that Gilson and his platoon would follow the Grimsby Chums at a distance of 150 yards. They had been warned that the Lochnagar mine to be exploded at La Boisselle would cause considerable 'concussion'. The massive explosion and the debris thrown hundreds of feet into the air

Photo of Robert Gilson (lower right) leading the 6th Platoon of C Company of 11/ Suffolks training at Ripon, North Yorkshire in 1915

must have boosted morale. Two and a half minutes after the 10/ Lincolns had commenced their attack over No Man's Land, Gilson blew his whistle and his platoon followed, walking at a steady pace into a hail of enfilading machine-gun fire from La Boisselle and Heligoland Redoubt. They had no chance and were slaughtered, scythed down before they had made any significant progress. The casualties were alarmingly high - 15 officers and 513 other ranks were wounded or killed. An artillery officer described how across No Man's Land 'line after line of dead men were lying where they had fallen.' Gilson managed to dodge the machine-guns and took over command from the wounded Major Morton but he, his batman Bradnam and Sergeant-Major Brooks, soon succumbed to a shell burst.

The Headmaster of King Edward's Birmingham heard the news of his son's death when about to present the prizes at Sports Day. Tolkien, a signalling officer in the 11/ Lancashire Fusiliers, heard the news of the death of his close friend when based at nearby Warloy. Lieutenant Andrew Wright, a friend of Gilson's, informed his father that he was leading his men forward 'perfectly calmly and confidently. It was the final but not the first triumph of determination over his sensitive nature - he alone is brave who goes to face everything with a full knowledge of his own cowardice.' 245 Old Edwardians are listed on the school's memorial plaques as having died in the Great War. **43**

Lieutenant Robert Gilson's grave

Robert Gilson plus eight old boys were killed on 1st July and a total of 54 lost their lives in the Somme offensive.

A message was received at Battalion HQ from Brigadier-General Gore of 101st Brigade: 'Their courage was magnificent as in spite of wave after wave being mown down they fearlessly pressed forward towards their objective … no troops could have done better… it will go down as one of the gallant actions of the war.' It had been a gallant but futile and ill-conceived action which ended the life of a talented artist and intellectual. Lieutenant Robert Quilter Gilson's grave is to be found in Bécourt Military Cemetery.

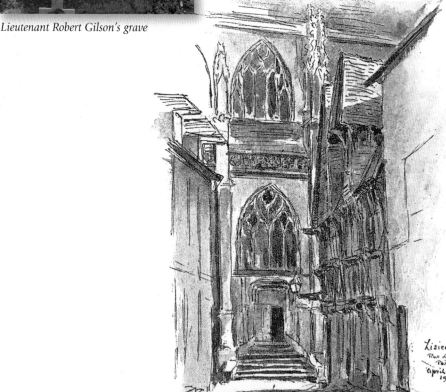

Robert Gilson's drawing of Lisieux in 1912. It was reproduced on a thank you note for people who wrote to the family after his death
Gilson Family Archive

Lieutenant-Colonel Edwin Sandys DSO
2/ Middlesex (Duke of Cambridge's Own), 23rd Brigade, 8th Division

'I have never had a moment's peace since 1st July'

Lieutenant-Colonel Edwin Sandys was CO of the 2/ Middlesex, a battalion of 'regulars' or professionals which had fought in 1915 at the Battles of Neuve Chapelle and Aubers Ridge. The Battalion was transferred to the Somme in April 1916 in readiness for the 'Big Push'.

TRAGEDY OF D.S.O.

Lieutenant-Colonel E. T. Falkner Sandys, D.S.O., who committed suicide. He was wounded five times, and told a friend he wished he had died with his men during the offensive. He was in the attack on July 1.

He was born into a military family on 9th January 1876 in Bareilly, Bengal, India where his father was serving as an officer in the Royal Artillery. Edwin followed in his father's footsteps and by 1911 was a captain in the Middlesex Regiment.

On 9th May 1916, Sandys drew up a scheme for a raiding party on German trenches between Ovillers and La Boisselle. It took place on 11th May although, for various reasons, it was not a great success and in his report the following day to 23rd Brigade Head Quarters, Sandys concluded 'I very much regret that the raid, as a raid, was a failure, but I am confident every man did his best and that if an entrance to the German trench had been humanly possible, these men would have effected it and reached the goal for which they were aiming.'

Edwin Sandys was, from that moment, conscious of the strength of German trenches and their defences and expressed concerns to his superiors in late June about whether the bombardment had caused the level of damage they hoped for. Although he was granted leave between 17th and 26th May, he was not in the greatest of health, being admitted to hospital from 17th to 21st June.

The Germans' view of Mash Valley. The 2/ Middlesex attacked from right to left through the dark green part of the field

In the days leading to Zero Hour, he would spend much time with his binoculars scanning the enemy trenches and their defensive barbed wire entanglements. He remained unconvinced that they or the Germans and their defences were being demolished. His warnings were not heeded - it was with a heavy heart that he awaited the time when his Battalion would attack a dangerously long distance of 750 yards up Mash Valley to objectives between Ovillers and La Boisselle with the aim of reaching Pozières.

At 7.28 a.m. a 40,000 lb mine was exploded at Y Sap to the west of La Boisselle which alerted the Germans to the impending attack. Numerous casualties to the 2/ Middlesex, 2/ Devons and 20/ Northumberland Fusiliers (1st Tyneside Scottish) were caused by untouched machine-guns from both fortified villages. Desperately concerned for his men, Sandys went into No Man's Land where he was badly wounded.

D.S.O. HERO'S DESIRE.

Wanted to Die with His Men in the Great Push.

A tragic story was told at a Westminster inquest yesterday on Lieutenant-Colonel E. T. Falkner Sandys, D.S.O., who died at St. George's Hospital as the result of a bullet wound.

On September 6 he took a room at the Cavendish Hotel and was found dead in bed with a revolver in his hand.

Captain Lloyd Jones said that Colonel Sandys, who resided at the Bath Club, had been wounded five times, and was greatly depressed and much distressed because in the attack on July 1 his battalion suffered severely.

He had never threatened suicide, but said he wished he had been killed with his men.

Witness received a letter from him, saying: " I have come to London to-day to take my life. I have never had a moment's peace since July 1."

The coroner said the case revealed a pathetic tragedy of a very distinguished soldier, who thought less of his own wounds than he did of the loss of his men.

Suicide whilst temporarily insane was the verdict.

Daily Mirror 15th September 1916

The whole exercise was a fiasco with a massive toll of dead and wounded: 23 officers and 517 other ranks. It was of little consequence to him that his concerns had been vindicated. The Battalion War Diary recorded that of those who took part in the attack 'a bare 50 answered their names in the early hours of 2nd July.'

Sandys returned to England to recuperate. He related in a letter to a friend that 'I have come to London to take my life. I have never had a moment's peace since 1st July.' On 6th September he was found in a bedroom in the Cavendish Hotel in London's Mayfair having shot himself. He was taken to St. George's Hospital where he died on 13th September. *The Daily Mirror's* headline of 15th September was a 'Hero's Desire to Die with his Men in the Great Push of 1st July 1916.'

Captain Lloyd-Jones stated that Colonel Sandys who resided at the Bath Club had been wounded five times … he had never threatened suicide but said he wished he had been killed with his men.'

At the inquest, the coroner concluded that the case 'revealed a pathetic tragedy of a very distinguished soldier, who thought less of his own wounds than he did of the loss of his men.' His verdict was that he had committed suicide 'whilst temporarily insane.'

Lieutenant-Colonel Sandys was awarded the DSO nine days after his death despite the contemporary shame surrounding suicide and in 1917 he was Mentioned in Despatches by Field Marshal Haig.

He was a CO who understood the importance of duty of care for his men - his failure to convince his superiors of the dangers that they would face, caused him such mental anguish that he decided he could no longer live with himself. He was deeply depressed by what had happened and the suggestion that he was 'temporarily insane' is to modern eyes, insensitive but at least it was officially recorded by the War Office that he 'died of wounds' on 1st July 1916.

He is buried in the Brompton Cemetery in London with 368 other First and Second World War casualties. The inscription on his grave states that he 'fell in France severely wounded on 1st July and died in London on 13th September 1916.'

Lieutenant-Colonel Sandys's grave in Brompton Cemetery, London

British view of Mash Valley. Sandys and his men attacked from left to right through the darker green part of the field towards the German front line where the houses are today

Sergeant James Turnbull vc
17/ Highland Light Infantry, 97th Brigade, 32nd Division

'A strong, forthright personality who would not suffer fools gladly'

A year after 'that awful day' on the Somme, a memorial service was held on 8th July 1917 in Glasgow Cathedral to honour 'the officers, non-commissioned officers and men of the 17/ Highland Light Infantry (Glasgow Commercials) who fell during the Battle of the Somme and elsewhere.' The service was led by the Reverend A. Herbert Gray, who had served as the Battalion's chaplain during the War. He praised 'the hundreds of young men … who dared to die in a great cause. Young, strong, and free, full of high hopes and great purpose, in love with life, and in a hundred ways fitted for mastery in it, they yet consented to deal with death … but because humanity called, they laid them all aside and went to the Great War. No such life was their choice, but because it was their destiny they accepted with a smile.'

Sergeant James Turnbull

The Service was attended by more than 1,200 including some of the Battalion's wounded soldiers - their sombre mood would have been in stark contrast to their disposition three years earlier when, on a tide of patriotic fervour, they had volunteered to fight for King and Country.

One of those prepared to join the great adventure in the late summer of 1914 was the 30 year old James Turnbull, the third son of James Turnbull, a well-known Glaswegian master joiner and his wife Elizabeth. James Youll was born on Christmas Eve 1883 and after his schooling at Albert Road Academy worked as a 'clothing warehouseman' for the speciality tailors Wallace, Scott and Co. and was a member of the local militia. He moved on to work for a similar firm in Oban on the west coast of Scotland.

James or 'Jimmy' as he was known was a keen sportsman. Tall and athletic he played rugby for Cartha Queens Park RFC and sailed at the Lorn Corinthian Yacht Club. After the declaration of war, he returned to Glasgow to enlist in the 'Citizens Army'.

Glasgow's Town Council raised two battalions - the 1st Glasgow, drawn mainly from the employees of the Tramways, and the 2nd Glasgow which was composed of former members of the Boys' Brigade. Other institutions in the city were keen to be involved and at a meeting of the Directors of the Chamber of Commerce, it was agreed to form a Glasgow Chamber of Commerce Battalion known as the 3rd Glasgow, composed of men from various trades and businesses in the city. In addition, students of the Royal Technical College were encouraged to sign up. James decided to join the Battalion and like many thousands of men in the country, he was not a professional soldier but he had, as the Reverend Gray had asserted in his address, been recruited 'simply by conscience and the claims of humanity.' The President of the Chamber of Commerce received a letter from the War Office dated 2nd November 1914 thanking him 'for having raised the 17th (Service) Battalion, Highland Light Infantry (3rd Glasgow) of which the administration has now been taken over by the military authorities.'

James and his comrades were introduced to army life with the issue of navy blue serge tunics for their training at Gailes. Later, at Troon, they were supplied with standard khaki uniform which they proudly wore when the Battalion paraded in the streets of Glasgow when, according to the History of the 17/ Highland Light Infantry 'the men marched between banks of faces, in a deep silence …' They were cheered enthusiastically when they reached the Main Square.

Their training in 1915 took them to Shropshire, Yorkshire and finally Salisbury Plain in Wiltshire. The sporting Turnbull would have enjoyed the periods of relaxation when the men played rugby, football, cricket and golf; the Battalion excelled in inter-unit rugby matches and they took on and beat Bath City at football.

In November the 17/ Highland Light Infantry crossed the Channel to Le Havre and made their way to the Somme area. They were underwhelmed by their initiation to life in the trenches which, up to their knees in water, they shared with memorably large rats. They soon acquired a reputation with their German opponents who dubbed them the 'Red Division' (so called because a red circle was worn on the soldiers' sleeves) on account of their regular shelling and constant raids.

In preparation for the 'Big Push' new trenches had to be dug and divisional exercises performed. James Turnbull may have been a member of a raiding party on 22nd April which successfully cleared dug-outs, destroyed machine-gun positions and took 13 prisoners. They were congratulated on their work by General Sir Henry Rawlinson.

Soon after arriving in France, James was promoted to the rank of sergeant. According to Duncan Peterson who served with him, he had 'a strong, forthright personality who would not suffer fools gladly. He took care of his men to the risk of being court-martialled for insubordination where their welfare was concerned.'

The build-up to the offensive on 1st July is well described by Private C.B. Meadows of the 17/ Highland Light Infantry. The terrific noise of the seven day bombardment of the German lines was so loud that the men were given cotton wool for their ears- not that it did them much good! The shelling took its toll on the Germans - for Private Eversmann of the 26th Reserve Division 'five nights has this hell-concert lasted. One's head is as a madman's; the tongue sticks to the roof of the mouth.'

Meadows described the equipment that men were to take with them in a haversack during the assault: a mess tin, small kit, two days' rations, 'iron rations' (consisting of preserved meat, biscuits and tea), a spare pair of socks, waterproof sheet, pouches with 120 rounds of ammunition, a bayonet, iron rations, four sandbags, a water bottle and another 100 rounds in bandoliers. Speed across No Man's Land was clearly not a priority.

In the early morning of 1st July the Battalion made its way to trenches near Authuille. The Battalion History records that 'nothing was real, men stood and waited as if in a dream' and after the guns had ceased firing 'in the death-like stillness was the warbling of birds in No Man's Land. The grim reality of it all was felt. With the lifting mist of the morning, the curtain rose.'

At 7.23 they left their trenches, crept into No Man's Land and advanced to within 60 yards of the barrage. According to Lance-Corporal McKechnie, James Turnbull was one of the first to 'go over the top' to assault the Leipzig Redoubt, a heavily fortified position in a chalk quarry known to the Germans as the 'Granatloch'. The Highlanders subdued the defenders inside and outside their dug-outs. James had been urged, during training, to keep an eye out during attacks for German stores of bombs - he noticed a large store.

Progress was halted by heavy machine-gun fire from another fortified position, the Wonder Work - the Scotsmen were now badly exposed on both flanks. The Leipzig Redoubt was a maze of trenches and in the chaotic fighting one officer was heard to shout 'every man for himself'.

By 9 o'clock, 22 officers and 400 other ranks were casualties. Bombers were striving to hold the flanks and it was at this stage that James came to the fore. In McKechnie's opinion 'he was a fellow who always took charge of affairs, but we all had the greatest confidence in his judgement. He had a splendid physique and was almost fearless. He was a fine cricketer and it was possibly this that made him such an expert bomber.'

Early in the afternoon Turnbull and his men were still holed up in the Redoubt but had seen off several counter-attacks; he was unwavering in his efforts to keep the Germans at bay, throwing bombs further than anyone else and encouraging men

Cigarette card of Turnbull VC

around him to supply him with more. When they were in danger of running out, he remembered the bomb store he had noticed earlier and sent men to fetch them. McKechnie was impressed: 'He kept this up for about sixteen hours, practically holding up the whole of the German flank and saving the battalion ... his stamina was really remarkable, as most of the others were quite fagged out with what they had gone through.' He had taken numerous risks and it was sadly ironic that he should be hit by a sniper when back defending the Battalion's trenches.

James Turnbull's body was recovered and is buried in Lonsdale Cemetery about 350 yards from the Leipzig Redoubt, alongside 30 comrades from the 17/ Highland Light Infantry. Sir Arthur Conan Doyle in his history of the War, wrote that 'in the desperate circumstances, it might well be considered a remarkable result that a stretch of the Leipzig Redoubt should be won and permanently held by the Highlanders, especially by the 17th Highland Light Infantry.'

James Turnbull was awarded the VC posthumously. The award was gazetted on 25th September 1916 to 'James Young (sic) Turnbull for most conspicuous bravery and devotion to duty, when, having with his party captured a post apparently of great importance to the enemy, he was subjected to severe counter-attacks, which were continuous throughout the whole day. Although his party was wiped out and replaced several times during the day, Sergeant Turnbull never wavered in his determination to hold the post, the loss of which would have been serious. Almost single-handed, he maintained his position, and displayed the highest degree of valour and skill in the performance of his duties. Later in the day this very gallant soldier was killed whilst bombing a counter-attack from the parados of our trench.'

The VC medal was presented to his father at Buckingham Palace on 2nd May 1917. A memorial tablet in his honour was unveiled on 11th September 1925 at the Lorn Corinthian Yacht Club at Oban where James had been an active member.

The recommendation for the award of the VC has to be issued by an officer and supported by witnesses. James Turnbull was one of only nine men awarded the medal following the momentous events of 1st July when there must have been many more acts of gallantry and courage - however, so many great deeds were not witnessed, due to the huge numbers of officers who were killed.

Grave of Sergeant Turnbull VC in Lonsdale Cemetery

Lonsdale Cemetery

Lieutenant-Colonel Frank Crozier
9/ Royal Irish Rifles (West Belfast), 107th Brigade, 36th (Ulster) Division

'The human corn stalks were falling before the Reaper'

The CO of the 9/ Royal Irish Rifles on 1st July 1916 was a maverick, a most unlikely candidate for meteoric promotion from being a private in August 1914 to lieutenant-colonel by 1st January 1916. An avowed Orangeman from a well-heeled Anglo-Irish family, he was involved in procuring German guns in early 1914 for the Protestant Ulster Volunteer Force for use against the British Government and its moves to introduce Irish Home Rule. A deteriorating situation in Ireland with Protestant and Nationalist militias at loggerheads was temporarily placed on hold with the outbreak of war in Europe. Frank Crozier deftly withdrew from his mutinous activities and threw himself into raising troops for the 9/ Royal Irish Rifles from West Belfast, known locally as the 'Shankill Boys.' Many of the recruits were members of the Ulster Volunteer Force but despite the tensions in Ireland, about 25% were Roman Catholics.

Crozier had risen to the rank of major by the end of September 1914. He was second in command of the Battalion, quite an achievement for someone whose career since leaving Wellington College had been somewhat chequered: he had worked on a tea plantation in Ceylon (now Sri Lanka), saw service in a cavalry regiment in the Boer War (cavalry because he was too short for the required height for the infantry), and his time in the Manchester Regiment came to an unhappy end due to his frequent failure to honour cheques. He farmed unsuccessfully in Canada before returning to Ireland.

When Crozier and his Battalion waited in Aveluy Wood to take part in the 109th and 107th Brigades' attack on the heavily fortified Schwaben Redoubt, his men knew by this stage that he was not to be trifled with - he had earned a reputation for his unbending and harsh leadership: he would send patrols out into No Man's Land for no good reason other than to foster a spirit of aggression. The 36th Division's CO, Major-General Nugent expressed concern about Crozier's 'roughness and ruthless way in which he handled his men' even if such traits were tempered by his unfailing courage and firm leadership. He thought nothing of shooting those who had 'the wind up' and his treatment of one of his young Shankill recruits, James Crozier, was a chilling warning to his men that desertion or cowardice would be punished by execution.

James Crozier, coincidentally with the same surname, was an apprentice in the Belfast dockyards - the Kitchener campaign for volunteers offered him an exciting opportunity to escape his humdrum existence. In the recruiting office, Frank Crozier allayed his mother's fears for her young boy and promised to keep an avuncular eye on him. James completed training at Ballykinlar, south of Belfast and at Seaford in Sussex before sailing to France in October 1915, a member of what Frank Crozier described as this 'immature, hastily trained army'.

In February 1916, Private James Crozier was arrested for having left his sentry post opposite Serre village. His CO stated that 'from a fighting point of view this soldier is of no value. His behaviour has been that of a "shirker" for the past three months. I am firmly of the opinion that the crime was deliberately committed with the intention of avoiding duty in the Redan.' Young Crozier's file made its way to the highest level and his death warrant was signed by General Sir Douglas Haig. James Crozier was shot at 7.05 a.m. on 27th February in Mailly Maillet with the Battalion behind the wall of the villa where the execution took place, expressly 'for the sake of example'. Lieutenant-Colonel Crozier had failed to fulfil his promise to James Crozier's mother - he was responsible for a cold blooded decision to have a boy 'shot at dawn' whose only crime was to be cold, miserable, homesick and quite probably shell-shocked. It was an event that would weigh heavily on Frank Crozier's shoulders for the rest of his life.

On the eve of the long awaited assault, the 9 and 10/ Royal Irish Rifles had crossed a causeway over the river Ancre and were on Speyside Avenue. Scottish regiments had originally held the line which explains why many of the positions in Thiepval Wood were named after places in the Highlands of Scotland - Gordon Castle, Elgin Avenue, Speyside and Blair Atholl, all of which reminded Crozier of 'happier days killing grouse instead of Germans.' He was confident that his men were well versed in what the assault would entail. They had practised in 'spit-locked trenches' (i.e. not fully constructed) and he had lectured the whole Battalion with a cloth map 20 feet square.

James Crozier 'Shot at Dawn' buried in Sucrerie Military Cemetery

Crozier and Colonel Bernard of the 10/ Royal Irish Rifles mulled over the task they faced resting against a tree trunk eating sandwiches and drinking tea, on what, significantly for them, would on the morrow, be the anniversary of the Battle of the Boyne when in 1690 the Protestant William of Orange had defeated the forces of the ousted Roman Catholic, King James II. Major-General Oliver Nugent their divisional commander, was of the opinion that 'no date could have been more auspiciously chosen for the day on which the Ulster Division was to prove its value as a fighting force … The cries of "No Surrender Boys", heard as the waves of the attack swept forward, showed how well the men appreciated the historical association of the day.'

Both were furious at orders received from Nugent, that, for safety reasons, commanding officers were not to accompany their units. Crozier, smoking his pipe as usual, bridled that 'the whole idea was repulsive. It cut across the foundations of mutual trust between private and officer … so Bernard and I agreed in private to disobey.' Bernard was concerned that the 34th Division might struggle to take Thiepval village to their right and asked the question, pertinent as the day unfolded: 'If that fails, where are we on the flank?' When they parted at 11 p.m. 'Bernard's "Good night old chap" were his final words, for nine hours later he went to his long rest to join the vast legion of happy warriors.'

Crozier could not sleep. He chose to walk round the trenches. He saw a small illegal light shining - it was young Private Campbell writing a letter home. 'Do you want to give the whole show away?' he asked. Campbell apologised and explained that he was writing his last letter home. His CO asked him why it would be his last communication: **53**

Re-created trench on the edge of Thiepval Wood on the original front line

'I feel I'm for it, Sir. One day's as good as another, and the sooner the better; all we fellows are bound to get it in the neck, sooner or later.' Crozier took the green envelope and promised to post it at the first opportunity.

Six battalions of the 36th (Ulster) Division manned the front line trenches from Thiepval Wood to the river Ancre and on the other bank to Mary Redan. Two of the 107th Brigade's Royal Irish Rifles Battalions, Crozier's 9th alongside Bernard's 10th, were to attack the Schwaben Redoubt, a strongly fortified stronghold, from the edge of Thiepval Wood in the third wave behind battalions of the 109th Brigade.

Crozier complimented the cook on the quality of the hearty breakfast, essential for a hard but hopefully short day's fighting: '… Rashers, fried bread, jam, Sir - they should be able to fight on that alright, and each man is to have cold tea and lemon in his water bottle.' There was no trace of rum, therefore, by order of the teetotaller officer who had lost his way earlier in life from frequent bouts of drunkenness.

The first wave of the 9 and 10/ Royal Inniskilling Fusiliers went over the top a few minutes before Zero Hour on the order of Major-General Nugent. They were, Crozier recalled, 'carrying the creeping barrage on their backs'. At Zero there was a furious German counter barrage but the 9/ Royal Irish Rifles were protected by the steep slope of Speyside where they had assembled. The Battalion then sang, a little nervously and moved off at a 'steady pace'. As they neared the fringe of Thiepval Wood, Crozier glanced to his right and saw 'rows upon rows of British soldiers lying dead or wounded in No Man's Land.' Visibility was poor but he saw enough to convince him that Thiepval was still held by the Germans and had not, as planned, been taken at 7.45 a.m. They were at the mercy of enfilade machine-gun fire from Thiepval. The sights to his right were horrific: 'The human corn stalks were falling before the Reaper.' He admitted to himself that 'Bernard was right' - but where was he? News arrived that he had been hit by a trench mortar shell and mortally wounded- the 50 year old ex-Indian Army Colonel is buried in Martinsart British Cemetery. Crozier claimed in *Brass Hat in No Man's Land* that he took over command of the 10/ Royal Irish Rifles although the evidence to corroborate this is limited.

Connaught Cemetery - the 9/ Royal Irish Rifles attacked from the edge of Thiepval Wood from left to right

The 9/ Royal Irish Rifles made their way to a sunken road (now the road from Thiepval to the Ulster Tower and not as 'sunken' as in 1916) where there was a modicum of cover. A wag behind Crozier shouted: 'This way to eternity.' Major George Gaffikin was in the sunken road - he was of a similarly bellicose disposition to his CO, from an Anglo-Irish family and educated at Uppingham, an English public school. He called out to Crozier 'Goodbye, sir, good luck, tell them I died a teetotaller, put it on the stone if you find me.' Gaffikin was referring to an earlier incident when Crozier had discovered him blind drunk, had given him a sound dressing down but had taken the matter no further. Crozier wished him good luck and chided him: '... don't talk rot, anyway you played the game.'

Crozier blew his whistle and the men attacked; Gaffikin led his men into No Man's Land, waving an orange handkerchief and shouting, so it was said, the Protestant cry of 'No Surrender!' He was part

Major George Gaffikin's grave

of 'a spirited dash across No Man's Land carried out as if on parade' but he never reached the German wire. He was wounded and rescued but died later that evening. His grave is in Bray Vale British Cemetery ... without any mention of his drinking habits on it!

Brigadier-General Frank Crozier

A few Royal Irish did manage to get within range of the German wire: Corporal G.A. Lloyd wrote that 'we were pinned down in the open just outside the German wire. It was just Hell; the British artillery were at us, the German artillery were at us, and there was rifle and machine-gun fire as well.'

The Battalion was pushed back and forced to retreat to the wood. Brutal but frank in name and thought - Crozier later wrote that 'the dead no longer count. War has no use for dead men.' But he expressed the hope that 'they will be buried later', one of whom would have been a retreating Irishman shot by a subaltern attempting to stem the flow: 'A young subaltern heads them off. They push by him. He draws his revolver and threatens them. They take no notice. He fires. Down drops a British soldier at his feet. The effect is instantaneous, they turn back to the assistance of their comrades in distress.'

Crozier decamped to a deep dug-out in the wood, allocated as an HQ only to find it full of dead and wounded: 'A wrong thing has been done ... I find the place full of dead and wounded men ... most are in agony, some there for days ... All were removed.'

The wounded from the battlefield were by now being taken to the wood in large numbers. He heard the name of Campbell and it reminded him of the green envelope - one can but hope he managed to post it.

Crozier managed to survive his defiance of orders not to go over the top. He saw 'the initial recommendation for a DSO for me, made out by Withycombe' (the brigade-general) but it had been 'scrawled across in red by Nugent (a great friend of mine) "rank disobedience of orders should be court martialled" !!' Crozier's copy book had not been blotted - he was promoted to the rank of brigadier-general in August.

At 10 p.m. 'the curtain rings down on hell. The cost? Enormous. I have 70 men left, all told out of 700.' He told of going out into No Man's Land to organise the evacuation of the wounded, about 700 dead and wounded in an area perhaps a quarter of a mile square. He had trained the 9/ Royal Irish Rifles in every detail from

September 1914 when they were 'only a mob in muffin'. All his work lay literally in tatters in No Man's Land - commanders at various levels, not least General Rawlinson had been anxious about the fighting qualities of, as Crozier described them, a 'hastily trained volunteer national army'. His view was that it was impossible for the battalions involved to take and hold the Schwaben Redoubt: 'They almost achieved a miracle by doing what they did with both flanks exposed.' As the morning wore on - what were the chances of success on 1st July 1916, given the military lack of experience amongst the 'immature' battalions of Kitchener's Army?

In 1914 Frank Crozier joined the Royal Irish Rifles without a rank; during the next four years he was awarded the DSO, CMG, CB, the Croix de Guerre and was mentioned several times in despatches. He ended the War as brigade-general for the predominantly Welsh 119th Brigade of the 40th Division on the recommendation of Brigadier-General Withycombe. Such success, however, was not replicated in the post war years. He acted briefly in 1919 as a military adviser to the Lithuanian Government and in 1920 for a year only, took command of the Royal Irish Constabulary Reserve Force, 'The Black and Tans', before resigning - disillusioned by the British Government's policy in Ireland. He found it difficult to find gainful employment thereafter and concentrated on writing two books *A Brass Hat in No Man's Land* (1930) and *The Men I Killed* (1937, the year of his death) which he dedicated to 'the genuine fighters of all nations who stuck it to the end in the front line, and to the genuine conscientious objectors of all nations who stuck it to the end in jail.' Rambling, repetitive and at times factually challenged, they reflected an extraordinary *volte-face* by one of the toughest hardliners of the Great War, as he sought to explain 'shot at dawn' executions, the shooting of those, like the Portuguese in retreat in 1918 but ultimately to denounce the concept of war: 'A lifetime of professional soldiering has brought me, by painful ways, to the realisation that all war is wrong, is senseless.' He joined the Labour Party in 1923 and turned to pacifism. Reminded of the lady who zealously handed out white feathers of cowardice early in the War, he hoped that 'this patriotic lady will work as hard in the cause of peace as she did in the cause of war.'

The James Crozier incident looms large in his writings. He concluded that 'he was no rotter deserving to die like that. He was merely fragile. He had volunteered to fight for his country … at the dictates of his own young heart he failed. And for that failure he was condemned to die … we never made up our minds for whom we were sorrier - him or ourselves. Such is war.'

Frank Crozier had his enemies; many found him bombastic, fractious and opinionated - his criticism of the High Command in the post war years was damning: Horne (XV Corps) 'could do little save touch his hat', Rawlinson (4th Army) was 'a circus clown' and Field Marshal Haig 'not worth a day's pay'!

Lieutenant-Colonel Frank Crozier could at least boast that on 1st July, he led his men heroically against insurmountable odds but the events of those few hours helped to shape his extraordinary rejection of war: 'The birds have gone, nature has been supplanted. The wood itself has disappeared; was there ever such a day? Not in my recollection.'

Private Anthony James (Jim) Stacey
1/ Newfoundland Regiment, 88th Brigade, 29th Division

'I could see no one moving, but heaps of khaki slumped to the ground'

Visitors to the Somme, with good reason, are drawn to see the Thiepval Memorial to the 72,000 'Missing of the Somme'. Thereafter they can experience the awe-inspiring Lochnagar Crater or the homely Ulster Tower Memorial to the fallen Irish, but one site, the Newfoundland Memorial Park, comes closest to offering a feel for and

Private 'Jim' Stacey   *Jean Edwards Stacey*

understanding of what the soldiers experienced on 1st July 1916. The British trench system, No Man's Land and the German front line can all be easily 'walked'. For the small former colony of Newfoundland, it is sacred ground where their Battalion on 1st July 1916 suffered the second highest percentage of casualties. Out of 801 men, only 68 answered roll call after the battle; one of their number 'Jim' Stacey survived the rest of the War to tell his tale.

Jim Stacey was born in Oxfordshire, on 17th November 1890 and at the age of 20, like many others at the time, decided to leave Britain for a new life abroad, following his brother Charles to Newfoundland where he had already settled. His first job was in a grocer's shop then as a waiter in a dining car with the Reid Newfoundland Railway Company.

When War was declared, he was one of the first to volunteer and thanks to his memoirs which he wrote in the 1960s we have a detailed and honest account of his experience as a private.

Newfoundland proudly held the distinction of being the oldest British Crown colony, the tie dating back to 1583. It was not until 1949 that independence from Britain was achieved when it became a Canadian province. In 1914 the Newfoundland Patriotic Committee was founded with the aim of enlisting and equipping 500 men promised to the Mother Country. Jim recalled that it was 'your duty in the hour of need.'

Due to the shortage of khaki puttees, the new recruits were issued with blue ones worn by their local Church Lads Brigade and thus was born the Regiment's nick name of the 'Blue Puttees'.

Jim and his mates sailed on the *Florizel* from the capital St. John's on 3rd October 1914 in a convoy of more than 30 ships which also transported the first contingent of Canadian troops. Jim considered himself fortunate to be put in charge of the Sergeants' Mess which guaranteed him better conditions on board.

The 'Blue Puttees' arrived on 14th October in England and underwent seven weeks of training on Salisbury Plain where the weather was wet and cold. Jim was in the 7th platoon of 'B' Company under the command of Lieutenant Charles Ayre. In December they were sent to Fort George in the Highlands where Jim celebrated the New Year a little 'too well' and found himself confined to barracks! By May 1915 the Battalion was up to strength and posted to Aldershot where they were reviewed by King George V and the great military hero, Lord Kitchener.

Young Jim Stacey was often getting into scrapes - he forged a signature to get a pass but was caught and confined to barracks again - for two days. Undeterred he managed to buy a pass from an impecunious mate and travelled home to Oxfordshire for ten days. He found on his return that the Battalion had sailed for Gallipoli! He was sent to Ayr in Scotland and joined the 2nd Battalion which was being formed as a reserve to provide reinforcements for the 1st. It was here that the Regiment acquired its mascot, a Newfoundland dog named Sable Chief.

Jim re-joined the 1st Battalion in the Gallipoli Peninsula in December during a storm which 'washed out the trenches and then froze.' He was now experiencing the grim reality of war, the sorry sight of Royal Scots frozen to death, cases of trench foot and 40 men killed mostly by disease and 'stray bullets and sniper-fire'. In January 1916, the Newfoundlanders were amongst the last of the 29th Division to leave which 'closed the chapter of that operation of that folly.'

After a tour of duty in the defence of the Suez Canal in March 1916, the Battalion under the command of Lieutenant-Colonel Arthur Hadow left for France. Transferred from the Norfolk Regiment ('The Holy Boys'), Hadow was a strict disciplinarian who instigated hard training programmes for the men but Jim nonetheless had great respect for him: 'He was a great organiser and ready to cut clear of red tape.'

They made him the subject of a ditty to the tune of the popular 'I'm Gilbert the Filbert' sung by Basil Hallam who was killed in the Somme when in August 1916 he fell to his death from a kite balloon.

> *I'm Hadow, some lad-o*
> *Just off the Staff,*
> *I command the Newfoundlanders*
> *And they know it - not half.*
> *I'll make them or break them,*
> *I'll make the blighters sweat,*
> *For I'm Hadow, some lad-o,*
> *I'll be a general yet.*

They arrived in the Somme in April and were billeted in Louvencourt: 'For the next three months we would stay a week in reserves, then move about two miles up toward the line for a week in supports at Englebelmer and from there to the front line' where their trenches were between the villages of Beaumont and Hamel. Compared to some, it was a reasonably quiet sector.

He was given the important but dangerous job as a runner, attached to Battalion HQ, 'to deliver messages to company commanders, medical officers, Transport section and Brigade HQs.' Life for runners was precarious, a high percentage of them were killed when executing their duties so Jim did well to survive another two years.

Three 1/ Newfoundlanders runners - from left to right Walter Thistle, Will Eaton and Jim Stacey
Jean Edwards Stacey

Activity increased in June. There were more raids, an increase in British shelling and more aeroplanes in the skies above. Jim counted 30 British machines in one day. On 26th and 27th June 57 men undertook trench raids under the command of the intelligence officer Captain Bert Butler. On the second night they just managed to reach the German front trench and found the barbed wire was more or less intact despite the days of bombardment. Four men were killed, 21 wounded and three missing.

Jim was not alone in being lulled into a false sense of security. His overconfidence was typical: 'Seeing so much activity from our side and so little from the enemy, one would think it would be a walkover.' At 9 p.m. on 30th June, the Newfoundlanders left their billets to play their part in the 'Big Push'. Their numbers had been increased on the day by the arrival of 66 reinforcements who were pitched into the action with a complete lack of preparation. The locals bade them farewell with tears in their eyes and as they marched, they broke into a rendition of 'Keep the Home Fires Burning.' They passed by Mailly Maillet and took up position in the St. John's Road trenches behind the front line by 2 a.m. Before dawn they were served a hot breakfast.

Newfoundlanders in St. John's Road Trench

At 7.20 a.m. the mine at Hawthorn Ridge was detonated. The Germans had been served notice that the attack was imminent and rushed their machine-guns into position. At Zero Hour thousands of men attacked across No Man's Land. The 1/ Newfoundlanders were the only Empire troops to attack and with the 16/ Middlesex (Public Schools) were the only non-regular units of the 'Incomparable' 29th Division that were awarded a record 27 VCs during the War.

The first wave to attack in front of the Newfoundlanders at 7.30 a.m. were the 2/ South Wales Borderers who were mown down in their own wire. They were followed by the 1/ Border Regiment who were demolished before clearing their own trenches. The RIR 119 were opposite and it was recorded in their War Diary that 'ahead of us wave after wave of British troops were crawling out of their trenches and coming towards us at a walk, their bayonets glistening in the sun.'

The Generals behind the lines were anxious for news and when soon after 8.30 a.m. a white flare was seen, it was assumed that the first objective had been achieved. In reality it was a German flare probably alerting their gunners to the fact that their shells were falling short. At 8.45 the Newfoundlanders and the 1/ Essex were ordered to attack. Jim conveyed the message to Captains Bruce Reid and Eric Ayre to advance.

The Essex took two hours to reach their jumping-off positions, delayed by the dead and wounded lying in the trenches. They never got beyond their own wire, mown down by machine-gun fire at a cost of more than 200 casualties. Meanwhile the Newfoundlanders had to move forward from reserve and support trenches across 250 yards before reaching the front line trenches and in so doing, like the 1/ Essex, sustained many casualties. Those who did reach the trenches and crossed into No Man's Land discovered that the wire had been cut to form zigzag lanes which became death traps for large numbers fired at by a machine-gun to their right. Nearly half way down the incline towards the German line, dead soldiers were heaped by a land-mark now known as the Danger Tree.

Walter Day who had volunteered in 1914 at the age of 15, was the youngest to go into battle. He survived to tell his story: 'I didn't get no more than halfway towards our own wire' when he came across a wounded man: 'I can't stop … I got to keep going.' The man replied 'I know that, sonny' as he was trying to bandage his wound.

Jim was with Lieutenant-Colonel Hadow lying down in the British wire trying to assess the situation. Jim 'could see no one moving, but heaps of khaki slumped to the ground.' Hadow ordered him to obtain information from a man seen crawling back. Jim failed to reach him because of the wounded in his way. He remembered their agonising cries vividly. Hadow ordered all those around to retreat. The Germans had started to fire their heavy guns which 'accounted for so many missing as H.E. shells blew the dead and wounded to pieces.' The supporting 4/ Worcesters lost 100 men to such shelling on their way to the front line.

Grave of 2nd Lieutenant Wilfrid Ayre, Knightsbridge Cemetery

At 9.45 a.m. Hadow reported to Brigade HQ that the attack had failed. Notwithstanding this, Brigadier-General Douglas Cayley directed him to renew the attack with whatever fit men he could find. Fortunately his order was countermanded by Corps HQ. Jim was sent to fetch any 'stragglers' and to bring them to Hyde Park Corner behind the line; some were badly shell-shocked. As darkness fell, Jim was by now exhausted, crawled into a dug-out and fell asleep.

CAPT. ERIC STANLEY AYRE, 1st. Nfld. Regiment, son of Mrs. Robt. Chesley Ayre, aged 28; educated at Methodist College and Leys School, Cambridge. Killed in action, July 1st.

CAPT. BERNARD PITTS AYRE, Norfolk Regiment, brother to Eric, aged 24, educated at Methodist College and Leys School, Cambridge. Took an Honours Degree in Medicine at Jesus, Cambridge University. Killed in action, July 1st.

LIEUT. GERALD WALTER AYRE, 1st. Nfld. Regiment. Son of Fred. W. Ayre, aged 25, educated at Methodist College and Rossall College. Killed in action, July 1st.

LIEUT. WILFRID DOUGLAS AYRE, 1st. Nfld. Regiment. Son of Charles P. Ayre, aged 21, educated at Methodist College and Leys School, Cambridge. Killed in action, July 1st.

The four Newfoundlander Ayre cou...

When he reported to HQ, he found he had been listed as missing. He was sent out as a guide for the relief battalion and, while delivering a message to the front line, he saw 'war at its worst, with the trench full of dead in all kinds of gruesome shapes'.

Only 68 men were at roll call on 2nd July. In the space of a mere half an hour the 1/ Newfoundlanders suffered about 700 casualties. All 25 officers were casualties, 14 of whom were killed (the CWGC records 12 and the BWD 14) , 221 other ranks were killed and 454 were wounded or missing. The average age of the casualties was 24. Two pairs of brothers were killed and four cousins of the Ayre family fell. Some stranded in No Man's Land waited for night-fall to crawl back to their trenches and one inched his way back five days later. The grim task of collecting and burying the dead had to be undertaken - Jim was tasked with finding a grave for Lieutenant Owen Steele, the billeting officer, who had died of wounds caused by shelling.

Back in Newfoundland, on 6th July the *Evening Telegram* reported candidly that 'it is too early to give any particulars of the fighting … The British casualties have so far been comparatively light according to official reports.' However on 13th July a full list of casualties was published with praise for the Battalion in *News from London*: 'The men behaved with completely noble steadiness and courage.'

The truth continued to percolate its way home. On 22nd July the paper published a letter from Bert Ellis who had written to his mother from his hospital bed in Wandsworth, London. He had been wounded in the leg during the attack which he described as 'like hell let loose' and 'the Regiment is about done … Only Dead! Dead! Everywhere … Our boys acted throughout like heroes. They went on top singing just as if they were going on a march instead of facing death.'

Newfoundland paid a high price during the war. Out of a population of 263,000 over 6,000 enlisted in the Regiment at a cost of 1 in 5 killed and 1 in 3 wounded.

The various reports on the actions of the 1/ Newfoundlanders reflect the attitudes, emotions and language of the time. Brigadier-General Cayley, GOC 88th Brigade: 'I cannot sufficiently express my admiration for their heroism nor my sorrow for their overwhelming losses.' The 29th Division's GOC Major-General Sir Henry de Beauvoir de Lisle lauded 'a magnificent display of trained and disciplined valour and its assault failed because dead men can advance no further.' Lieutenant-General Sir Aylmer Hunter-Weston, commanding VIII Corps referred to the 29th Division's attack as 'a magnificent display of disciplined courage.' A cable was sent to the people of

Newfoundland by Commander-in-Chief General Sir Douglas Haig: 'Newfoundland may well feel proud of her sons. The heroism and devotion to duty they displayed on 1st July has never been surpassed … their example will live.' The Regiment's motto was 'Better than the Best'. Faced with such odds, no one could have done any better.

The Official History of the 29th Division compiled in the 1920s viewed the day in a very different light: 'The attack (first waves) had failed. What would be the fate of the 88th Brigade? If they went forward, they went to certain death, but when the military machine gets in motion, it is hard to divert or stop' and of the Newfoundlanders 'these men from a foreign land spent their blood like water for their distant kindred, their love of justice and the Pax Britannica.'

In *The Fighting Newfoundlander*, the official Regimental History, Colonel Nicholson quotes an observer, Major Arthur Raley who witnessed the men under attack: 'The only visible sign that the men knew they were under terrific fire was that they instinctively tucked their chins into advanced shoulder as they had so often done when fighting their way home against a blizzard.'

The remainder of the Battalion were joined by 130 reinforcements and when they returned to the trenches on 14th July, there were only 271 in the unit.

Jim's war took him to major battlefields to Ypres and back to the Somme. The Battalion distinguished itself at Monchy-le-Preux east of Arras in April 1917 and returned to Ypres. In September the title of 'Royal' was bestowed on them by King George V - the only one in the First World War. In November it took part in the Battle of Cambrai and in 1918, after a period of rest, it provided the Guard of Honour for General Haig at GHQ in Montreuil.

The veterans of the 'Blue Puttees' were at last granted home leave. Now a sergeant, Jim left France on 25th July 1918 and arrived in Newfoundland on 4th August via England and New York. His war was over … A friend of his in the Regiment, Corporal John Hillier invited him to dinner where he met Blanche, one of John's sisters, a seamstress whom he married in 1920. They ran two restaurants and a mobile fish and

chip van, probably the first in Newfoundland and had time to bring up 12 children! Jim turned his hand to farming and passed away coincidentally on 2nd July 1969, 53 years after so many of his comrades fell.

Jim and nine fellow veterans made the long return journey to the battlefield at Beaumont Hamel for the unveiling of a commemorative plaque to the Newfoundlanders on 1st July 1961. The sight that greeted him was very different to the one he had left behind in 1916.

Jim and Blanche Stacey with 7 of their 12 children
Jean Edwards Stacey

The story of the Newfoundland Memorial Park is unique. After the War, the Newfoundland representative on the Imperial War Graves Commission, the Reverend Lieutenant-Colonel Thomas Nangle negotiated the purchase of the land where so many Newfoundlanders had fallen. In the process he had to deal with a significant number of farmers to acquire the 74 acre site. The Dutch-born Rudolph Cochius was chosen as the landscape architect. He felt

The bronze caribou statue and the Newfoundland Regiment memorial tablets, surrounded by British communication and support trenches J Kerr

that 'the sternness and the tragedy of War are passed from the scene. Where there was conflict, now is peace.'

A bronze statue of a caribou, the regimental emblem, was erected on a mound of Newfoundland granite in between the support trenches where the men emerged to face the German fire. It was designed by an Englishman, Basil Gotto, and is one of five caribous to be found along the Western Front. A sixth is located in St. John's, the capital of Newfoundland. At the base of the mound there are three bronze tablets with the names of 814 Newfoundlanders who died on land and at sea, who have no known grave. More than 5,000 trees native to Newfoundland were planted around the site.

The Memorial Park was officially opened by Field Marshal Sir Douglas Haig on 7th

The opening of the Newfoundland Memorial Park in 1925

June 1925- Lieutenant-General Hunter-Weston and Major-General de Lisle were present. Haig referred to the site in his speech as a place 'where courage, devotion and self-sacrifice were poured out, as it seemed at the moment, for no good purpose'. Is there an element of contrition when he spoke of 'a scene which, in July 1916, seemed to many remarkable for the failure of British arms' a view with which Jim Stacey and other survivors would have concurred.

The Prime Minister of Newfoundland, Sir Edward Morris, was scathing in his assessment of what had happened on the site which he visited in late July 1916. In his report to the Governor, Sir Walter Davidson, he asked: 'Why the war? What is all this for? After you have been to the Front and seen, got right up against this indescribable horror of war through which the nations are now passing, the question that is irresistibly borne in upon you is: Who is responsible for this titanic struggle? It is the greatest blunder in history.'

Sergeant Arthur Cook

1/ Somerset Light Infantry, 11th Brigade, 4th Division

'It looked so easy on the ground'

Sergeant Arthur Cook and men of the 1/ Somerset Light Infantry were in 'excellent spirits and full of hope' for their impending attack on the Quadrilateral, a German fortified position they called Heidenkopf, south of the village of Serre. For the majority it would be 'a welcome change from lying in a trench and taking everything without the opportunity of hitting back.'

Arthur Cook was born on 22nd November 1888 into a large family in the village of Wroughton near Swindon. Henry Cook, a carrier and barber, and his wife Mary were poor but the children were brought up according to sound Christian principles. Arthur was a talented musician; he played the piano, organ and trombone, as well as singing baritone in the church choir. He worked on the railways after school but disillusioned with the nature of the work and his prospects, he applied to join the Somerset Light Infantry in 1910 at the age of 22. He wrote that 'his chest would not expand to the required inches for my age so I was sent away for a fortnight to "blow out my chest"'. That failed but Company Sergeant-Major Drake, not wanting to lose his recruiting fee, 'advised me to put my age back 13 months. This I did and so entered this grand regiment with a false statement on my attestation paper.' He described it as 'a lapse' but one he never regretted: 'It gave me a home in the finest regiment in the Army.' During the first years of his service, his musical skills came to the fore in the regimental band.

He impressed his superiors; by November 1914 he was promoted to the rank of corporal and during December was based in the Plugstreet Wood area south of Ypres. He was unimpressed by his first taste of life in the trenches: 'I sat down in a little dug-out about large enough for a decent single rat, changed my socks, had my tot of rum and went to sleep just as I was, with plenty of fleas.' His description of the 11th Brigade assault involving the 1/ Somerset Light Infantry, 1/ Hants and 1/ Rifle Brigade at Plugstreet on 19th December 1914 makes for interesting reading in view of what would happen to the Brigade 18 months later on the Somme on 1st July: he was scathing in his criticism of the operation: 'It was a bad day's work for the Somersets, there were very heavy casualties and nothing in reward for it… precious lives were thrown away in an attempt to take a few yards of ground, not worth the death of one British Tommy… It was an awful day and I was very glad when it was over, the groans of the wounded were terrible especially at night.' He concluded that the day had been 'very disastrous to the regiment'. The odds were dead against us but in spite of that, a very brave attempt had been made only to end in failure and saddest of all, the loss of valuable lives.' The Battalion War Diary maintained that 80 yards were gained 'which was our objective'.

Just five days later the Battalions opposite the Germans at Plugstreet Wood were involved in the Christmas Truce, Cook marvelling at 'this fantastic situation … it is quite amusing to think that a few hours ago, they were at one another's throats.'

By the time the 4th Division and 11th Brigade were directed south to the Somme, Cook had been promoted to sergeant. He had known since 23rd May 1916 that a major offensive was being planned. The Fourth Army that went into action on 1st July was a remarkable achievement for the authorities; 2/3rds of the battalions that

Christmas Truce at Plugstreet Wood as depicted by
Bruce Bairnsfather who was also present
The Estate of Barbara Bruce Littlejohn

participated consisted of volunteers who less than two years earlier had little or no experience of military life. The 1/ Somerset Light Infantry was one of 47 battalions of regulars to fight on 1st July. There were also 31 Territorial battalions who in the main fought in the north end of the Somme Front.

On 11th June, the 1/ Somerset LI moved from billets at Bertrancourt to Beauval where they underwent special training 'for the Somme attack'. He told of how 'a special model plan of the area or sector we had to attack was made on the ground, showing the objectives we were supposed to take. It looked so easy on the ground'.

It was planned that the Battalion would stay in billets at Mailly Maillet but there was fear of shell fire so they withdrew to a nearby wood to bivouac. Cook noted that a number of German observation balloons were in the air - those manning them, before being harried by the RFC, cannot have failed to spot below, the unmistakeable heightened activity and the build up to a major attack. The British bombardment that commenced on 24th June and lasted a week was 'never silent day or night, advertising the fact that an attack was coming'.

The 'great attack' had been planned originally for 29th June but as Cook noted 'due to incessant rain and the shocking state of the trenches, it would not now take place till July 1st'. The Battalion paraded at 9.45 p.m. on 30th June marching to the assembly trenches which were reached at midnight. Orders were carried out to 'put ladders in position for scaling the trenches, also bridges for troops behind us to cross over' and then they were told to 'get a couple of hours sleep'. Like Arthur Seanor at Montauban, Arthur Cook found that 'sleep was out of the question'.

Breakfast was served at 5.30 a.m. An hour later the artillery bombardment was 'terrific, enemy lines were a cloud of smoke … and it seemed impossible for anybody to live in such a hell. It was a wonderful and inspiring sight'.

Cook and his platoon took a risk by standing on the trench parapet to view the action and cheered all the direct hits. They were ill advisedly overconfident: 'Not a soul could be seen' which confirmed the message emanating from the Generals that the operation would be trouble free or as Cook himself wrote: 'not a soul could be seen, and the enemy guns were strangely quiet, we all thought this was going to be a cakewalk'.

Eight minutes earlier than elsewhere, a massive explosion went up on the Hawthorn Ridge less than a mile south of the 1/ Somerset LI who were to follow the 1/ Rifle Brigade and attack the Quadrilateral scarcely 200 yards opposite. The force of it rocked their trenches. Those about to go 'over the top' had every reason to be confident of success and Cook and fellow soldiers were perhaps too eager to 'get into the fray', not waiting the scheduled ten minutes before following the Rifle Brigade: 'With a prayer on our lips … we went over the top.'

rare photograph of British troops in No Man's Land   Le Miroir No.138 July 1916

Arthur Cook's description of the attack on the Quadrilateral is vivid and captures the horrors for those involved. Everything was going smoothly; the 1/ Rifle Brigade had nearly reached the German front line when they were 'met by a murderous gun-fire'. There was no cover as 'every approach to the enemy lines had been cleverly covered by the machine-guns. Men were falling like nine-pins and the battleground was soon a mass of dead, dying and wounded.' Cook lost his platoon officer and was now in charge. Showing composure and taking the initiative, he realised that he needed to swing his men to the left as 'it was impossible to approach our objective direct for it would have meant going over some high ground which was already covered with dead and dying and was absolutely impassable.' He and the remnants of his platoon reached the German second line but thereafter he lost control of his men as they rushed from shell-hole to shell-hole. They were caught by enfilade fire … the whole scenario was 'terrifying'. It was clear they could advance no further.

Cook recalled amid the maelstrom that an order to retire was given, followed by panic. He and others tried in vain to prevent the retreat. Colonel Hopkins of the Seaforth Highlanders 'seemed to be the only officer in the area' and probably on his order, a bugler, Private Ritchie, sounded the charge for which he was awarded the VC. There were many casualties amongst those who had retreated: 'I had never seen so many dead in so small an area. Hundreds were lying on top of each other where the machine-guns had caught them … There were no hopes of getting them back in daylight.'

Cook's description emphasises how the assault had turned to total chaos. He and his men were short of water and ammunition but it was 'bombs we wanted and men.' A furious life and death struggle took place in a second line German trench for nearly three hours: 'Only Providence can say how many of us escaped the grim struggle …' The Germans retreated but the men were subjected to shell-fire. They were relieved at 11 p.m. and ordered back to their trenches; not surprisingly Cook considered that 'it was very disheartening to have to go back to the very trench we had left, so full of hope in the morning after all our efforts over there.'

On his way back he stumbled across the Battalion's signalling sergeant, Sam Imber, who had commandeered six helmets as souvenirs, contrary to regulations. No Man's Land was covered by a 'devastating barrage of German shells.' He soon lost Imber and his helmets but survived the barrage. 'I jumped from shell-hole to shell-hole, fell headlong over barbed wire and dead bodies. My clothes were torn to ribbons.' When he stumbled into a trench, he saw looming above him a sentry threatening him with a bayonet. He thought that in the darkness he had lost direction and returned to the German lines. To his relief the sentry barked in English 'Who are you?' and once his identity had been established he comfortingly said, 'You are lucky I didn't shoot you when you fell in.' It was symptomatic of the breakdown in communications on 1st July, that the sentry had been incorrectly informed that 'there were no English troops in front.'

Beefeater Arthur Cook   *South West Heritage Trust*

The remainder of the 11th Brigade was ordered back to Mailly Maillet which was reached at 3.30 a.m., the men pleased and thankful to be alive but 'absolutely beaten'.

Arthur Cook was one of a small and illustrious band of British soldiers who miraculously survived front line action from 22nd August 1914 right through to 11th November 1918 and was the only one in the Somerset Light Infantry to do so.

He was wounded just nine days before the Armistice was signed on 11th November and was sent to York Military Hospital to recuperate. He received the Distinguished Conduct Medal for his actions during the Battle of the Selle near Le Cateau: 'During the advance on Preseau, on 1st November 1918, the line was held up by the heavy fire from two machine-gun posts. He organised a small party and rushed them one after another, killing the teams, and capturing the guns. He then returned to his company, re-organised them and led them on to their final objective. He set a splendid example throughout of courage and good leadership.'

Cook was highly regarded and on Armistice Day in 1920 was selected to represent the Somerset Light Infantry at the funeral of the Unknown Soldier in Westminster Abbey. He served for the 2nd Battalion in India and in 1926 at Khartoum. He was chosen in 1928 as one of the few "Old Contemptibles" who had fought throughout the War, to represent the Regiment again at the opening of the spectacular memorial for those who died during the 1914 campaign on the Aisne at La Ferté-sous-Jouarre (designed by George Goldsmith and unveiled by Lieutenant-General Sir William Pulteney.)

In 1932 he was discharged from the Army after 22 years' service and in 1934 applied for and was accepted as a "Beefeater" at the Tower of London. Within just nine years he had been promoted to the highest rank of Chief Warder, a post he held with distinction until retirement in 1954. He died two years later in Hastings after a major operation.

2nd Lieutenant Kenneth Perkin

12/ York and Lancaster Regiment (Sheffield City), 94th Brigade, 31st Division

'I am very confident that I shall come through all right'

Kenneth Perkin must have hoped that the assault by the Sheffield Pals on the village of Serre would be met without too much German resistance. He was a gentle young man for whom even killing animals was unappealing. Over Christmas 1915 when at a training camp on Salisbury Plain, he was asked by a local landowner if he would like to go rabbit shooting and declined, saying he preferred 'not to kill the little things'.

It was through a deep sense of patriotic duty to his country that he joined thousands of young men in 'middle class' occupations who answered the call in August 1914. Living and working in Sheffield, he and friends and colleagues were inspired by appeals to enlist made by the Duke of Norfolk, who like Lord Derby in Liverpool, used his considerable influence and business interests in the city to spearhead the Kitchener campaign for volunteers amongst the business and manufacturing classes.

(Philip) Kenneth was born on 26th February 1894 in Tiverton, Devon, where his father Emil was the Principal of the Tiverton Technical, Science and Art School. He was educated at Blundell's, a public school in the town where he prospered but without being a prolific prize winner due, his father believed, to 'the lightning speed at which he worked.' His musical talents were nurtured at the school where he sang in the choir and played violin and piano. He impressed his family greatly one evening during Christmas leave from the Front in 1915 when, accompanied by his aunt on piano, he whistled from memory the whole of Verdi's *Il Trovatore*.

2nd Lieutenant Kenneth Perkin
Rotherham Archives

As a young boy Kenneth was obsessed with cricket - his knowledge of players and their statistics was encyclopaedic and his father's tennis court at 'The Wilderness' in Tiverton, witnessed his efforts to emulate the feats of his heroes, C.B. Fry, Gilbert Jessop and his favourite, Prince Ranjitsinhji. It would be surprising if Kenneth was unaware that two of the finest contemporary cricketers were on the Front Line, 2nd Lieutenant Major William Booth of the 15/ West Yorks, Yorkshire's leading all rounder had toured South Africa with MCC in 1913 and was killed on 1st July. Percy Jeeves of the 15/ Royal Warwicks, a fine Warwickshire player on the verge of selection for England, immortalised later for being the inspiration for the name of P.G. Wodehouse's famous fictional character, was killed on 8th July.

Kenneth decided at the age of 16 that he did not wish to pursue his academic studies and was not interested in a career in the professions or in Government service. He was determined to go into manufacturing or commerce, a decision that embarrassed his parents who had no suitable connections, family or otherwise, to help him on his way.

Kenneth the young officer   *Rotherham Archives*

Kenneth was fortunate that an Old Blundellian was looking out for a young man with potential to receive training at William Hutton and Sons, an eminent silversmiths company with factories in Sheffield, Birmingham and London. He started at the firm in 1911 and experienced work in the toolmaking, silversmith and sales and marketing departments and attended evening classes in design at the Sheffield School of Art.

He found life in Sheffield congenial. He played rugby, turned out for two cricket clubs and was a member of the Hallamshire Golf Club. His integration into life in the city led his father to note that 'he had cultivated an unusually (for a southerner) accurate acquaintance with the Yorkshire dialect…' When the call came, he and hundreds of other young businessmen, professionals and students joined up at the City Hall. He had not been a robust child and his chest measurement was not sufficient for military service. He sent a telegram to his father reporting that 'Doctor rejected me for special reserve and territorials chest measurement 2 ½ inches small nothing doing shall I come home?' He decided against rejection and ensured that he was examined by a duty doctor that he knew well, who overlooked his chest size and passed him fit to serve with the York and Lancaster Regiment; he was assigned to 'A' Company of the 12/ York and Lancaster (Sheffield City) Battalion, one of four battalions in the 31st Division's 94th Brigade.

Unless they had been in the OTC at school or university, training for volunteers like Kenneth Perkin was a long drawn out affair - in 18 months he received training at Redmires, Cannock Chase, Formby, Blyth, Salisbury Plain, Catterick and Clipstone. He was singled out to train as a sniping scout and spent time training on the Yorkshire moorlands after which he suffered a severe chest complaint. He performed well enough to be gazetted on 13th September 1915 as a 2nd Lieutenant. His wait to get to the Front ended on 15 April 1916 when he saluted his father and mother Isabell at Charing Cross Station and bade his final farewells.

Kenneth Perkin and parents Emil and Isabell
Rotherham Archives

The 12/ York and Lancaster were billeted at Colincamps in the Somme region, about three miles behind the front line. Their trenches were opposite the 1st July objective of Serre. Trench life came as a shock to the Battalion; Leonard Duke recalled that 'we were filthy and fed up and were wondering what we were doing there, in the line like that for 5 days and nights at a stretch … then out, short rest, shaved and clean, then all over again.'

It soon became apparent to Kenneth that trench life was dangerous; it was common for men to write home preparing their family for the worst and in his letter dated 22nd April the warning was clear: 'I want to tell you how grateful I am for all you have done for me throughout my life.' He admitted that he was not perturbed by what was

happening at the Front, 'just interested'. Four days later he continued in the same vein: 'We will soon be in a hard struggle with the Germans. I am very confident that I shall come through all right but it is better to be prepared, so I will write now and give the letter to the padre to forward in case of anything happening to me. You already have one sealed letter from me but I feel I must write again and express once again my gratitude for all you have done for me throughout my life.' He asked that they buy from his 'estate' a luminous watch for his best friend Lieutenant Tommy Storry.

'A' Company marched from their billets late in the evening of 30th June. As they approached the local sugar beet factory on the road from Colincamps, they were confronted by a mind-numbing sight, a masterstroke of morale boosting. They marched past large, recently dug, burial trenches …which are now in the Sucrerie Military Cemetery.

Sucrerie Military Cemetery

By 2.40 a.m. on 1st July, the first and second waves of the Company were in position in the assembly trenches which were in 'an exceedingly bad condition owing to the heavy rain, in places the water was well above the knees.' The Battalion's CO, Major Plackett, had set up his HQ at John Copse which German artillery started shelling at 4.05 a.m.

At 7.20 a.m. Perkin and his platoon mounted the parapet and went down to lie in front of the barbed wire. He and fellow officers were under the impression that tape had been laid in No Man's Land to help guide the attack but during the night it had been taken up by the Germans. The Germans clearly knew an attack was due. Their guns were still firing. The portents were not good.

When the British artillery stopped, Perkin and his men made their way through the gap cut in their barbed wire overnight - in the post-dawn daylight the gaps had been observed by the Germans. The 12/ York and Lancaster were easy targets. They were surprised to find that the German machine-guns had not been silenced as had been confidently predicted; on the contrary, they were being used to savagely good effect. Perkin was amongst the few that did reputedly reach the German barbed wire only to find that it was virtually uncut by British artillery fire.

Musketier Karl Blenk, IR 169, was concerned when he saw such huge numbers of British soldiers emerging from their front line. He was fearful they would soon invade their trenches. However, he had to pinch himself to confirm what he was seeing … men walking slowly in open order being mown down, as Leonard Duke described it 'like corn in a wheat field.' Blenk was astonished by the ease with which the British assault was brought to a standstill.

In many obituaries and letters of condolence, accounts of an officer's death were a well-considered surfeit of the truth. In 1914 a Royal Warwicks captain, Charles Bentley, was killed when allegedly urging and driving his men on, whereas the reality of his death was less heroic; he was hit by a shell when being arrested for drunkenness. Private Foxon's account in a letter to Emil Perkin may or may not be reliable: 'I saw two of your son's platoon fellows at night and they said that when Captain Clarke was killed (leading the second wave) your son got on top of the German parapet and shouted "Come on Lads" and that he fired three or four shots and then fell. He had been shot three times previously.' Foxon heard much the same report from Captain Clarke's batman Private Hunter but he felt compelled to stress that 'I cannot vouch for the truth of the facts I have stated but think they are pretty nigh correct.' Private Barker stated that Kenneth was shouting encouragement at the same time as 'trying to work his way through the wire when a hand bomb which the Bosches were throwing at us, burst close to him. He reeled and half fell but most pluckily pulled himself together for another effort but another bomb burst which brought him down.' Faced with uncut wire and machine-gun fire Kenneth Perkin had little chance.

From Emil Perkin's album of his son Kenneth's life
Rotherham Archives

It is evident from the extraordinary album that he compiled about his son's short life, that Emil Perkin was heartbroken. It was Emil and Isabell's record of their 'dearly cherished and courageous son.' It is one of the most poignant of personal memorials to a loved one killed in the Great War- an out pouring of grief, 'a brief and imperfect account of his life, full of promise, sweetness and beauty; which was so tragically ended before it had begun.' Emil found it hard to come to terms with his loss and that his son's body was never identified. Official confirmation of his son's death did not arrive until 8th January 1917 and a telegram from the King and Queen expressing their condolences followed soon after. Emil Perkins's response bore no malice whatsoever. He asked the Keeper of the Privy Purse at Buckingham Palace to 'convey to their Majesties the King and Queen our sincere gratitude for their most gracious message and sympathy in our great grief and the assurance of the loyal devotion and humble duty of myself and family.'

Like Rudyard Kipling who lost his 18 year old son John at the Battle of Loos in September 1915, Emil was desperate to find out what had happened to his son. He wrote many desperate letters in the vain hope that he was still alive or at least might be able to unearth information about his final moments. His letter to Private Barker was in the form of a questionnaire: how near to his son was he when he was killed? Did he see him killed or after he was killed? If he saw the killing would he please say what happened? Could his body have been taken by the Germans at night? Barker answered the questions as best he could but left blank the space for an answer to 'Can you please say where the fatal wound was?' Finally Emil asked if he could name any landmark in front of Serre village near the spot where Kenneth fell, so that later 'if we go there, we can very generally recognise the neighbourhood.' Barker promised to send him a map with the location pinpointed. The Perkins made their sad journey to Serre in 1930 and picked some wild flowers from the spot and included them in the album.

Emil Perkin's caption: 'Flowers gathered in "No Man's Land" in front of Serre - probably where the attack on the German trenches was made approaching "Luke Copse" and Railway Hollow' Rotherham Archives

When the War started there were 117 chaplains in the regular Army, a number that increased dramatically during the War on the Western Front to about 2,000, partly explained by the huge amount of burials that had to be conducted and the letters of condolence to be written to grieving families. The Battalion's chaplain Rev. Frank Ford wrote to Emil on 14th July with the unwanted news that 'I think there is no doubt your brave son was killed.' He commented on Kenneth's 'calmness and coolness' and was impressed 'that he was the first officer to invite me to tea when I first joined the Battalion… He made his first communion before going into action.'

Major Plackett* in his letter of condolence was unable to offer the Perkins family much hope: 'I fear the worst for all our missing.' He concluded with news about himself which may or may not have been appropriate for the grieving Perkins: 'On Monday 3rd July I was sent out suffering from shell-shock and nerve strain; the wonder is that any of us were spared. My nerve has gone completely and the loss of so many officers and men I knew so well has been very distressing.' Sensibly at this stage he called a halt to his woes: '… but enough of me …' He admitted that 'I am afraid I am to blame for his inclusion in the attack' of which he was fiercely critical- the way it was planned and how it was conducted on the day.

Tommy Storry, Kenneth's 'pal' from Sheffield, contacted Emil and thanked him for sending his dead friend's bequest of the watch: 'I value it very much and hope to show it to you some day.'

73

Emil and Isabell Perkin never came to terms with their son's death and how and why it happened. It was something they could not comprehend and Emil's album of remembrance to his son conveyed in greater detail the sentiment displayed on a number of graves in the Somme: SOMETIME WE'LL UNDERSTAND

The name of Philip Kenneth Perkin, aged 22, can be found on the Thiepval Memorial.

*Major Alfred Plackett was born on 25th November 1880 in Chesterfield. He worked in the Civil Service from 1896-1898 and then joined the Army for four years as a corporal in the York and Lancaster Regiment. He spent a year and eight months in South Africa fighting the Boers, after which he left the Army and joined the London Joint Stock Bank in Chesterfield. He signed up on 23rd October 1914 and because he had, at one time been an acting captain, was gazetted as an officer and by 30th June 1916 was a temporary major.

He took over command of the 12/ York and Lancaster when the CO Lieutenant-Colonel Crosthwaite was taken ill. Plackett suffered greatly from combat stress on 1st July as a result of which he was sent home on 4th July due to 'shell-shock and nervous breakdown'. His papers in the National Archives highlight his personal battle for financial compensation for his incapacity but it is clear that the War Office would not accept shell-shock and breakdown as valid reasons for compensation. He was scrupulously courteous in his correspondence; on 6th December 1916 after four months of sick leave he wrote 'as my incapacity was received in action, I beg therefore to apply for a gratuity, as some compensation for the heavy expenses consequently incurred.'

In response to another request, an official at the War Office responded: 'I am directed to acquaint you that, as the Medical Boards by which you were examined did not regard your wound as still of a very severe nature, you are not entitled … to any pension.' Note the reference to Plackett's mental illness as a 'wound'. On 22nd June 1917, almost a year after the first day of the Battle of the Somme, he lost his personal battle with the War Office. It had been decided there was 'no alternative but that he should relinquish his commission on the grounds of ill health contracted on active service.' At least it was accepted that he was suffering from ill health rather than a wound but the case was now closed. He applied for a Silver Badge on 27th August - in September 1916, King George V authorized the Silver War Badge to honour soldiers who had been discharged because of wounds or illness. It was a small, silver circular badge bearing the King's initials, a crown, and the inscriptions 'For King and Empire' and 'Services Rendered'. His request was now, however, tinged with sarcasm: 'I should be obliged if you would send me this as a 'memento of "the extreme dangers and the painful service rendered for a thankful country"!' Alfred Plackett returned to his civilian career in banking with bitter memories of 'that awful day' itself and his subsequent treatment.

The Reverend Julian Bickersteth

**Army Chaplains Department 4th Class 1/12 London (Rangers)
and 1/14 London (1st London Scottish), 168th Brigade, 56th (London) Division**

*'The courage, self-sacrifice and endurance of countless numbers of men will be
an inspiration to me for all time'*

'I have been surrounded for three days with nothing but blood, blood, blood.' The fighting on 1st July 1916 and its immediate aftermath left an indelible impression on the Reverend Julian Bickersteth who, in February 1916, had exchanged the ease of existence as chaplain to the Church of England Grammar School in Melbourne, Australia, for what must have been the unimaginable contrast of military life on the Somme Front as chief chaplain to the 1/12 London (Rangers) and 1/ 14 (1st London Scottish) Battalions of the 168th Brigade.

At a time when many Australians had or were in the process of volunteering for action to defend their Mother Country, Julian wrote: 'How all my English blood courses through my veins when I read of England's responses to the great call' and 'I can't bear being out of it all.' A man of action and moral rectitude, he wanted to play his part against an enemy that had perpetrated many evils - against the Belgians in particular in the summer of 1914 and he was keen to offer support to those engaged in the 'moral crusade' on the Western Front. He left his post in Melbourne in February 1916; the

London Scottish on the march

boys gave him a cheque to buy a communion set for use in his new role and teaching colleagues presented him with fountain pens, a cheque and, thoughtfully, plenty of socks.

Julian Bickersteth was an engaging and inspirational character. His final report by the Headmaster of Rugby School paid tribute to his 'transparent sincerity', 'abundant energy' and 'strength of will and character', qualities that were to serve him well on the Western Front for over two years.

He believed his role was to offer spiritual encouragement and solace for men caught in the harsh environment of trench warfare; he was also keen to foster Christian worship, to awaken men to 'the great truths of Christianity' and he emphasised the importance of the Sacraments and especially Holy Communion.

He had no wish, however, to be restricted to a spiritual and pastoral role and like Charles Doudney (see *Stolen Lives* by Hamilton and Reed), a chaplain killed near Lijssenthoek in Belgium in October 1915, Bickersteth was prepared to roll his sleeves up and help dealing with the wounded. In fact, at one stage, he was so dedicated to the cause, that he contemplated becoming a combatant. Neither he nor Doudney were the

type of chaplain castigated by double VC Noel Chavasse who regretted his failure to 'galvanise our padre, the Rev "Washout" into a little activity' who was 'absolutely useless and never visits the men unless they go to hospital.' Julian made a point of wearing his white collar 'so that the wounded and others would recognise me at once' and was amused to be equipped with one of the recently introduced steel helmets.

The Bickersteths were compulsive letter writers and the family received regular updates from three of the six brothers who served at the Front. In July 1916 Burgon Bickersteth wrote of his frustration with the monotonous training of his cavalry regiment at Le Touquet; Morris was with the 15/ West Yorks (Leeds Pals) opposite Serre and Julian was based in the next sector at Hébuterne opposite Gommecourt. Ella Bickersteth coordinated the letter writing of her six sons and husband Sam, the vicar of a parish in Leeds.

Brothers at the Front Rev. Julian Bickersteth (above) and Morris Bickersteth (below)

Julian informed the family in mid-June that chaplains had been told 'to be ready for anything' and that he had served communion, 'the bread of life' to 400 men on Sunday 18th June. It was clear there would be casualties in due course and Julian believed he should help men 'to prepare to meet their God' and to give them help and encouragement 'when they come to us for confessions.'

By 26th June it was an open secret that the 'Big Push' would take place in a few days. He wrote of his happiness 'at being able to be in the Great Effort … I only hope that I may be able to be of some use.' False modesty, of course - Julian would play a crucial role on 1st July.

The three brothers managed a rendezvous on Thursday 29th June at the HQ of the 15/ West Yorks. Morris recorded that 'the first thing we did was to laugh for about five minutes as it was so extraordinary all of us meeting together.' For Julian, 'our meeting of the three brothers was really historical … it put us all in an excellent humour.' Their meeting was interrupted by an inspection of the 15/ West Yorks by the 31st Division's CO Lieutenant-General Sir Aylmer Hunter-Weston who 'spoke encouraging words to the men.'

Two days later on 1st July, Morris Bickersteth was dead. The 15/ West Yorks had been slaughtered on their way across No Man's Land to capture the village of Serre. Every wave of the attack was met by sweeping enfilade machine-gun fire. Few of the Leeds Pals even reached the German front line. The tally of casualties was horrendous: 24 officers and 504 other ranks were casualties.

The news of Morris's death, for a tightly knit, Christian family, was the hammer blow they had feared. Julian was able to console himself that he had never felt 'so strong in my faith that the dear lad isn't dead but lives,' and he spoke for all the family when he expressed 'thankfulness to God that he didn't suffer at all - that he passed away at once' and was not left to die of wounds in the searing heat of the midday sun.

Julian found himself confronted by the same predicament as the Reverend Chappell, the chaplain of Morris's Leeds Pals' Battalion, who confessed to a feeling of despair and that he was broken-hearted at the loss of so many 'brave men I knew and loved.' He was not the first chaplain to muse that the War was a 'supreme test of our faith.'

The London Rangers and London Scottish were in the first wave of the 56th Division's attack on the German lines at Gommecourt, the northernmost sector of the Somme Front. It was in effect a diversionary tactic to draw German troops and artillery away from the main area of assault further south.

Troops left Hébuterne at 8.00 p.m. the night before, and when entrenched, Julian went round a number of platoons, calming men and raising a laugh: 'Every now and again a man would come up to me and hand me a letter or some valuables with instructions for them to be sent to relatives in case of their death.'

The grave of Morris Bickersteth in Queens Cemetery. Julian wrote 'His grave is all the world, and his memory is ours to cherish for all time and he isn't far from us.'

Julian engaged in conversation with Major Lindsay of the London Scottish who spoke of his young son who prayed for him every night: a poignant moment. Lindsay was killed during the morning of 1st July. His body was not recovered and his name is to be found on the Thiepval Memorial.

The Reverend's involvement on the big day was as he had wished as he and two other chaplains, Crisford and Palmer, worked tirelessly throughout the day and for most of the night, based at the Advanced Dressing Station and were allowed to move forward at their own discretion to the Regimental Aid Post. At 2.00 a.m. he and Crisford made their way to the ADS where they found three doctors enjoying comparative calm before the storm with a game of poker. They were joined by Palmer and snatched a couple of hours' sleep, waking at 4.00 a.m. German guns, supposed to have been taken out by the week-long pre-attack bombardment, were causing many casualties. The stretcher-bearers were already busy.

Julian was given various tasks by a doctor - to get away the walking casualties, superintend the loading of cars for the wounded, to see that the worst cases had "Oxo" or hot tea to prevent collapse, then to clear out a couple of dug-outs which in the rush had been filled with the wounded. He noticed that those with the worst wounds appeared to feel less pain than those with lesser wounds and noted there was scarcely

Many chaplains helped with the wounded - this one on the La Boisselle to Albert road in July 1916
IWM Q000721

a complaint or a groan from the men. He would find it difficult for the rest of his life to forget the eerie cries, laughter and tearfulness of the shell-shocked and the failure, despite all his efforts, to calm them down.

Before midday 15 wounded Germans were brought in. True to his Christian ideals, he 'felt no animosity towards them ... we did all we could for them.' The chaplains worked continuously during the day and night only returning to Hébuterne after dawn on Sunday 2nd July. Later in the day the rush of wounded abated. Crisford had been wounded so Bickersteth and Palmer found themselves by default dealing with the 'saddest task of identifying the dead. We removed all personal property and placed it in a sack and identified the body by the identification disc or the pay book, and then marked it carefully by writing details on a label ... All the time the words beat in on my brain "The living, the living shall praise Thee".'

Common sense prevailed, as it had done on Christmas Day in 1914 in many sectors of the front line, when a brief armistice was observed to clear No Man's Land of the wounded. Germans appeared from their trenches waving white flags and some of the doctors 'waved us to come over' at which point 'every man available went out with stretchers right over the top of the trenches into the open and began feverishly collecting our wounded.'

Burying such large numbers of the dead was a pressing and immediate problem. The chaplains found themselves in charge. Single graves were out of the question as there was a shortage of men to dig them until the Chief of the Military Police sent 30 men who dug a 26 feet long trench by 6 foot 6 inches wide. They had only gone down to 4 feet in depth when the cemetery was bombarded by the Germans with the chaplains and gravediggers lying flat in the bottom of the grave for 30 uncomfortable minutes.

Julian Bickersteth remained at the Front until November 1918. His diary contains moving accounts of the last few hours spent by two men condemned to death, 'shot at dawn' for desertion, executed by their own side for 'the sake of example'. 'Our modern civilisation had done little' for one of the men whose religious interest was at first a closed book but Julian managed to encourage him to sing … 'How we sang! Hymn after hymn … all night I sat by his side …we knelt together in prayer. I commended him to God and we said the Lord's Prayer … he ate a really good breakfast… we had about 300 yards to go to a deserted and ruined house just outside the village … I whispered in his ear "Safe in the arms of Jesus"… in three or four seconds the Firing Party had done their work … Poor lads - I was sorry for them … another chaplain arrived … we gave his body a Christian burial.'

On another occasion he spent a night with a 19 year old before his execution- 'there are few deaths I have witnessed which so wrung my heart strings as this one … as they bound him I held his arm tight to reassure him - words are useless at such a moment and then he turned his blindfolded face up to mine in a voice which wrung my heart "Kiss me, Sir, kiss me" and with my kiss on his lips and, "God has you in his keeping" whispered in his ear, he passed into the Great Unseen.'

Julian's beliefs helped him to come to terms with the horrors of the War and its effects on those who suffered losses of family and friends. Exactly nine months after the death of his brother Morris, he visited the Somme battlefield in Holy Week

Burying such large numbers of the dead was a pressing and immediate problem - British dead awaiting burial

of 1917: 'I placed a cross within a few yards of where Morris must have been when he was struck, and took careful note of the place. In the midst of the desolation and the endless circles of shell-holes, I read the Burial Service aloud and scattered earth to the north, east, south and west when I came to the words of the committal. I felt that I was standing on Holy ground, sanctified for ever by the blood of heroes.'

The Reverend Julian Bickersteth deservedly received an MC in 1919 from King George V for his work on the Somme, at Arras, Cambrai and Passchendaele. He returned in the same year to the Church of England Grammar School in Melbourne as Headmaster and in 1933 moved on to Felsted School in Essex, receiving plaudits at both schools for his reforming zeal. He became Archdeacon of Maidstone and a canon of Canterbury Cathedral in 1943. His final post in 1953 was as chaplain to the new young Queen, Elizabeth II, until his retirement in 1958. He died in 1962 after a full and varied life.

Julian Bickersteth witnessed the pouring of more blood on 1st July than he can have imagined possible, yet for him 'rising out of this sea of misery and pain, human nature, the spirit of man, has won the day… The courage, self-sacrifice and endurance of countless numbers of men will be an inspiration to me for all time, though I may never blot out from my eyes the hideous realities of these dreadful days.' He conceded that 'this War may bring out the best qualities in man, but the evil it does is incalculably greater. The whole thing is utterly devilish.'

Major-General Edward James Montagu-Stuart-Wortley
Commander of 46th (North Midland) Division

'I am not prepared to accept him as a Divisional Commander in this country again'

Major-General Edward Montagu-Stuart-Wortley
NPG P 1700

The day after the appalling events of 1st July 1916, the Commander of VII Corps, Lieutenant-General Sir Thomas D'Oyly Snow, sent a confidential note to his superior, General Sir Edmund Allenby of the Third Army, stating that one of the divisions under his command 'in yesterday's operation showed a lack of offensive spirit' and its commander would be 'better utilised for training purposes than in a position which requires the energy only possessed by a younger man.' Snow's damning assessment had been reached in indecent haste before he had even received a report of the events. The commander concerned was Major-General the Hon. Edward J. Montagu-Stuart-Wortley and his Division was the 46th (North Midland).

Within two days General Sir Douglas Haig had sent a letter to the Secretary of the War Office informing him that 'I have relieved Major-General Montagu-Stuart-Wortley from his command and underlined in red: 'I am not prepared to accept him as a Divisional Commander again in this country.' It was a decision made on the same day that Snow had ordered a Court of Inquiry into the actions of the 46th Division on 1st July.

There are interesting similarities in the two men's early years and careers. Lieutenant-General Snow variously nick-named 'Slush', 'Snowball' and 'Polar Bear', and 'Eddie' Stuart-Wortley were born within scarcely a year of each other, the latter in July 1857 and Snow in May 1858. They both attended Eton College and were commissioned as officers within two years of each other. Their military grounding was in Britain's colonial wars, Snow against the Zulus and Stuart-Wortley in Afghanistan. During the Nile Expedition of 1884-1885 to relieve General Gordon at Khartoum, both took part in the Battle of Abu Klea when a force of 13,000 Sudanese was repelled within 15 minutes. Snow was wounded during the campaign but Stuart-Wortley arrived in Khartoum, two days too late ... after the town had been taken by the Mahdi, self-styled redeemer of the Islamic faith and responsible for the massacre of over 10,000 people in the town and its garrison, including General Gordon.

By the late 1890s both men had been promoted to the rank of major and took part in the Second Nile campaign when Stuart-Wortley commanded some Arab irregulars in successfully holding the east bank of the Nile in the Battle of Omdurman against the Mahdist Army which was mown down by machine-guns, which would prove as deadly 18 years later when the British Army would succumb to them on the Somme. Stuart-Wortley was awarded a DSO for his actions, a distinction that Snow would never achieve.

Thereafter Snow was rapidly promoted to lieutenant-colonel in 1903, brigadier-general in 1906, and by 1914 was a major-general in command of the 4th Division. Stuart-Wortley meanwhile took part in the relief of Ladysmith in 1900 during the Boer War after which his career took an interesting turn when as a lieutenant-colonel he was appointed Military Attaché in Paris at an important time in Anglo-French relations culminating in the signing of the Entente Cordiale on 8th April 1904. He made a notable impression there and on leaving Paris in July, Edmund Monson, the British Ambassador, wrote to the Marquess of Lansdowne, the Foreign Secretary about 'the universal popularity of Colonel Stuart-Wortley … whose personal qualities have won him deservedly general recognition … I trust that he has a long career of utility and distinction before him.'

The German view of the Entente Cordiale

In 1907 and 1908 Stuart-Wortley unwittingly played a role in the down-turn in Anglo-German relations. Kaiser Wilhelm II paid a visit to England in 1907 after which he expressed a wish to take a holiday on or near the Isle of Wight. Remarkably the Kaiser, whose actions played an important part in causing the War, held the rank of Field Marshal in the British Army! King Edward VII suggested Highcliffe, a Gothic revival castle in Dorset, the home of Stuart-Wortley, who acquitted himself as the perfect host. They went on regular walks and visits to nearby towns. On his return to Germany, the Kaiser conveyed his thanks on a postcard: 'I am quite in love with your lovely place. Shall only be too glad to come again' and he invited him to attend his army manoeuvres in Lorraine which the Germans had annexed from the French in 1871.

The two had talked at length about how Anglo-German relations could be improved and to that effect Stuart-Wortley wrote an article for *The Daily Telegraph* about his conversations with the Kaiser. Prior to publication, he sent it to the Kaiser for approval who passed it on to his Chancellor, von Bülow, who it is generally believed, returned it approved but unread. The article appeared anonymously in October 1908 entitled: 'The German Emperor and England- Personal Interview - Frank Statement of World Policy - Proofs of Friendship.' It provoked a storm of protest.

Not known for his tact and diplomacy, the Kaiser was quoted as claiming: 'You English are mad, mad, mad as March hares, what has come over you that you are so completely given over to suspicions quite unworthy of a great nation? … My heart is set upon peace and it is one of my dearest wishes to live on the best of terms with England.' He blamed the British press for the perceived mistrust and warned that many sectors of German society disliked the English; he declared that, during the Boer War, he had supported Britain against France and Russia. He tried to allay European fears

The Kaiser emerging from St. Mark's Church at Highcliffe   *Illustrated London News*

about the rapid increase in the size of the German fleet by asserting that he wished to protect German commercial interests and contribute towards potential aggression from Japan. The article succeeded in souring Germany's relations with Britain and Japan and von Bülow was forced to resign in July of the following year. Stuart-Wortley's article provoked more reaction than he had intended.

Snow and Stuart-Wortley were divisional commanders when war broke out in 1914: the 4th and 46th (North Midland) respectively. The 4th Division successfully covered the retirement of the B.E.F. at Le Cateau in August 1914 - Snow's performance was highly criticised by Aylmer Haldane GOC of the 10th Brigade: 'He showed what a poor spirited man he was when troublous times were upon us.' Three battalion commanders were 'sent home' but Snow survived. He was moved to the 27th Division in April 1915 which supported the Canadians at Ypres during the Germans' first use of poison gas. He was created a KCB and was handed command of VII Corps in July.

Stuart-Wortley's 46th (North Midland) was a Territorial Division. Their first action was in October 1915 at Loos in a costly attack against the Hohenzollern Redoubt. He had been overruled by Lieutenant-General Richard Haking, Commander of XI Corps. When he suggested a bombing attack, he was ignored and ordered to organise a frontal attack, described by the *Official History* as 'a tragic waste of infantry' which incurred nearly 4,000 casualties.

Stuart-Wortley followed his disagreement with Haking by irritating Haig who was irked by his regular correspondence with King George V about the doings of his

Division. In Stuart-Wortley's defence, the King had asked him to send him weekly bulletins which had been rubber-stamped by Sir John French, the then Commander-in-Chief of the B.E.F.

When in 1916, Haig and Rawlinson planned the Fourth Army's offensive in the Somme, a cornerstone of their strategy was a diversionary assault at Gommecourt, about a mile from the main attack. Gommecourt was the most western point of the German line in France and was marked with a tree named the 'Kaiser's Oak'. The village formed a salient which like other villages on the Somme front was turned into a fortress. The aim was to divert German men and weapons from the south of the Front and to make it obvious to the Germans that an attack was planned there. The attack on Gommecourt was to be carried out by the Third Army's VII Corps of which Stuart-Wortley's 46th (North Midland) Division was part. Once the British had made their attacking intentions clear, the Germans duly reinforced their position with more soldiers and artillery.

Two Territorial Divisions would be used in a pincer movement on Gommecourt, the 46th (North Midland) from the north and the 56th (London) from the south commanded by Major-General C.P.A. Hull. The Londoners found the wire had been well cut and quickly overran the first two lines of German trenches before encountering resistance in the third. The 46th Division's attack, however, was a disaster from the outset. The wire had not been well cut and the attackers were halted by machine- guns and a heavy barrage.

It became clear to Stuart-Wortley, after a series of unsuccessful attempts to renew the attack that there was little chance of success. He was no doubt dismayed to receive orders in the afternoon to organise another attack. Realising the hopelessness of another assault, he ordered a token action by only two companies but in the event only one platoon of twenty men attacked with the loss of all but two men- a disaster foreseen by Stuart-Wortley but importantly, his decision saved the lives of several hundred men.

Lieutenant-General Sir Thomas D'Oyly Snow

The 56th Division were dependent on meeting the 46th behind Gommecourt, but without their support, were driven back to their trenches by mid-evening. Casualties were heavy for the 56th: 4,300 but markedly less for the 46th: their total of 2,450 was the 'lightest' on the day and in marked contrast to the highest figure of 6,400 suffered by the 34th Division at La Boisselle.

In his note to Allenby on 2nd July, Snow inferred that Stuart-Wortley was not fit enough to command a division and was too old for the job which was a bit rich from someone who was virtually the same age! There is evidence, though, that Stuart-

Wortley was suffering from sciatica and was described by Brigadier-General Frank Lyon of VII Corps Staff as a 'worn out man'.

Stuart-Wortley was unimpressed with Snow's allegation that his division had 'lacked offensive spirit' and his reaction was immediate: 'I beg most respectfully to protest not only on my own behalf, but also on behalf of this Division … my orders were carried out with dash and determination under very difficult conditions.' He could not resist a side-swipe: he reminded Snow of what had happened at Loos.

Stuart-Wortley took Snow and Haig's comments as unfair insults and fought for the rest of his life to clear his name and put the official record straight. The file held by the National Archives on 'Appeals regarding removal from command of 46th Division in 1916' makes for fascinating reading as Stuart-Wortley's angst and distress are laid bare in the face of official stone-walling.

In view of Snow's comments on 2nd July, his message to Stuart-Wortley's men on 3rd July is remarkably disingenuous: 'The Corps commander wishes to congratulate the troops of 46th Division for the manner in which they fought ... The purpose of the attack, which was mainly to contain and kill Germans, was accomplished.' Contrast that with another attack on Stuart-Wortley on 5th July in a note to Sir Cecil Lowther, Military Secretary at GHQ in France that the 46th Division 'showed a lack of offensive' and that 'on account of his physical capability and age' Stuart-Wortley was not 'able to go to the Front Trenches as much as necessary for a Divisional Commander.' He toned down his comments, a sensible move as things turned out, by making it clear that he did not infer any criticism of his military career and that he felt he would be well employed in training troops as 'all his preparations and training in the back lines was as good as it could be but he could not be constantly tramping through long and muddy trenches.'

In his Account of Operations of VII Corps on 1st July dated 10th July, Snow candidly reported that 'the main object of the attack (of diverting troops) was fulfilled.' The failure to achieve the second objective, the capture of the salient, he blamed on 'the large amount of artillery', the distance between the opposing trenches and, tellingly, 'the faulty organisation on the part of the 46th Division in allowing the men of the rear waves of the assault to advance through communication trenches rather than in the open,' so had the men crossed in the open as suggested, the casualties would have been much increased. Snow absolved himself from any responsibility by concluding that 'there was no excuse for the uncut state of the wire not being known' and, stating the obvious that 'it would have been better not to order a fresh attack,' he was in effect condoning Stuart-Wortley's 'lack of offensive spirit'. After the War, Snow admitted that 'the Gommecourt Salient had proven stronger than anticipated.'

Stuart-Wortley continued his crusade on 18th July with a letter to the War Office in which he pointed out that Snow's note of 2nd July 'was written before any report on the operation had been received' with the inference that Snow's comments were of 'a personal nature.' Lacking a satisfactory reply, in desperation Stuart-Wortley turned to the King in October 1916 detailing the unfairness of his sacking. The King's Private Secretary, Stamfordham, sent a non-committal reply: 'His Majesty was very sorry when he heard that you had come home from the Front … no one would dare to cast the slightest reflection upon a Divisional General who proved unable to bear the constant strain and general demand upon his powers with (sic) such a command untails (sic)' and of Snow's decision which 'must have been most painful to him.'

He was put in command in early 1917 of the 65th (2nd Lowland) Division in Ireland, responsible for home defence and training, a far cry from the challenges of the Western Front, a role that he felt was not commensurate with his ability and experience and that prompted him to continue his private battle for personal redress. By now he was running out of options and turned to Sir John French, who had also suffered the agony of dismissal when replaced by Haig as Commander-in-Chief of the B.E.F. in December 1915. He showed a willingness to support him 'to get some better acknowledgement of your services out of the government.' Whatever French may have done for him, it came to nothing but he offered some solace by revealing his own sense of grievance: 'In the past I have suffered in the same way myself very severely.'

The deep sense of injustice is evident in Stuart-Wortley's letter to Haig in December 1918: 'I have had to suffer a most humiliating and heart-breaking criticism for having been sent back from France.' He refers to his unblemished military career and to his health, angrily pointing out 'that I was not an aged cripple.' He was deeply aggrieved that he was 'almost the sole General Officer omitted entirely from any sort of mention, honour, or decoration during the war.' His humiliation and despair were so great that he concluded: 'In fact, I could not suffer a more ignoble and heart-breaking fate had I been tried by Court Martial or had I committed some egregious blunder.' There is no evidence of a reply in the file.

Stuart-Wortley retired from the Army in 1919. He could now concentrate his efforts on his 'campaign'. The War Office was his target. He wrote at length to Henry Wilson, the Chief of Imperial Staff but received no comfort from the reply: 'I cannot … bring any pressure to bear from personal knowledge … if there is any comfort in it, you may remember that you are not alone in your ill-fortune and that many another good man and true keeps your company.' Stuart-Wortley bombarded the War Office with more letters like one sent in November 1919 in which he opined that 'rewards are nothing in value compared with professional reputation … reputations should not be liable to indelible stain by obvious injustice.'

In a final throw of the dice, he articulated his case once more, at length, to Winston Churchill, Secretary of State for War in May 1920. He introduced the usual detail but on this occasion intimated that Sir John French and Sir William Robertson, the Chief of General Staff, had promised him the command of a Corps in 1915 but this had come to nothing when French was replaced by Haig. Of the action at Gommecourt, he declared that the attack was made 'on a position of exceptional strength which the French had failed to take after ten attempts.' He did not hold any punches when it came to blame for his 'great sense of injustice … For five months (before 1st July) pressure had been brought to bear by superior authority on Generals Allenby and Snow to get rid of me and the failure to take Gommecourt was finally decided upon as a sufficient reason' and he highlights the contradictions in Snow's reports. His predicament, he bitterly complained, was 'the outcome of personal antipathy' and he deplored the fact his Army career could 'just be wiped out by an act of injustice or the stroke of an unjust pen.'

Churchill in his reply attempted to mollify Stuart-Wortley and reassure him that there is no 'grave reflection' on his military career and with reference to Snow's note he considered that 'the only person who can withdraw it is General Snow himself.' He offered 'to instruct the Military Secretary to ask General Snow if he would be prepared to withdraw or modify his report.' It was an offer that Stuart-Wortley could not entertain: 'The evil that it did remains.'

Four years on, in December 1924, approaches were made by Colonel Sir Charles Burn, aide-de-camp to George V, to the new Secretary of State for War, Sir Laming Worthington-Evans, on behalf of Stuart-Wortley who 'deserves recognition.' Worthington-Evans replied that he was unable to help as 'it is so long ago now that it would be impossible to arrive at any very satisfactory and independent conclusion.' With that response the file was well and truly closed with a loud thud. Stuart-Wortley's efforts for redress had come to nothing. The reputation of his 46th Division remained tainted until their success in crossing the St. Quentin canal in September 1918 when their honour was restored.

Stuart-Wortley must have been touched by an element of deeply satisfying *schadenfreude* on hearing the news that his nemesis Snow had been replaced, partly on grounds of age as Corps Commander following criticism of his and others' leadership during the German counter-attack at the Battle of Cambrai in November and December 1917. It is ironic that Snow's successor was Lieutenant-General Walter Congreve VC, who had been the most successful Corps Commander on 1st July 1916, when he had overseen the advance and capture of Montauban. It would indeed be interesting to know if Stuart-Wortley was aware of suggestions that Snow was replaced on account of his age!

Stuart-Wortley died in 1934. Sad and embittered by his wartime experiences and his failure to clear his name, his sense of despair was heightened by the death in 1926 of his only son Nicholas, an MC and a brilliant flying ace in the Royal Flying Corps.

The indecent haste with which he was summarily dismissed from his command on seemingly spurious grounds does prompt one to wonder what had happened between Stuart-Wortley and Snow in days gone by at Eton and encounters during the Nile Expeditions. Perhaps there had been an element of jealousy when Wortley was in Paris.

Haig's fingerprints are definitely to be found on the case. He had felt threatened by Wortley's close relationship with King George V and it is likely that Allenby and Snow were happy to pander to Haig's dislike of Stuart-Wortley and to besmirch him to cover their own backs. Snow's note written on 2nd July 1916 appears to be an attempt to deflect attention and blame from himself following the disaster at Gommecourt, despite ultimately being responsible for his Corps' performance. He had also incurred Allenby's displeasure in that he had taken a ten-day leave before the offensive and was not involved, therefore, with all the preparations.

There has been much debate over the years as to the real reasons for a controversial decision so hastily taken. It has been argued that Stuart-Wortley was made a scapegoat to deflect criticisms of the Generals who planned the 'Big Push' on the Somme.

Whatever the reasons for his downfall, it was clear that by 1st July 1916, Major-General the Hon. Edward James Montagu-Stuart-Wortley was 'a marked man'. His manic crusade to seek redress for his perceived sense of personal injustice is a moving and troubling story of intrigue at the highest level.

Lochnagar Crater during a 1st July ceremony

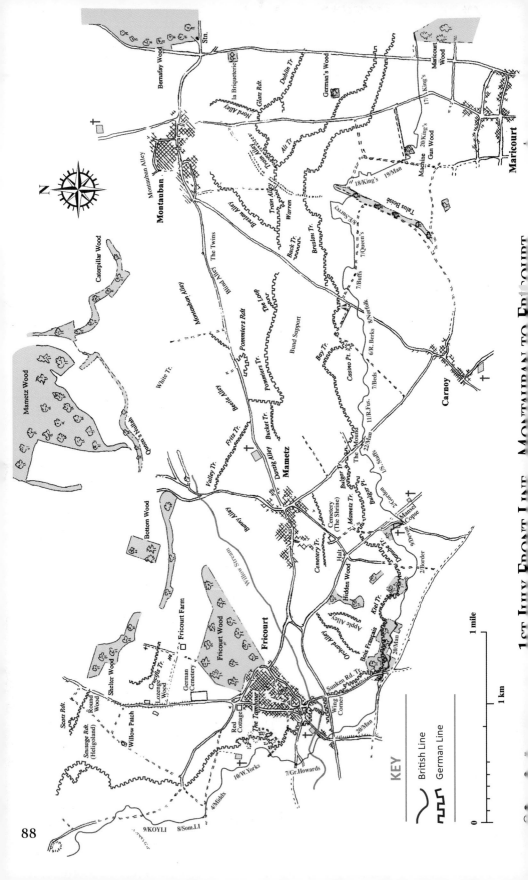

88

KEY

British Line

German Line

1 mile

1 km

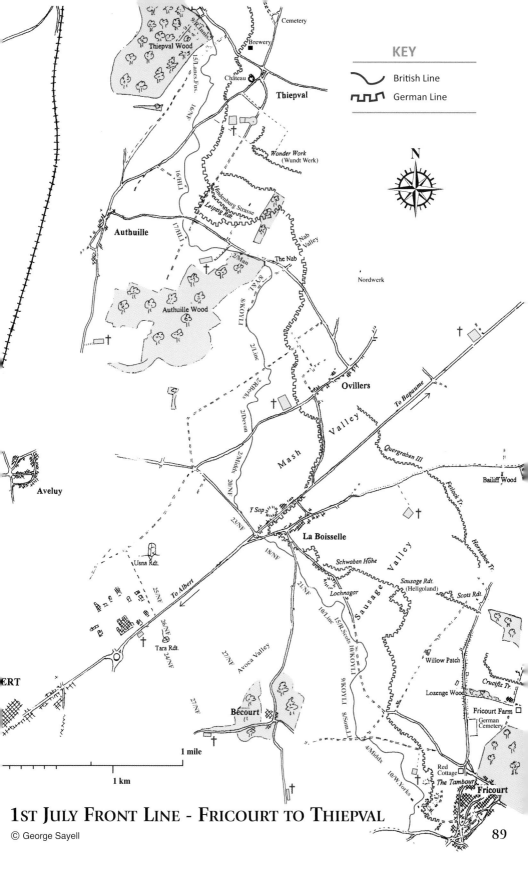

1ST JULY FRONT LINE - FRICOURT TO THIEPVAL

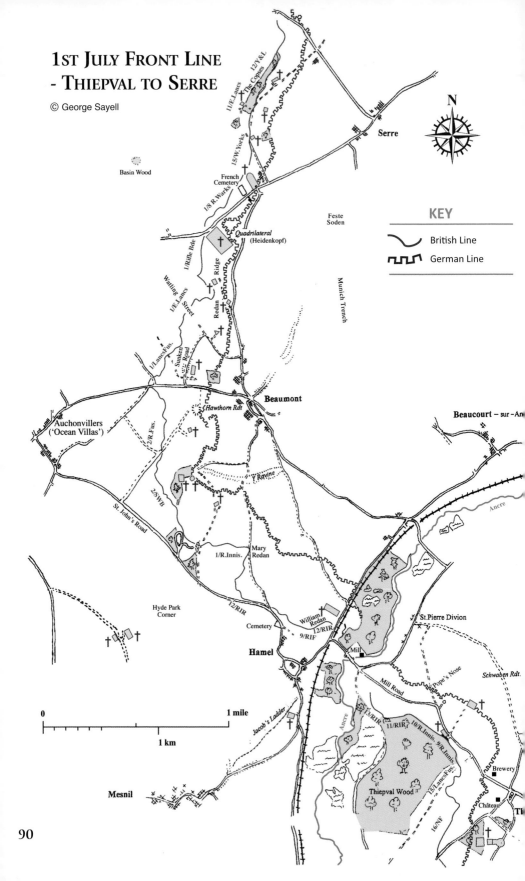

1st July Front Line
- Thiepval to Serre

© George Sayell

Basin Wood

Serre

French Cemetery

12/Y&L

11/E.Lancs
The Copses

15/W.Yorks

1/8 R.Warks

Feste Soden

Munich Trench

Quadrilateral
(Heidenkopf)

1/Rifle Bde

Redan Ridge

1/E.Lancs

Watling Street

Sunken Road

1/Lancs.Fus.

Beaumont

Beaucourt – sur – Ancre

Auchonvillers
('Ocean Villas')

Hawthorn Rdt

2/R.Fus.

2/SWB

Y Ravine

St. John's Road

Mary Redan

Ancre

1/R.Innis.

Hyde Park Corner

12/RIR

St.Pierre Divion

William Redan

Cemetery

12/RIR

9/RIF

Hamel

Mill

Mill Road

Pope's Nose

Schwaben Rdt.

Jacob's Ladder

Ancre

13/RIR

11/RIR

10/R.Innis

9/R.Innis

15/Lancs.Fus.

Brewery

Mesnil

Thiepval Wood

16/NF

Château

Th

KEY

〜 British Line

⊓⊔⊓ German Line

N

0   1 mile

1 km

1st July Front Line - Serre to Gommecourt

© George Sayell

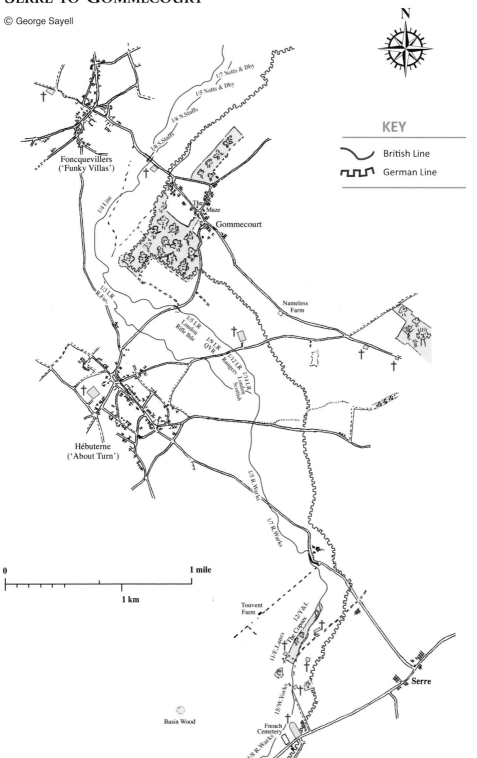

KEY

British Line

German Line

Foncquevillers
('Funky Villas')

1/7 Notts & Dby

1/5 Notts & Dby

1/6 N.Staffs

1/6 S.Staffs

1/4 Line

The Maze

Gommecourt

1/3 L.R
R.Fus.

Nameless
Farm

1/5 L.R
London
Rifle Bde

1/9 L.R
Q.V.R.

1/12 L.R
Rangers

1/14 L.R
London
Scottish

Hébuterne
('About Turn')

1/5 R.Works

1/7 R.Works

0   1 mile

1 km

Touvent
Farm

11 E.Lancs

12 Y & L

The Copse

15 W.Yorks

Serre

Basin Wood

French
Cemetery

1/8 R.Works

LT. COLONEL
F. C. HENEKER.
LEINSTER REGIMENT
1ST JULY 1916 AGE 43

HE DIED THE NOBLEST DEATH
A MAN MAY DIE

LIEUTENANT COLONEL
A. DICKSON.
SOUTH LANCASHIRE REGT.
ATTD.WEST YORKSHIRE REGIMENT
1ST JULY 1916. AGE 41

LIEUTENANT COLONEL
L. M. HOWARD.
TYNESIDE IRISH N.F.
2ND. JULY 1916

LIEUTENANT COLONEL
W. BURNETT D.S.O.
N. STAFFORDSHIRE REGT.
3RD JULY 1916 AGE 36

MAJOR
J. N. BROMILOW
COMDG. 1ST BN
ROYAL LANCASTER REGIMENT
2ND JULY 1916

COLONEL
HERBERT CLIFFORD BERNARD
4TH RATTRAY'S SIKHS
COMDG. ROYAL IRISH RIFLES
1ST JULY 1916

LIEUTENANT COLONEL
H. ALLARDICE.
36TH JACOBS HORSE
1ST JULY 1916

LIEUTENANT COLONEL
CHARLES EDMUND BOOT
N. STAFFORDSHIRE REGT.
1ST JULY 1916 AGE 41

IV

Countdown to Zero

*'My God! All we'll find in Thiepval when we go across
is the caretaker and his dog'*

Major-General William Rycroft, 32nd Division

'Lucky Jim', a 12" Howitzer on 1st July   IWM Q 000004

The Endless Wait:

Lieutenant Robert Gilson, 11/ Suffolks (Cambridgeshire), maintained that 'the real strain is the strain of waiting. Always waiting with the knowledge that waiting cannot end the war, and nothing stirring to take our minds away from petty worries.' For Frank Bastable, 7/ Royal West Kents, 'going over the top at last 'was a sort of relief. In a way we were frightened or excited at the same time.'

The daily grind of life in trenches with all its discomforts tested the patience. The rains in the week before 'Z' Day dampened the spirits further. Charles Moss, 18/ Durham Light Infantry, felt that 'the main thing we all looked forward to was to get away from the trenches to fight in open country and to get on the move.' Sergeant Arthur Cook, 1/ Somerset Light Infantry, reckoned that the planned assault would be a welcome change from lying in a cramped trench and Private Ralph Miller, 1/ 8 Royal Warwicks, thought the 'quicker the bloody whistles go the better … We got so browned off with the waiting'; some regulars, however, like a number in the 1/ Lancashire Fusiliers, were not as enthusiastic about the 'Big Push' as some of the New Army Battalions. George Ashurst was to take part in the assault on Beaumont Hamel and recalled that the Division's GOC, Major-General Beauvoir de Lisle 'briefed the Lancashire Fusiliers who were taking part in an advance that might mean the end of the war and that nothing was being overlooked to ensure its success. So many guns would take part in the bombardment that if placed side by side "they would stretch from the English Channel to the Alps. The guns would not leave a single German soldier to bar our progress" … he knew he could trust us to do our duty … then he wished us goodbye and good luck and rode off to tell our neighbouring battalion the same story.' Ashurst wondered if the General was aware of the ugly murmurings amongst the ranks during his speech. 'Had he heard the remarks of the men when they were dismissed off parade, he would have thought they were not so enthusiastic about the big push …' In contrast the official cinematographer, Geoffrey Malins, was more impressed and noted the faces of the men 'shone with a new light.'

Major-General Beauvoir de Lisle 'briefed the Lancashire Fusiliers who were taking part in an advance that might mean the end of the war …'   IWM Q 000738

Canny regulars knew how to catch a 'Blighty', an injury bad enough to be sent home, but not as obvious as self-harm. Ashurst recalled that 'the day of our return to the trenches was dreaded by most men, and during our games of football, men fervently hoped that their legs would be broken and actually risked seriously crippling themselves in order to gain admission to hospital, and even in their calmer moments deliberately devised the means to get dysentery or blood poisoning.' Private Miller was pleased to go over the top, in the hope he would catch a 'blighty wound'. His prayer was answered as he was hit by shrapnel in his hand and arm, and lost two fingers. He came-to in the University Hospital, Birmingham. Siegried Sassoon, the poet and author, was somewhat more high-minded in comparison: 'I don't often descend to the desire for a "blightie one" which everyone talks about.'

The Germans had been in trenches on the Somme since 1914 and they too were keen for the deadlock to be broken - Hauptmann Hensel of IR 60 wrote on 27th June that 'everyone was longing for the attack to begin.'

Training and Practice:

Much of June was spent training and practising for 'Z' Day. General Rawlinson visited the divisions under his command to cast his eye over their preparations which often did not match his expectations. The 1/ 5 London (1st London Rifle Brigade) were due to take part in the 56th (London) Division's attack on the Gommecourt Salient. Rifleman Aubrey Smith recalled that 'eventually it became known that the battalion would advance in waves, the details of which were worked out carefully. Indeed, it was clear that the battalion were to be well versed in what they were expected to accomplish, for, in course of time, shallow trenches were dug in neighbouring wheat-fields, modelled exactly upon the German defences as revealed by aeroplane photos. The British front line and the German first, second and third lines were indicated by little flags, and time and again the whistles would blow and the various waves, advancing through the corn, would take the successive lines of imaginary trenches. Every battalion that was attacking rehearsed on the same lines, each reproducing a different section of German fortifications, and making itself thoroughly conversant with them. If this went on throughout the attacking divisions … it says much for the care that was taken to make the advance a success.'

Care and attention to detail were the watch words; the 18th (Eastern) Division spent considerable time training in a trench system specially built well behind the lines, an exact copy of their objective and Sir Arthur Conan Doyle, whose son Kingsley fought on 1st July, considered that 'every operation of the attack was practised on similar ground behind the lines.' An 18 year old from Peckham, Thomas Gay, 2/ Royal Scots Fusiliers, believed mistakenly that 'we knew what we were doing because we'd trained hard for the Big Push in the months before, going over mock battlefields …'

A practice attack by the London-based Battalions of the 168th and 169th Infantry Brigades of the 56th Division took place on the morning of 26th June. Detailed instructions were issued by 56th Division's General Staff stating that the practice attack would be 'under cover of smoke' and the Brigades 'would be assembled previous to the attack on what would represent our own trench system. The various waves of assaulting troops will start at exactly the same distances as they would in reality. Surplus officers from battalions will be placed in each of the German trenches to take the exact time at which the leading wave passes, so that the times laid down by artillery lifts can be checked and amended if necessary. Watches will be synchronised … 8.55 a.m. Smoke begins … 8.57 a.m. First waves leave trenches where necessary,

and lie down within 250 yards of German trenches ... 9 a.m. Assault ... In addition to the smoke barrage the Special Brigade RE will reinforce the smoke barrage by the employment of trench mortars ... Practice in communication with aeroplanes will be carried by means of red and yellow flares, and illuminating lights ... In addition troops will make use of the Vigilant Periscopes which have already been issued. These will be fixed to the bayonets during the assault.' There was commendable emphasis on timings and synchronisation with the artillery, but once confronted with real machine-guns, rifles and shelling, detailed schedules would count for nothing.

Raiding Parties:

Throughout the month before 'Z' Day raids and patrols were executed along the German front line to assess the strength of the trenches and barbed wire entanglements and to ascertain how well manned they were. The aim was also to keep the enemy on their toes. A good example of a raid was reported by 2nd Lieutenant J.B. Karran, 2/ South Wales Borderers: 'I left our lines near sap 3 at 10.20 p.m. on the 29th June with a party of one sergeant and 5 other men. We moved forward to Q10 while it was still dusk and waited

' ... the employment of trench mortars' known to the troops as 'Toffee Apples' or 'Plum Puddings'

in the sunken road about half an hour until it was properly dark, and then crept up to the enemy's wire. I left 3 men here to keep a look out, and the sergeant and I crept forward followed by the other two men at about 5 paces distance. I arrived on the parapet immediately over the entrance to the dug-out where there was no fire step. Almost as soon as I

'The trench was about 7ft broad at the top and from 8-10 ft deep.' One hundred years on, a German trench in Newfoundland Memorial Park is still deep. J Kerr

arrived a German appeared out of the darkness about 10 yards to my left, and then passed immediately below me. He was about 2 yards from me, and turned to go round the traverse. I fired at him with my pistol and he fell with a grunt. I moved along the parapet to find a way down into the trench, and heard sounds of the occupants coming out …We got back to our own trench at about 12 midnight …The trench was about 7ft broad at the top and from 8-10 ft deep … The parapet was much knocked about by our shells, but the bay did not seem to be much damaged. The entrance to the dug-out appeared to be larger than those of our deep dug-outs. The trench appeared to be quite dry. I went in through a good gap in the wire, about 4 yards wide. The rest of the wire at this point appeared fairly strong.'

It is interesting that Karran should mention the large entrance to a dug-out but his final comment was the most telling - that the wire still seemed uncut with only 30 hours or so until Zero Hour … Karran was killed on 1st July and is buried in Y Ravine Cemetery. He was probably hit by machine-guns trained on the gaps in the Battalion's wire.

This trench at Pozières emphasises how deep and well-constructed German trenches were

On the night before, reports from battalions sent to 29th Division HQ were detailing the same observations:

86th Brigade: Copies of the reports were also sent to VIII Corps HQ

- 16/ Middlesex (Public Schools) reported that the wire was not very well cut and a large body of men would have difficulty in getting through

- 1/ Lancashire Fusiliers: 'The wire was found insufficiently cut to allow the passage of a large party … it appears the line is strongly held at night'

- 2/ Royal Fusiliers found there was a row of wire that had not been touched

A General Staff memorandum to 86th Brigade admitted that 'owing to the heavy rains rendering observation difficult, there appears to be little likelihood of the wire on the enemy's front line being properly cut. Complete cutting by means of Bangalore Torpedoes and parties with wire cutters.'

2nd Lieutenant J.B. Karran's grave in Y Ravine Cemetery

87th Brigade:

- 1/ Border raiding party found a thick belt of wire uncut

88th Brigade:

- 1/ Newfoundlanders reported there was no need for a Bangalore Torpedo to cut the wire as this was from all accounts practically non-existent

On 29th June a Special Wire Cutting Report was collated for 31st Division:

93rd Brigade:

- 15/ West Yorks: 'At no point was there a clean gap but what was left was low'
- 16/ West Yorks: 'Wire was very thin in many places and would not be a serious obstacle'
- 18/ West Yorks: 'Wire much damaged but no clean gaps cut. With wire cutters the wire would be easily passable for infantry'
- 18/ Durham LI: '… regular gaps - where no gaps wire very much cut about'

Mixed messages were being received, therefore, but the number of reports that suggested, at such a late stage, that the German wire would pose attackers great problems, lends weight to the argument that at Corps level and above, it was decided to ignore the findings. The momentum was such that there could be no turning back…

Last Letters:

Many soldiers who knew their battalions would be involved in the imminent attack, wrote letters home to family and loved ones to prepare them for the worst. Private John Scollen, 27/ Northumberland Fusiliers (4th Tyneside Irish), wrote to his wife Tina: 'I have done my duty to my King and Country … I hope justly in the sight of God … It is hard to part from you but keep a good heart dear Tina and do not grieve for me, for God and his blessed mother will watch over you and my bonny children and I have not the least doubt that my country will help you … My Joe, Jack, and Aggie, not forgetting my bonny little twins Nora and Hugh and my last flower baby whom I have only had the great pleasure of seeing … Good bye and think of me in your prayers … I know hard words to receive but God's will be done … From your faithful soldier, husband and father … Good bye my loved one … DON'T CRY …'

John Scollen was killed during the attack on La Boisselle. His body was never identified; his name is to be found on the Thiepval Memorial.

2nd Lieutenant Eric Heaton, 16/ Middlesex (Public Schools) wrote on 28th June to his father, the Reverend Daniel Heaton, who ministered to a parish in Hove, Sussex. As yet the attack had not been postponed by two days because of the poor weather: 'Tomorrow we go to the attack in the greatest battle the British Army has ever fought. I cannot quite express my feelings on this night and I cannot tell if it's God's will that I shall come through - but if I fall in battle then I have no regrets save for my loved ones I leave behind. It is a great cause and I came out willingly to serve my King and Country. My greatest concern is that I may have the courage and determination necessary to lead my platoon well.' There is a valedictory finality about his concluding comments: 'No one had such parents as you … my life has been full of faults … If I fall do not let things be black for you, be cheerful …' Eric Heaton went over the top with his Battalion and it is possible that the 20 year old who aspired to be a doctor or a dentist, featured in the film shot by Geoffrey Malins of the Battalion following the 2/ Royal Fusiliers and 1/ Lancashire Fusiliers as they attacked the Hawthorn Ridge Redoubt which had been blown up by 40,000 lbs of ammonal explosive at 7.20 a.m. His body was buried not far from where he fell, in Hawthorn Ridge Cemetery No.1.

Captain Charles May, 22/ Manchesters (7th Pals) wrote to his wife: 'If I have to go I am ready, but the thought I may never see you or our darling baby again turns my bowels to water.' He was keen, like Heaton, to perform creditably as a soldier: 'For myself Maudie, I pray to God in all humility that I do my job well, achieve my objectives, hold them and generally carry out my orders correctly and successfully.' She responded that 'my heart thumps with fear … I am trusting in God and praying, baby with me, that you will be spared to come through these terrible days of fighting safe and well and return, my darling man.' The 27 year old Dunedin-born New Zealander was killed during the Battalion's attack on Danzig Alley, east of Mametz. He is buried in Dantzig Alley Military Cemetery and was Mentioned in Despatches. In a letter to her husband's batman, Private Bunting, Maude May was eager for answers to questions about whether her husband suffered, if he had been conscious at any stage, where his wounds were and what his dying words were - she asked him to tell her everything 'my heart aches to know.'

2nd Lieutenant Eric Heaton, 16/ Middlesex (Public Schools)

Eric Heaton's parents by his grave in Hawthorn Ridge Cemetery No. 1

Later she received her husband's belongings which reached her 'quite in order. The heart-breaking task of unpacking the valise and touching his clothes seemed to bring home to me more than ever this dreadful calamity. I don't know how I shall go through life without him - the loving care and devotion he showered upon baby and me was greater than I could ever put in words. Can there be anything in life for me again?' One presumes so, because Charles had asked his friend Captain Earles to look after his wife and daughter Pauline in the event of his death … which he duly did by marrying Maude after the War.

Corporal Alfred Kettle, 24/ Northumberland Fusiliers (1st Tyneside Irish), wrote to his wife and family on 27th June: '… by the time you get this I will be in the thick of it, so Dear I will want all the prayers I can get from you all … but I can tell you I am going into it with plenty of confidence and have good hopes of coming out of it all right, and if it had not been for you and the little ones, I would not care a rap about what happened to me … if the worst does happen it cannot be helped and it will be just as God wills it.' A Roman Catholic, he was 'at church last night and after

Benediction I went to Confession and I received communion after.' On 1st July he was in the attack on La Boisselle; he was probably killed by machine-gun fire and his body destroyed by shelling. His name is on the Thiepval Memorial.

God's Will:

Religion had offered comfort to Alfred Kettle. 2nd Lieutenant John Engall, 16/ London (Queen's Westminster Rifles), in a letter to his parents written on 28th June told them: 'I took my communion yesterday … I place my soul and body in God's keeping … should it be God's holy will to call me away, I am quite prepared to go.'

2nd Lieutenant Sam Oakes, 12/ York and Lancaster (Sheffield City) wrote on 13th July 1916 to Miss Green of the Christian Endeavour Society, expressing the hope that 'it will be of interest to Endeavours to know that in some parts of the battalion, before we went forward into what seemed certain death, the hymn *Lead Kindly Light* was sung softly by the men. The roar of the shells was deafening and the air was black with flying earth and debris; men were constantly being literally blown to pieces, yet amidst it all, the men found comfort in that significant hymn.' Private Arthur Seanor of the 18/ King's (2nd Liverpool Pals) 'asked God at early communion this morning to forgive me all my sins.'

Over Confidence:

Commander-in-Chief Sir Douglas Haig and commanders of the Fourth and Third Armies were optimistic: Haig's diary entry for 30th June was positive: 'With God's help I feel hopeful. The men are in splendid spirits … The wire has never been so well cut, nor the artillery prepared so thoroughly … Nothing could exist at the conclusion of the bombardment in the area covered by it.' General Sir Henry Rawlinson of the Fourth Army felt 'pretty confident of success…' and General Sir Edmund Allenby of Third Army was 'quite satisfied with the artillery bombardment and wire cutting'.

At Corps level the majority of commanders were similarly confident, at least outwardly. Lieutenant-General Aylmer Hunter-Weston, VIII Corps, wrote to Major-General the Hon. Sir William Lambton, Commander of the 4th Division: 'We now have a long and glorious battle before us and with my old comrades of the 4th Division in the centre, we are sure of winning.' He was 'satisfied and confident.' Lieutenant-General Sir Thomas Morland of X Corps was 'quietly confident of success'.

Divisional leaders appeared buoyant: Major-General Rycroft, 32nd Division, standing at the edge of Aveluy Wood, saw that Thiepval château had disappeared and believed the bombardment had been so successful that he commented to his brigade commanders: 'My God! All we'll find in Thiepval when we go across, is the caretaker and his dog!' 7th Division's Major-General Herbert Watts wished his men good luck: 'There is not a German left in their trenches, our guns have blown them to hell.'

Brigadier-General H.C. Rees, 94th Brigade of the 31st Division, declared that 'You are about to attack the enemy with far greater numbers than he can oppose you with, supported by a huge number of guns.' Brigadier-General Jackson of the 18th Division's 55th Brigade was gung ho: 'The Germans are now outnumbered and out-gunned and will soon go to pieces if every man goes into the fight tomorrow determined to get through whatever the local difficulties may be. Let every man remember that all England and all the world is watching him. GOOD LUCK, WE WILL

MEET AGAIN IN MONTAUBAN.'

So confident was Lieutenant-Colonel William Lyle, 23/ Northumberland Fusiliers (4th Tyneside Scottish), that he went into No Man's Land with a walking stick in his hand ... He was killed on 1st July and is buried in Bapaume Post Military Cemetery outside Albert. Major Irwin took over command of the 8/ East Surreys three days before 'Z' Day: 'We were very young ... I took it for granted that the wire would be cut ... we were all very optimistic.'

A medical officer to the 2/ Royal Welch Fusiliers, Captain J.C. Dunn, was of the opinion that 'the French people about here are quite sure the War will be over in a few weeks, and our Staff is full of CONFIDENCE in itself this time.' Lieutenant Russell-Jones, commander of a 30th Division trench-mortar battery, confidently predicted that 'we're within a few minutes of what is to be the beginning of the end of German culture.'

2nd Lieutenant Percy Boswell, aged 22, 8/ KOYLI, wrote to his father '... The Hun is going to get consummate hell just in this quarter & we are going over the parapet tomorrow, when I hope to spend a few merry hours in chasing the Bosch all over the place ... I am absolutely sure that I shall get through all right, but, in case the unexpected does happen, I shall rest content with the knowledge that I have done my duty - and you can't ask more.' Charles Douie, a 2nd lieutenant in the 1/ Dorsets, believed that 'few of us had the smallest doubt' about success: 'We had at last the men and the guns. Confidence reigned supreme.' Private Laidlaw, 17/ Highland Light Infantry (Glasgow Commercials), confidently wrote to his wife: 'O my darling! I hope I am home soon ... O there is no doubt about it Germany is finished.'

Men all along the line were left in no doubt as to the ease with which the Germans would be overcome. Archie Rutherford, 16/ Northumberland Fusiliers (Newcastle Commercials): 'We were told that after our barrage nothing would be left alive in the German lines. One officer actually said in a lecture that we would almost be able to throw our rifles away and go across with walking sticks.'

2nd Lieutenant E.D. Shearn, 1/ Hants, commented that 'we all thought and indeed were told there would be nothing left alive in the German lines and our attack would in fact be a "walkover". We were all pretty confident ... As soon as I got out of the assembly trench I discovered that the story was a myth. We went over literally into a hail of machine-gun fire.' A young Cornishman, Cyril José who had joined the 2/ Devons as a 15 year old in 1914, was due to attack Ovillers: 'We were told that it would be a walkover - our artillery had their machine-guns and batteries all weighed off and would splash them all out in the last few hours of the bombardment.'

Lieutenant J.F.E. Moncton recalled a visit by Commander-in-Chief General Sir Douglas Haig: 'He asked me what I thought of the new steel helmets, and also said that the dull life of the trenches would soon be over ... we were lulled into thinking that nothing could possibly survive such a tornado.'

German defenders of IR 169 at Serre were struck by the quality of the men who attacked and their misplaced confidence; some, they reported, were carrying their washing and shaving equipment! The IR180 defending the line between Thiepval and Ovillers recorded that the British 'came on at a steady pace as if expecting to find nothing alive in our front trenches. Some appeared to be carrying Kodaks to perpetuate the memory of their triumphal march across the German defences.' They were unlikely to have been carrying cameras but the impression given by the British soldiers was one of calm assurance. The Germans were in awe of their enemy: 'The British soldier has no lack of courage and once his hand is set on the plough, he is not easily turned from his purpose.'

Imbued with such confidence, the first few minutes after Zero Hour must have come as a massively unwelcome surprise to the thousands that were caught by German machine-gun and artillery fire as they made their way to the front line trenches or when they poured into No Man's Land.

Scepticism:

Many officers and men who survived, writing with the benefit of hindsight, criticised the handling of the offensive on 1st July; there were some, however, who raised their concerns in the days beforehand - Captain Duncan L. Martin was fearful that the 9/ Devons attacking Mametz would be hit by machine-gun fire from the 'Shrine' in the civilian cemetery. When on leave he made a plasticine model of the ground to be covered and the dangers involved. It had been thought that the model's message was ignored by his superiors but recent research suggests otherwise. Brigadier-Major Foss wrote to all Brigades in 7th Division: 'A contoured model in plasticene (sic) has been made by Captain Martin … showing the whole area to be attacked by the 20th Infantry Brigade … The model may be seen at any time on application to 20th Division HQ.' It is doubtful much notice was in practice taken of the model, given that Martin and 150 members of the 8 and 9/ Devons Battalions fell and are buried in Devonshire Cemetery at Mansel Copse.

Lieutenant-Colonel Edwin Sandys, 2/ Middlesex, had severe misgivings about his Battalion's chances of attacking 750 yards up Mash Valley to Ovillers, as perusal of the Germans' barbed wire through his binoculars, showed it to be uncut. Lieutenant-Colonel E.K. Cordeaux, 10/ Lincolns (Grimsby Chums) asked about the effect of bombardment on 'the Boche' but was inclined to think that 'their dug-outs are too deep for him to have suffered much.'

Brigadier-General H. C. Rees, 94th Brigade, was concerned that his men faced 700 yards of No Man's Land to negotiate, up a 'decided rise' at the top of which the Germans had a clear view. Lieutenant-Colonel Reginald Bastard, 2/ Lincolns, wondered 'how many of us will be here tomorrow night'- at least he survived the attack on Ovillers.

Before the War, Rifleman Percy Jones, 1/ 16 London (Queen's Westminster Rifles), was a journalist; when waiting to attack at Gommecourt, he queried the effectiveness of the barrage: 'I do not see how the stiffest bombardment is going to kill them all. Nor do I see how the whole of the enemy's artillery is going to be silenced.'

Zero Hour Approaches:

Despite being assured that when they went over the top, it would be a 'walkover', most men were nonetheless nervous and reacted in different ways. Some were silent, some prayed. Many enjoyed what would prove to be their last breakfast. One man shot himself in the knee. Lieutenant-Colonel Frank Crozier and his 9/ Royal Irish Rifles enjoyed a substantial breakfast. Colonel Laidlaw and men of his 16/ Highland Light Infantry 'breakfasted on the contents of the night before - baked beans and biscuits, tinned salmon and shortbread all washed down with water.' The 1/ 2 London (Royal Fusiliers) enjoyed a hot mug of pea soup at 5.00 a.m. The 11/ Suffolks had tea laced with rum and some overdid the ration! Gilbert Hall, 13/ York and Lancaster (1st Barnsley Pals), was more circumspect, accepting just one tot from Captain Currin and a group of NCOs, preferring to keep his wits about him. Captain Flatau, 8/ East Surreys, spent the night writing letters to his family post-dated to 2nd July-

optimistically as it turned out … he was killed early in the attack on Montauban and is buried in Carnoy Military Cemetery. Fellow officer Lieutenant Ackerley read Joseph Conrad's *Lord Jim* for the fifth time.

A member of the 13/ York and Lancaster (1st Barnsley Pals) went for a bathe in the Ancre (near Bus Wood) and was asked what he thought he was doing. He replied that 'I want to appear clean before my maker.' He was killed on 1st July.

The 8/ Norfolks Battalion War Diary recorded that 'artillery activity of both sides was marked after dawn. The demeanour of the men was admirable; an atmosphere of quiet confidence and determination prevailed amongst all ranks which augured well for the success of the undertaking.'

The feelings of Captain William Henry Bloor, Royal Field Artillery, 30th Division, 'are tonight mixed somewhat - we are sure that Boche is going to get the most terrific hiding of his life … but we also know what we are about to undergo and nothing is more certain that very many will never live to see who is victorious.'

Overworked Infantrymen:

General Haig allocated only 5,000 men to Rawlinson for manual work. As a result many infantrymen were called on to carry out 'fatigues' which left them exhausted. It was not ideal preparation for 'going over the top'. Captain James Jack, 2/ Cameronians, complained that 'frequently our infantry were overworked by High Command till shortly before assaulting. Exhausted troops can hold a position, but men must be fresh to produce the energy needed to attack.' The History of the 5 and 6/ North Staffs recounts that the men had to dig assembly trenches and clear communication trenches concluding: 'No wonder they were soon worn out.' Captain 'Billie' Nevill, 8/ East Surreys, in a letter to his sister Elsie on 27th June, informed her that 'for twenty two days on end, we've been working hard, all hours day & night, my personal sleep time being from 2 a.m. to 3.30 and from 4.00 a.m. to 8.00 usually but that's when I'm lucky.'

On the day, many men were worn out by Zero Hour. The 1/ Essex were, according to the Battalion War Diary 'much fatigued by the long time, 9.30 p.m. to 3.30 a.m. to get into position and the heavy equipment carried.'

A journalist who had served on the Somme recalled that 'we had trudged a long way heavily laden up a seemingly never ending communication trench, often up to our knees and once or twice waist deep in mud and water. We were tired.'

'The Germans Knew We Were On The Way...'

As early as 26th May, General Fritz Von Below noted that 'the British have been reinforced so strongly north of the Somme there can hardly be any remaining doubt concerning their plans for an offensive.' Other ranks from their front line trenches could not fail to see much of the British build-up to 'Z' Day during June. The Germans entrenched opposite the 5/ North Staffs at Gommecourt, had hoisted up placards with the taunt: 'Come on, we are ready for you.'

The attack by the 46th (North Midland) and 56th (London) Divisions was a decoy to draw German infantry and weapons away from the south and Major-Generals Montagu-Stuart-Wortley and Hull had been actively encouraged to make sure that the Germans realised that the attack would take place in that sector. Private Victor Wheat

General Fritz von Below

of a 1/5 North Staffs wiring party was captured at 4.00 a.m. on 27th June and provided valuable intelligence as to where the assault would be aimed, based on practice raids carried out in trenches behind the lines at St. Léger. The Germans were even told which Battalion would lead the attack - it would be the 6/ North Staffs as the 5/ North Staffs had attacked first at Loos the previous year! The interview led the Germans to conclude that 'the soldiers have little faith in the success of their attack.'

Aubrey Smith, 1/5 London (1st London Rifle Brigade), was convinced that 'the Germans were prepared for us - there was little doubt of that. How could they help being so when we dug assembly trenches and gun-pits under their very noses and advertised to the French and to the world in general that we were about to take the offensive?'

German intelligence did not have to rely on prisoners' information. In early June it was widely reported and picked up in Germany that the Labour member of the Coalition Government, Arthur Henderson, admitted the Government wished to postpone the end of May Bank Holiday and asked factory munitions workers in Leeds to delay their holidays until after the beginning of July.

The 16/ Highland Light Infantry were in trenches with Thiepval village to their left and the Leipzig Redoubt to the right: 'The enemy knew what to expect. He could afford to jest … as he had done when he erected a board in No Man's Land asking when the strafe was to begin. The element of surprise was entirely absent.'

Captain Harry Bursey, Royal Horse Artillery, wrote that on the day before the bombardment began, the Germans held up a board above the front line trenches. Humour was at a premium by this stage of the War but pinned on it was: 'We know you are going to attack. Kitchener is done. Asquith is done. You are done. We are done. In fact we are all done!' It must have been quite a large board.

A deserter from the 29th Division due to attack at Beaumont furnished the Germans with information about which battalions would be in the attack, their tactics, what would happen in the days before the attack and even the detail of the colours of flares that would be sent up for the artillery. The Germans may well have used such intelligence, as there were occasions when they sent up similarly coloured flares which confused British commanders with devastating consequences.

On 24th June a Bavarian regiment had been briefed by intelligence officers that 'an attack by British and French units is to be expected shortly on both banks of the Somme.' Captain J.C. Dunn, 2/ Royal Welch Fusiliers, although not present on 1st July, pointed out that 'every prisoner taken in raids on this front knew where we would attack.' General Haig was a staunch believer in the need for surprise - it would appear that the greatest surprise would have been if the British had decided against an offensive at the last moment.

The War Diary of the German RIR 91 at Gommecourt, makes it clear that it was a case of when rather than if the attack took place: 'The new British assembly trenches, the pushing forward of saps, the frequent bombardment of important points, the appearance of heavy trench mortars, and increased artillery fire left no doubt as to the intention of the enemy.'

If the Germans needed any further confirmation of the imminence of the attack, it was provided by a listening post at La Boisselle, codenamed Moritz, which intercepted an order in the early hours of 1st July from 34th Division that the 'infantry must hold on obstinately to every yard of ground that is gained. Behind it is an excellent artillery.' That was the confirmation the Germans welcomed - that the offensive was, at last, to begin a few hours later …

As the Germans were ready and waiting for the British to attack, it is doubtful that an order from 56th Division General Staff would have made any difference: 'Brigades are warned not to fix bayonets until shortly before the assault in order that they should not show over the parapet and give warning to the enemy.'

Bombardment:

The Germans did not have to be masterminds to realise that the intensive British bombardment was the prelude to a major assault. For Rawlinson, who had managed to convince Haig of the need for five days of barrage, its effectiveness was essential to the success of the offensive. Captain A.J.M. Barmby, 7/ Yorkshire (Green Howards), was upbeat about the bombardment: 'Such a concentration of guns had never been seen before in the history of the World.' During the week of bombardment over 1,500 guns fired 1,732,872 shells which, reputedly, could be heard across the Channel:

British Howitzers in the Somme   *The Times History of the War*

possibly but surely not in 10 Downing Street as was claimed? The post 1915 French mantra that 'the artillery conquers and the infantry occupies' was soon to face the sternest of examinations.

Described by a German as a 'hell concert', Rawlinson hoped that it would break enemy morale. Captain Charles May, 22/ Manchesters, wrote to his wife: 'Mametz they tell us has ceased to be.' The bombardment was 'calculated to shake the morale of the finest troops in the world. It destroys sleep and interferes with rationing. Lack of either of these always affects a soldier. If his old machine-gunners have only suffered in proportion to his other ranks, we should not be too seriously hurt doing our job.'

Captain A. Radclyffe Dugmore, KOYLI, recalled that after a lull 'suddenly hell would be let loose, for every gun as though activated by one invisible hand, would spit forth its deadly shot, and the air would vibrate with the roar as of ten thousand peals of thunder ...'

The Germans had other ideas: 'The torture and fatigue, not to mention the strain on the nerves, were indescribable ... You made a good job of it you British! Seven days and seven nights you rapped and hammered on our door! Now your reception was going to match your turbulent longing to enter!' A soldier of the IR 180 made his feelings clear: 'If the British believe that their fire has shaken and unnerved us, they have deceived themselves.' A soldier serving in the RIR 109 at Mametz recalled that 'thirst made one almost mad. Luckily it rained yesterday and the water in the shell holes mixed with the yellow shell sulphur tasted as good as a bottle of beer.' Kurt Westmann, a trainee doctor, remembered 'down below, men became hysterical ... even the rats panicked and sought refuge in our flimsy shelters; they ran up the walls and we had to kill them with our spades.'

British troops attacking Mametz   *Sir Douglas Haig's Great Push*

V

'Over The Top'

Men of 26/ Northumberland Fusiliers (3rd Tyneside Irish) about to clear Tara Hill seconds before being hit by machine-gun fire   IWM Q 000053

Into No Man's Land:

Soldiers of some battalions crawled out into No Man's Land to get nearer to the German front line trenches to reduce the distance they would have to negotiate. Most experienced their first taste of action at 7.30 a.m. when whistles, bugles and in one case a flute were blown and they climbed over their parapets, went through specially cut gaps in the wire and made their way generally in extended order towards the enemy. Many in following battalions did not even reach their own front line trenches. Experiences were not dissimilar except in the south during the 30th Division's successful assault on Montauban where the loss of life was less. Lieutenant J.R. Ackerley, 8/ East Surreys, vividly describes his Battalion's attack on Montauban: 'The air when at last we went over the top in broad daylight, positively hummed, buzzed and whined with what sounded like hordes of wasps and hornets but were of course bullets.' Men were caught by enfilade machine-gun fire or hit by shells from guns that were supposed to have been silenced. Men fell in their hundreds.

Descriptions by those who survived, paint a picture of bloody devastation:

- Sergeant Arthur Cook, 1/ Somerset Light Infantry: 'During nearly two years of war, I had never seen so many dead in such a small area. In places where enfilade fire caught them, they were three to four deep, and all looked to be asleep, except for their painful expressions. Their bodies at the time were whole, as machine-gun fire does not dismember the body, this will start when shells begin to fall among them … the sight of some of the dead was ghastly … life here was more fit for devils than human beings'

- 16 year old Frank Lindley, 14/ York and Lancaster (2nd Barnsley Pals): 'It was all right the Generals saying "You will walk across". Even if we had run across we would have been in the same fix because we couldn't have got through their wire … I remember seeing the lads laid in rows just as if they had gone to sleep. The machine-guns just laid them out. I was lying in a shell-hole and could see piles of dead where they had made for the gaps in the wire. Some were caught up on the wire and their bodies were being knocked about by bullets, legs and arms were flying about all over the place'

'…the sight of some of the dead was ghastly …'   *British dead outside a dug-out*

- Jack Cratchley, 12/ York and Lancaster (Sheffield City): 'We walked over heaps of dead just as if it were a carpet laid for us'

- George Coppard, Machine-Gun Corps: 'Hundreds of dead, many belonging to the 137th Brigade (46th Division) were strung out like wreckage washed up to a high water mark. Quite as many had died on the enemy wire as on the ground, like fish caught in a net. They hung there in grotesque postures. Some looked as though they were praying: they had died on their knees and the wire had prevented their fall … It was clear there were no gaps in the wire at the time of the attack'

- Private W.J. Senescall, 11/ Suffolks: 'A very large shell fell some yards to my left. With all the bits and pieces flying up was a body. The legs had blown off right to the crutch. I have never seen a body lifted so high'

- Private W. Roberts, 18/ Durham Light Infantry: 'The sights I saw are too terrible to write about and men almost blown to pieces were lying side by side unable to proceed further'

- Daniel John Sweeney, 1/ Lincolns: 'You cannot realise what it is like to see poor lads lying about with terrible wounds and not being able to help them'

A significant number of descriptions compare men's deaths to skittles being knocked down or corn and grass being cut or scythed:

- Lance-Corporal Thomas Higgins, 1/ 5 North Staffs at Gommecourt: 'Men were falling like skittles, bowled over'

- A soldier of 1/ 2 London (Royal Fusiliers) at Gommecourt: 'Men were being bowled over like skittles'

- Frederick Francis, 11/ Border (Lonsdales): 'The Germans just mowed us down like grass in a hay field'

- Corporal R. Harley, 11/ Suffolks: 'A great many of our brigade, not being bulletproof, fell before they reached the German line, for the Germans were mowing the grass with machine-gun fire'

- Leonard Duke, 12/ York and Lancaster (Sheffield City): 'All went down like corn in a wheat field'

- Lance-Corporal H. Bury at Serre saw comrades of his in the 11/ East Lancs (Accrington Pals) being 'mown down like meadow grass … I felt sick at the sight of this carnage and remember weeping'

- An officer led the first wave of men brandishing his sword … 'It flashed in the sunlight … he fell to the ground. His men undaunted battled on to be mown down … like autumn corn before the cutter'

- Leutnant Alfred Frick, 6th Battery Reserve Field Artillery Regiment, defending Ovillers: 'The fifteen remaining undamaged machine-guns in this sector of RIR 110 poured into the oncoming columns so that the assaulting forces went down like ripe corn before the scythe. In consequence the enemy casualties were simply enormous'

- Private James Walton, 11/ Suffolks: 'The (Lochnagar) mine had never touched the German machine-guns and there were so many of them, and they were placed so they cross-fired and the infantry went down in front of their murderous fire just like corn in front of a farmer's reaper ... I've never seen anything like it before and I hope nobody ever sees anything like it again'

German machine-gunners Rudolf Stadelbacher and Otto Schüsele of Machine-Gun Company RIR 111: 'When early 1st July the enemy lifted the fire, we knew the attack was not far off ... So we put down a hail of fire on the attacking enemy. Two companies of British who attempted to assault from Fricourt Station were quickly caught by our machine-gun and suffered dreadful casualties. We were not untouched, suffering two wounded and one killed. We fired 22,000 rounds during the day. We were each given a bottle of mineral water which cheered us up.'

German machine-gun crew   IWM Q061038

Many German soldiers could scarcely believe their eyes when they saw the enemy coming slowly towards them in 'extended order' and saw them mown down. There were several instances of Germans helping British wounded or offering an armistice to tend to them.

Losses were so great that officers and men could not believe the situation they found themselves in- Lieutenant-Colonel Ritson, 16/ Northumberland Fusiliers (Newcastle Commercials) at Thiepval was heard to exclaim tearfully and repeatedly: 'My God, My Boys, My Boys' as he surveyed the wreckage of his Battalion. Private Dodd, 23/ Northumberland Fusiliers (4th Tyneside Scottish) at La Boiselle, heard his lieutenant disbelievingly shout 'God, God, where's the rest of the boys?'

Opposite the London Rifle Brigade, one combatant recalled an incident 'which shows we had a decent lot of Huns opposite and which would prove a source of consolation to the relatives of the missing. At about 9.45 p.m. a German came out to us and as I saw his red cross, I prevented our men from firing ... he stopped one of their machine-guns. I think this action showed pluck and augurs well for our wounded which we had to leave behind.'

'I beg to report' wrote the diarist for the 1/ East Lancs 'that at 9.20 p.m. I saw two Germans removing our wounded back to their lines from No Man's Land.' Defenders of Hawthorn Crater attacked by the 86th Brigade did not fire on British soldiers carrying their seriously wounded lieutenant back to his trench and Captain Adjutant A. J. W. Barmby, 7/ Yorkshire (Green Howards): 'In the evening and overnight, the Germans did not molest us and no casualties occurred removing the wounded.'

A member of 4/ Worcesters at Beaumont Hamel tended to a wounded member of the Battalion and at dawn the two soldiers realised that they were just a few yards from the Germans' front trench. They were asked by a German officer if they wanted to be taken prisoner or allowed to return to their own lines and the answer was as respectful as if in answer to one of their own officers: 'I'll go back to my own trenches, Sir.' Stretcher-bearers were permitted later to bring in the wounded man.

Unteroffizier (Corporal) Otto Lais IR 169 at Serre was appalled by the scene in No Man's Land as First Aid men appeared with Red Cross flags: 'Whimpering and moaning confronts them from almost every square metre. Our own first-aiders who are not required elsewhere, go forward to bandage the wounded and deliver the enemy carefully to their own people.'

There were, however, reports of less conciliatory Germans. George Ashurst, 1/ Lancashire Fusiliers recalled that: 'As I lay there watching their painful efforts to get back to our line, I noticed these poor fellows suddenly try to rise on their feet and then fall in a heap and lie very still. Surely Fritz wasn't killing these unfortunate men? Shells whistled over my head and dropped amongst the poor fellows, blowing dead men into the air and putting others out of their agony.' The 94th Brigade War Diary recorded that at Serre 'at odd intervals and for the rest of the day, small groups of Germans were seen in the front line standing on the fire step sniping at any of our men in No Man's Land who showed any sign of life, and making target practice of dead bodies.' Brigadier-General Ternan wrote in *The Story of the Tyneside Scottish*: 'Not one man was taken prisoner and losses were unnecessarily high due to the fact the Germans deliberately fired at and killed any wounded lying in front of their trenches.'

Such cruelty was not the sole preserve of the Germans as the War Diary of the 8/ York and Lancaster testifies: 'It is reported that an enemy machine-gun was found in the front line with two Germans chained to it. Both were dead, one having been bayoneted and the other apparently killed by the butt of a rifle.'

A quiet looking soldier in the 8/ East Surreys was pointed out as one who had requested that a companion hold his rifle for a moment while he polished off a Boche with his fists. He explained that 'the bloke was too old to shoot in cold blood and too thin to bayonet.'

Dealing with the Wounded:

General Rawlinson had estimated there would be 10,000 casualties per day and had insisted on 18 Ambulance trains being on hand to transport the wounded. In the event only five were operational which made it impossible to move sufficient numbers of men to Base Hospitals. During the first 24 hours of the battle over 25,000 wounded were removed from the battlefield. According to one stretcher-bearer working in the Basilica at Albert, 'wounded flooded in on foot, or were brought in by stretchers, wheelbarrows, carts, anything … those who were not expected to survive were put on one side and left. It was hard to ignore their cries for help but we had to concentrate on those who might live.' Sister Edith Appleton on 3rd July recorded 'we had a couple of train loads of wounded - 1,100 in all - 153 officers - very dirty. The London Scottish kilts were a sight to behold.'

On 1st July, a chaplain, the Rev. John Walker was in a Casualty Clearing Station. Later in the day the staff were dealing with 1,500 'and still they come, 3-400 officers, it is a sight - chaps with fearful wounds lying in agony, many so patient, some make a noise, one goes to a stretcher, lays one's hand on the forehead, it is cold, strike a match, he is dead - here a Communion, there an absolution, there a drink, there a madman … O I am tired, excuse my writing.' On the following day he went 'twice to bury, we used the trench we had prepared in a field adjoining. I first held a service of consecration, when I turned round, the old man labouring in the field was on his knees in the soil. I buried thirty-seven but have some left over till tomorrow.'

Matron-in-Chief Emma Maud McCarthy's War Diary highlighted the huge demands placed on the doctors and nurses at the Front. On 3rd July there were 'still demands for nurses. The present staffs, MOs, nurses and men have been working day and night, and unable entirely to cope with the work.' The following day she left at 7 a.m. to visit seven Casualty Clearing Stations. At two of them, Numbers 36 and 38,300 German wounded were waiting on stretchers to be evacuated. Her day concluded with a visit to Fourth Army HQ at Querrieu where 'everyone was pleased with the news of the excellent work which has been done by all ranks in medical units.'

A chaplain taking details of the wounded   IWM Q 004060

Hospitals were not places for the squeamish. Edith Appleton dealt with 'horribly bad wounds … some crawling with maggots, some stinking and tense with gangrene.' She described one poor young lad whose eyes had been shot through: 'They were all smashed up with the eyelashes. He was quite calm and very tired. He said "Shall I have an operation? I can't see anything." Poor boy, he never will.'

Journalist Philip Gibbs vividly described his visit to a hospital at Corbie: 'I found myself trembling in a queer way. The hospital was christened the Butcher's Shop by a colonel of the RAMC: "We lop off limbs here all day long, and all night. You've no idea." I saw and was sickened. In one long, narrow room there were about 30 beds, and in each bed lay a young British soldier or part of a young British soldier … I walked stiffly out … past a stench of mud and blood and anaesthetics, to the fresh air of the gateway where a column of ambulances had just arrived with a new harvest from the fields of the Somme.'

Edith Appleton articulated the view that must have been prevalent amongst the medical units on the Somme: 'It is to be hoped that our attacking is doing useful work for the war as we are paying a tall price … The surgeons are amputating limbs and boring through skulls at 30 a day - not a day passes without Death taking its toll.' And the Somme battlefield in 1916 took its toll on the RAMC - 400 doctors were casualties, many unsurprisingly from stress.

'As If On Parade':

As 94 battalions of inexperienced New Army troops were to take part in the offensive, there was understandable anxiety amongst the Generals about how they would cope in battle - hence the decision by some generals to maintain order and discipline by making men walk in rows side by side across No Man's Land. The intention was that men arrived at the objective together and in a fit state to take on the enemy … An extraordinary number of accounts after the event refer to the men walking to their deaths 'as if on parade', and that they were disciplined and unfaltering.

Major-General Nugent, 36th (Ulster) Division wrote to his wife on 2nd July: 'The whole Army is talking of the incomparable gallantry shown by officers and men. There has been nothing like it since the New Armies came out. They came out of the trenches, formed up as if on the barrack square and went forward with every line, dressed as if for the King's inspection, torn from end to end by shell and machine-gun fire.' Major-General Ingouville-Williams ('Inky Bill') recorded that his troops in the 34th Division attacking La Boisselle 'advanced as if on parade …' 54 year old Ingouville-Williams was killed on 22nd July 1916 when reconnoitring the terrain over which his Division would attack. He is buried in Warloy Baillon Communal Cemetery Extension.

Lieutenant E.W. Wilmer, 17/ King's (1st Liverpool Pals) was in the attack at Montauban: 'At 7.30 a.m. our barrage lifted from the German front line and waves of British troops left the trenches and walked out into No Man's Land, in extended line, with bayonets fixed, and rifles at the carry.' The attack on the Schwaben Redoubt by Lieutenant-Colonel Frank Crozier's 9/ Royal Irish Rifles, was a 'spirited dash across No Man's Land, carried out as if on parade and has cost us fifty dead and seventy disabled.'

Brigadier-General H.C. Rees, 94th Brigade: 'I have been through many battles in this war and nothing more magnificent has come under my notice. The waves went forward as if on drill parade. I saw no man turn back or falter.'

Company Sergeant-Major Crawford was with the Tyneside Irish at La Boisselle: 'It was glorious to see these men advance under a perfect hail of machine-gun fire and shells. They went on and on never faltering as if on an ordinary parade.' The 109th Brigade War Diary in an attempt to wash away the horror of what happened at Thiepval recorded for posterity that 'The Brigade moved off as if on parade nothing finer in the way of an advance has ever been seen.'

The Germans were amazed. Unteroffizier (Corporal) Paul Scheytt, RIR 109 at Mametz remembered 'the English came walking, as though they were going to the theatre or as though they were on the parade ground. We felt they were mad. Our orders were given in complete calm and every man took careful aim to avoid wasting ammunition.'

The Dead:

When it came to dealing with the dead, Jack Cratchley, 12/ York and Lancaster (Sheffield City), wrote that 'corpses were taken to an old disused French trench near an old building at Red Farm. There we had to dump the corpses one on top of another till the trench was nearly full. This job we carried on for three nights and three days. We was told that every dead body had to be fetched before we was relieved, but that was impossible, as scores of bodies were buried and could not be found without digging, which would have taken weeks.'

Over 18,500 British soldiers died on 1st July. The following figures are taken from the CWGC records of those in the British Army who died on 1st July on all fronts, but the large majority died on the Somme. Many died of wounds in the following days and months:

No Rank:

12,218	privates
1,587	riflemen
16	drummers
6	buglers
4	pipers
13,831	

NCOs:

1837	lance-corporals
776	corporals
793	sergeants
99	company sergeant-majors
3,505	

Officers:

558	2nd lieutenants
215	lieutenants
198	captains
22	majors
20	lieutenant-colonels
2	colonels
1	brigadier-general
1,016	

Others:

4	Machine-Gun Corps
21	RAMC
137	Royal Engineers (including 91 sappers)
91	RFA
13	RGA
3	RHA
6	RFC
275	

18,627

This is a 'ball park' figure but reasonably accurate we believe; added to it would be those who died of wounds later and those of units we have overlooked so we have an overall figure of in the region of 19,000 deaths caused by the actions on 1st July 1916.

In percentage terms, huge numbers of officers were killed, most of them as they led their troops either towards their own front line trenches or into No Man's Land. The highest ranked soldier to fall was Brigadier-General Charles Bertie Prowse (see *Stolen Lives* and *Meet at Dawn, Unarmed* by Andrew Hamilton and Alan Reed) of the 11th Brigade as it attacked the Redan Ridge, north of Beaumont Hamel.

When war broke out, Prowse had reached the rank of major and fought with the 1/ Somerset Light Infantry which was part of the 11th Brigade in the 4th Division. Like the Royal Warwicks of the 10th Brigade, the Somersets in November and December 1914 were located near 'Plugstreet Wood' in Belgium and were involved in the Christmas Truce at St.Yvon.

Charles Bertie Prowse was a career soldier. After leaving Marlborough College he joined the Somerset Light Infantry in 1892 with whom he served in the Boer War from 1899 to 1902. He did so with great distinction, being Mentioned in Despatches three times. He took part in the operations in Natal, Cape Colony, Orange River and Transvaal and was involved in the actions at Ladysmith and Spion Kop.

He fought in the early battles in northern France - at Le Cateau on 26th August 1914 when the British Expeditionary Force was forced into retreat and in the Marne and Aisne offensives. He was mentioned in Sir John French's first despatch for saving the British lines at St. Yvon and was promoted to brevet lieutenant-colonel, the first brevet of the War. He took on the leadership of the 1/ Leinster Regiment on 19th January 1915 but was swiftly promoted on 29th April to GOC of 11th Brigade. He commanded the Brigade at the 2nd Battle of Ypres in late April 1915 and during the battle was placed in command of 15 battalions, three of which were French.

Vandyk

Brig.=Gen. C. B. Prowse, D.S.O.

Killed in action on July 1, aged forty-seven years. He had previously served in the South African War, and was three times mentioned in despatches. He held the Queen's medal with five clasps and the King's medal with two clasps

Prowse had risen from the rank of major to brigadier-general in less than a year. Promotion prospects before the War were limited but as the War unfolded, opportunities suddenly improved.

On 1st July Prowse was in command of the 11th Brigade, entrenched north of Beaumont Hamel. Captain G.A. Prideaux recorded in the Somerset Light Infantry Regimental History that 'at about 9.45 a.m. the General decided to move his HQ into the German front line, thinking that it was cleared of all Germans. Just as he was getting out of our front line trench, near "Brett Street", he was shot in the back by a machine-gun in the Ridge Redoubt and died in the afternoon.' Prowse had been

Battalion commanding officers who died on or soon after 1st July who have graves in the Somme (others are on p. 92)

assembling men of the Seaforth Highlanders; Lieutenant G.A Robinson of the 1/ Rifle Brigade commended the brigadier-general for showing 'great gallantry in his efforts, ignoring the great breaches in our parapets and exposing himself to great danger.'

Brigadier-General Prowse's body was recovered thanks to the brave efforts of a Seaforth Highlander, Private W.R. Bailey, who wrote to Mrs. Violet Prowse detailing her husband's final moments. He described how a fellow Seaforth Highlander rushed off to find a doctor or stretcher-bearers and to inform Headquarters: 'I myself did all in my power for my beloved master holding my hand over his wound for quite some half an hour or so to keep the blood in … We then started on a journey back, after we had procured a stretcher, which took a considerable time. It was a terrible journey moving up these small trenches … He was conscious and happy until we reached Divisional Headquarters when he grew weaker. We got to the hospital as soon as possible. He practically died in

Brigadier-General Prowse's grave   A Reed

my arms, breathing his last at the hospital.' Bailey may not have survived the War himself as a Private W. Bailey of the 2/ Seaforth Highlanders died on 4th October 1917 and is commemorated on the Tyne Cot Memorial.

The Brigadier-General who was awarded a DSO during his time on the Western Front was buried at Louvencourt Military Cemetery, amongst other ranks and fate would have it that he was buried near Private Harry MacDonald, a soldier 'shot at dawn' for desertion.

Lieutenant-General Sir Aylmer Hunter-Weston, VIII Corps, wrote to Mrs. Prowse on 2nd July: 'The grave of my dear friend, your husband, looks so peaceful, pretty and happy with its carpet of green. I cannot express the sympathy I feel for you. His life was a great and notable one. He did his Duty and it is better to be his widow than anyone else's wife. He was a man. A gentleman and a soldier.' Lieutenant-General Snow, VII Corps, sent his condolences: 'As an old friend of your husband's and one of his greatest admirers, I write not to offer sympathy as that is useless, but to tell you that your husband was one of the bravest men I have ever known.'

Prowse Point Military Cemetery near 'Plugstreet Wood' in Belgium was set up on 14th November 1914 by the 2/ Royal Dublin Fusiliers and 1/ Royal Warwicks and was named after Prowse in recognition of his deeds in the area; it is unique in the Ypres Salient for being the only cemetery named after an individual.

As well as Brigadier-General Prowse, 29 lieutenant-colonels and majors (battalion commanders), were killed or died of wounds, rather more than popular mythology would have us believe.

Nature:

Despite the thunderous noise, the exploding shells and the ensuing smoke and dust, the natural world of skylarks, flowers and poppies still co-existed with Man as he continued hell-bent to destroy fellow Man in June and July 1916.

Charles Douie, 1/ Dorsets, painted a pretty spring-time picture: 'The Thiepval trenches ran through the garden of Thiepval Chateau and in the absence of shell fire there was much that was attractive in the view over the valley of the Ancre and the woods of Thiepval, Aveluy and Authuille on each side, now beautiful in the glory of spring. Flowers were often to be found growing in the sides of the trenches and in No Man's Land.'

Poppies in No Man's Land by the Sunken Road with the Ulster Tower in the background

The 14/ Royal Irish Rifles at 1.10 a.m. on 1st July experienced 'a lull which seemed to settle over all the earth, as if it were a mutual tightening up for the great struggle shortly to commence. A water hen called to its mate midst the reedy swamp and a courageous nightingale made so bold as to treat us with a song.' The Battalion War Diary marvelled at how 'anything can live under such a hail of shells.'

Gilbert Hall, 13/ York and Lancaster (1st Barnsley Pals) recalled looking up and seeing the coarse grass growing along the parapet flying into the air as the bullets' stream hit it … 'the intense bombardment was interspersed with the incongruous sound of the larks singing in the air above them.'

The poet Will Streets, 12/ York and Lancaster (Sheffield City): 'I hear between the bursts, the sweet lyric of the lark who is lost in the clouds. He is simply an ecstasy of emotion beyond the din of the strife. And my soul goes up with him and loses itself in the dreams, the altitude of life. I sit here where Death is taking his toll, reaping his red harvest of youth … sweet flowers of the trenches you lead me back to life.'

Private G.E. Waller, 16/ Highland Light Infantry (Glasgow Boys' Brigade): ' I suppose a shell hole is not the best place from which to admire anything but believe it or not, waving about just above my head were two full blown red poppies which stood out in pleasant contrast against the azure blue sky.'

Lieutenant Edward Living, 1/ 12 London (Rangers) remembered when 'a hare jumped up and rushed towards and past me through the dry, yellowish grass, its eyes bulging with fear.'

Colonel Laidlaw, 16/ Highland Light Infantry watched a small tapeworm wriggle up the side of the trench and 'high above, the larks circled gaily, singing songs of peace. The poppies in the fields behind swayed gently in the cool morning air, shaking the dewdrops onto the grass below. Nature was at her best.'

The Rev. Ernest Crosse, chaplain to the 8 and 9/ Devons, was impressed by a magpie in Mansel Copse which had built its nest there and hatched out its young, oblivious to the regular bombardments which seemed to have hit every other tree except that one: 'It afforded me an illustration just before the battle, of an animal who carried on its job despite the danger of it …'

A soldier journalist writing in the *Sheffield Telegraph* on 30th June 1916 remembered that 'the air was sweet with the faint scent of wild flowers growing in the trench sides … big brazen dandelions and delicate golden buttercups were nodding tremulously radiant with dew in the sunny morning.'

Captain A. Radclyffe Dugmore, KOYLI, heard the voice of a cuckoo in the woods behind Fricourt sounding 'strangely out of place.' Normally associated with the tranquillity of the countryside 'here it was mingling its sweet notes with the ghastly droon (sic) of the passing shells, and the terrific explosions which shook the very earth.'

Humour:

Given the hellish conditions faced, humour, with the exception of Bruce Bairnsfather's cartoons, was in short supply. Lance-Corporal Fred Sayer, 11/ East Lancs (Accrington Pals) was part of the assault on Serre when 'there was much sadness at our failure, and for once humour, that paragon of the British Army was absent' but a soldier's natural inclination to gallows humour was not entirely extinguished. Several 2nd Tyneside Irish dragged a wounded sergeant on a groundsheet: 'When in our trenches dying, as further waves of troops were advancing and stepping on him as he lay there, he joked "It's bad enough being wounded but when you buggers walk on you as well …"'

LES ARTILLEURS ANGLAIS SONT PLEINS D'HUMOUR

'Humour Britannique'   *Le Miroir, July 1916*

Behind the lines some officers dealing with paperwork for the 8/ East Surreys playfully decided to indulge in some tomfoolery:

'Trench topics:

Intelligence Report: A fatigue party of 15 inch trench rats, left by the Buffs, have entrenched themselves in Mr. Soames's haversack

News: A certain liveliness on the British Front. German weather cock reports 'wind up'   **119**

Things we want to know:

1. How many German privates reported sick this morning

2. How many Germans have no privates

3. Have the Germans started playing football yet

4. When the war will end'

Hell:

There might have been some occasional examples of gallows humour prior to going over the top but for most the whole experience was hellish. 'Hell' was a much used word during the Great War- Captain Robert Hamilton, the author's grandfather, described the mobile warfare for the 1/ Royal Warwicks on the Marne in 1914 as 'the hell' and Private William Tapp, of the same regiment, before the Christmas Truce recounted that he 'once or twice had a glimpse of hell.' The type of warfare had changed 18 months later on the Somme to the static and attritional but the description was just as apt: Temporary Lieutenant-Colonel Archie Gavin-Jones, 2/ Middlesex, survived the disastrous attack on Ovillers and when back in the trenches was subjected to a hurricane bombardment which was like 'hell let loose. Men were blown to pieces … I never expected to see the light of day but I am alive and not hurt. Somewhat shaken …'

Corporal Dick Read, 8/ Leicesters, witnessed the return of the South Staffs later in the day - they looked 'dishevelled, dirty, hollow-eyed and grime-streaked … We sensed somehow that these men had seen hell'. Captain James Jack, second in command of the 2/ Cameronians (Scottish Rifles) believed that 'the loss of so many friends, coupled with almost continual personal strain of one kind or another, made the War a "living hell".'

Drummer G. Gatley, a runner during the Staffordshires' attack on Gommecourt Wood, penned a simple but heart-felt poem to those killed:

> *Many a brave hero fell,*
> *We did our duty though it was like being in hell,*
> *Good luck to the Staffords, I wish them success*
> *God bless them and grant them happiness.*

Private John Garner, 11/ Suffolks, was involved in the attack on the Lochnagar Crater at La Boisselle maintaining that 'I do not want to experience hell again… The charge was the worst ever made by the British and they were still going forward.' Corporal G.A. Lloyd, 9/ Royal Irish Rifles (West Belfast Volunteers) attacked the Schwaben Redoubt and neatly summed up the awesome challenge faced by the assaulting British: 'It was just hell, the British artillery were at us, the German artillery were at us and rifle and machine-gun fire as well.'

VI

'One Day We Will Understand'

'You can't teach an old dog new tricks'

R.C. Sherriff author of *Journey's End*

Plaque at Foncquevillers

On 1st July 1916, 25 Generals were responsible for the Somme offensive - 16 Division and 6 Corps commanders, the commanders of Third and Fourth Armies and the Commander-in-Chief, General Sir Douglas Haig. Their average age was 53; a number were near retirement age; most had been educated at public schools, five at Eton, four at Harrow, two at Clifton and one each at Charterhouse, Haileybury, King's Peterborough, Reading, Rugby, Sedbergh and Wellington. Three studied at Oxford and one at Cambridge and eight were trained at the Royal Military College, Sandhurst.

Their training had been for a type of open warfare that had served them well in colonial wars when they had performed with skill and courage. Most fought in South Africa against the Boers between 1899 and 1902 and had been on colonial duty in the imperial outposts of India, Egypt, Sudan and West Africa prior to the outbreak of hostilities in 1914. The warfare conducted on the Western Front bore little resemblance to colonial skirmishes towards the end of the 19th century. The South African War against well-armed Boer farmers was challenging but what unfolded after 1914 was the first major industrialised war with the use of weapons designed to kill in great numbers; the machine-gun and heavy artillery would cause massive losses to men and damage to defensive positions as the nature of the warfare changed from mobile fighting to attritional and static trench combat. Soldiers of all armies involved and at all levels were lacking in meaningful experience of this type of fighting.

Many officers had been cavalry trained but advanced weaponry reduced the usefulness of men on horseback - Major-General David Campbell, youngest of the Divisional officers at 47, had received and recovered from a lance wound on 7th September 1914: nearly two years later, there was no danger of such a wound being inflicted by the Germans on the first day of the Battle of the Somme.

Captain Robert Sherriff MC, 9/ East Surreys, whose play *Journey's End* examined the effect of trench warfare on those who had, with innocence and fervour, signed up for King and Country, argued that when the stalemate came 'it needed men with resilient, imaginative minds who could discard all the old outdated methods and adapt themselves to new ones. But you can't teach an old dog new tricks, and that went for the generals.' The extent and speed with which they adapted to the new challenges is fundamental to an appraisal of the first day of the Battle of the Somme.

After the War, many of those who took part were ferociously critical of the way the offensive had been planned and executed. The 2/ Devons lost 177 men during their attack on Ovillers - Private Cyril José, survived to vent his scorn on the Generals who planned and implemented the Battle. After being badly wounded, he sheltered behind the body of his platoon commander for hours within feet of the German trenches, then took 18 hours to crawl 600 yards back to his own lines. Writing after his experience, he had little complimentary to say about his leaders: 'Such a pity that Haig and his Brass Hats did not lead us into battle instead of urging us on from their safe positions in the rear … They might not have survived to sacrifice hundreds of thousands more of my generation. So many lives wasted to cover up their incompetence. So many less to witness the great betrayal by our politicians.' José was so consumed with anger at the way thousands of Tommies had been sacrificed on 1st July that he became a lifelong communist. His resentment and antagonism are understandable - but to what extent was his trenchant and bitter criticism of the Generals justified?

Huge efforts had underpinned the planning and organisation of the attack on 1st July. Soldiers had to be billeted, fed and watered, trained and given practice for their specific roles. Supplies of guns and ammunition had to be manufactured and transported to the front. Railways were built to transport munitions, men and supplies; trenches were dug and 7,000 miles of telephone cables laid. Horses were still the main form of transport; 100,000 on the Western Front needed fodder which was sent over from Britain, as not surprisingly the locals were reluctant to relinquish their own stocks. Hospitals and medical facilities for the 10,000 casualties per day as predicted by Rawlinson, required to be constructed and organised.

It was a huge logistical challenge which was met by a relatively small administrative machine. Their success was recognised by the Germans: RIR 55 that faced the 46th and the 56th Divisions remarked that 'it must be acknowledged that the equipment and preparation of the English attack were magnificent. The assaulting troops were amply provided with machine-guns, Lewis guns, trench mortars and storming ladders.' Captured British maps, sketches and aerial photographs received praise and a long list of arms and equipment 'gives an idea of the excellent preparations.'

Despite the attention to detail in preparing for the big day, it was not long after Zero Hour that assaulting troops along the front were in a state of abject confusion. The methods of communication available to them had not kept in step with the developments in artillery.

In the 1/5 North Staffs Battalion War Diary it was admitted that the assault on RIR 55 degenerated into confusion: 'When the 5th wave arrived at the advance trench, they found the 4th wave had not left their line, although considerably overdue; considerable confusion ensued and in spite of all efforts from the officers, the 4th wave could not be persuaded to go forward. The 5th wave therefore went through the 4th wave and advanced through them towards the German wire; on arriving there this wave had all its officers killed or wounded and a large number of men knocked out … By 11.00 am things then got in utter confusion … Burnett could not be found …' Lieutenant-Colonel Burnett had been killed so a report of the action was compiled by a 'Captain Commanding 1/5 N Staffs', the narrative being based on reports from the few officers to have survived. The confusion at Gommecourt was replicated at many points along the British line of attack.

Lieutenant F.P. Roe wrote that 'every single yard of the communication trench up to the front line was impassable and the confusion was indescribable' and Jack Cratchley, 12/ York and Lancaster (Sheffield City) was damning in his assessment: 'I don't believe that any man knew what he was doing or saying.' A private in the 1/ King's Own Scottish Borderers 'cursed the generals for their useless slaughter, they seemed to have no idea what was going on.' A sergeant in the 22/ Manchesters recalled that 'the worst of it was the confusion; one didn't know how many of us were living or where they were.'

The 8/ East Surreys' War Diary displays the problems experienced in receiving accurate information: 'At 8.40 a.m. the Adjutant again reported heavy fire from the left causing us a large number of casualties.' The officer commanding the 7/ Queens to their left was asked whether the craters had been taken, and the reply received at 8.47 was that 'he believed the craters had been taken, but as it turned out later, this was not the case.'

It was hardly surprising that order should turn to disarray so quickly. Communications were rudimentary; the chances of different waves of men communicating with each other and their HQs were limited.

In one sector Germans were astonished to see some British soldiers carrying picnic baskets … which they later realised contained carrier pigeons. Each brigade in the 4th **123**

Division, according to the War Diary, 'had 8 pigeons distributed amongst its battalions but these do not seem to have been used, as only one pigeon came back and that carried no message of any value. Having failed in their duties all pigeons have been returned to the loft with the exception of four birds'!

Carrier pigeon

It was clear from an operational order from 31st Division to 12/ York and Lancaster that each battalion would be issued with four carrier pigeons to be kept at Battalion HQ. However, they were to be used only as a last resort but it must have been comforting to know that 'these birds are trained to return to Divisional HQs at Bus-les-Artois.' The fact that pigeons were considered at all for use, does underline the limited scope of communication available to the B.E.F.

'Runners' were the most widely used form of communication on 1st July. Drummer G. Gatley of the North Staffs Regiment, was entrenched opposite Gommecourt Wood and in one of his poems described his role:

> *The company runner I professed to be*
>
> *Taking messages then was my duty*
>
> *A message was given me so to Headquarters I ran,*
>
> *It is always my motto to do the best I can.*

A message was sent from 31st Division to 94th Brigade: 'It appears that 12/ York and Lancaster, 11/ East Lancs and three companies of 13/ York and Lancaster have gone forward and you have no news of them. GOC wishes you to use every endeavour to get in touch with them as soon as possible by means of runners if no other method is available.' Use of runners was unreliable as many were hit by machine-gun or shell fire when delivering their messages. The staff of the 1/ Dorsets had little idea how their men were faring as 'none of the runners sent by companies reached Headquarters, they were all killed or wounded' and as a result were 'unable to get in touch with anyone on our right or left.'

Messages took a long time to reach their destination in the heat and danger of battle and crossed with others. The 2/ Seaforth Highlanders reported that 'a runner brought two messages with no time of despatch, one stating that "the battalion must hold on at all costs" and the second "return to front line"'. Captain A. Radclyffe Dugmore, KOYLI, understood the risks that runners faced: 'God knows, for these trusty runners who bring word across the open shell-torn area pay a heavy price for their splendid work. Yet they do not hesitate, for on them depends the welfare of many of their comrades.'

For two hours some optimistic reports came through to all levels of command, ridiculously so, as matters transpired but based on patchy communications.

Aeroplanes of the Royal Flying Corps were utilised to determine positions of troops on the ground who were to keep in touch with them by use of various methods. In an order from their CO, Lieutenant-Colonel H.G.L. Ferguson, 8/ Norfolks were told that: 'Flares will be used first; mirrors if flares fail to attract attention. The firing of a white Very light by aeroplanes signifies "Where are you?" and means that the aeroplanes are ready to receive a message which can be observed if you light your flares and flash your mirrors.'

There was plenty of scope for misinterpretation as the 2/ South Wales Borderers of the 87th Brigade found to their cost: 'Prior to the attack it had been arranged that companies on reaching enemy's trenches should fire Very lights to let the Brigade know but shortly after we advanced, the enemy put up lights and for some time it was thought we had taken the front line and also pushed on, consequently our barrage was not put back onto the enemy's front line.' The lifting of the barrage had fatal consequences. With no protection from counter barrage, the Welshmen were cruelly exposed to machine-gun and shell-fire - 131 were killed. The Battalion War Diary mentions that 'Single white flare = unit halted,   Objective gained = 3 white flares … in the confusion it was difficult to tell…'

Signalling was practised endlessly during training behind the lines in the month preceding the attack. The 8/ East Surreys were to wave red and yellow flags 'to denote the position of our leading wave.' But there would prove to be an obvious failing in the system as described by George Ashurst, 1/ Lancashire Fusiliers: 'Lieutenant-Colonel Magniac called for a signaller. One stepped up to him. "Get to the top of that road and signal for reinforcements quickly" he thundered. Without a moment's hesitation the signaller obeyed, but as he raised his flags to send the first letter, the brave fellow dropped back into the road riddled with bullets.'

2nd Lieutenant Turnbull, 10/ Lincolns (Grimsby Chums), was unimpressed with the RFC: 'For some unknown reason, our Artillery started shelling us with whizz bangs. Our planes were sailing close overhead, and though I shone a mirror up they took no notice. In the end I sent an orderly to Colonel Howard (he died on 2nd July of his wounds and was buried in Ovillers Military Cemetery) to ask for permission to use a *red flare*, which he gave. As soon as we lit it, our planes went straight off home.'

The communication between 1/8 Royal Warwicks and the RFC was equally unproductive. Private Sidney Williamson recalled that 'Lance-Corporal Beard joined me and asked me to hold down a ground signalling sheet so that he could get a message to the observing aeroplane flying overhead. He asked for "MORE BOMBS" and the pilot asked "Code please". This was flashed back and the aeroplane flew away.' It must appear somewhat comical to the British Army in 2016 to learn that 100 years earlier an RFC pilot would fly over his troops and give them a long blast on a klaxon which signified the question 'Where are you?' and the reply was to be transmitted by coloured flares!

RFC pilot Cecil Lewis accepted that the methods of communication between the front line troops and the battalion and brigade headquarters were inadequate. In theory 'an aeroplane patrolling at low altitude could easily see the red flares the men carried and were instructed to light when necessary. An observer could mark the positions of the flares on the map, write down their co-ordinations on a slip of paper, put it in a weighted message-bag and, swooping down over the Battalion headquarters (whose position was known by a semi-circular sheet of white cloth pegged out on the ground) drop the message-bag.' But he conceded that there was a 'gap between theory and practice … when an attack was launched, men in the front line (not unnaturally) shrank from lighting fireworks which would give away their position to any German machine-gun for miles around. Besides they had other things to think of and so, during the first phase of the attack Contact Patrol was pretty useless.' Lewis recorded damningly in his logbook on 1st July: 'From our point of view an entire failure. Not a single ground sheet of Battalion or Brigade Headquarters was seen. Only two flares were lit on the whole of both Corps fronts … There must be a colossal lack of organization somewhere. Our patrol was n.b.g.'

Methods of communication between troops and the artillery behind them, were basic and liable to fail. Thomas Gay, 2/ Royal Scots Fusiliers, wrote that 'before the attack, we were given a sheet of tin to put between the straps on the back of our pack. One side was painted white and the other was shiny. If it was sunny, we was to turn the tin plate with the shiny side upwards but if it was a dull morning we put the painted side up so the artillery half a mile back could see us and fire over our heads.' Problems may have been faced when the early morning mist gave way to brilliant sunshine ...

One of the main causes of communication breakdown was the loss of officers: wounded or killed. The 13/ Royal Irish Rifles' attack on the Schwaben Redoubt was, according to their CO, Colonel Savage, compromised as 'almost no information was received during fighting due to most officers having become casualties.' Nor could there be any telephone contact as 'signalling wire was impossible to lay down.' Consequently 'the situation was quite confused and very conflicting reports were coming in.'

The catastrophic frontal attack on Fricourt by 7/ Yorkshire (Green Howards) at 2.30 p.m. was based on over optimistic reports despite the Green Howards having issued a warning that the situation was desperate. Brigadier-General Gordon ordered a hopeless attack only to be told by 8th Division's commander, Major-General Hudson, to attack again. He witheringly replied on the telephone that 'You seem to forget, Sir, that there is now no 70th Brigade.' The four battalions - the 8 and 9/ York and Lancaster, the 8/ KOYLI and 11/ Notts and Derby (Sherwood Foresters) had suffered near wipe-out with a total of 863 having been killed. Of those, 604 have no known grave and are listed on the Thiepval Memorial and there were, of course, hundreds of wounded.

It would be unfair to attach too much blame on the Generals for the confusion caused by communication breakdown as methods were basic and the transmitting of messages via aeroplanes was likely to prove unreliable in the heat, dust and smoke of battle.

As we have seen, for Generals Haig, Rawlinson and Allenby, success of the operation was dependent on the bombardment which started on 24th June and was most prolific from 6.25 a.m. on 1st July. Major-General Rycroft, 32nd Division, believed the bombardment had been so successful that he happily conveyed the impression that he expected to see just 'the caretaker and his dog in Thiepval'. Unfortunately, 'the caretaker and his dog' were in the company of hundreds of German troops who climbed up from their unaffected dug-outs and proceeded to man machine-guns and trench parapets.

The 16/ Lancashire Fusiliers were part of Rycroft's 32nd Division's attack on Thiepval. The Battalion War Diary reported that 'it is evident that the bombardment failed to dislodge the protected machine-guns in the Thiepval defences and it is probable that some of these were in advanced positions nearer to our lines than we supposed; there must have been some machine-guns with a commanding view, for men crawling, were instantly detected and fired on. During one bombardment before the attack, enemy machine-guns could be heard firing from several positions.' A machine-gun in the Brewery Position at Thiepval fired 18,000 rounds on the day.

As early as the night of 3rd to 4th June the Lancashire Fusiliers reported to VIII Corps that the German dug-outs were about '20 feet deep and connected'. These were 'stollen', deeply mined and usually located behind the front line, as opposed to shallow 'unterstände' which were constructed in the firing trenches.

Throughout the week preceding 'Z' Day, raiding parties crossed No Man's Land to assess the damage being caused by the bombardment to dug-outs, barbed wire, artillery and trenches. Too often their reports were ignored. Captain Leetham of the 8th Division mused: 'After a raid which found the Boche line so strongly occupied, it made me doubt whether all this bombardment was doing much good. It was all a very fine exhibition of what our Artillery could do but what was the use of bombing Boches 30 feet below the level of the ground?'

2nd Lieutenant Charles Meeres, Royal Field Artillery, was pleased that 'acres of ground had been so ploughed and ploughed that not a blade of grass remained, nor was there any sign of the trenches which had been there.' What he and others could not be sure of, was how well the German dug-outs would stand up to the bombardment. When the British did make inroads after 1st July, they would be amazed at how well constructed and appointed the dug-outs were.

'I had no idea how comfortably the Hun lived in his deep dug-outs' (at Fricourt)   IWM Q 001384

The Germans were confident that their fortifications would withstand the worst of the British bombardment. Leutnant M. Gerster, RIR 119 at Beaumont, asked: 'Had the Tommies gone off their heads? Did they believe they could wear us down with shrapnel? We, who had dug ourselves deep into the earth? We who had moled down into the innards of the enemy's territory? The very thought made the infantry smile.'

Meeres believed that 'nothing but the enemy's numerous deep dug-outs saved his harassed troops from complete annihilation.' When he walked into Fricourt he was stunned when he went into an officer's dug-out with its neat sliding doors concealing shelves for cups. When it was quiet, Thomas Gay and other 2/ Royal Scots Fusiliers, 'were able to have a look around and we saw marvellous dug-outs with three flights of stairs forty feet deep with beds at the bottom' and T.F.C. Downman, 1/ 5 Notts and Derby (Sherwood Foresters), was taken to a 'large dug-out about 40 feet deep, fitted with beds, tables etc. I was also taken to a dressing station about 50 feet below the surface, fitted with an operating table, equipment and instruments of all kinds.'

'They were proper wooden steps'- captured German dug-out near Montauban   IWM Q004307

Many dug-outs were fitted with heavy stoves; some troops were employed as charcoal burners. Huge amounts of concrete were transported by rail from Germany to provide shell and bullet-proof protection in not only dug-outs but also cellars of houses in the villages.

In the opinion of Charles Douie, 1/ Dorsets: ' … the German troops were in no way superior to the British. What was superior beyond any doubt was the enemy trench system, built in thorough German fashion to a proper standard of strength and efficiency, and defended with large numbers of machine-guns. It was the strength of this system that was seriously under-estimated … the Leipzig Redoubt was fortified by the Germans with the utmost ingenuity and resource … a labyrinth of underground passages leading from the deep cellars of the village in all directions … Such was the strength of the fortifications, that even the massed artilleries of the Somme could not obliterate them.' Sir Adrian Carton de Wiart, 8/ Gloucesters, VC: 'I had no idea how comfortably the Hun lived in his deep dug-outs. We had nothing to compare with them.' Rifleman Aubrey Smith, 1/5 London Regiment (1st London Rifle Brigade) went over the top at Gommecourt where the Germans had been 'lurking in huge dug-outs under the ground … huge underground caves … which had survived the bombardment and were now disgorging bombers by the hundred …'

Most of the above were discovered during attacks after 1st July. Dug-outs captured on 1st July tended to be at Mametz or Montauban, the only objectives taken. Private Gregory, 18/ King's (2nd Liverpool Pals) witnessed the capture of Glatz Redoubt in front of Montauban: '… then a German came up, we thought, out of the ground, but he was coming up some steps. They were proper wooden steps, about 12 or 13. They led down to a huge dug-out with wire beds in three tiers - enough beds to take about one hundred people.'

Later in July captured dug-outs in Fricourt were opened up for the Press to view, an ideal propaganda opportunity. John Masefield wrote of '… stairs with wired treads, the bolting holes, the air and escape shafts, the living rooms with electric light, the panelled walls, covered with cretonnes of the smartest berlin patterns, the neat bunks' and interestingly 'the signs of female visitors …'!

The British should not have been surprised by the impregnability of the German dug-outs. There had been plenty of clues provided by patrol and raids' reports and they had taken over from the French, Touvent Farm opposite Serre, which had been in German hands. It did not pass unnoticed how solidly constructed the dug-outs were.

If troops did manage to cross No Man's Land, in many cases they were confronted with uncut barbed wire entanglements. In his *Official History of the Great War* Brigadier-General J.E. Edmonds asserted that 'after Neuve Chapelle, the Germans had taken every precaution to strengthen defences in depth and particularly to improve wire in quantity and quality. There were acres and acres of wire to cut.'

Many Seaforth Highlanders came to an ugly end vividly described by Private J.S. Reid, 2/ Seaforth Highlanders: 'I could see that our leading waves had got caught by their kilts. They were killed hanging on the wire, riddled with bullets, like crows shot on a dyke.'

According to their War Diary the Newfoundlanders were warned that 'many more gaps in the (German) wire were required than had been cut.' In the event it made no difference due to the problems being posed by their own wire ... they found there were four belts to get through. The wire had been pre-cut with zigzagging gaps to conceal the operation from the enemy. There were too few of them to get through and the Germans had observed the first waves trying to go through them earlier and could train their machine-guns on the bunching-up groups. Colonel Hadow in the Regimental War Diary summed up the ensuing decimation of the only Empire Battalion to take part on 1st July 1916: 'Men were mown down in heaps.'

The 1/ Royal Dublin Fusiliers were one of a number of battalions challenged by their own wire which was 'cut at intervals of about 40 yards and by this time, the Germans had machine-guns trained on these gaps, the result being that our casualties were very heavy and only a few of our men got through our wire.'

George Coppard, in his *With a Machine Gun to Cambrai* pertinently asked: 'How did our planners imagine that Tommies, having survived all other hazards ... would break through the German wire? Had they studied the black density of it through their powerful binoculars? What made them think that artillery fire would pound such wire to pieces? Any Tommy could have told them that shell fire lifts wire up and drops it down, often in a worse tangle than before.'

Too much emphasis had been placed on the bombardment. There were sufficient reports to have prompted the Generals to question the effectiveness of the bombardment, the failure of which (except in the Mametz and Montauban attacks) meant that, safe in their dug-outs the Germans could quickly emerge and man their machine-guns and that uncut barbed wire would pose assaulting troops a major and in many cases an insurmountable barrier.

Colonel Laidlaw of the 16/ Highland Light Infantry left no scope for misinterpretation in his piece in the Regimental History entitled *The Shambles of the Somme*. He commented that 'every step cost dreadful casualties but it is conceivable that the Battalion could have stubbornly pushed its way to the German trenches but for one dire factor - the stacked belts of barbed wire had been imperfectly cut.'

Most battalions went across No Man's Land at a steady walk rather than at a run. General Rawlinson's pre-assault Tactical Notes advised that 'the assaulting troops must push forward at a steady pace in successive lines ... occasions may arise where the rapid advance of some lightly equipped men on some particular part of the enemy's defences may turn the scale.' It would appear that there were few instances of a 'rapid advance' by lightly equipped men. A disbelieving Musketier Karl Blenk IR 169 at Serre, who witnessed hundreds of British troops slowly walking towards his position, suggested that things might have been different 'If only they had run', a comment echoed in the *Official History of the Great War*: 'It may be that there would have been complete victory everywhere on 1st July had the infantry been ordered to cross No Man's Land at the fastest speed possible instead of at a "steady pace" although there was no creeping barrage to help them in this first stage.' This may have been successful in sectors where No Man's Land was less than 200 yards wide - the element of surprise would have been greater.

An important feature of pre-assault practice had been ensuring that trenches taken were 'mopped up' or cleared of Germans. In the general maelstrom, too often it did not happen, and those that had successfully taken first line trenches were then hit from behind by enemy survivors. A message was sent from Third Army's VII Corps at 11.27 a.m. to 56th (London) Division: 'Reports from Fourth Army show that in some cases our troops did not sufficiently clear dug-outs and that Germans have reappeared and retaken their front line trenches.' Reports received by 34th Division soon led HQ to conclude that 'our infantry had left a number of the enemy behind in his trenches … several enemy machine-guns in emplacements had also been left behind … The result of this was that carrying parties were unable to move up after the advancing infantry …' The 8/ Devons complained that 'the nature of engagements was affected by mopping up parties not clearing the trenches, leaving machine-guns and snipers who caused practically all their casualties.'

Machine-gun and shell-fire meant that support troops encountered difficulties in bringing supplies to the first wave of troops. There are many examples of pleas for reinforcements and for more bombs. The 9/ Royal Inniskilling Fusiliers reported: 'Small bodies of men reached the German wire and charged the trenches, in places the Germans held up their hands to surrender but realising there were no support troops resumed the contest till there were only a handful of our men left.' The 1/ 8 Royal Warwicks felt that 'we did well but none of the support battalions could get to us … No bomb supply' and Rifleman Aubrey Smith, 1/5 London (1st London Rifle Brigade) recounted that 'time went on and no fresh waves appeared …'

One of the objectives of the 36th (Ulster) Division was the heavily fortified Schwaben Redoubt to the north of Thiepval village. Promising progress was made but to consolidate the Redoubt they were in need of more men and bombs. Requests for reinforcements were initially refused by General Sir Thomas Morland of X Corps; when they did eventually reach the Schwaben Redoubt at 6 p.m., it was too late.

In the rush to supply the demand, as many as a third of the shells sent out to the Western Front proved to be 'duds'; those from the U.S.A. had been fitted with faulty fuses. A soldier in the 1/ 6 North Staffs' attack on Gommecourt saw hundreds of unexploded mortar bombs which he described as looking like oranges and he doubted that any of them had exploded. The 2/ Essex were hindered by an inadequate supply of bombs although they resourcefully used grenades found in the German trenches and the 8/ Royal Inniskilling Fusiliers 'at 10.20 p.m. having no bombs and very little ammunition left, our men withdrew …' Sergeant Arthur Cook 1/ Somerset LI believed that the Germans had been provided with a 'superior supply of bombs.'

Captain Sparks, 1/ 14 London (1st London Scottish), was faced with a challenging dilemma- he had only just taken over from his CO Major Lindsay who had been killed: 'I am faced with this position; I have collected all bombs and SAA from casualties, every one has been used, given the enemy's continued barrage fire none can be brought to me … I am faced with three alternatives: a) to stay here with such men as are alive and be killed   b) to surrender to the enemy   c) to withdraw such of my men as I can. Either of the first alternatives is distasteful to me. I propose to adopt the latter.'

On 2nd July an instant appraisal of the previous day's events was communicated from GHQ in France by CIGC General Sir William Robertson to Major-General F.B. Maurice, Director of Military Operations based in London: 'Apparently some of the new divisions were a little too reckless and as was to be expected through want of adequate military experience they failed to meet unexpected situations correctly. All our troops, however, fought with the utmost gallantry and today all are in excellent spirits.' It was a view that would not have been shared by many of those who had participated in 'that awful day.'

After 1918 there was no shortage of harsh criticism of operations from all ranks on 1st July and from 'some of the new divisions.' Major Alfred Plackett CO of one of them, the 12 / York and Lancaster (Sheffield City), returned to England on 4th July suffering from shell-shock and nervous exhaustion. He was scathing about

A third of the British shells sent out to the Western Front proved to be 'duds'; a British dud behind German lines plus dog, with the caption 'Liebesgabe'- love's gift

the War Office's refusal to grant him compensation for his illness and was equally dismissive of the planning and execution of the assault. He was critical of poor telephonic communication which from the outset with the Brigade was cut and the only means of communication throughout the day was by runner. He believed that as the enemy artillery had become active as soon as it was daylight, it appeared likely that the Germans had been warned of the attack by observing gaps in his battalion's own wire and tapes laid out in No Man's Land, which in his opinion, gave at least 3½ hours warning of the attack. Guiding-tape laid during the night had apparently been removed: 'It served no purpose at all except to give the enemy warning. The wire in front of our lines had been cut away too much and as the gaps were not staggered our intention to attack must have been quite obvious to the enemy.'

He believed the failure of the attack was, without question, due to the wire not being sufficiently cut. Had this been effected, the enemy's machine-guns could have been dealt with by the men who managed to reach the front line.

He was adamant that the assault should have been made in 'double time'. The waves were too far apart, the distance between them allowing the enemy to pay attention to each wave before the next came up. He concluded that 'the general opinion was that officers, NCOs and machine-gunners were marked men.'

Brigadier-General Tuson GOC of the 25th Brigade argued that his men had been 'deprived of artillery support and that it was futile bombarding distant objectives if we **131** ourselves are unable to maintain our hold on the enemy's front line.' He questioned the validity of the timetable utilised by III Corps which involved Pozières, over a mile behind the German front line, being bombarded at the time that 8th Division was being destroyed in No Man's Land. He was, in effect, questioning General Haig's strategy of bombarding objectives several thousand yards beyond the German front line.

There are several reports of the proceedings before and on 1st July put together by those commanding divisional attacks. Major-General H. B. de Lisle, 29th Division, articulated a number of trenchant criticisms in cataloguing the 'Causes of Failure' in his *Reports on Operations 1st July 1916* :

1. The enemy were undoubtedly prepared for the attack … they had brought up many additional machine-guns kept under cover in deep dug-outs … Beaumont Hamel, moreover, is undermined with large caves with some 30 feet of chalk above them, and capable of accommodating some two battalions.

2. The sector allotted to this Division had been converted by the enemy into a first class fortress … more success would probably have attended our efforts had we surprised the enemy by an attack at dawn and had we concentrated all our artillery fire on the first objective, leaving the second objective to be dealt with in a subsequent operation.

3. Speed in crossing the area between our front trenches and the enemy's is essential. The leading troops should therefore be lightly equipped.

4. It is essential that the first line system of trenches should be completely demolished and it would appear advisable for certain heavy howitzers to be allotted to the Divisional front for this duty.

5. The explosion of the mine (Hawthorn Ridge) warned the enemy of the time of the assault.

6. The performance of the Stokes Mortars was most disappointing.

He concluded that 'no fault can be found with the behaviour of our troops who did all that was possible. Their bravery and the severity of the engagement are best evidenced by the casualties, which I regret to state were very severe, amounting to some 200 officers and 5,000 men.' It is noteworthy that he should have described the operations on the day as a 'Failure'.

He added at the bottom of the page in a handwritten note: 'The spirit of the troops is good, but the physical fatigue among the young soldiers who form three quarters of the Battalions is marked compared with the stamina of the original troops of earlier days.' Regular soldiers might have covered the ground quicker and performed more sophisticated manoeuvres but an analysis of them in Chapter VIII indicates that they did not perform noticeably better or suffer less casualties than their volunteer brothers-in-arms.

Major-General C.P.A. Hull, 56th (London) Division, came to the same conclusion in his report of 17th July 1916, requested by Lieutenant-General Snow, VII Corps, that the attack had been a failure. The main reason he gave for the inability to retain ground won, was the shortage of grenades which was caused by the enemy's barrage preventing supplies being carried across No Man's Land which he believed was too wide. 'It was only when grenades became scarce that the enemy were able to push us back.'

His main proposal was to increase and improve the counter battery. It would be better to employ heavy 9.2″ and medium 3″ Howitzers for counter battery work than smaller calibre 4.7″ guns. It was vital that an adequate supply of ammunition be made available from Zero Hour onwards.

It was important to strike out as near as possible to the enemy: 'I believe it to be a generally accepted axiom that trenches should be pushed forward to within 150 yards of the enemy's position before an attack … On 1st July I am sure my trenches were too far away from the enemy's front line. It was unavoidable but another month was needed to prepare. The concealed approach of a Russian sap is required - it could be well stocked with stores of grenades and SAA. Grenades should be carried forward with the assaulting troops and should be easily detached from casualties.' It was important to 'seek out German grenade stores in dug-outs and trenches and for the future, actual samples of all patterns of German grenades should be kept at bombing schools and dummy German grenades made for actual practice at the schools.'

The preliminary bombardment on the German trenches had been significant, so much so that assaulting troops found it hard to recognise their various objectives when they reached them. However, the effect on enemy morale had not been as 'great as one would have hoped, probably owing to the fact that the enemy had time to realise that his deep dug-outs were proof against the heaviest artillery fire.'

He expressed doubts about very long bombardments, which he believed gave the enemy time to recognise the points selected for attack. Shorter preliminary bombardments would provide sufficient time for wire cutting. The Germans decided to soak up pressure and not reply to the bombardment, thereby saving ammunition for use on the day of the attack.

He was critical that the intense bombardment prior to the assault lasted 65 minutes, considerably longer than any other during the week before. He favoured 'as many false attacks as possible but there should be no difference between the procedure on the day of attack and that adopted in the false attacks.'

He may have been at variance with his men on the ground but he felt that wire cutting had been 'very satisfactorily performed'.

The decision to detonate a smoke screen caused a difference of opinion after the event. Some held that smoke caused troops to lose their bearings and hampered observation but for others it minimised the danger of hostile machine-gun fire. If smoke were to be used he advised that it should not go off too early as experience had shown that machine-guns had opened fire two to three minutes after the emission of smoke.

The time for the assault had exercised the minds of Haig, Rawlinson, Joffre and Fayolle in the preceding weeks. Hull would have preferred to start as soon after daylight as possible, there being a risk of discovery especially where trenches had been demolished.

In practice it had been noticeable to many that German bombing parties were unencumbered with equipment, except for a bag of bombs which put his bombers at a disadvantage. 'I think we have a tendency to overload our men and that to get the best out of bombers in particular they must be as lightly equipped as possible and free to use their arms.'

The 46th (North Midland) Division's report unlike the reviews of the operations of the 29th and 56th Divisions was not signed off by the GOC: Montagu-Stuart-Wortley had been unceremoniously sacked on 4th July. Points of interest in the report include the difficulty met by rearward waves in getting through a heavy and accurate barrage on the British front trenches: 'It is suggested that more attention might be paid to counter-battery work, which is the only means of checking this hostile barrage.'

Lieutenant Ashford of 46th (North Midland) Division had been asked to submit his views on the Gommecourt attack; in his letter he admitted it was easy to criticise after the event but pointed out that 'The wire was not cut uniformly ... and on the night of 29th June I examined it personally and reported it uncut. The actual attack was preceded by an intense bombardment of the hostile positions which drove the enemy out of Gommecourt Park, many of them surrendering to 56th Division. If this bombardment had been closely followed up, the attack might have succeeded. As it happens there was an interval (according to plan) between the lifting of the barrage and the launching of the attack, during which a smoke screen was discharged between the lines. This interval allowed the enemy to mount his machine-guns and to man his trenches and, in my opinion, was a fatal mistake.'

He watched the attack from a specially constructed observation post: 'It was impossible to see much due to smoke ... After the attack was abandoned, I examined the scene from the branches of a tall tree on the outskirts of Foncquevillers village and could see the dead and wounded like a high water mark, close to the German wire ... I stumbled over many bodies which were out of sight beneath the mud.

The strength of the enemy artillery appears to have taken us by surprise. Up to the actual time of the attack there was very little reply to our fire and registration was carefully concealed. The result was that our counter battery work was ineffective.'

He explained in his summary that the failure of the attack was due to extensive 'advertising' to the Germans beforehand, poor weather conditions in the preceding days, uncut wire, the interval between Zero Hour and attack, smoke which hid the gaps in enemy wire, overloading of men, congestion in the trenches and exhaustion of the men.

Lieutenant-General Snow's Report of the 46th (North Midland) Division's attack dwelled on the need for better counter battery work and limiting the first objective to the first line of trenches, in effect criticism of Haig's strategy of attacking in greater depth.

To what extent were the three main generals, Haig, Rawlinson and Allenby, culpable for the long list of criticisms after the event? Could anything have been done differently?

The timing of the attack provoked much post battle discussion. Private Cyril José, 2/ Devons, wrote on 16th July to his mother from his hospital bed in Plymouth: 'Some "big bug" thought it a great idea to go over in broad daylight instead of crawling up as near their parapet in the night under cover of the bombardment so that we could then dive in the trench with hardly any losses in going across. Result: Johnny spots us coming over the parapet and we have to go about 600 yards. What brains old Douglas must have. It made me laugh when I read his despatch yesterday "I (underlined 5 times) attacked"... Old women in England picturing Sir Doug in front of British waves, brandishing his sword at Johnny in the trenches ...'

In fairness to General Rawlinson, he had protracted discussions with the French about timing; he was in favour of going as dawn broke allowing troops to get into place in darkness. The French wanted to attack in the afternoon, the decision, therefore, to go at 7.30 a.m., was a compromise that was not necessarily the most prudent.

The wastage of ammunition on secondary, distant objectives was Haig's decision-concentration on front line trenches and dug-outs might have made a difference although evidence suggests that the fortified redoubts in particular were relatively 'bomb proof'.

Troops crossing No Man's Land at 'double quick time' could have caught the Germans by surprise in some areas despite the raking machine-gun fire but the decision was taken by most Corps and Divisional generals to go at walking pace because of their lack of confidence in their raw New Army recruits. It was an understandable and acceptable reaction and Haig, in particular, had wanted to delay the attack several weeks to train his troops better as well as to boost supplies of guns and ammunition. Whether or not more training and practice would have had an impact in the face of intense machine-gun fire is doubtful.

Rawlinson had won the argument with Haig about a long and intensive bombardment - the success of the offensive was over dependant on it. Had Haig stood his ground and insisted on shorter bombardment bursts, the Germans would have been kept guessing as to where attacks would take place and when.

Despite the difficulties faced by commanders, there were examples of poor leadership and decision making on the day. Lieutenant-General Hunter-Weston's decision to blow the Hawthorn Ridge Mine eight minutes earlier than the other mines was a costly and crucial mistake. It was unfortunate for him that his order to lift the barrage on the crater area to protect the attacking troops was extended, for whatever reason, to the front from Serre to Y Ravine thus compromising the effectiveness of the attacks by the 31st, 4th and 29th Divisions.

Major-General de Lisle's decision to order the 1/ Essex and 1/ Newfoundlanders into the fray was catastrophic, in part due to the inadequacy of communications, based on erroneous reports that the first waves had been successful - the Germans had sent up white flares which were the same as white British flares which signalled 'success'.

Given the failure of the bombardment and various tactics adhered to on the day, the British troops had little chance. Brigadier-General Williams of 137th Brigade did not mince his words with reference to the attack on Gommecourt: 'I do not think that any troops could have taken the enemy line as held on that morning' and machine-gunner George Coppard was as categorical: 'The very manner of their death is proof that our assault troops on those first terrible days hadn't a dog's chance … Someone had blundered about the wire … Any element of initiative or surprise had already been ruined by the long bombardment of the enemy trenches … Jerry thus had ample time to repair and strengthen his defences and lay doggo in deep dug outs waiting for us.'

In stark contrast to the disasters from Gommecourt to Fricourt, the 18th and 30th Divisions commanded by Major-Generals Maxse and the largely unsung hero Shea, managed to achieve their objectives at Mametz and Montauban and had their troops not been halted by the cautious decision taken by General Rawlinson to consolidate rather than press on, serious inroads could have been made.

On 1st July, five French Divisions attacked from Maricourt, across the river Somme and four miles to the south of it. XX Corps of 64 year old General Emile Fayolle's Sixth Army, achieved all its objectives. The French had learned lessons from the conflict at Verdun, appreciating now the importance of utilising heavy guns, 87 per mile as opposed to the British ratio of 32 to the mile. The French sent their assaulting infantry forward in small groups rather than in the long lines favoured by the British. Their losses were significantly lower, about 1,600. Their task was made easier because the Germans were taken by surprise believing the French, otherwise engaged heavily at Verdun, could not also mount an offensive successfully in the Somme. In the first ten days of the campaign, the French advanced over six miles, a distance not achieved by the Allies since the Battle of the Marne in September 1914. It took the British 20 weeks to achieve a similar distance in the Somme.

The 18th and 30th Divisions benefited from the effective French bombardment of Montauban from their right. Major-General Maxse was younger than most of the generals and more forward thinking. On his 18th (Eastern) Division's front, he implemented the use of flame projectors (two of which were set off east of Casino Point, designed to confuse and disorientate the enemy), the detonation of three mines at Casino Point and the digging of Russian saps to get troops and mines as near to the German line as possible. He also managed to mastermind an effective 'creeping barrage' and to protect men in assembly and front line trenches, he concentrated more on a defensive counter barrage than most on the 18 mile front.

Maxse was more confident in the 'New Army' troops than Haig and Rawlinson and other Corps and Division commanders, having faith in their ability and enthusiasm. In his division he believed in telling his subordinates 'as much as possible of impending operations long before they occur.' He considered it was better to risk leaks of information from captured soldiers than to 'run the greater risk of ordering infantry over the parapet unacquainted with what they are expected to do or where they are to go.'

He paid tribute to his men for their achievements on 1st July: 'Well done, it's what I expected. Now hold on to what you gained so splendidly for the Fourth Army.' Military historian Captain Basil Liddell-Hart, who at the age of 20 served in the War, lauded him for always being 'ready to encourage and make use of new ideas.'

General Rawlinson was not as prescriptive about tactics as is sometimes assumed. Maxse was given a free rein but one wonders whether the outcome of the 1st July would have been different if all sectors had pursued Maxse's strategies and tactics.

In Haig and Rawlinson's defence, there are several mitigating factors to consider. Haig was bounced into action sooner than he would have liked - the German attack on Verdun on 21st February was a 'game changer' and the significance of the threat was commented on by both men in their diaries. Haig had favoured a major offensive in Belgium and reluctantly acquiesced to one in the Somme from which the French proceeded to withdraw divisions at a rapid rate. The British inherited from the French a wide front with, in places, significant distances of up to 800 yards of No Man's Land to attack across.

Haig had, in effect, been handed a poisoned chalice. The Germans had strengthened their defences on the Somme with redoubts and barbed wire, in well-chosen positions with good observation of the British lines and on higher and more easily defended ground. For the British troops, attacks were literally an uphill struggle.

Haig and Rawlinson exercised little control over the quality of soldiers at their disposal. Kitchener's Army of young, exuberant, keen and, in fairness, innocent volunteers were unlikely to adapt as quickly as regulars and be confident and skilful enough to undertake more sophisticated manoeuvres; many who volunteered with patriotic enthusiasm were not cut out to be soldiers; Albert Goodwin wrote of his son Harold that he had settled into Army life during 'the present distress ... though he is much more at home school mastering.' In comparison, conscripted German troops were well trained and more efficient. It is easy to understand, therefore, why many generals chose to maintain order and discipline by pursuing steady forward movement likened on so many occasions to being 'on parade'. The failure of the bombardment would make a mockery of such a tactic.

The shortage of ordnance and the poor quality of shells in particular, were problems that caused great concern but over which they had no control. The poor weather before 'Z' Day was unhelpful - an extra two days meant the munitions had to be spread more thinly and the bombardment in the final hour before the assault was not as intense as originally planned.

Confidence in the bombardment was so fervent that insufficient thought was given to the manoeuvrability of the men; weighed down by equipment, weapons and supplies, as they struggled across cratered terrain, they were easy targets to pick off. If fast moving troops had attacked in the first waves, followed by carriers with grenades and provisions, and men whose sole responsibility was to clear trenches of Germans, outcomes along some sectors of the front line might have been different.

Not enough thought was given to assess the effect of the much heralded bombardment after it had exploded into life on 24th June. 'What if the bombardment fails to destroy the enemy defences and firepower' was the risk assessment that no one dared to undertake. The evidence was compelling but it was ignored. Captain D.L. Martin's plasticine model of the danger from a machine-gun near Mametz and Lieutenant-Colonel Sandys's cautionary caveats of uncut barbed wire at Ovillers were warnings that were not isolated examples of concern; others must have progressed beyond Staff pending trays. Haig, Rawlinson and Allenby had been forewarned but time pressures were such that they had little option than to propagate and instil in their troops an unquestioning confidence in the outcome of the imminent attack. The momentum of operations in June was such that there was no turning back. France had to be saved. Despite their misgivings, Haig and Rawlinson could not at this late stage, delay proceedings. The bombardment would work. It had to work.

So numerous are war diary accounts of enemy shelling on 30th June and in the early hours of 'Der Tag', that British soldiers of all ranks must have approached their tasks with a deep sense of foreboding.

Haig and Rawlinson's spirited public utterances camouflaged their innermost anxieties: concerns about the quality of some divisional commanders, the inadequacy of some of the training and practice, the inexperience of the Kitchener troops who had yet to experience 'going over the top' and shortage of and poor quality of ordnance and guns. Hunter-Weston who was roundly criticised before and after 1st July by Haig and Rawlinson wrote to General Sir William Robertson on 2nd July: 'A contributory cause (of the lack of success) was the inadequacy of the artillery and of the ammunition available ... We always have to be saving our guns ... This latter reason is for your ear alone, it is inadvisable to give currency to such unpleasant and dangerous facts.' Such a comment and the treatment of Montagu-Stuart-Wortley suggest that after 1st July there was a significant blame game being played by the senior commanders.

The debate as to whether or not such high numbers of casualties could have been reduced, is one that is unlikely to wane in intensity. Division and Corps commanders and to a certain extent Rawlinson expressed heart-felt regrets at the tragic consequences of the few hours of carnage on 1st July 1916. A similar level of remorse was not articulated by Haig. After all, in the wider context, he had France to save and a war to win. Notwithstanding the huge losses sustained during this most bloody of encounters, the offensive of 1st July initiated the slow decline of German morale and the grinding down of their Armies.

Our concentration in *Where are the Boys?* is on the human aspect of the events, the personal stories and accounts, some of the many depressing human tragedies and the effects of them on loved ones and communities blighted by losses and wounded lives. The day was a calamity and catastrophe of breathtaking proportions that inevitably prompts the question as to how it could have happened. Could the consequences have been less disastrous with one or two tactical tweaks? It is easy with the benefit of hindsight and for those with no military experience to suggest that it might have been prudent to have bombarded closer targets, concentrated attacks on specific weaker sectors, dug more saps nearer to enemy trenches, to have utilised different attacking formations and so on: indeed to have used the sort of tactics advocated and advised in reports and reviews of the actions by those involved, which begs the question as to what extent those who contributed to reviews like Lieutenant Ashford, Major-General Hull and Lieutenant-General Snow raised such points in the build up to the day of the attack. It is noticeable that they were all remarkably wise after the event.

Hard as it is to disentangle oneself from the horrors of what took place, the First Day of the Battle of the Somme must be assessed in the wider context of the four years of the War and heed should be taken, difficult though it is, of Gary Sheffield's exhortation that 'the horror of the battle should not blind us to its importance.' Haig asserted on 23rd December 1916 that 'the campaign in the Somme was 'the opening of the wearing out battle.' As the War staggered its way to a conclusion, he was justified in his belief that the Germans would buckle eventually under sustained pressure: the Battle of Albert was, after all, one day and one battle in a four year long bloody conflict.

Stand in Mill Road Cemetery near the sites of the Schwaben Redoubt and the Ulster Tower, and it is not difficult to imagine the attacks of the Irish battalions coming towards you on the German front line; a cacophony of sound - bugles, men shouting, guns blazing, shells exploding as British soldiers made their way towards you through the early morning haze, the cries and screams of the wounded and dying hit by enfilading machine-guns from your right and left. Captain Basil Liddell-Hart wrote disparagingly of the attack as a military failure, but extolled it as 'an epic of heroism, and, better still, the proof of the moral quality of the new armies of Britain, who, in making the supreme sacrifice of the war, passed through the most fiery and bloody ordeals with their courage unshaken and their fortitude established.' For Martin Middlebrook 'the only good to emerge from that terrible day was the display of patriotism, courage and self-sacrifice shown by the British soldiers ... Theirs is a memory that their country should always cherish.'

There are 93 1st July burials in Mill Road Cemetery including Corporal J. Dunbar, 9/ Royal Inniskilling Fusiliers, Private R. White aged 42 and 2nd Lieutenant P.E. Wedgwood, 16/ Royal Irish Rifles. They may have fallen during their uphill attack to the German front line. Little is known of them … we can but wonder why they joined the British Army, and how successful they were as soldiers. They are just three of King George V's 'silent witnesses to the desolation of war' and the shocking events that unfolded on 1st July 1916.

For those who took part the attack on 1st July was an abomination with virtually nothing to show for it territorially. In some respects it was a success in that significant numbers of Germans had been killed and morale shaken. The week-long bombardment exacted its toll in fraying nerves and soldiers tired in body and mind questioned their defensive strategy. Fighting would continue in the Somme for another 140 days culminating in the final day of the Battle of the Ancre on 18th November. Gains achieved on the right flank were quickly exploited; Fricourt fell on 2nd July and La Boisselle on 4th July. Villages for ever associated with 1st July gave way strategically to woodland areas which in the next phase of operations were names linked to more British troop losses but at least some territorial gains - Bernafay, Trônes, Bazentin, Mametz, Delville (Devil's) and High (London).

Since the beginnings of trench warfare, the British Army had been engaged in a gradual learning curve; many recommendations in the reviews of the operations on 1st July were introduced in due course - night time attacks by men more lightly equipped, greater concentration on counter battery, shorter preliminary bombardments on a narrower front and the use of flexible and better trained assault troops. The creeping barrage, effectively utilised by Major-Generals Maxse and Shea on 1st July, was executed more often and more efficiently. Greater use was made of Lewis guns and rifle grenades and there were marked improvements in organisation, command and tactics, exemplified by the successful night attack on 14th July between Bazentin and Longueval after which 6,000 yards of German lines were taken.

One reason Haig had wanted a delay in the start of the Somme offensive was to introduce tanks to help break the deadlock. Slow and unreliable, they made their entry in September when 11 out of 49 managed to cross the British front line and one tank played an important role in the capture of Flers.

Progress was made in September when Maxse's 18th (Eastern) Division took Thiepval, the graveyard of 1,500 soldiers of 32nd Division on 1st July. The Schwaben Redoubt followed in mid-October. Autumnal mud hampered operations until the final attack started on 13th November when Beaumont was stormed by the 51st (Highland) Division and Beaucourt was seized by the 63rd (Naval) Division. Serre, however, was not taken in 1916.

The Newfoundlanders had been the only fighting Empire troops on 1st July. Thereafter Empire troops were brought in as reinforcements: South Africans, Australians, Canadians and New Zealanders. The Australians were mobilised for the disastrous diversionary attack at Fromelles, between Arras and Ypres, on the 19th and 20th July when 5,500 casualties out of 7,000 were Australian. Later at Pozières, on the Albert to Bapaume road, the Australian Imperial Force sustained 23,000 casualties - their highest number during the War.

During this period the British gained a maximum of 6 miles over a 20 mile front while the numbers of casualties continued to mount up, the British suffering about 420,000, the French 204,000 and the Germans over 500,000. There was much unease in London about the ever increasing numbers of casualties highlighted in a letter from General Sir William Robertson to Haig on 29th July when he cautioned: 'the Powers that be are beginning to get a little uneasy in regard to the situation. The casualties are mounting up and they are wondering whether we are likely to get a proper return for them.' The pressure on Haig to deliver a breakthrough on the Somme was intensifying.

Haig's offensive after 1st July slowly wore down the Germans- forced to come out and counter-attack on over 300 occasions, they lost increasing numbers of men and importantly their morale began to be adversely affected. Captain Hans von Hentig of the Guards Reserve Division came to the conclusion that 'the Somme was the muddy grave of the German Army' and it was clear to newly-appointed Chief of Staff General Erich Ludendorff, that their troops would be unable to withstand British and French pressure indefinitely.

The Great War was fought to the bitter end. The future military historian Leutnant Gerhard Ritter was shocked enough to conclude that the warfare had been 'monotonous, mutual mass murder'. The artist Albert Goodwin who had lost his son Harold summed up the feelings of the thousands who had suffered personal losses: 'The War has made us see how cheap life has got to be.'

When the sun set on 1st July 1916 the battlefield was littered with the wounded and the dead. The Danger Tree in No Man's Land at the Newfoundland Memorial Park symbolises the calamitous losses; it was here that hundreds of South Wales Borderers, Borders and Newfoundlanders fell

Picture to right:
'There's some corner of a foreign field that is forever England'
Rupert Brooke 'The Soldier'

VII

'Remembrance'

The Cemeteries and the Thiepval Memorial to The Missing Of The Somme

If you were to take any of the Walks along the 1st July battlefield in Chapter IX you could not fail to be impressed by the beauty and tranquillity of the British cemeteries as fitting final resting places for those who fell on the Somme. They are a far cry from the reality of what happened on 1st July.

Gommecourt Wood New Cemetery

To have buried and commemorated in excess of one million soldiers of the Great War with such methodical efficiency and sensitivity, was a tribute to the prime movers of the Imperial War Graves Commission, later renamed 'Commonwealth' in 1960.

The driving force behind the Commission's formation in 1917 by Royal Charter, and its organisation until a year before his death in 1949, was Sir Fabian Ware. He was a visionary with a social conscience whose tenacity in the face of many hurdles ensured a dignified final resting place or commemoration for the British and Imperial soldiers who died fighting for their King and Country.

Sir Frederic Kenyon, Director of the British Museum, was appointed as the Commission's first architectural adviser. He oversaw the designs of the four principal architects: Edwin Lutyens, Reginald Blomfield, Herbert Baker (all three were knighted for their work) and Charles Holden.

The celebrated author and chronicler of the British Empire, Rudyard Kipling, offered his literary expertise to the Commission, inspired by the loss of his only son John who died at the Battle of Loos in 1915, aged only 18. He chose the memorable wording for the cemeteries' Stones of Remembrance: THEIR NAME LIVETH FOR EVERMORE taken from the Old Testament's Book of Ecclesiastes Chapter 44, Verse 14; for graves of the unidentified: **A SOLDIER OF THE GREAT WAR KNOWN UNTO GOD**, and for the Thiepval Memorial: **THE MISSING OF THE SOMME**. Kipling's contribution was acknowledged by Ware who wrote that he offered his genius 'freely and wholeheartedly in the service of the commemoration of the dead.'

Stone of Remembrance at Bernafay Wood British Cemetery

The philosophy of the Imperial War Graves Commission was underpinned by a number of principles which have been zealously adhered to ever since. Equality of treatment, regardless of rank, was the overriding aim of the Commission. In Carnoy Military Cemetery for example, seven officers serving with the 8/ East Surreys are buried with 'other ranks'.

Linked to the belief in equality of treatment, was the view that bodies should not be repatriated, for if families of officers who died on 1st July had insisted on repatriation of their loved ones' bodies, the Somme cemeteries would have become the odd preserve of 'other ranks'. By an Act of Parliament, passed in 1920, the principle of 'No Repatriation' was confirmed in law.

In the cemeteries, it was agreed to adopt Sir Edwin Lutyens's design for the headstones that would replace the original wooden crosses which marked bodies where they were buried on or near the battlefield. They were to be of a uniform height, 2 feet and 8 inches (81 cm) and shaped with a curved top and straight sides. White Portland stone from Weymouth in Dorset was used in preference to red Corsehill or Lochabriggs stone which, as can be seen in the photograph on page 272 of Martinsart British Cemetery was unappealing in comparison.

Inscriptions were designed in a Roman style by Macdonald Gill; a serviceman's regimental badge would be engraved at the top of the stone, under which there could be an appropriate religious symbol.

Families were allowed to choose an inscription and the Commission appears to have acceded to families' wishes.

Private monuments were forbidden. It was established that, wherever possible, a marked grave would be provided for every soldier whose body could not be identified. On the Western Front 580, 346 graves were identified and 185, 254 were not. Serre Road Cemetery No. 2 is the largest in the Somme: there are 7,127 burials of which 4,944 were of unidentified soldiers - a staggering 70%. Such a high proportion emphasises the brutality of the warfare; bodies were so badly mutilated by shell-fire in particular, as to make identification impossible, or named graves on or near the battlefield were destroyed in later actions.

One of Fabian Ware's greatest achievements was to reach an agreement over the standard design for cemeteries. For those

Cross of Sacrifice at Ovillers Military Cemetery

with more than 400 burials, a cemetery's design would incorporate a non-religious Stone of Remembrance designed by Lutyens. Ware bowed to pressure from Anglican lobbyists who campaigned for the installation of a Cross of Sacrifice, the eye-catching design of Reginald Blomfield: a dark sword set into a white stone cross.

The understated simplicity of the cemeteries' design is a tribute to Ware's team and provided peaceful havens like Fricourt New Military which on 1st July was a shocking scene of slaughter. The aim was to create in the cemeteries, a little corner of England in 'foreign fields'. Great thought went into doing so in the image of an English garden, ablaze in summer with colour. Red roses, a myriad of flowers, manicured grass lawns, hedges and trees have, for nearly a century, been lovingly nurtured by Commonwealth War Graves Commission gardeners. Fabian Ware sought the advice of the garden designer Gertrude Jekyll whose expertise was harnessed for several of Lutyens's initial cemetery designs like Louvencourt, 8 miles from the front line.

Today the focal point of the battlefield is Lutyens's Thiepval Memorial to 'The Missing of the Somme' which is even more dominating than the Menin Gate in Ypres, due mainly to the need to find space for nearly 18,000 more names. The original intention was for a memorial to straddle the Albert to Bapaume road which was unacceptable to the French Government. On its eventual and current site at Thiepval, it

Ancre British Cemetery

stands on the German front line which proved so impenetrable during the first stages of the Somme offensive. It overlooks the killing fields below in the Ancre Valley where, on 1st July 1916, 19,000 British and Newfoundland troops were killed and about 39,000 wounded. The structure was dedicated 'Aux Armées Française et Britannique l'Empire Britannique reconnaissant' (To the French and British Armies, from the grateful British Empire) and behind the Memorial there is a cemetery for French and British soldiers.

The Thiepval Memorial was completed in 1932 and inaugurated on 1st August by the Prince of Wales, the future Edward VIII. The Memorial does not glorify victory over the Germans; it has a timeless quality that impressively rises above the senseless brutality of the battlefield on which it stands. From whichever direction one approaches it, the memorial makes a statement - its size alone, accommodating 72,255 names of men for whom there was no known grave, condemns those that failed to end the mind-blowing slaughter. The Thiepval Memorial is a shocking indictment of those who were unable to call a halt to it.

12,397 of those named on the Thiepval memorial died on 1st July. Amongst them there were:

8,183	privates	510	sergeants	89	captains
1,247	lance-corporals	207	2nd lieutenants	10	majors
518	corporals	105	lieutenants	6	lieutenant-colonels

When one peruses the panels of the Menin Gate and Thiepval Memorials, it is impossible to comprehend the enormity of how men's lives and achievements were reduced to a mere inscription. Row upon row of gravestones in cemeteries are at least more tangible illustrations of the 'outrages that took place.'

Bruce Bairnsfather's 'sketch' following the unveiling of the Memorial in August 1932

" Yer know, Bert, I shouldn't be surprised if they puts up a memorial for us around 'ere some time "

However appalling the effects of the Great War were, at least Sir Fabian Ware, Rudyard Kipling and the architects of the cemeteries and memorials, created remarkable tributes to those whose lives were sacrificed. King George V expressed the hope that 'the existence of these visible memorials, will eventually serve to draw all peoples together in sanity and self-control.'

It was tragic that the sight of all the cemeteries and memorials in northern France and Belgium - British, Belgian, French and German, failed to prevent further human folly two decades later in 1939. Captain Robert Hamilton fought with the 1/ Royal Warwicks in the opening phases of the War dolefully and wearily recorded in his diary on August 24 1939 that 'the war news is hopeless. I do not see what is to prevent another European War.'

The unveiling of the Thiepval Memorial in 1932

1420 PRIVATE
S. PEARSON
WEST YORKSHIRE REGIMENT
1ST JULY 1916

WAR'S BITTER COST
A DEAR LIFE LOST
BUT MEMORY STILL REMAINS
FROM HIS WIFE LIZZIE

2497 LANCE CPL.
NORMAN WILLIAM HARPER
ROYAL WARWICKSHIRE REGT.
1ST JULY 1916 AGE 24

SLEEP ON DEAR SON
AND TAKE YOUR REST
WE MISS YOU MOST
WHO LOVED YOU BEST

CAPTAIN
B. S. SMITH-MAST
ESSEX REGIMEN
1ST JULY 1916 AGE

OBEDIENT UNTO DE
FOR GOD, KING AND CO
REQUIESCAT IN PA

18824 PRIVATE
EDWARD JAMES JOHN
ROYAL SCOTS
1ST JULY 1916 AGE

18600 CORPORAL
G.E. EBBS
MACHINE GUN CORPS (INF.)
1ST JULY 1916 AGE 27

A SOLDIER OF THE KING

3185 PRIVATE
HARRY SHAW
S. STAFFORDSHIRE REGT.
1ST JULY 1916 AGE 19
A LOVING SON
A DEVOTED BROTHER
ONE OF GOD'S BEST
FOR HOME & MOTHER

4992 PRIVATE
E. ADAMS
N. STAFFORDSHIRE REGT.
1ST JULY 1916 AGE 18
ONLY A BRITISH SOLDIER
ONLY HIS MOTHER'S PRIDE
FOR GOD, KING AND COUNTRY

2966 LANCE CPL.
T.C. WOODFORD
NOTTS. & DERBY REGIMENT
1ST JULY 1916

NO MORE
WITH SPRINGING FEET ILL
THE DEAR FAMILIAR
HILLS OF HOME

17691 C. SERJT. MAJOR
W. RAWLEY
ROYAL INNISKILLING FUS.
1ST JULY 1916 AGE 41

BLOW OUT YON BUGLES
OVER THE RICH DEAD
THEIR SONS THEY GAVE
THEIR IMMORTALITY

18/596 PRIVATE
W. WHITAKE
WEST YORKSHIRE RE
1ST JULY 1916 AG

A BOY IN YEARS
MAN IN SHIELD

Families were allowed to choose inscriptions on their loved ones' headstones

VIII

'A Trying Day On The Somme'
(1/ Essex Battalion War Diary)

How 1st July unfolded

Row of Newfoundlanders in Knightsbridge Cemetery

- The battalions, brigades, divisions and corps are listed in order of attack from Montauban in the south to Gommecourt in the north. Apart from the battalions that went 'over the top', we also include those in reserve which sustained casualties on 1st July

- We incorporate points about each unit. There is a shortage of information about some battalions as many of the officers were casualties and unable to file detailed reports

- Many quotes not acknowledged are taken from the various unit war diaries

- It is difficult to give precise figures for casualties - if known we have used figures from war diaries; for deaths we have given details from CWGC records for 1st July 1916 only

FOURTH ARMY
General Sir Henry Rawlinson

NAM 1202

XIII CORPS
Lieutenant-General Walter N. Congreve

IWM Art 001791

➤ Objective: Montauban

➤ Plan of operations for 15th June: Flame Projectors: 'A certain number of the non-portable type, if available, will be installed at selected points at the end of Russian sap-four on 30th Division's front and four on 18th Division's front. The saps will be opened up a few minutes before the assault and the machines used against the front and support trenches ... The Carnoy craters will be dealt with in this way. Use will also be made of any portable flame projectors which are available - 16 have been asked for'

Livens Flame Projector   IWM Q 014938

➤ Flame Projectors were designed by Captain W.H. Livens RE. They were 56 ft long, installed under No Man's Land. They were fired 150 ft from the enemy and the projector's head was raised 3ft from the ground. They were heavy (2.5 tons) and difficult to install, had a range of over 100 yards and the aim was to cause confusion, casualties and affect morale. GHQ had ordered 22 - only 8 arrived - four were sent to the front line of which two were successfully fired east of Casino Point, a third destined for Casino Point was damaged by shell-fire and the fourth was damaged on its way to the front line west of Mansel Copse. Six Vincent flame projectors, smaller than the Livens type, were ordered but none arrived

➢ Six Russian saps, used for creating advanced positions for machine-guns, observation and to help troops across No Man's Land, were dug by 183rd Tunnelling Company of the Royal Engineers

➢ The topography was such that the British artillery had a better view of the German front line than other Corps

➢ XIII Corps gave a high priority to counter battery work and were encouraged by the neighbouring French to use a 'creeping barrage.' An order from Corps HQ: 'The field artillery barrage will creep back by short lifts - the infantry will follow close behind the barrage as safety admits'

➢ The Corps artillery in conjunction with the French XX Corps was four times greater than the Germans'

➢ Lieutenant-General Congreve went to the front line on 1st July to see for himself how the offensive was progressing. He was able to inform General Rawlinson of the successes achieved by the 30th and 18th Divisions. He asked if the Corps should press on but Rawlinson, cautious as ever, told him to hold the ground gained, arguably one of many errors of judgement on 1st July 1916. XIII Corps was in control of their gains by nightfall

➢ Congreve: 'Please convey to all units my intense appreciation of their splendid fighting which has attained all asked from them and resulted in heavy losses to the enemy, nearly 1,000 prisoners have already passed through the cage'

➢ Memo from General Rawlinson to XIII Corps: 'Whilst regretting heavy casualties … I commend their determination and gallantry'

➢ The French 6th Army's 39th and 11th Divisions on the right flank under General Fayolle achieved all their objectives

IWM Art 1575

30th DIVISION

Major-General John S.M. Shea (Congreve's brother-in-law)

➢ Objective: The eastern half of Montauban and the German trenches running to the Maricourt road at the end of which was the Dublin Redoubt which was a French objective. It took the Division just one hour to achieve their objectives

➢ One reason for the success of 30th Division was their use of the 'creeping barrage' described on 30th June by Captain William Bloor of the Royal Field Artillery: 'Just had word that the day of the assault is tomorrow, and the hour 7.30 a.m. We are going to shell the front trenches until 7.30 a.m. then 'lift' to the second line, then just before the infantry get to the second line, we are to shell the third line. This is from 7.36 to 7.46 a.m., we then lift on to Glatz Alley. What happens after that is yet to be seen and depends upon the fortunes of war'

➢ Lieutenant-Colonel Neil Fraser-Tytler who commanded an RFA Howitzer Battery supporting the 30th Division confirms the success of the 'creeping barrage': 'The line advanced steadily, scarcely meeting any opposition in the first three lines of trenches. Every point was reached at scheduled time, so the automatic artillery barrage was always just in front of the infantry. At 9 o'clock we could see our flags waving in the trench behind German's Wood, and by 8.20 the formidable Glatz Redoubt was captured, an advance of 700 yards with very little loss. This redoubt had been submitted to a terrific bombardment and the infantry reported that the maze of strong points, machine-gun emplacements etc. had been swept away, and that the trenches were crammed with the dead. By 8.40 a.m. we had captured Casement Trench, and from there a dense smoke barrage was created with a view to hiding the advance of the second wave, their objective being Montauban village. They went across in perfect formation up to Glatz Redoubt; there they made a short pause, and then continued the attack and captured the whole of the village of Montauban by 10 a.m.'

Major William Congreve MC, DSO, VC (posthumous) Rifle Brigade killed in the Somme 20th July aged 25. He is buried in Corbie Communal Cemetery Extension

➢ 'Brigades were in No Man's land before Zero and attacked at the double - 21st and 89th Brigades were into the enemy's front line before they could organise themselves'

➢ Official History: 'Thanks to the very efficient artillery support and careful rehearsals, the 30th Division had most successfully and expeditiously accomplished the first phase of its task, reaching and holding its second objective. Failure on other parts of the British battle line led to Major-General Shea being ordered to delay the instigation of further phases'

➢ In his diary Major William Congreve, son of the Corps Commander, wrote that Major-General Shea's 30th Division wanted to go on: 'Congreve wanted them to go on. He even telephoned Rawlinson for permission to do so, but permission was refused … Congreve regretted that he was unable to comply. Rawlinson's orders were clear - capture and consolidate the definite objectives allotted to each corps.' It was a golden opportunity missed to advance further into German held territory. As far as Congreve and his father were concerned 'by the early hours of the next morning, the gap created by XIII Corps had healed.' They should have capitalised by pressing on to Bernafay and Trônes Woods and Guillemont

➢ The wire was well cut. The Germans had been starved of rations for six days

- German dug-outs in this sector were not as well constructed as elsewhere. The Germans did not believe the French would attack as they were committed at Verdun. One German unit, the 6th Bavarian RIR was virtually annihilated - only 500 survived out of 3,500

- Casualties were conspicuously less than those in other Divisions along the Front, but still significant: over 3,000: 36 officers were killed and 76 wounded, 800 other ranks killed and 2,042 wounded

Pioneers: 11/ Prince of Wales's Volunteers (South Lancashire) (St Helen's Pioneers)

Killed: Officers 1   ORs 20   Nos on Thiepval: 8

- Dug communication trenches to German front line during the day

89th BRIGADE

- Objective achieved was the line of trenches between Montauban and Dublin Redoubt

- There were less than 60 men of the brigade killed a significant contrast to those involved at Fricourt

17/ King's (1st Liverpool Pals):

Killed: Officers 1   ORs 15   Nos on Thiepval: 13

- Dublin Trench objective taken at 8.30 a.m. and held

- The one officer to die was Lieutenant D.H. Scott who died of wounds in a French hospital

Lt Colonel
Bryan Charles FAIRFAX

- 'Perfect liaison existed between the French and ourselves.' Lieutenant-Colonel Bryan Fairfax and Commandant Lepetit of the 3rd Battalion of the 153rd Regiment were reputed to have walked arm in arm into No Man's Land and arrived together in Dublin Trench

- 'Some shelling but very slight infantry resistance- little machine-gun fire encountered, the work of the artillery having been very effective on the German trenches'

- 'Advanced in double quick time'

- German casualties were heavy in this sector, RIR 109 losing 42 officers and 2,105 men which emphasises the effectiveness of the bombardment

- The soldiers were well rewarded for their successes with a hot lunch served at Dublin Trench

'German casualties were heavy in this sector' - dead Germans at Montauban   IWM Q065441

20/ King's (4th Liverpool Pals):

Casualties: 80   Killed: Officers 1   ORs 21   Nos on Thiepval: 16

- La Briqueterie was taken at 12.35 p.m. by 4th Company after artillery bombardment

- Compared to the majority of battalions on 1st July the numbers of deaths is low

- 'Lines advanced through enemy's artillery fire as though on parade in quick time'

2/ Bedfords:

Killed: Officers 0   ORs 6   Nos on Thiepval: 2

- Followed 100 yards behind 17 and 20/ King's. Wire was 'very well cut'

- Captured trenches in front of Montauban

- A new trench was dug from German's Wood to La Briqueterie as part of a consolidation exercise

- 'Mopping up' was successful. 300 prisoners of RIR 62 and 4 machine-guns were captured

19/ King's (3rd Liverpool Pals):

Killed: Officers 0   ORs 15   Nos on Thiepval: 7

- Followed 2/ Bedfords acting as carriers

- Signaller Nelson Mills: 'The boys got over the top and simply walked across … as if on manoeuvres in Sefton Park.'

21st BRIGADE:

19/ Manchesters (4th Pals):

Casualties: 191   Killed: Officers 1   ORs 59   Nos on Thiepval: 54

- Crawled into place before 7.30 a.m. Attacked Glatz Redoubt with 18/ King's
- Reached Glatz Redoubt by 8.35 a.m

18/ King's (2nd Liverpool Pals):

Casualties: Estimated by Lieutenant-Colonel Trotter DSO as over 500
Killed: Officers 9   ORs 160   Nos on Thiepval: 110
Dantzig Alley British Cemetery 50

- Attacked Dublin Trench and Glatz Redoubt which was reached by 8.35 a.m.
- **Private Arthur Seanor** was involved - for his story see page 27
- The attack benefited from intense and accurate bombardment by the French artillery to their right
- Private Pringle: 'Just as we were halfway to the first trench Captain Brockbank of 'No. 1' Company was hit by a machine-gun concealed somewhere to our left … but he kept marching and encouraging us with cries of "Go No. 1". We encountered no opposition at the first trench. Our artillery had peppered it far too well and we saw German bodies lying all along …' Charles Brockbank was killed and is buried in Dantzig Alley British Cemetery
- Lieutenant-Colonel Trotter: 'Every fighting officer was hit by enemy's bullets or shells except one and he was accidentally bayoneted as he crossed a trench.' Trotter was killed by a shell on 8th July and is buried in Péronne Road Cemetery. His brother Reginald fell in 1915

2/ Yorkshire (Green Howards) (Alexandra, Princess of Wales's Own):

Casualties: 200   Killed: Officers 4   ORs 62   Nos on Thiepval: 27

- In support, they reached and consolidated German front line
- A looting victor was shot, mistaken for a German as he was wearing a pickelhaube helmet

2/ Wiltshire (Duke of Edinburgh's):

Killed: Officers 1   ORs 4   Nos on Thiepval: 2

- 7.40 a.m. in support, 3 companies following the Green Howards acting as carriers of water rations and material

90th BRIGADE:

➢ Battalions went at 8.30 a.m. to Montauban passing through 21st Brigade
➢ Lieutenant-Colonel R.K. Walsh CO of 2/ Royal Scots Fusiliers had been 'previously appointed OC Montauban'

17/ Manchesters (2nd Pals):

Casualties: 348   Killed: Officers 5   ORs 114   Nos on Thiepval: 99

- In support, they reached Montauban at 10.20 a.m.

- All Company Commanders were casualties

- Private Albert Hurst: 'By this time (when in Montauban) we were too exhausted from carrying so much gear to start digging trenches'

- Major C.L. MacDonald, adjutant, about the artillery: 'They failed to silence the enemy batteries which were causing us such heavy losses. It was noticeable that when an aeroplane was making observations, the enemy's artillery fire almost ceased'

- CO Lieutenant-Colonel Johnson was wounded

16/ Manchesters (1st Pals):

Killed: Officers 0   ORs 77   Nos on Thiepval: 61

- Passed through 21st Brigade, reached Montauban Alley by 10.30 a.m. then consolidated

- They were the first men to enter a deserted Montauban. They were greeted by a solitary fox, according to the Official History

- 'Captured two guns with 16/ Manchester Regt. written on them, also were names of men who captured them.' They were thought to be the first guns to be captured on 1st July

- Counter-attack by Germans in the evening was checked

18/ Manchesters (3rd Pals):

Casualties: 176   Killed: Officers 0   ORs 38   Nos on Thiepval: 32

- Acted as carriers for 90th Brigade. Problem with weight of loads carried

- Private Pat Kennedy: 'I could see the French troops advancing on our right. It was a splendid sight to see them with their coloured uniforms and long bayonets. They advanced in short, sharp rushes … Their artillery was giving them plenty of support …' Note the different tactics being used compared to the British

- The CO Lieutenant-Colonel William Smith (36) died of wounds on 9th July, hit by the same shell as Lieutenant-Colonel Trotter, 18/ King's. Smith is buried in Corbie Communal Cemetery Extension

2/ Royal Scots Fusiliers:

156   Casualties: 170   Killed: Officers 3   ORs 44   Nos on Thiepval: 34

- At 8.30 a.m. passed through 21st Brigade. Reached Montauban by 10.05 a.m. and Montauban Alley soon after

- 'We moved up as close as possible to our artillery barrage'

- BWD: 'Only waterproof sheets and rations for one day - besides emergency rations - were carried and on each man's pack was a yellow patch - 30th DIV - and a metal disc'

NPG 21275

18th (EASTERN) DIVISION
Major-General Ivor Maxse

➤ Objectives: Pommiers Redoubt and Montauban Alley

➤ General Maxse is generally agreed to have been one of the more forward thinking of the Generals on 1st July 1916. He implemented:

- Artillery 'creeping barrage'

- Detonation of mines

- Flame projectors were fired in front of the 8/ Norfolks' front, to the right of Casino Point (Kasino Point was the German spelling)

- Use of Russian saps dug across No Man's Land

- Effective counter battery work

- The History of the Queen's Regiment records the Maxse dictum: 'Kill Germans'

➤ At 7.27 a.m. three mines were exploded at the end of saps at Casino Point, one of 5,000 and two of 500 lbs, as a result, a number of Germans surrendered

➤ When digging a Russian sap the Royal Engineers broke into a German dug-out. Fortunately for them, the Germans did not hear them- BWD 23rd June: 'Bored into enemy dug-out ... loud talking heard. Plugged hole. Enemy seems not to have noticed'

➤ The wire was generally well cut apart from in front of Pommiers Redoubt

➤ 55th and 53rd Brigades were to go either side of the cratered area

➤ 'The best thing that can be said about the Division is that it captured all its objectives and held them'

➤ Over 3,000 casualties: 40 officers killed and 70 wounded - 870 other ranks killed and 2090 wounded

Pioneers: 8/ Royal Sussex:

Casualties: 95   ● Killed: Officers 0   ORs 12   Nos on Thiepval: 9

- Consolidated strong points and dug communication trenches. 'A' Company was involved in fighting at Montauban Alley and 'D' Company supported in the capture of the Loop

55th BRIGADE

➢ Brigadier-General Jackson issued a tub thumping message on the eve of battle: 'The Germans are now outnumbered and out-gunned and will soon go to pieces if every man goes into the fight tomorrow determined to get through whatever the local difficulties may be. Let every man remember that all England and all the world is watching him. Good luck!'

8/ East Surreys:

Casualties: 446   ● Killed: Officers 7   ORs 132   Nos on Thiepval: 98

- 'The enemy shelled trenches from midnight' suggesting the week long bombardment had failed

- Hand to hand fighting for a long time in German trenches. 12.22 a.m. dug in on Mametz Road west of Montauban

- **Captain 'Billie' Nevill**, attached from East Yorks, encouraged his men to follow two footballs kicked into NML. For his story see page 31

- On 6th June the Battalion had practised the 'abnormal attack on trenches laid out to represent German trenches'

- '… later Lance-Corporal Brame turned up with a bottle of champagne to be drunk in Montauban "ON DER TAG". This bottle was sent round from officer to officer, to all those who had not been killed or wounded.' How typically British! The champagne was followed by something less alcoholic: 'In the afternoon HQ Officers put their kit on the firestep in Mill Trench and had only just finished tea when the first of a number 5.9 shells landed … At 9 p.m. a party of Suffolks reported with 25 canvas buckets of water which were extremely welcome' but not as welcome as the champagne one can safely assume …

- 'Two Huns ran into the trench crying for mercy…'

- CO Major Irwin was put out that his written recommendation of a VC for Captain Gimson, RAMC, was criticised by Major-General Maxse for being too 'journalistic' and proceeded to re-write it. Irwin felt that Gimson would not have missed out on the VC if his original piece had been submitted!

- Brothers Private John and Sergeant William Abrey were both killed and are commemorated on the Thiepval Memorial. A total of 33 pairs of brothers were killed on 1st July 1916 and three sets of three brothers

7/ Queen's (Royal West Surreys):

Casualties: 532   Killed: Officers 6   ORs 154   Nos on Thiepval: 71
Dantzig Alley British Cemetery 73

- Crept into NML and at 7.30 a.m. 'advanced in line'. Montauban/ Mametz road by 2 p.m. By 6.45 p.m. consolidated its gain in Montauban Alley

- There is a story about a German being found chained to a machine-gun in Breslau trench. According to a witness, Captain M. Kemp-Welch, 'the man was wounded in the thigh; a real "tough" who obviously chained himself to his gun out of sheer bravado but not by order.' Myth or truth? Either it was a case of 'bravado' or the chain was actually a harness for carrying the gun …

7/ Buffs (East Kents):

Killed: Officers 2   ORs 49   Nos on Thiepval: 31

- Two platoons went forward at 7.30 a.m. to clear the muddy crater area in front of their trenches and the rest moved towards west Montauban by midday and Montauban Alley by 5.15 p.m.

- Three Hayesmore brothers, all privates, died on the Somme in 1916. Frederick died of wounds on 2nd July, Hubert on 1st July and Louis on 18th November. Frederick and Louis are to be found on the Thiepval Memorial and Hubert is buried in Dantzig Alley British Cemetery

7/ Royal West Kents (Queen's Own):

Casualties 183   Killed: Officers 1   ORs 27   Nos on Thiepval: 21

- Reinforced the 8/ East Surreys. Some arrived at Montauban Alley at 11.45 a.m.

- 'The weather became decidedly hot'… 'At 3 p.m. the men were much exhausted and SAA and water needed urgently'

53rd BRIGADE

➢ Faced little opposition due to the mine exploding at Casino Point and the effect of two flame projectors which cleared resistance on the western edge of Carnoy craters. The mine under Casino Point of 5,000 lbs was near the surface and threw up a great deal of chalk which scattered widely and wounded many 6/ Royal Berks and 10/ Essex

➢ The German artillery fired all day

➢ By-passed 'crater zone' where machine-guns still operating

8/ Norfolks:

Casualties: 345   Killed: Officers 3   ORs 101   Nos on Thiepval: 86

- 'Wire completely demolished by the artillery'

- 'Teas were brought up from Carnoy and served out in Assembly trenches'

- '7.27 a.m. a mine and two Russian saps were exploded on our front'- i.e. the Casino Point mine. Two Companies crawled into NML then proceeded calmly at 'walking pace' to the south west of Montauban.

- Reached Pommiers Trench at 10.30 and Montauban Alley at 5.45 p.m.

6/ Royal Berkshire (Princess Charlotte of Wales's):

Casualties: 350   Killed: Officers 7   ORs 84   Nos on Thiepval: 71

- Crept out 30 yards into NML before 7.30 a.m. Slow and steady pace

- Advanced through the debris of Casino Point mine. Pommiers Redoubt captured at 9.30 a.m. Montauban Alley at 5.40 p.m.

- The 5,000 lb Casino Point mine was exploded 20 seconds late, the debris thus causing some casualties amongst the Battalion. Captain S. Fenner CO reported that 'the moral effect of the mine on the Huns was very noticeable and many rushed out towards our men holding up their hands … The success of this operation was due to the thorough grounding everyone had in this work.' NCOs and men were able to carry on according to their programme when officers became casualties

- A. J. Gosling: 'I saw the first batch of Hun prisoners come and surrender. I still have a cigarette given me by one of them'

10/ Essex:

Killed: Officers 1   ORs 27   Nos on Thiepval: 16

- 'At 5.30 a.m. the men were served with substantial breakfast of hot tea and rum, bacon and bully beef'

- '7.27 Mine under Casino Point was blown.' This was near the surface and threw up a great deal of chalk which was widely scattered and wounded many men of the Berks and Essex

- Assisted advance of Norfolks and Royal Berks. In the evening detailed 'to hold the Pommier Line to the last man'

- 'Rations came up Carnoy-Montauban Road on pack animals - this method proved very satisfactory'

- Good telephone communication was established

8/ Suffolks:

Casualties: 21   Killed: Officers 0   ORs 10   Nos on Thiepval: 5

- Provided carrying parties to forward areas all day

54th BRIGADE

7/ Bedfords:

160   Casualties: 321   Killed: Officers 2   ORs 87   Nos on Thiepval: 52

- Into NML at 7.30 a.m. with 11/ Royal Fusiliers

- Successful assault on the right at 9.30 am on Pommiers Redoubt with 11/ Royal Fusiliers

- Telephones, visual signalling and runners unsatisfactory

- Heavy loss of officers wounded, leading waves had to be led by NCOs

- 'Machine-gun fire was very galling'

- Private Jack Cousins: 'Our platoon officer said "You'll find the barbed wire in front of the German trench blown away." Nothing of the sort!'

- 'Every platoon will carry two red and two yellow artillery flags. These flags will be waved for a short period by the leading line to show how far the attack has progressed'

- Reasons for success according to the BWD: 1. Successful wire cutting by Artillery 2. Training and attention to detail 3. Clear and concise orders received 4. Successful mopping up by Northants 5. Good supply of bombs by carrying parties 6. Speed with which assistant battalions left the trenches 7. Close cooperation of all units in assaulting waves

- 'A truly wonderful performance when it is taken into consideration that their training had not reached its second year. Both during the preliminary bombardment when the weather was very bad and the men were living in trenches filled with water day and night … the cheeriness and high morale of all ranks was remarkable'

11/ Royal Fusiliers (City of London Regiment):

Casualties: 227   Killed: Officers 2   ORs 57   Nos on Thiepval: 48

- Attacked with 7/ Bedfords. First two Companies advanced in 'four waves in extended order' and next two companies followed up in 'artillery formation'

- Rapid advance to Pommiers Trench. Fierce hand to hand fighting at Pommiers Redoubt

- Telephones not working - good work by signallers 'by means of shutter and flag'

- Official History: 'Advance over Mametz spur so rapid that a halt had to be made in front of the Pommiers trench as the artillery had not yet ceased firing on it'

6/ Northants:

Casualties: 160   Killed: Officers 0   ORs 34   Nos on Thiepval: 3

- Artillery barrage when in assembly trenches
- Reinforced Royal Fusiliers and Bedfords in Pommiers Redoubt

12/ Middlesex (Duke of Cambridge's Own):

Casualties: 38   Killed: Officers 2   ORs 4   Nos on Thiepval: 2

- Into NML at 12.45 p.m. from Carnoy

Bedfords
2nd and 7th

Border
1st, 2nd and 11th

Buffs
7th

Devons
2nd, 8th and 9th

Dorset
1st

Duke Of Wellington
2nd

Durham
Light Infantry
15th and 18th

East Lancs
1st and 11th

East Surreys
8th

East Yorks
1st, 7th, 10th and 11th

Essex
1st, 2nd and 10th

Gordon Highlanders
2nd

Hants
1st

Highland
Light Infantry
15th, 16th and 17th

King's (Liverpool)
17th, 18th, 19th and 20th

King's Own
(Royal Lancaster)
1st

162

XV CORPS
Lieutenant-General Henry S. Horne

NPG 154582

➤ Objective: Mametz and Fricourt Salient

➤ 'Gas was let off from the centre of the Corps to fool the enemy. Smoke was discharged at 7.26 a.m.'

➤ Generally a more effective bombardment was aided by better observation and the majority of troops were ordered into NML before Zero

➤ HQ was taken in by overly positive reports of progress made by 21st and 7th Divisions which resulted in the decision for a frontal attack on Fricourt, one of the largest and best defended villages. The 7/ Yorkshire (Green Howards) warned that the situation was parlous

➤ Three mines were laid at the Tambour of 25,000, 15,000 and 9,000 lbs, one of which failed to detonate because the mine was flooded. According to Peter Barton a tambour is 'an ancient military term meaning a construction attached to a stockade or wall that projected outwards to present enfilade defensive fire'

➤ The Corps' success can be explained by the ineffectual German shelling and a shortage of grenades

7th DIVISION
Major-General Herbert E. Watts

IWM Art 1830

➤ Objective: Mametz and south east of Fricourt

➤ The Division had been at the Front since 1914

➤ Fricourt held out but Mametz was captured. The men were too exhausted to go any further

➤ Most battalions went into NML before Zero and crawled to within 70-100 yards of the German wire

➤ 'At 7.32 2/ Border and 9/ Devons reached German front line'

➤ 'The services rendered by the Divisional Artillery were admirable throughout the operations. The wire was very well cut although in places it presented exceptional difficulties'

➤ 'Medical Services were admirably carried out. The German prisoners very readily offered themselves as stretcher-bearers'

➤ 7th Division Report: 1,600 prisoners were taken including 23 officers. Their evidence elicited 'no doubt that the enemy's morale has been severely shaken. They have been unanimous in stating that had it not been for their deep dug-outs, it would have been impossible for them to hold the line in the face of our sustained bombardment'

➤ By 6.00 p.m. most of Mametz was in British hands

➤ There were 3,300 casualties

Pioneers: 24/ Manchesters (Oldham Comrades):

Casualties: 8   Killed: Officers 1   OR 1   Nos on Thiepval: 0

- Made strong points, cleared roads, opened up blown-in German trenches and removed barbed wire

91st BRIGADE

➤ Objective: to capture head of Mametz Spur and ground east of Mametz

22/ Manchesters (7th Pals):

Casualties: 472   Killed: Officers 7   ORs 194   Nos on Thiepval: 140

- Special Order: 'The use of the word "retire" is absolutely forbidden and if heard can only be a ruse of the enemy and must be ignored'

- Gas was let off at 7.15 a.m. and smoke at 7.26

- Attacked east of Mametz. NML only 100 -200 yards wide. Danzig Alley taken by 8.15 a.m.

- **Lieutenant Roy Mellor** was killed in the first wave. For his story see page 36

- High rate of casualties due to machine-guns positioned at Mametz and Danzig Alley

- Sergeant R.H. Tawney who later made his name as an economic historian: 'We went forward, not doubling but at a walk'

1/ South Staffs:

Casualties: 310   Killed: Officers 6   ORs 84   Nos on Thiepval: 60

- Attacking south of Mametz with 22/ Manchesters

- Front line trenches taken quickly - 700 yards in 15 minutes as far as Cemetery Trench. Entered Mametz and captured west end of Danzig Alley at 1.40 p.m.

- A 2000 lb mine at Bulgar Point failed to explode because, according to Peter Barton in *The Somme, The Unseen Panoramas*, a British trench mortar accidentally cut the detonator wires

A captured German dug-out at Danzig Alley used as an Aid Post - note the stretchers on the right
IWM Q 000814

2/ Queen's (Royal West Surreys):

Killed: Officers 6   ORs 50   Nos on Thiepval: 43

- In support of 22/ Manchesters. Danzig Alley reached at 3.30 p.m.

21/ Manchesters (6th Pals):

Killed: Officers 2   ORs 61   Nos on Thiepval: 48

- 'B' and 'C' Companies assisting 1/ South Staffs on outskirts of Mametz. Danzig Alley occupied by 1.40 p.m.

20th BRIGADE

➢ Objective: south west of Mametz

2/ Gordon Highlanders:

Casualties: 461   Killed: Officers 5   ORs 119   Nos on Thiepval: 13
Gordon Cemetery 94

- The Battalion went over 'as if on parade'
- Attacked the west side of Mametz to the right of the railway. Wire was partly uncut.
- Problem of heavy machine-gun fire from the 'Shrine' south of Mametz

- Example of success by a battalion of regulars

- Came across large numbers of unexploded shells or 'duds' as they were known

9/ Devons:

Casualties: 464   Killed: Officers 7   ORs 158   Nos on Thiepval: 43

- At 7.27 a.m. left their support trenches and attacked through Mansel Copse. German front line reached by 7.32, then Shrine Alley from where German prisoners were brought back

- Hit by artillery barrage at the outset, machine-gun fire from 'The Shrine'- all but one officer had fallen by 7.40 a.m.

- 50% of casualties were caused before Mansel Copse was reached

- Private H.L. Wide: 'The sun went down that first evening back over our old trenches, in gold which turned to blood and it seemed symbolic'

- Captain D.L. Martin's prediction that a machine-gun located in the civilian cemetery south of Mametz would inflict great casualties on his Battalion, proved correct. He is buried in Devonshire Cemetery

- Also buried in the cemetery is the poet Lieutenant William Hodgson MC who ended his final poem *Before Action*: 'Help me to die, O Lord.' He and his batman were killed and buried near each other

- Two brothers Privates Sidney and Thomas Copp were killed, the former was in the 2/ Devons and both are listed on the Thiepval Memorial

- Lieutenant H. Pearse: 'Our Devon men walked through (the intense artillery barrage) in perfect line'

2/ Border:

Casualties: 343   Killed: Officers 2   ORs 86   Nos on Thiepval: 36

- A 500 lb mine was exploded in the German trench ahead of the Battalion

- 'Walked through German barrage in perfect line'. All objectives taken and consolidated by evening - Danube Trench, Shrine Alley and Apple Alley

- Heavy toll from enfilading machine-guns in Mametz and Fricourt

8/ Devons:

Killed: Officers 4   ORs 39   Nos on Thiepval: 2

- Followed 9/ Devons and 2/ Gordon Highlanders. Went through Mansel Copse

- Cleared dug-outs in Danzig trench, all objectives achieved. Heavy machine-gun at the 'Shrine', Mametz

- All officers of 'B' Coy were casualties so the men were led by Company Sergeant-Major Helwill

  - A sixteen year old, Private Bathurst, was put in charge of 60 prisoners

A German dug-out that the British artillery had failed to destroy on 1st July   IWM Q 000870

- A chaplain, Rev. Ernest Crosse, watched the action from above Mansel Copse: 'The road was strewn with dead … in every shell-hole all across the valley and up to the German saps were the badly wounded. I bandaged up a few as best I could and then returned with stretcher-bearers.' At 6 a.m. on 2nd July he conducted a burial service for about 60 men in the front line trench in the presence of the General. It is now the Devonshire Cemetery with the plaque 'The Devonshires held this trench, the Devonshires hold it still'

22nd BRIGADE

➢   In Division's centre attacked south of Fricourt

20/ Manchesters (5th Pals):

Casualties: 326   🔴 Killed: Officers 6   ORs 118   Nos on Thiepval: 24

- At 2.30 p.m. attacked to right of Fricourt. Held a long stretch of front line trench along Bois Français to south of Fricourt. High casualty numbers in Sunken Road Trench due to heavy machine-gun fire from Wing Corner

- CO 35 year old Lieutenant-Colonel Harold Lewis, attached from 37th Lancers (Baluch Horse) is buried in Dantzig Alley British Cemetery. From *Sir Douglas Haig's Great Push*: 'A pathetic incident in the attack on the Danzig trench was the death of the Manchesters' pet dog, who had accompanied his master in the charge. Both master and dog were killed at the same moment, and were found afterwards lying a few paces apart.' The dog's owner was Lewis

- 'I heard two pistol shots. I feel sure that these two unfortunate boys had been executed for cowardice'

- To the Battalion's right, three mines were blown up along Kiel Trench of 500 lbs each

2/ Royal Warwicks:

Killed: Officers 3   ORs 2   Nos on Thiepval: 2

- In the afternoon, moved forward into Shrine Alley and helped the 2/ Gordon Highlanders to capture the ruins of Mametz. Reached Danzig Alley

2/ Royal Irish Regiment:

Casualties: 50   Killed: Officers 1   ORs 6   Nos on Thiepval: 1

- At 10 p.m. they were sent to consolidate troops in Mametz and to repel counter-attacks

1/ Royal Welch Fusiliers 'A' and 'C' Companies:

Casualties: 39   Killed: Officers 0   ORs 4   Nos on Thiepval: 2

- At 4.20 p.m. in open order (fire and movement) supporting 20/ Manchesters, 'pushed up via craters'. Bombers worked up Sunken Road Trench towards Fricourt

- Corporal Harry Shaw: 'Whatever was gained, it wasn't worth the price that the men had paid to gain that advantage. It was no advantage to anybody. It was just sheer bloody murder'

- 200 prisoners taken

- One canister machine was claimed as a trophy, the German crew having been killed

17th (NORTHERN) DIVISION
Major-General Thomas D. Pilcher
(attached to 21st Division)

➤ Pilcher was unequivocal in his criticism of strategy in early July: 'It is very easy to sit a few miles in the rear and get credit for allowing men to be killed in an undertaking foredoomed to failure, but the part did not appeal to me and my protests against these useless attacks were not well received'. It will not be a surprise to learn that he was sacked by Haig on 12th July 1916 after the disasters that befell the 17th Division on 7th July

➤ Casualties: Over 1,100

Pioneers: 7/ York and Lancaster:

- Not involved on 1st July

50th BRIGADE

➤ Objective: west of Fricourt

➤ The 7/ Yorkshire (Green Howards) were to attack Fricourt from the west, the 10/ West Yorks were to assault the left flank and the 20/ Manchesters of the 7th Division's 22nd Brigade were to come in from the right

➤ At 7.28 a.m. the three Tambour mines of 30,000, 15,000 and 8,000 lbs were fired to distract the enemy but one, thought to be the largest, failed to explode because of flooding

7/ Yorkshire (Green Howards) (Alexandra, Princess of Wales's Own):

Casualties: 351   ●   Killed: Officers 5   ORs 101   Nos on Thiepval: 9

- At 2.30 pm 'D', 'B' and 'C' Companies (apart from 'A' Coy) went over. State of wire was uncut at the Tambour due to bad fuses in shells. Hit by machine-gun fire from the Tambour and Red Cottage

- One of the greatest blunders on the day is described by Captain A.J.W. Barmby: 'The Battalion was ordered to assault Fricourt at 2.30 p.m. but before this order reached us at Battalion HQs we heard with consternation that 'A' Company had attacked at 7.45 a.m. … an unexplainable mistake on the part of their OC (Major Kent) … the men were mown down in lines and the dead lay as they fell one line behind the other.' The majority of them fell before they had gone 20 yards, 108 out of 140 were casualties. The reward for Major Kent was promotion to Lieutenant-Colonel!

- 'The enemy could clearly be seen in the (Tambour) mine craters'

- In the afternoon the CO decided against any further action

10/ West Yorks (Prince of Wales's Own):

Casualties: 772   ●   Killed: Officers 10   ORs 295   Nos on Thiepval: 113 Fricourt New Military Cemetery 134

- Failure of the third Tambour mine to explode did not help their cause. Supporting companies were seriously hit by machine-guns brought out from dug-outs firing from the Tambour area and Fricourt

- Major James Knott DSO (33) was buried in Fricourt New Military Cemetery near the spot where he was killed. However, after the war his body was moved to be next to his brother, Captain Henry Knott (24) in Ypres Reservoir Cemetery. The inscriptions on their graves: 'Devoted in life. In death not divided.' There are few other instances of such a move

- The Battalion suffered the highest number of casualties on 1st July - a complete disaster … according to the War Diary 22 officers and approximately 750 other ranks. It was virtually a wipe-out of the whole unit

169

- CO Lieutenant-Colonel A. Dickson is buried in Fricourt New Military Cemetery

- Brothers Harold (Fricourt New Military Cemetery) and 18 year old John Lowes (Thiepval Memorial) were killed

- 2nd Lieutenant Francis Joseph Hicking, aged 19 (see page 2) was killed on 1st July and buried in Fricourt New Military. His brother George, an articled clerk in 1911, was in the 8/ York and Lancaster and is remembered on the Thiepval Memorial. Both went to Uppingham School and were sons of grocers and wine merchants Joseph and Kate Hicking of Halsey House, Pittville, Cheltenham

7/ East Yorks:

Casualties: 178   Killed: Officers 4   ORs 36   Nos on Thiepval: 2

- In support at the start of the Fricourt assault

- At 4.20 p.m. the CO of 7/ Yorkshire (Green Howards) informed Brigade HQ that another advance was impossible without a further bombardment

21st DIVISION
Major-General David G.M. Campbell

- ➤ Objective: north of Fricourt, which was in British hands by noon on 2nd July

- ➤ Consisted of mainly New Army units and had been at Loos in September 1915

- ➤ 2nd Lieutenant Meeres RFA: 'We had so effectively destroyed the entanglement that there was no wire left for them to blow up'

- ➤ 'Bombardment of Fricourt was unsuccessful due to failure of 9.2" shells to explode, the fuses having come out during flight.'

- ➤ Casualties were 4,200

Pioneers: 14/ Northumberland Fusiliers

Killed: Officers 1   ORs 4   Nos on Thiepval: 5

- Assisted 63rd and 64th Brigades. They followed some way behind and were tasked with consolidating captured trenches

63rd BRIGADE

4/ Middlesex:

170   Casualties: 488   Killed: Officers 13   ORs 79   Nos on Thiepval: 36

- 'A' and 'B' Companies into NML five minutes before Zero. Forced to retire immediately, went forward again at 7.29 a.m. When 'C' and 'D' Coys reached German front line they were reduced to a strength of 4 officers and about 100 other ranks. Immediately swept by 6 machine-guns, 4 from northern Fricourt and 2 between German front and support trenches

- There were 83 deaths on 2nd July, the third highest for that day

- All officers in 'A and 'B' Companies were killed except 2nd Lieutenant Simpson.

- 'Due to losses it was decided at 8.15 a.m. to consolidate and hold ground gained'

8/ Somerset Light Infantry (Prince Albert's):

Killed: Officers 9   ORs 107   Nos on Thiepval: 73

- 'B' and 'C' Companies crept into NML before Zero but 'leading companies were disorganised and had lost all their officers.' Sunken Road and Lozenge Alley were taken and retained. Moved forward to Patch Alley on 3rd July and were relieved on 4th July by the 12/ Manchesters

- The only Germans found in the trenches were machine-gunners who were killed. Bombers cleared dug-outs

10/ York and Lancaster:

Casualties: 305   Killed: Officers 4   ORs 13   Nos on Thiepval: 15

- In support, they were following 4/ Middlesex. Got to Sunken Road beyond first line trenches and Lozenge Alley. Relieved on 4th July

8/ Lincolnshire:

Casualties: 51   Killed: Officers 2   ORs 14   Nos on Thiepval: 11

- 8.40 a.m. to support 8/ Somerset LI in Fricourt attack. At 9.15 a.m. went through 8/ Somerset LI to Lozenge Alley and the Sunken Road. They were relieved at 2 a.m. on 4th July

- 'All officers will carry rifle and bayonet and revolvers and will wear clothes as far as possible like the men. Badge of rank will be worn on the shoulder'

64th BRIGADE

➤ Attacked north of Fricourt up the gentle slope of Fricourt spur

➤ Brevet-Major Graham Bosanquet (30) MC and Légion d'Honneur was killed on the Fricourt-Contalmaison road near Crucifix Trench and is buried in Gordon Dump Cemetery

9/ King's Own Yorkshire Light Infantry:

Casualties: 497   Killed: Officers 14   ORs 163   Nos on Thiepval: 115

- 7.30 a.m. crept into NML then advanced in line with 10/ KOYLI

- State of wire: 2nd Lieutenant Charles Meeres R.F.A. attached to 29th Division recalled that the wire was cut in front of Crucifix trench and 'we were equally successful with the wire along Gin Alley but the thick, heavy masses before South Sausage Redoubt proved very difficult … fortunately for our reputation (when a party of sappers with a Bangalore torpedo went out to cut a lane) they found we had effectively destroyed the entanglement so there was no wire left for them to blow up.' Bangalore Torpedoes were sections of pipe, with an explosive charge in the end piece. They were pushed out into No Man's Land, screwing section onto section like a chimney-sweep's brush to blow gaps in the enemy barbed wire. They were designed in Bangalore, India, by Captain R. McClintock of the RE in 1912

- Two lines of trenches were taken in only ten minutes, the Sunken Road and Crucifix Trench were reached by some men and consolidated. They were relieved on the following day

- '… greeted by a hail of machine-gun and rifle fire'

- In the general chaos, Captain Liddell-Hart, later a military historian and strategist, found himself in charge of what remained of a neighbouring battalion

- Two brothers died during the action, Samuel and Lawrence Cooper, both remembered on the Thiepval Memorial

- CO Lieutenant-Colonel Colmer Lynch is buried in Norfolk Cemetery. So unpopular was he with his officers that at a meal before 'Z' Day, they refused to raise their glasses to him, a situation rescued by 24 year old Captain Gordon Haswell who proposed a toast to 'When the Barrage Lifts.' Haswell was also killed on 1st July and is buried in the same cemetery

- Brigadier-General Headlam joined the men in the Sunken Road but was forced to return to Brigade HQ for communication purposes

10/ King's Own Yorkshire Light Infantry:

Casualties: 502   Killed: Officers 9   ORs 156   Nos on Thiepval: 146

- 7.30 a.m. crawled into No Man's Land with 9/ KOYLI on their right. Took Crucifix Trench that morning and held it until relieved

15/ Durham Light Infantry:

Casualties: 388   Killed: Officers 7   ORs 128   Nos on Thiepval: 100

- Into NML at 8.30 a.m. 200 yards of NML to negotiate at rapid pace following 9/ KOYLI. Wire was well cut. Crucifix Trench taken by 8.30 a.m. and consolidated. Relieved on the evening of 3rd July

- Private W. Roberts: 'The short but terrible rush through the fierce curtain fire I shall never forget … the sights I saw are too terrible to write about … at night I saw dead and wounded lying side by side. Some were moaning and others had so far lost their reason that they were laughing and singing'

1/ East Yorkshire:

Casualties: 499 ● Killed: Officers 6 ORs 114 Nos on Thiepval: 103

- 8.30 a.m. in support of 9 and 10/ KOYLI attacking Fricourt at rapid pace. Captured Crucifix Trench and Sunken Road

- 32 year old Lieutenant-Colonel Montague Bruce Stow died of his wounds on 2nd July and is buried in Daours Communal Cemetery Extension

62nd BRIGADE

➢ In reserve

10/ Yorkshire (Green Howards) (Alexandra, Princess of Wales's Own):

● Killed: Officers 1 ORs 41 Nos on Thiepval: 37

- Followed 4/ Middlesex to Crucifix Trench and consolidated

- Out of 5 officers and 117 other ranks in 'B' Company that went into action, only 1 officer and 27 men returned

- Information is scarce 'owing to Colonel Eddowes being sent to England sick and having taken the fuller details with him'. William Eddowes was wounded on 2nd July by shell fire

- VC: Major Stewart Loudoun-Shand (36) was hit and wounded when trying to help his men out of their trench under fierce machine-gun fire. To encourage his men of 'B' Company forward, he insisted on being propped up rather than being tended to but died soon after. He is buried in Norfolk Cemetery

13/ Northumberland Fusiliers:

Casualties: 158 ● Killed: Officers 1 ORs 7 Nos on Thiepval: 7

- After 12 noon, they moved to captured German trenches and provided supplies and ammunition to troops ahead

- Their CO, attached from 36th Jacob's Horse (Indian Army), 30 year old Lieutenant-Colonel Harry Allardice was killed and is buried in Dartmoor Cemetery

1/ Lincolnshire:

Casualties: 119 ● Killed: Officers 2 ORs 10 Nos on Thiepval: 7

- Into NML at 8.00 a.m. Carrying parties including some Bermuda Volunteer Rifle Corps. Consolidated captured positions at Crucifix Trench

- Private Daniel John Sweeney: 'Kirk the best officer we had in this company called for volunteers to go with him over to see Fritz to see what damage our artillery had done, every man would follow this officer anywhere but he only took ten of us - they always expect us Regulars to go on these 'trips' as we are

173

supposed to be experts at the game ... (on 1st July) We took hundreds of prisoners that day and they were glad to be prisoners but we made them work ...When I think of my dear old chums who have fallen, I could cry ...'

12/ Northumberland Fusiliers:

Killed: Officers 0   ORs 12   Nos on Thiepval: 12

- Moved to reserve line - the evening was spent unloading railway wagons

III CORPS
Lieutenant-General Sir William P. Pulteney

➤ The Corps gunners had stated that the Germans' wire would not necessarily be cut due to lack of ammunition which was also unreliable. An officer noted that there were huge numbers of duds lying on the ground

➤ The main Amiens-Albert-Bapaume (old Roman) road cut through the centre of the Corps' front

➤ There was not a proper trench at the Glory Hole due to the mine craters, the front being held by a line of posts

34th DIVISION
Major-General Edward C. Ingouville-Williams

➤ Objectives: Fricourt Spur, Sausage Redoubt and La Boisselle as far as Contalmaison and Pozières. La Boisselle was captured on 4th July

➤ No Man's Land at La Boisselle varied in distance from as little as 75 yards at the Glory Hole up to 800 yards at Mash Valley

➤ Message sent from the front line on 26th June: 'Situation at Y Sap ... much wire still remains ... still requires a great deal of attention'

➤ 30th June: Patrols were sent out to assess the effect of the bombardment on the enemy's trenches and wire ... they found the front line trenches occupied and were fired on with machine-guns. The wire was found to require further attention from the artillery in several places

➢ The Division's chances were not helped by a message being intercepted at 02.45 a.m. on 1st July by the Moritz listening post or phone tap at Contalmaison: 'Infantry must hold onto every yard of ground gained …' News of an impending assault did not take long to spread along the 18 mile German front

➢ **Mines:** To aid the capture of La Boisselle, four mines were laid, the largest Lochnagar to the south, Y Sap to the north and two others were prepared of 8,000 lbs each, the purpose to destroy and gas the German tunnel system near the Glory Hole

- The **Lochnagar Crater** is probably the largest ever man-made crater. One of 19 mines laid for 1st July, its aim was to destroy a fortified stronghold - the Schwaben Höhe. Two adjacent chambers were filled with ammonal explosive, one with 36,000 and the other 24,000 lbs, a total of 27 tons. They were fired at 7.28 a.m. Nine German dug-outs were blown up and in each there would have been one officer and 35 men. The noise of the explosion was awe-inspiring. The result was a massive crater 300 feet (91 m) in diameter and 70 feet (21 m) in depth

  Miners of the 179th Tunnelling Company had been working since March 1916 after taking over from the 185th who had started operations in November 1915. A shaft had been sunk from Lochnagar Street Trench, 300 feet behind the British front line, to a depth of 95 feet and a tunnel 1,030 feet long was mined towards the German front line. As they approached it, silence was essential, so picks were no longer used and work had to be carried out with bayonets, a painfully slow process. A 15 foot lip was created by the explosion which protected assaulting troops from machine-guns in La Boisselle

  Attacking battalions waited two minutes for the debris to settle: a fatal delay during which time the German machine-gunners were able to get into position

  That the crater is still in existence and not filled in like the Y Sap Crater, is thanks to the foresight and perseverance of Richard Dunning who bought the site on 1st July 1978 and has, with the Friends of Lochnagar, preserved it as a permanent memorial dedicated to 'peace, fellowship and reconciliation between all nations who fought on the Western Front'

- **Y Sap**: The tunnel to the explosives' chamber was just under 1,000 ft long going at right angles from the crossroads at La Boisselle to avoid deep German dug-outs. The last section of the tunnel was 4.5 x 2.5 feet. The mine had a limited impact as the trenches in the vicinity had been evacuated

- Once the dust and debris had settled, from the skies above, RFC pilot Cecil Lewis was stunned by the 'two white eyes of the craters'

➢ 'The first reports received from brigades showed that the leading lines moved over the enemy's front line trenches in perfect order'

➢ 'The GOC watched the first part of the advance and noted that the enemy barrage on our front line trenches was intensely heavy and accurate. He was proud to see

The result of work by Tunnelling Companies in the chalk of the Somme   A Reed

the steady manner in which the troops advanced through this barrage without hesitation or confusion and the lines went on in perfect order towards the enemy's front line trenches where they were met by machine-gun and rifle fire.' An acceptance here, therefore, that the week-long bombardment had failed to destroy German artillery and machine-guns

➤ From reports received it soon became evident that 'our infantry had left a number of the enemy behind in his trenches... several enemy machine-guns in emplacements had also been left behind. .. The result of this was that carrying parties were unable to move up after the advancing infantry...'

➤ 2nd July: 'As soon as it was daylight, it became evident that La Boisselle was in the hands of the enemy'

➤ The Division suffered the largest number of casualties on 1st July - 6,380 for virtually no ground gained. Leutnant Alfred Frick of RIR 110 emphasised the importance of the survival of their machine-guns: 'The fifteen remaining undamaged machine-guns in the sector of RIR 110 poured fire into the oncoming columns so that the assault forces went down like ripe corn before the scythe. In consequence the enemy casualties were simply enormous'

➤ A telegram was received by the Division: 'General Rawlinson wires as follows: "Please convey to the 34th Division my hearty congratulations on their successes. Whilst regretting their heavy casualties I desire to express my gratitude for and admiration of the determination and gallantry with which they carried out their difficult task"'

➤ In just 10 minutes 4/5 of the men in the advance battalions were casualties

➤ The Regimental History of the 9/ Cheshire (in the reserve 19th (Western) Division) on relieving men holding Lochnagar Crater noted that 'the scene beggars description. Every shell-hole held a killed or wounded man. The whole area was littered with all the debris of a battle with equipment, clothing, timber, stores and dud shells'

➢ Major-General Edward Ingouville-Williams (54) DSO was killed on 22nd July by shell-fire when visiting a potential location for attack. He was buried in the Warloy-Baillon Communal Cemetery Extension. He was a hands-on commander, who on one occasion before 1st July rescued a wagon of shells from German artillery fire

Pioneers: 18/ Northumberland Fusiliers (1st Tyneside Pioneers):

Killed: Officers 0   ORs 13   Nos on Thiepval: 10

• Actively assisted 101st and 102nd Brigades

101st BRIGADE

➢ Brigadier-General Gore: 'The use of the word "retire" is forbidden in the 101st Brigade, unless it is in writing from an authorised person'

➢ 'Assisting a wounded man to the rear is a court martial offence'

➢ 'A mine will be exploded. All ranks to be warned that the concussion will be considerable'

➢ The Brigade attacked up Sausage Valley

➢ 'Too much credence should not be given to the opinions of wounded men'

➢ 'All men to carry the following: Rifle and equipment … 2 extra bandoliers of SAA … 2 Mills bombs … 1 Iron rations … 1 Day rations … Waterproof cape … 4 sandbags … 1 Gas helmet and pair of goggles … 1 Gas helmet pinned to shirt … Yellow triangle inverted on haversack …1 Pick or shovel … Oil can and bottle … Field dressing … No papers or orders apart from a 1/ 5000 German trench map … Officers will carry a rifle and not a stick. Also a Very pistol … Officers to dress like the men. Badges of rank to remain and all must wear puttees'

➢ Carrying companies failed to get across No Man's Land as their loads were too heavy

15/ Royal Scots (1st Edinburgh City Pals) (Lothian):

Killed: Officers 9   ORs 221   Nos on Thiepval: 201

• 7.30 a.m. attack south of La Boisselle. Crept forward into NML under cover of the barrage. Reached Scots Redoubt at 7.48 a.m.

• Brothers Lance-Corporal Charles and Sergeant William Capstick are recorded on the Thiepval Memorial

• 'The men went over with great heart and in grand form'

• Many Royal Scots were burnt to death by flame throwers

King's Own
Scottish Borderers
1st

KOYLI
2nd, 8th, 9th, 10th
and 12th

Lancashire Fusiliers
1st, 2nd, 15th, 16th
and 19th

Lincolns
1st, 1/ 4th, 2nd, 8th
and 10th

London Kensington

London
Queen Victoria's Rifles

London Queen's
Westminsters Rifles

London Rangers

London Royal Fusiliers

London Scottish

Manchesters
2nd, 7th, 8th, 16th, 17th,
18th, 19th, 20th, 21st,
22nd and 24th

Middlesex
2nd, 4th, 12th and 16th

Newfoundlanders
1st

Norfolks
8th

Northants
6th

North Staffs
1/ 5th and 1/ 6th

10/ Lincolns (Grimsby Chums):

Casualties: 502 ● Killed: Officers 5 ORs 163 Nos on Thiepval: 130

- At 7.28 a.m. when the Lochnagar mine exploded, a private braced himself against the trench wall and the force of the explosion was so great that his leg was broken and was later amputated. At least he survived the day unlike 168 of his unit

- 7.30 a.m. Crept forward into NML under cover of the barrage. Small parties reached the Lochnagar crater where they consolidated their position but failed to cross the German front line. Heavy shell fire and machine-gun fire from La Boisselle and Heligoland Redoubt made reinforcement impossible during the day

- The Battalion advanced with 'the utmost steadiness and courage, not to be surpassed by any troops in the world'

- 4th Army Diary: 'at 8.46 a.m. a wounded captain from 10/ Lincs reports "Germans had had heavy casualties … Lincs have got over No Man's Land with very few casualties"'. They had in fact lost 500 men

- 'No Man's Land was littered with men apparently lying down. At first it was difficult to realise that they were all casualties'

- Brigadier-General R.C. Gore wrote to the Battalion's commander Lieutenant-Colonel E. Cordeaux: 'No troops could have done better and it was no fault of theirs that they did not reach their allotted objective'

- 2nd Lieutenant Turnbull: 'Goodness knows how many machine-guns fired on us'

16/ Royal Scots (2nd Edinburgh City Pals also known as McCrae's Battalion or the Scottish Sportsmen's):

● Killed: Officers 2 ORs 209 Nos on Thiepval: 174

- Into NML at 7.35 a.m. following 15/ Royal Scots in attack south of La Boisselle. One unit got to Contalmaison further than most battalions on the day, over a mile and a half

- Breakfast was 'issued to men at 2.30 a.m.'

- Three of the 16 recruits of the Hearts (Heart of Midlothian) football team were killed and all are to be found on the Thiepval Memorial - Sergeant Duncan Currie (23) and Privates Ernest Ellis (30) and Harry Wattie (23). In the Battalion there were 500 Hearts supporters and professional footballers from Raith Rovers, Dunfermline and Falkirk. It was raised by the CO, Sir George McCrae Kt. DSO, who had made his fortune in textiles

- Two pairs of brothers died - Privates Robert (Thiepval Memorial) and William Archibald (Gordon Dump Cemetery) and Private Alexander (Thiepval Memorial) and Lance-Corporal John Laing (London Cemetery)

11/ Suffolks (Cambridgeshire):

Casualties: 528 ● Killed: Officers 7 ORs 181 Nos on Thiepval: 147

- At 7.30 a.m. aim was to pass through 10/ Lincs within two minutes of the barrage lifting and go on to Lochnagar Crater. 'Wave after wave were mown down'

- **Lieutenant Robert Gilson** was killed in the attack. For his story see page 42

- 'No water to be drunk in Contalmaison until the source has been confirmed.' It proved not to be a problem…

- About 80 Suffolks going up Sausage Valley reached Heligoland Redoubt and were burnt by flamethrowers

- 'Private Billson one of the Battalion orderlies had been sent forward to remind Companies to wave their Artillery flags'

- Private Eric Haylock: 'They was going down like corn in a field. The last time I looked to see who was with me, there wasn't anybody within the length of a cricket pitch on either side. And I thought to myself well, I'm not going to face this lot alone'

102nd BRIGADE (Tyneside Scottish)

➤ Many were 'Geordie' miners. Each battalion had a pipers' band

➤ Brigadier-General Trevor Ternan who took part wrote in the Brigade History: '… losses were unnecessarily high due to the fact that Germans deliberately fired at and killed any wounded lying in front of their trenches'

➤ Piper George Griffiths told of 'fellow piper Willie Scott, a shipyard worker from Elswick in Newcastle, was still ahead of me playing. When I reached the German trenches and jumped in, the first man I saw was Willie, dead but still holding his pipes. If ever a man deserved a VC Willie did.' His name is on the Thiepval Memorial

➤ Brigade casualties: of 80 officers who went into attack, only 10 returned- all four Battalion COs were killed, and all seconds-in-command and adjutants were casualties. About 4/5ths of other ranks were casualties. The Brigade casualties were some of the worst on 1st July

21/ Northumberland Fusiliers (2nd Tyneside Scottish):
Killed: Officers 8   ORs 123   Nos on Thiepval: 117

- 7.30 a.m. attacked south of La Boisselle followed by 22/ NFs. At night 150 men were holding German trenches

- CO Lieutenant-Colonel Frederick Heneker (43) is buried in Ovillers Military Cemetery. He was from the Leinster Regiment

- Thought to be one of the tallest men in the British Army at 6' 5", 2nd Lieutenant William Furse, was shot in No Man's Land when, apparently, he stopped to light his pipe . He lived in School Road, Moseley, Birmingham, was educated at Solihull Grammar School (now Solihull School) and was a clerk at Lloyd's Bank, Stirchley. He is buried in Bapaume Post Military Cemetery just outside Albert. He left a widow, Beatrice

20/ Northumberland Fusiliers (1st Tyneside Scottish):

Casualties: 584   Killed: Officers 15   ORs 305   Nos on Thiepval: 267

- At 7.30a.m. attacked up Mash Valley a wide part of NML with 23/ NFs

- The Battalion was almost completely wiped out within minutes of going 'over the top' due to enfilade machine-gun fire from Ovillers

- Lieutenant-Colonel Charles Sillery was killed and is buried in Bapaume Post Military Cemetery. Aged 54, he was a 'dug out' from the Indian Army

- 'The pipers had continued to play until either killed or wounded.' Two pipers died on the day - Ernest Boyce and John Fellows, both 21 and remembered on the Thiepval Memorial

- Every officer and sergeant were casualties

22/ Northumberland Fusiliers (3rd Tyneside Scottish):

Casualties: 537   Killed: Officers 7   ORs 155   Nos on Thiepval: 144

- Moved up with 21/ NFs. 150 men in German line at nightfall

- CO 53 year old Lieutenant-Colonel Arthur Elphinstone (Mentioned in Despatches) is commemorated on the Thiepval Memorial

23/ Northumberland Fusiliers (4th Tyneside Scottish):

Casualties: 630   Killed: Officers 10   ORs 230   Nos on Thiepval: 213

- 7.30 a.m. with 20/ NFs up Mash Valley. A few got to the German lines but fell back because of counter-attacks

- Lieutenant A.O. Terry: 'One feels numb about the affair. It is most incredible that we won't see half the battalion again and we won't be anything as a fighting unit for some months'

- Lieutenant-Colonel William Lyle (40) fell, last seen with a walking stick in hand and is buried in Bapaume Post Military Cemetery

103rd BRIGADE (Tyneside Irish):

➤ The 103rd Brigade was in support of the 101st and 102nd Brigades. Most of the Brigade when marching along the unprotected and open Tara and Usna Hills, was wiped out before reaching the British front line. 2,200 of the Brigade's 3,000 men were wounded or killed

➤ Brigadier-General N.J.G. Cameron was wounded

27/ Northumberland Fusiliers (4th Tyneside Irish):

Casualties 538   ☙ Killed: Officers 5   ORs 139   Nos on Thiepval: 122

- From Tara Usna Line in support of 15 and 16/ Royal Scots. Only 30% reached German front line, small parties getting as far as Contalmaison but had to retire

24/ Northumberland Fusiliers (1st Tyneside Irish):

Casualties: 626   ☙ Killed: Officers 5   ORs 148   Nos on Thiepval: 128

- Advanced from assembly positions in Tara Usna line in support of 101st Brigade. Into NML at 7.40 a.m. attacking up Sausage Valley. Some men battled to Lochnagar Crater and a handful nearly reached Contalmaison

- Lieutenant-Colonel Louis Meredith Howard died of wounds on 2nd July and is buried in Ovillers Military Cemetery

26/ Northumberland Fusiliers (3rd Tyneside Irish):

Casualties: 489   ☙ Killed: Officers 8   ORs 162   Nos on Thiepval: 147

- Marched from assembly trenches near Tara Redoubt about 1,000 yards behind the British front line. Only a few got as far as the German front line

- 'Men advanced as if on parade under heavy machine-gun and shell fire'

- Only two 2nd lieutenants answered at roll call, Fortune and Downend

- CSM Gavin Wild was hit by a machine-gun in the hip and the arm. A friend dragged him into a shell-hole but was shot through the head. Wild lay for 16 hours in the burning sun with Jackie his pal: 'You can imagine my feelings, lying there with one of my best chums who'd given his life to save me'

- CO Lieutenant-Colonel M. Richardson was wounded

25/ Northumberland Fusiliers (2nd Tyneside Irish):

Casualties: 487   ☙ Killed: Officers 3   ORs 140   Nos on Thiepval: 131

- Into NML at 7.45 a.m. Very few remained to attack towards the strongly held La Boisselle. A handful reached German front line

- Tom Easton: 'Casualties were dropping on all sides as we struggled forward and I remember getting to the German barbed wire, though how, I will never know and scrambling into the German front line. The enemy had withdrawn'

- 'Only a few scattered soldiers were left standing, the discipline and courage of all ranks being remarkable'

   - CO Lieutenant-Colonel J. Arden was wounded

8th DIVISION
Major-General Havelock Hudson

- ➢ Objectives: defences north of Bapaume Road-Mash Valley and Ovillers and to Pozières and Mouquet Farm

- ➢ 27th June- 'Units are warned that when the mine explodes, dug-outs which have not been strutted are unsafe'

- ➢ The wire was mostly uncut

- ➢ Eight minutes before Zero, the leading waves were 300 yards into No Man's Land but were instantly hit by machine-gun fire

- ➢ The Division's battalions attacked Ovillers up Mash Valley and were enfiladed from Ovillers on the left and La Boisselle to the right. No Man's Land was 750 yards wide. Only a handful of men reached German trenches

- ➢ Report of the action 1st July: 'At 7.22 a.m. our Stokes Mortars opened a hurricane bombardment on the enemy's front line and continued it until 7.30 a.m. A few minutes prior to the time fixed for the assault our Infantry left the front line trenches and crept forward under cover of our Artillery barrage. As soon as our troops emerged from the barrage, they were met by a heavy machine-gun and rifle fire from the front, probably from the enemy's reserve lines as well as from the flanks'

- ➢ The Germans of IR 180 suffered 300 casualties during the British bombardment. 'Again and again the extended lines of British infantry broke against the German defence like waves against a cliff only to be beaten back. It was an amazing spectacle of unexampled gallantry, courage and bulldog determination'

- ➢ Colonel H. W. Hill CMG, DSO of the RFA: 'An attack on a valley from which good observation for defending machine-guns is obtainable for a distance of about 500 yards should not be regarded as a reasonable Military operation but as a serious criminal offence'

- ➢ The Division suffered 5,121 casualties of whom 1,927 were killed

Pioneers: 22/ Durham Light Infantry (3rd County Pioneers):

- • Not involved on 1st July

23rd BRIGADE:

- ➢ No Man's Land in Mash Valley was at least 750 yards wide

2/ Middlesex (Duke of Cambridge):

Casualties: 540   Killed: Officers 11   ORs 260   Nos on Thiepval: 235

- Had to cross a huge length of NML. 'Before anyone reached the German line, the original wave formation ceased to exist'

- About 200 reached German front and second lines but by 9.15 a.m. were forced to retire into NML

- Casualties caused by machine-gun fire from both flanks at Ovillers and La Boisselle. Only one officer and 50 other ranks returned for roll call

- **Lieutenant-Colonel Edwin Sandys**'s prediction of huge casualties was correct. For his story see page 45

- Temporary Lieutenant-Colonel Gavin-Jones was in charge of the reserves but witnessed the Battalion's attack: 'At midday an order came from our Brigadier to collect every available man and make another attack at 12.30. It was certain death and we knew it. At 12.15 the Brigadier learnt of our condition and cancelled the order. I never expected to see the light of day next day'

2/ Devons:

Casualties: 431   Killed: Officers 10   ORs 167   Nos on Thiepval: 126

- At 7.22 a.m. crawled forward into NML. Advanced up Mash Valley in 'open order' (fire and movement) to within 100 yards of enemy trenches - the few that reached the German front line were soon killed

- Observation difficult at 6.30 due to mist. The enemy used a lot of lachrymatory shells

- Regimental historian C.T. Atkinson: 'Onlookers from British trenches at first thought leading waves were lying in NML awaiting another chance to go forward'

- 17 year old Cyril José: 'We went over with the feeling in us of the song "over the top, over the top and never come back again"'. He was hit by a sniper at 7.35 a.m. 'I couldn't get back to our own lines until next morning … I didn't eat anything, but lived on pulling off dead men's water bottles'. He overestimated the casualties when he wrote in a letter 'I heard that out of our battalion, 27 answered roll call after the battle'

- 'Heavy hostile machine-gun fire told its own tale'

2/ West Yorks (Prince of Wales's Own):

Casualties: 506   Killed: Officers 7   ORs 101   Nos on Thiepval: 100

- 21 officers and 702 other ranks breakfasted at 5.30 a.m. 'B' Coy followed 2/ Middlesex at 7.42 a.m. and 'A' at 7.52. Wire mostly uncut. Withdrew after heavy fighting around Ovillers. German barrage on front line and enfilade machine-gun fire from La Boisselle as soon as they advanced from their assembly trenches

184   - '280 casualties in traversing 600 yards'

- Sidney Rogerson in *Twelve Days* recalls the dead 'hanging thick on the German wire'

2/ Cameronians (Scottish Rifles):

Casualties: 71   Killed: Officers 1   ORs 5   Nos on Thiepval: 5

- Made way to front line trenches via communication trenches rather than across open ground. Orders received not to go into NML

- 'Terrible blast from enemy howitzers'

- Captain James Jack: 'The strain on the waiting men was very great, so I took to joking about the dirt scattered over my well-cut uniform, while dusting it off with a handkerchief … men driven out of the German trenches took what cover they could in shell-holes amid the long grass decked with sunlit scarlet poppies on our side of the enemy's wire entanglements. These men remained still, as the dead avoid drawing fire, till darkness should screen their escape …'

- A message had been received from the 2/ Middlesex requesting help. Jack wrote: 'Feeling that we must honourably try to reinforce him, I stepped back several paces to take a running jump on the parapet, sound my hunting horn and wave my men on, when a signaller thrust into my hand a message, timed 9.45, from the adjutant (the telephone lines being broken) saying that no further advance was to take place without fresh orders. What a relief to be rid of such a grim responsibility!'

25th BRIGADE:

2/ Royal Berkshire (Princess Charlotte of Wales's):

Casualties: 464   Killed: Officers 10   ORs 149   Nos on Thiepval: 102

- Attack on Ovillers: 'A small group succeeded in getting in the German front line but were bombed out'

- 'Our own wire was not sufficiently cut and parties were immediately sent by companies to clear it'

- Half of the battalion were casualties by 9.00 a.m.

- Captain Jack of the 2/ Cameronians about Germans at Ovillers: ' During the night of 25th and 26th June, the 2/ Royal Berks successfully executed a surprise raid on the Germans and found some of the enemy not accounted for in their trench, singing happily in dug-outs 30-40 feet below earth notwithstanding our bombardment'

- CO Lieutenant-Colonel Arthur Holdsworth (40) was wounded and died of his wounds on 7th July and is buried at Etaples Military Cemetery

2/ Lincolnshire:

Casualties: 471   Killed: Officers 8   ORs 128   Nos on Thiepval: 100   **185**

- In position at 3.30 a.m. Leading waves into NML at 7.25 a.m. 'Open order advancing in rushes and returning fire' attacking Ovillers. 200 yards of German trench taken by 7.50 a.m. after fierce fighting

- Lieutenant-Colonel Reginald Bastard DSO and Bar performed heroics crossing NML four times under fire. He and only one other officer were left and 'we had bullet holes in our clothing.' A Bar to his DSO was awarded for his efforts on 1st July

1/ Royal Irish Rifles:

Casualties: 403   Killed: Officers 4   ORs 58   Nos on Thiepval: 52

- 'A' and 'B' Companies never got beyond their own front line. 'C' may have got to German front line and 'D' fought through to German 2nd line - both forced to withdraw

- 'The German trenches had been completely bombed by our bombardment but excellent use had been made of the cellars in Ovillers ... the trenches were thickly manned'

- Lieutenant-Colonel Carroll Charles MacNamara (41) was treated for his wounds at No. 24 General Hospital, Etaples and was transferred to Fishmonger's Hall Hospital in London where he died of his wounds on 15th July. He is buried in the churchyard of Christ Church, Chorley Wood, Hertfordshire. Captain G.J. Gartlan, himself wounded, in a letter of condolence to the family wrote: 'His whole thought was "to go on, go on" ... The Colonel's whole anxiety was how the Battalion had got on'

- The remnants of the Battalion came under the command of Lieutenant-Colonel Reginald Bastard, 2/ Lincolns

2/ Rifle Brigade (The Prince Consort's Own):

Casualties: 135   Killed: Officers 0   ORs 26   Nos on Thiepval: 21

- In reserve. When in own trenches hit by intense shell-fire

70th BRIGADE:

➤ The Brigade suffered the most losses in the 8th Division - in the region of 2,000

➤ When Brigadier-General Herbert Gordon was pressed by Major-General Hudson to attack again he replied on the telephone: 'You seem to forget, Sir, that there is now no 70th Brigade'

8/ King's Own Yorkshire Light Infantry:

Killed: Officers 14   ORs 268   Nos on Thiepval: 202

- Attacking north of Ovillers. 'German wire was completely cut easily through the front line.' Cleared German front line and entered second and a few men reached the third line. Other attacks were led by NCOs (and officers of 2/ Lincs) as all officers were casualties. No notice had been taken of an 8.30 a.m. order to retire 'possibly originating from the enemy'. Withdrawal took place at about 6 p.m.

- 'No casualties occurred from our own artillery. The German wire offered no obstacle'

- The BWD report was put together from evidence taken from NCOs and other ranks only as 'no officer taking part in the operations being available'

- After withdrawal in the evening only the medical officer and 110 other ranks were left

8/ York and Lancaster:

Casualties: 600   ●   Killed: Officers 12   ORs 279   Nos on Thiepval: 189

- 'No smoke was liberated on our front as the wind was unfavourable'

- Into NML with 8/ KOYLI attacking north of Ovillers. 'First wave in perfect order'. Wire was 'in places still uncut and many Officers and men were shot down whilst cutting it'

- About 70 men reached the enemy trenches and some of those got to the third line but only one returned. The remainder were held up in the German front line, only three returning

- According to the Official History of 8th Division, 680 NCOs and other ranks and 23 officers attacked: of these, only 68 men returned, all officers were casualties. The casualty list was about the fifth highest on the day

- 2nd Lieutenants James and Leslie Ekin MC were brothers; 19 year old James is buried in Lonsdale Cemetery and 22 year old Leslie in Blighty Valley Cemetery. Both were originally from Sydney, Australia

- Lieutenant George Hicking was killed about 2 ½ miles from his brother Francis who died attacking Fricourt. George is remembered on the Thiepval Memorial and Francis is buried in Fricourt New Military Cemetery

- CO Lieutenant-Colonel B.L. Maddison attached from 2/ Yorkshire (Green Howards) was killed in No Man's Land on 1st July and is buried in Blighty Valley Cemetery

- 'It is reported that an enemy machine-gun was found in the front line with two Germans chained to it. Both were dead, one having been bayoneted and the other apparently killed with the butt of a rifle'

9/ York and Lancaster:

Casualties: 423   ●   Killed: Officers 6   ORs 158   Nos on Thiepval: 120

- After manoeuvres the Battalion would make merry in cafés in Doullens: 'In one at the corner of a street, Madame the propriétaire, had lost two sons at Verdun and poor woman, she never tired of talking about them.' *Sheffield Telegraph* 30th June 1917

- 'The attack was rehearsed time after time on a full size scale flagged course behind the lines. The troops, marching through growing crops, were instructed to advance as if on parade … No thought was apparently given to enemy resistance. All that was to have been dispersed by our artillery'

- Almost half of the men in NML were hit by machine-gun fire from Thiepval Spur

- The History of the Battalion: 'So ends the Golden Age'

- CO Lieutenant-Colonel Arthur Addison (49) is buried in Bécourt Military Cemetery, one of 11 Haileybury old boys to die on 1st July. Also killed was Major Harry Lewis (54) DCM and Mentioned in Despatches who is commemorated on the Thiepval Memorial

- Brothers Private Arthur (Blighty Valley Cemetery) and Private Charles Payling (Thiepval Memorial) were killed

- There is very little detail about the Battalion in their War Diary as the adjutant, Lieutenant McCallum was wounded. This is a good example of a shortage of information due to the casualties amongst the officers

- 'German machine-guns were stored on lifts by which they could be hoisted into their fire positions which consisted of concrete cupolas placed low in the ground with a slit through which the gun could traverse a raking fire from ankle to chest'

11/ Notts and Derby (Sherwood Foresters):

Casualties: 529   Killed: Officers 5   ORs 121   Nos on Thiepval: 93

- In reserve - 2 waves went across

- They were promised a hot meal when they reached the objective of Mouquet Farm. The advance died out before the German front line was reached

- CO Lieutenant-Colonel Harold Watson walked 'diagonally across the front collecting men as he went, he gave a fresh impetus to the advance by his personal example but the advance died out before the 1st line was reached, he and others being wounded'

X CORPS

Lieutenant-General Sir Thomas L.N. Morland

➢ The Corps constantly reported that it was difficult to ascertain the exact effect of guns on the wire … The houses in Thiepval and the Château (called Grand Sapin, owned by the Count of Breda) were destroyed by the bombardment but cellars, reinforced with concrete, housed machine-guns which survived and caused huge casualties with enfilade fire on 36th and 32nd Divisions. The British also found German defensive systems like the Schwaben Redoubt, the Wunderwerk and the Leipzig Redoubt difficult to attack and consolidate

IWM Art 001816

A house cellar at Pozières reinforced by the Germans with concrete - part of their second line of defence

➤ The situation was not helped by Morland's refusal to send reinforcements for his struggling Divisions

➤ The Corps' attack was almost a complete failure. Casualties were 9,000

➤ A brigadier-general admitted 'I am convinced that the German lines are full of men but they will be in their dug-outs'

➤ On 3rd July Lieutenant-General Morland congratulated his men for their 'dash and gallantry and he regrets the heavy and inevitable losses'

➤ In the Official History Brigadier-General James Edmonds stated that 'only bullet proof soldiers could have taken Thiepval that day'

32nd DIVISION
Major-General William. H. Rycroft

➤ Objectives: Leipzig Salient (known by the Germans as 'Granatloch', their word for shell-hole) and Thiepval Village

➤ The Division consisted of 9 New Army Battalions and 4 Regulars

➤ Rycroft exclaimed to three of his brigadier-generals: 'All we'll find in Thiepval when we go across, is the caretaker and his dog'

NPG 185084

189

➤ The wire was cut in places

➤ 'If gallantry could have availed, the Division would have succeeded on 1st July'

➤ The Division sustained nearly 4,000 casualties

➤ Progress was severely hindered by incorrect reports from the RFC that British helmets were seen in Thiepval. Later reports indicated that Thiepval had been taken prompting orders to stop shelling - a fatal mistake

Pioneers: 17/ Northumberland Fusiliers (Newcastle Railway Pals)

Killed: Officers 0   ORs 4   Nos on Thiepval: 0

- Main role was digging communication trenches

14th BRIGADE:

➤ The Brigade attacked Thiepval which, according to Charles Douie, 1/ Dorsets, 'had been fortified by the Germans with the utmost ingenuity and resource'

2/ Manchesters:

Killed: Officers 7   ORs 207   Nos on Thiepval: 146

- In the afternoon they helped to consolidate the Leipzig Salient and held it against counter-attack

- 'At about 9.30 a.m. it was found that our front line was full of Dorsets, Lancs Fusiliers and Borders who were under the impression they were in the enemy line'

- Prisoners were taken ... 'considerable enjoyment was given to our troops by Lieutenant Robertson who made the prisoners run across the open through their own Artillery Barrage, upon reaching our line these men were kept out of our dug-outs by the sharp end of a bayonet'

1/ Dorsets:

Casualties: 501   Killed: Officers 1   ORs 67   Nos on Thiepval: 35

- 8.45 a.m. in support of 11/ Border. They struggled to get out of Authuille Wood (also known as Blighty Wood) as they were hit by machine-gun fire from Nordwerk Redoubt. Some got into German front line where they remained until relieved at 2 a.m. on 2nd July

- 'Observation difficult early on due to a mist that drifted over from enemy line. Germans used lachrymatory shells which caused a great deal of inconvenience to anyone not wearing goggles ... Our bombs ran out ... we were unable to get in touch with anyone on our right or left ... the enemy's artillery bombarded us continually all afternoon and by 5 p.m. his fire became so intense and accurate that our position was almost untenable ...'

- 'It was during the dash across country from Authuille Wood to our front line trench that at least half our total casualties were sustained … the ground up to our front line trench was covered with our killed and wounded'

- Drum Major Kerr played the regimental march past on his flute in No Man's Land to encourage men forward. Later his arm was shattered by a bullet

- Charles Douie mourning the loss of many comrades: 'They sleep. Many of them, on the uplands of Picardy. They asked no reward, no sunlit fields of heaven … yet perhaps, as they sleep, they hear a voice across the ages "Well done".'

- Sergeant-Major Ernest Shephard in his diary entry for 2nd July pointed out that his Division was adversely affected by the 8th Division's failure to secure the Dorsets' right flank: 'If our General did know and yet decided that we should carry on, he is not fit for his job'

19/ Lancashire Fusiliers (3rd Salford Pals):

Casualties: 268   Killed: Officers 5   ORs 38   Nos on Thiepval: 27
- 'The smoke barrage on our right flank … considerably aided our advance'

- Followed 1/ Dorsets to Leipzig Redoubt but only two officers and 40 men were able to join the remnants of the Dorsets

- '… of the bomb carriers very few got across the fire-swept zone with their buckets. This was due to the fact that the men could not advance quick enough with the loads they had to carry and they, probably being more conspicuous, were singled out.' When the bomb supply was exhausted it was 'found necessary to make use of all the German bombs in the trench, some 700 or 800 being used'

15/ Highland Light Infantry (Glasgow Tramways):

Killed: Officers 0   ORs 8   Nos on Thiepval: 6

- Reserve Battalion for the Brigade, did not go over the top but sustained casualties by shell-fire and lachrymatory shells in Authuille Wood

- From the BWD report on the village of Thiepval: 'The Chateau facing West is an important building, the cellars of which are very large and are used by the Germans for lodging soldiers and are always full … Thiepval farm is used as a grenade store … It is estimated that there is accommodation for 1,500 underground'

97th BRIGADE:

17/ Highland Light Infantry (Glasgow Commercials):

Casualties: 469   Killed: Officers 12   ORs 168   Nos on Thiepval: 115

- Two companies crept into NML at 7.23 a.m. to within 30-40 yards of the enemy front line, then rushed the Leipzig Redoubt in 'open order' at 7.30 a.m. but their advance was stopped by fire from the Wunderwerk

- VC: **Sergeant James Turnbull** was awarded the VC for his role in the attack on the Leipzig Redoubt and its consolidation. For his story see page 48

- Two brothers were killed - Lance-Corporal James and Private John Rogerson (both Thiepval Memorial)

- Lieutenant-Colonel David Morton wrote to the Glasgow Chamber of Commerce's President, James Murray: 'Up until now I have made it a rule to write to the next of kin … but in the present circumstances it is beyond me to continue this practice. I have, therefore, no course open to me but to ask you to send this letter to the Glasgow papers …'

16/ Highland Light Infantry (Glasgow Boys' Brigade):

Casualties: 554　　Killed: Officers 7　ORs 241　Nos on Thiepval: 173

- On 30th June a 5.9 shell dropped into the encampment and burst between the goalposts during a football match. One man was killed and another wounded

- From the History of the 16/ Highland Light Infantry, a chapter entitled *The Shambles of the Somme*: 'The men were singing and whistling as if they were going to a football match instead of one of the most serious encounters in the world's history'… 30th June: 'This afternoon the Battalion chafed under the strain of waiting. All was ready; equipment packed, identity discs examined and iron rations inspected … The buff field cards had been pencilled and posted bearing that ironic message "I am well" …'

- Before 1st July it was, according to the Battalion History 'like living on the edge of a thunderstorm'

- 'For the past few days it has been quite impossible to maintain telephone communication with Brigade and we have to rely entirely on messengers'

- 7.30 a.m. platoons crept over the parapet and lay down in shell-holes. They were armed with Bangalore torpedoes to cut wire which was found to be imperfectly cut despite a midnight patrol having earlier reported that the German wire was well cut and it was anticipated that there would be no difficulty in getting through. Torpedo parties went out but none survived

- Colonel David Laidlaw: 'The Bosche artillery thundered; every foot of Wunderwerk spouted machine-gun bullets; the enemy parados was manned by bombers at intervals of two paces. Yet the 16th advanced in face of this withering fire. Every step cost dreadful casualties but it is conceivable that the battalion would have stubbornly pushed its way to the German trenches but for one factor - the stacked belts of barbed wire had been imperfectly cut … concealed and protected machine-guns bristled like spines on a hedgehog'

11/ Border (Lonsdales):

Casualties: 500　　Killed: Officers 9　ORs 173　Nos on Thiepval: 98

- 8.30 a.m. moved out from Authuille Wood to 'mop up' in the Leipzig Redoubt. Majority failed to get to the front line trenches of the Leipzig Salient

- Brothers Sergeant Samuel, 24, and Corporal Claude Bryan, 22, both fell and their names are to be found on the Thiepval Memorial

- 22 year old Frederick Francis: 'As we filed out the colonel, Colonel Machell patted me on the back and said "Best of luck son". Before the battle he said that if we met with stiff opposition, he would come and lead the men himself. We met with stiff opposition … so he came out. Bullet in the head. Finish'. 54 year old Percy Machell DSO is buried in Warloy-Baillon Communal Cemetery

2/ King's Own Yorkshire Light Infantry:

Casualties: 340   Killed: Officers 5   ORs 69   Nos on Thiepval: 57

- In support of 16 and 17/ Highland LI at 7.30 a.m.

- Supply of bombs ran short but all available men, including cooks and servants were organised into carrying parties

- Many casualties were suffered before reaching their own front line

96th BRIGADE:

➢ ' … in solid lines without gaps, in faultless order led by its officers carrying little flags and sticks - wave after wave was shot down by well-aimed fire … a wall of dead British was piled up on the front.'

16/ Northumberland Fusiliers (Newcastle Commercials):

Casualties: 378   Killed: Officers 7   ORs 124   Nos on Thiepval: 94

- The Battalion included miners, Newcastle United footballers and County rugby players. Prominent footballers who died included 26 year old England international Corporal Dan Dunglinson and Private Thomas Goodwill (22) the club's outside left. Sergeant Ralph Noble (25) was a rugby player who also died. All three are remembered on the Thiepval Memorial

- Failed to get to German front line

- CO Colonel William Ritson CMG: 'You will be able to get over the top with a walking stick, you will not need rifles'

- Lance-Corporal Stan Henderson: 'It was suicide, a massacre. You could hear the wounded shouting! Ritson with tears streaming cried out "My men! My men! My God, my men!" We had to restrain him from going over the top himself'

- Rugby or football? According to the *Official History*, a football was followed into battle at Zero Hour. A.H. Farrar-Hockley claims that the Battalion's attack was launched 'behind a rugby football, drop-kicked in a high arc from the assembly trench'

- The Battalion History claimed that the enemy stood on their parapet inviting the men to come forward then picked them off with accurate rifle fire

- 'Advanced in perfect formation - the dead being later found in straight lines as if "dressed" for parade'   193

- Arthur Rutherford: 'Haig and his generals should have been shot - the pride of the British race died that day and yet they continued with the massacre. We were told that after our barrage nothing would be left alive in the German lines'

15/ Lancashire Fusiliers (1st Salford Pals):

Casualties: 470   Killed: Officers 16   ORs 258   Nos on Thiepval: 206

- Assault on Thiepval. 'Certain officers, NCOs and men penetrated the line … it is presumed that they gave a good account of themselves'. Mopping up parties were overcome by German counter-attack

- 'It was obvious by 9 a.m. that further efforts were only a useless waste of life' - 75% were casualties

- An under-age messenger boy on 1st July survived the battle. The CO replied to a letter from his mother arguing that he thought he should not be discharged because he was physically fit and strong. As he was capable of the work he should stay at the Front especially in view of the fact he had come through on 1st July

16/ Lancashire Fusiliers (2nd Salford Pals):

Casualties: 231   Killed: Officers 1   ORs 22   Nos on Thiepval: 18

- In support of attack on Thiepval

- 'It is evident that the bombardment failed to dislodge the protected MGs in the Thiepval defences'

2/ Royal Inniskilling Fusiliers:

Killed: Officers 0   ORs 17   Nos on Thiepval: 11

- Held up in No Man's Land. One company to Thiepval at 8.55 a.m. Another attack failed at 1.00 p.m.

Cavan County Museum

36th (ULSTER) DIVISION
Major-General Sir Oliver S.W. Nugent

➤ Objective: From Thiepval Village to St. Pierre Divion including the Schwaben Redoubt

➤ The Ulster Division was made up mostly of Protestants but there was a significant body of Roman Catholics in the Battalions

➤ A raid on the night of 26th /27th June found the wire cut and the trenches 'were so knocked about as to be unrecognisable in places' but on 29th 'on the right bank of the Ancre river there were many gaps but the wire was not destroyed as on the left bank'

- 29th June: 'The wire cutting has been proceeding well everywhere. In this, the postponement (by two days) is rather more satisfactory than otherwise for us'

- At 3.0 a.m. the Ulster Division was shelled by the Germans. This must have rung alarm bells as the week long bombardment was supposed to have knocked out the enemy's guns

- 'The enemy's retaliation to our bombardment was again pretty severe'

- The Division benefited from a supply of French guns

- The Division assembled in Thiepval Wood where seven miles of assembly trenches were dug from March 1916. There were stores for 4,800 trench mortar rounds, 22,000 grenades and two million rounds of SAA

- Bugles were blown to sound the advance. 'The men ran and didn't walk'

- 'The troops began to leave their assembly trenches some half an hour before the time of the assault and by 7.30 a.m. the leading Battalions were lying in the open within 200 yards of the enemy's trench'

- The Division War Diary: '… the failure of the Divisions on either flank (i.e. the 29th on the left and the 31st on the right) to advance or to silence the machine guns which made communication with the ground captured almost impossible, did us very great ill-service. Our men gradually fell back as the day wore on from the ground gained'

- At 8.32 a.m. Major-General Nugent asked of Lieutenant-General Morland whether 107th Brigade should move through 109th Brigade. He was slow to reply that he wanted to delay their attack but by the time the message was received they had advanced

- The Schwaben Redoubt was recaptured by admiring Germans at 11 p.m. when 'The British corpses of 700 courageous members of the Ulster Division littered the Redoubt, every foot of which was soaked in blood'

- Some Bavarians in the Schwaben Redoubt escaped soon after being taken prisoner there but not before the Ulstermen had removed from them their watches, money and rings

- Major-General Nugent: 'The advance across the open to the German line was carried out with the steadiness of a parade movement under a fire both from front and flanks which could only have been faced by troops of the highest quality'

- An Ulster Division officer wrote that 'Major-General Nugent addressed us after the battle and said "Men you've done very well, but you might have done better". It was an unbelievable comment given the disaster that unfolded on 1st July which was not the fault of those who went into the attack …

- King George V: 'Throughout the long years of struggle … the men of Ulster have proved how nobly they fight and die'

> The Germans opposite recorded that 'many an Irish mother's son lay down to the eternal sleep from which there is no awakening … The dawn of a new day revealed to us, in the form of great piles of dead and wounded, some of the success of the violent work we had achieved in conjunction with our machine-guns'

> The Division suffered over 5,000 casualties

Pioneers: 16/ Royal Irish Rifles (2nd County Down)

Casualties: 20   Killed: Officers 0   ORs 2   Nos on Thiepval: 0

- An attempt to dig communication trench during attack was abandoned, thereafter they were employed bringing in wounded and carrying supplies. Helped to hold British front line

109th BRIGADE:

> The Brigade 'moved off as if on parade. Nothing finer in the way of an advance has ever been seen'

9/ Royal Inniskilling Fusiliers (County Tyrone):

Casualties: 535   Killed: Officers 10   ORs 211   Nos on Thiepval: 162

- The Battalion held a final practice on 22nd June. Lieutenant Godson noted that 'we were in high fettle looking forward to accomplishing something - may be even the end of the war'

- Crept into NML then advanced in line before Zero. At 7.30 a bugle sounded the assault which was 'carried out as if it was a parade movement'. The wire was well cut. At 8 a.m. front of Schwaben Redoubt taken. Some got to German 3rd line

- When advancing on the second line hit by machine-gun fire from deep unmopped-up dug-outs in Thiepval. Low on water and ammunition. In the evening pushed back to German front line. Difficulties getting supplies across NML

- VC: Temporary Captain Eric Bell (20), attached to a Trench Mortar Battery, was awarded the VC posthumously for his actions in the Schwaben Redoubt when he killed a German machine-gunner, on three occasions threw bombs at the enemy in their trenches and when out of bombs, he used his rifle to keep at bay counter-attackers. He was killed when organising troops who had lost their officers. He was one of four 36th Division VCs on the day. He is remembered on the Thiepval Memorial

- 2nd Lieutenant William Hewitt was killed, as was his brother Lieutenant Holt Hewitt of the Machine-Gun Corps. William's name is on the Thiepval Memorial and Holt is buried in Mill Road Cemetery

10/ Royal Inniskilling Fusiliers (County Derry):

196   Casualties: 418   Killed: Officers 5   ORs 124   Nos on Thiepval: 103

- 'At 7.15 a.m. the leading companies went through gaps in our wire each platoon deployed in extended lines with about three paces interval … crept cautiously up till the leading line was within 150 yards of the German 'A' line, where it lay down to await the signal for the assault.' At 7.30 a.m. the regimental bugle call was followed by the 'Advance'- company and platoon leaders blew their whistles … The spectacle of those lines of men moving forward, with rifles sloped and the morning sun glistening on their fixed bayonets, keeping their alignment and distance as well as if on a ceremonial parade, unfaltering, unwavering - this spectacle was not only impressive, it was extraordinary'

- 'Not a single man of our battalion had occasion, as far one can learn, to use his wire cutters, of which each company carried a supply'

- 'Hardly a man was seen to fall and the front line trenches of the enemy were reached with incredibly few casualties at first …' Some reached the third line. Counter-attacks meant 'a retirement became inevitable'

- Leading Companies were hit by British bombardment as they were ahead of schedule. BWD: 'terrible shelling and enfilade machine-gun fire from Thiepval … running out of supplies particularly water - six four gallon petrol tins were sent over'

- 2nd Lieutenant Spalding (25) was killed by one of the Rifle Regiments as he was coming out of a dug-out he had just bombed, mistaken for a German. His name is to be found on the Thiepval Memorial

- Prisoners were captured: 'They seemed for the most part dazed and bewildered by the fury of our bombardment' The first batch were so keen to reach the safety of the British front line that they outstepped their escort and 'meeting our reinforcing lines coming forward, were bayoneted by them in the heat of the moment'

11/ Royal Inniskilling Fusiliers (Donegal and Fermanagh):

Casualties: 589　　Killed: Officers 7　ORs 224　Nos on Thiepval: 158

- Followed 9/ Royal Inniskilling Fusiliers

- Reached Schwaben Redoubt where Germans 'quickly threw up their hands'

- Enfilade machine-gun fire from Thiepval. Confusion in the afternoon. Many German prisoners were mixed up with British troops

- Two pairs of brothers fell on 1st July. Privates Andrew and Ezekiel Smyth from Donegal, both named on the Thiepval Memorial and Privates Samuel (Connaught Cemetery) and William Watson (Thiepval Memorial)

14/ Royal Irish Rifles (Belfast Young Citizens):

Killed: Officers 5　ORs 83　Nos on Thiepval: 67

- In support of 10/ Royal Inniskilling Fusiliers '… moved off as if on parade', hit by 'a deadly crossfire'

- Some men reached the German third line

- VC **Rifleman William McFadzean** gave up his life to save his pals when he threw himself onto a box of grenades which was about to explode. He was the first VC of 1st July

- At 7.45 a.m.: 'Report from CSM Lowry of 'C' Coy that they had reached the Sunken Road known as the "Bloody Road" as the corpses were piled high here … at 6 p.m. I met a company of a territorial battalion. On enquiries being made I found they were my love list and much sought after reinforcements going the wrong way. The boy in command did not know in what direction he was to go, so I put him right'

108th BRIGADE:

➤ An operational order listed the equipment the men were to take with them into No Man's Land: waterproof sheet, wool waistcoat, a rifle, 170 rounds of ammunition, two Mills bombs, two sandbags, one iron ration, two smoke helmets and goggles. Those in leading waves were to be 'equipped as lightly as possible' which was not always the case

11/ Royal Irish Rifles (South Antrim):

Killed: Officers 2   ORs 140   Nos on Thiepval: 120

- Took 2nd line at 7.50 a.m. Casualties caused by own barrage during advance to 3rd line which was occupied at 8.46 a.m. but gradually had to withdraw to British lines by 11.45 p.m.

- Heavy shelling at 7.15 a.m. on assembly and front line trenches. Shortage of water in the afternoon. Later in the day troops were 'utterly exhausted'

- Captain Craig M.P. was taken prisoner, interned in Holland and repatriated on 4th October 1918

13/ Royal Irish Rifles (1/ County Down):

Casualties: 595   Killed: Officers 8   ORs 222   Nos on Thiepval: 177

- Into NML 15 minutes before Zero and 'laid down on the tape'

- Shortage of supplies of ammunition and bombs

- Riflemen James, John and Samuel Donaldson, all in 'B' Company, were killed and are remembered on the Thiepval Memorial. They are one of three sets of three brothers who died on 1st July

9/ Royal Irish Fusiliers (County Armagh, Monaghan and Cavan) (Princess Victoria's):

Casualties: 532   Killed: Officers 7   ORs 215   Nos on Thiepval: 151

- Many casualties before reaching gaps in own wire. Withdrew in the evening to Hamel

- 'Wire cutting was well carried out and effective lanes were cut'

- Lieutenant-Colonel Stewart Blacker: 'I am heartbroken … I am still dazed at the blow and the prospect in front of us all …'

- VC was awarded to Lieutenant Geoffey St. George Cather (25) for rescuing wounded soldiers from No Man's Land in the evening and next morning. When trying to help a wounded man, he was shot through the head. His name is on the Thiepval Memorial

- Three Hobbs brothers were killed, all named on the Thiepval Memorial, Privates Andrew and David and Sergeant Robert. A fourth, Herbert, was wounded on the same day

- Lieutenant Arthur Hollywood and his brother 2nd Lieutenant James of the 12/ Royal Irish Rifles are commemorated on the Thiepval Memorial

12/ Royal Irish Rifles (Central Antrim):

Killed: Officers 7   ORs 132   Nos on Thiepval: 106

- Based on the north side of the Ancre, they were manning trenches between the William and Mary Redans but 'B' Company were in support of 9/ Royal Irish Fusiliers

- Wire was uncut, men came across 'great rolls of wire with barbs as long as a man's thumb'

- VC: Private Robert Quigg (31), a batman, was awarded the VC for going into No Man's Land to look for his officer 20 year old Sir Edward (Harry) MacNaghten Bt. whom he failed to find but he managed to bring in seven wounded men under fire. After a seven hour search, he had to give up due to exhaustion. MacNaghten, the 6th Baronet, is commemorated on the Thiepval Memorial and his brother Arthur who became the 7th Baronet, was killed on 15th September 1916. When presenting Quigg with his VC in January 1917, it was believed that the King complimented him on being 'a brave man' to which Quigg replied 'You're a brave wee man yourself Mr. King.' The King then asked him if he was married and the reply was 'No Sir but after what has happened to me, I suppose I soon will be.' In fact, he never married and died in May 1955. He is buried in Bushmills, County Antrim. He was also awarded the French Croix de Guerre and the Order of St. George of Russia

- Two pairs of brothers from Ballymena are remembered on the Thiepval Memorial - Lieutenant Arthur and 2nd Lieutenant James Hollywood and Riflemen James and John McGowan

107th BRIGADE:

➤ It was a support Brigade for the 108th and 109th Brigades. By 10 a.m. leading lines were within 100 yards of the second line but ran into the British barrage which did not lift for 10 minutes. Heavy casualties were caused by 'friendly fire' corroborated by Felix Kircher of the German 26th Artillery: 'At 9 o'clock I was down in a dug-out (in Stuff Redoubt) when someone shouted down to me in an amazed voice - "The Tommies are here." I rushed up and there just outside were 10 or 20 English soldiers with flat steel helmets. We had no rifle, no revolver, no grenades … We were purely artillery observers. We would have to surrender but then, the English artillery began to fire at our trench but a great deal of the shells fell too short and hit the Englishmen and they began to fall back'

10/ Royal Irish Rifles (South Belfast):

Killed: Officers 7   ORs 101   Nos on Thiepval: 85

- Advanced at 8 a.m. 'in artillery formation'. Reached the Schwaben Redoubt

- CO Lieutenant-Colonel Herbert Bernard (50) was killed by a shell at 7.10 a.m. when leading his men to the front line trenches. He is buried in Martinsart British Cemetery

8/ Royal Irish Rifles (East Belfast):

Killed: Officers 3   ORs 4   Nos on Thiepval: 6

- Reached 2nd line at 9.40 a.m. and 3rd line at 10.10 and 4th line at 11 but position untenable. Men became mixed up with other units around the Schwaben Redoubt. They withdrew to Thiepval Wood during the night

- Casualties were low for 1st July but on 2nd July, 124 are recorded as having died, the highest number for that day

9/ Royal Irish Rifles (West Belfast):

Killed: Officers 3   ORs 95   Nos on Thiepval: 83

- **Lieutenant-Colonel Frank Crozier** was their controversial CO. For his story see page 52

- Assembled in Thiepval Wood. Heavy casualties while waiting and crossing NML at 8.05 a.m. Bugles blew the advance. Reached the Schwaben Redoubt - some men got as far as the 4th line

- Ran out of supplies especially of water and ammunition, so had to withdraw at 10.30 p.m.

- Corporal G.A. Lloyd: 'We were pinned down in the open just outside the German wire which was covering their 2nd line. It was just Hell; the British artillery were at us, the German artillery were at us and machine-gun fire as well'

- 'If it had not been for our barrage, we could have taken the Grandcourt Line'

- During afternoon counter-attacks, the Germans out threw the British bombers 'possibly owing to many of the men throwing their grenades instead of bowling them. At this juncture a catapult did good work and demonstrated the usefulness of this weapon'

15/ Royal Irish Rifles (North Belfast):

Killed: Officers 5   ORs 75   Nos on Thiepval: 64

- Followed 11th and 13th/ Royal Irish Rifles

- There had been a successful raid on evening of 26th and 27th June. Wire found to be well cut and the trenches so knocked about as to be unrecognisable in places

- At 7.45 a.m. reached front line, then the third line was captured and 4th line penetrated. Returned to their own line in the evening

49th (WEST RIDING) DIVISION
Major-General Edward M. Perceval

➤ They were in reserve to assist the 36th and 32nd Divisions in the capture of Thiepval

➤ There were about 600 casualties

Pioneers: 1/ 3 Monmouths:
- Not involved until the evening when they were positioned behind 36th Division

146th BRIGADE:

1/ 5 West Yorkshire (Prince of Wales's Own):

Casualties: 61　　Killed: Officers 0　ORs 10　Nos on Thiepval: 8

- Moved into Thiepval Wood 10 a.m. Small party assisted the occupation of the Schwaben Redoubt

1/ 6 West Yorkshire (Prince of Wales's Own):

Killed: Officers 1　ORs 31　Nos on Thiepval: 26

- From Thiepval Wood 9.00 a.m. Failed in attempt to reach Thiepval. 'No one advanced more than 100 yards'

- Private J. Wilson: 'We went forward in single file through a gap in what had once been a hedge; only one man could get through at a time. The Germans had a machine-gun trained on the gap. What I saw when I got to the other side shook me to pieces. There was a trench running parallel with the hedge which was full to the top with men who had gone before me. They were all dead or dying'

- CO Lieutenant-Colonel Henry Wade was wounded

1/ 7 West Yorkshire (Prince of Wales's Own) (Leeds Rifles):

Killed: Officers 0　ORs 11　Nos on Thiepval: 11

- To Thiepval Wood 9.00 a.m. 'C' and 'D' Coys sent to reinforce 36th Division in Schwaben but withdrew during the night

- VC: Corporal George Sanders (21) was south of the Schwaben Redoubt near Thiepval in support of the Ulster Division when he and a party of 30 men found themselves isolated. He organised the defence of their position ordering men to hold it at all costs. Under his leadership they repelled German counter-attacks, rescued prisoners taken by the Germans, and after 36 hours without food and water, the party was relieved on the morning of the 3rd of July. Sanders brought his 'party' now 19 strong back to the British line. He was promoted later to captain and during the German Spring offensives of 1918 he was taken prisoner. He died in April 1950 and was cremated at Cottingley Crematorium, Leeds

1/ 8 West Yorks (Prince of Wales's Own) (Leeds Rifles):

Killed: Officers 0   ORs 6   Nos on Thiepval: 6

- In support of 36th (Ulster) Division. No advance made and many casualties sustained

148th BRIGADE:

1/ 5 York and Lancaster:

Killed: Officer 1   ORs 12   Nos on Thiepval: 13

- Moved in reserve into Thiepval Wood. 'A' and 'B' Coys moved to north of the Ancre to hold the British front line. 'C' and 'D' Coy were south of the Ancre - some got to the German front line and attempted to reach the 3rd line. At midnight the order was given to withdraw

IWM Art 001811

VIII CORPS

Lieutenant-General Sir Aylmer G. Hunter-Weston

➢ Objectives: 1st and 2nd trench systems and the fortified village of Beaumont Hamel, Redan Ridge and Serre

➢ Bulletin from VIII Corps at noon on 30th June: 'Aerial reconnaissance yesterday reports general wrecking and obliteration of enemy defences throughout … The enemy reply was feeble and ineffective … Prisoners who have surrendered or been captured state that our bombardment kept them without food or water or sleep for 3 days and nights and that they longed for the attack to be launched in order that they might give themselves up. All accounts go to show the great effect the long bombardment had on the enemy morale'

- From OPERATIONAL ORDERS:

  - 'Disposal of Bodies: If the dead are buried in large pits, the bodies should be laid about one foot apart, the intervening space being filled with earth. There should also be one foot of earth between layers. The earth acts as an absorbent and prevents liquid matter percolating through the ground and contaminating sources of water supply'

  - Cheering: 'Cheering should be avoided as it only warns the enemy we are coming'

- It was hoped the 16 Pals Battalions of VIII Corps (including Pioneers and Newfoundlanders) would in the words of Lyn Macdonald 'oil the hinge that would open the door to Bapaume'

- German observation over the whole of the VIII Corps line was formidable

- The Corps Commander Lieutenant-General Hunter-Weston was 'extremely optimistic telling everyone that the wire had been blown away although we could see it standing strong and well, that there would be no German trenches and all we had to do was walk into Serre'

- The Germans opposite:

29th Division:	RIR 119
4th Division:	RIR 121
31st Division	IR 169

- Hunter-Weston's decision to lift the barrage after the Hawthorn Ridge mine had exploded at 7.20 a.m. was a serious error as it gave the Germans ample time to take up their firing positions without the need to rush. The CO of the German RIR 119 recorded that 'the entire garrison was able to occupy battle positions then open fire'

- Bulletin from Hunter-Weston noon 3rd July: 'It is abundantly clear that the VIII Corps contributed very materially to the success of the offensive as a whole … large numbers of prisoners taken together with the ground won, and the heavy casualties inflicted on the enemy points to a very substantial allied success'

- General Haig, however, was unimpressed with VIII Corps' performance: 'I am inclined to believe from further reports that very few of VIII Corps left their trenches.' A harsh assessment. The Corps suffered from a failure of the artillery to knock out enemy barbed wire, dug-outs, machine-guns and artillery

- According to the regular soldier Arthur Cook of the 1/ Somerset Light Infantry, Hunter-Weston was 'one of the finest soldiers and gentlemen you could wish to meet.' On the other hand, Charles Carrington of the 1/5 Royal Warwicks, 19 years of age in 1916, later described 'Hunter Bunter' as a 'figure of fun'

- By end of 1st July VIII Corps had nothing to show for its massive losses (13,000 failed to answer at roll call, the worst Corps casualties) except for presence in and near the Quadrilateral (Heidenkopf) which was abandoned the following morning **203**

NPG 121062

29th DIVISION 'The Incomparable'
Major-General Henry de Beauvoir de Lisle

➤ Objective: Beaumont Hamel

➤ The wire was mostly uncut

➤ Consisting mostly of regulars, apart from the 16/ Middlesex (Public Schools) and 1/ Newfoundland, the Division arrived from Gallipoli where they had been commanded by Hunter-Weston. They formed part of VIII Corps to the north of the river Ancre opposite Beaumont Hamel

➤ 'Armageddon started today and we are right in the thick of it'- Captain Cuthbert Lawson, observation officer

➤ Three Russian saps were mined under No Man's Land, one as a communication trench to the Sunken Lane and the others to within 30 yards of the German front trench. One was opened up for use by Stokes mortars

➤ The assault was notable for three major blunders:

• The Division's battalions were severely disadvantaged by the decision to explode the mine at Hawthorn Ridge eight minutes before zero which alerted the Germans to the impending assault. Machine-guns were in position and caused mayhem. RIR 119: 'This explosion was a signal for the infantry attack and everyone got ready and stood on the lower steps of the dug-outs rifles in hand, waiting for the bombardment to lift. In a few minutes the shelling ceased and we rushed up the steps and out into the crater positions. Ahead of us wave after wave of British troops were crawling out of their trenches and were coming forward towards us at a walk, their bayonets glistening in the sun.' Geoffrey Malins filmed the mine exploding and wrote that 'The ground where I stood gave a mighty convulsion. It rocked and swayed. I gripped hold of my tripod to steady myself … the earth rose like a gigantic sponge … The sight was stupefying … How in the world anything could live in such a maelstrom of explosive it is difficult to conceive.' It caused limited damage to the Germans

• The supporting barrage was lifted so as not to hit the attacking battalions

• De Lisle ordered two reserve battalions, the 1/ Essex and the 1/ Newfoundlanders forward as a result of erroneous reports received that the assault had been successful. White flares sent up by the Germans were mistaken for similar British flares which signified success. 1/ Essex were delayed by general confusion in their trenches and machine-gun fire to their right so the 1/ Newfoundlanders left assembly trenches alone at 9.05 and without artillery support were doomed. Their casualties were catastrophic

➤ Soldiers wore a triangle cut from a biscuit tin, sown onto their haversacks to aid tracking their movements from the air. The sun shining on the metal, however, increased the numbers of casualties

> De Lisle memorably wrote to the Prime Minister of Newfoundland that 'it was a magnificent display of trained and disciplined valour and its assault only failed of success because dead men can advance no further.' The Division's losses were 5,240 and not a yard was gained

> For de Lisle's Report on Operations see page 132

Pioneers: 1/ 2 Monmouths:

Killed: Officers 0   ORs 28   Nos on Thiepval: 19

- From the History of the Battalion: 'Only 200 men could be issued with helmets. The remainder (wearing their soft caps) were instructed to replace these with helmets taken from the dead as soon as possible'

87th BRIGADE:

> By 8.00 a.m. the Brigade was at a standstill

1/ Royal Inniskilling Fusiliers:

Casualties: 549   Killed: Officers 5   ORs 227 Nos on Thiepval: 139

- At 7.30 a.m. advanced south of Y Ravine towards Beaumont Hamel 'in admirable order'

- '… soon cut down by machine-gun fire from front and both flanks'. No reinforcements could be sent

- Regimental History: 'In that field of fire, nothing could live'

- General Staff War Diary: 'Rumour that the Royal Inniskilling Fusiliers had completely disappeared and no news has been heard of them'

- 4th Army Report on Operations: 'Some of the Royal Inniskilling Fusiliers on the right were seen to march up to the enemy's first line, as if on parade, place their trench bridges and cross the trench … the bulk of the battalion was held up on the line of the German wire'

- CO Lieutenant-Colonel Robert C. Pierce was killed and is buried in Ancre British Cemetery

The Hawthorn Ridge Mine explosion at 7.20 a.m. as filmed by Geoffrey Malins

Northumberland Fusiliers incl. Tyneside Irish
7, 12, 13, 14, 16, 17, 18
24, 25, 26 and 27

Northumberland Fusiliers - Tyneside Scottish
20th, 21st, 22nd and 23rd

Notts and Derby
1/ 5th, 1/6th, 1/ 7th,
1/8th and 11th

Queen's
2nd and 7th

Royal Berks
2nd and 6th

Royal Dublin Fusiliers
1st and 2nd

Royal Fusiliers
2nd and 11th

Royal Irish Fusiliers
1st and 9th

Royal Irish Regiment
2nd

Royal Irish Rifles
1st, 8th, 9th, 10th, 11th,
12th, 13th, 14th
15th and 16th

Royal Inniskilling Fusiliers
1st, 2nd, 9th, 10th
and 11th

Royal Scots Fusiliers
2nd

Royal Scots
15th and 16th

Royal Warwicks
1st, 2nd, 1/ 5th, 1/ 6th,
1/ 7th and 1/ 8th

Royal Welch Fusiliers
1st

Royal West Kents
7th

2/ South Wales Borderers:

Casualties: 368    Killed: Officers 7 ORs 124   Nos on Thiepval: 74

- Started to try to get through their own wire at 7.20 a.m. Objective Y Ravine (an ancient dry river bed)

- 'German wire appeared fairly strong'

- Most did not get much further than their own wire. The Battalion was obliterated by 7.35 a.m.

- One of few units to attack downhill on the day because the Germans were making good use of Y Ravine for dug-outs

- 17 Lance-Corporals were killed

- Y Ravine: 'Enemy fired heavy shrapnel over the wounded and men lying out in the open'

e Germans were making good use of Y Ravine for dug-outs

1/ King's Own Scottish Borderers:

Casualties: 552   Killed: Officers 10 ORs 122   Nos on Thiepval: 89

- Followed Royal Inniskilling Fusiliers at 7.40 a.m. in attack on Beaumont Hamel. 'Did not succeed in even reaching the few Fusiliers who were lying out in No Man's Land'

- Private F. H. Cameron: 'I cursed the generals for their useless slaughter, they seemed to have no idea what was going on'

- In one company there were 202 casualties out of 219

1/ Border:

Casualties 554   Killed: Officers 9   ORs 193   Nos on Thiepval: 121

- Followed South Wales Borderers towards Y Ravine crossing British front line over wooden bridges - 'Advanced at a slow walk'

- Raiding party had found a thick belt of wire uncut so their Bangalore torpedoes had little effect

- Misled by the Germans firing white flares which were to have been the British signal that the first objective had been reached. The Brigadier ordered them to proceed … Attack ceased at 8 a.m.

- Machine-gun fire wiped out most of the men 'in our own wire'

- 'At 23.00 one officer and 20 men were digging a grave at Knightsbridge'

- CO Lieutenant-Colonel Archibald Ellis was wounded

86th BRIGADE:

➤ None in the Brigade reached German front line apart from Royal Fusiliers who reached the Hawthorn Ridge mine crater

➤ Raids were carried out on the night of 27/ 28th June by 2nd Royal Fusiliers: 'Machine-guns very active … further row of wire had not been touched'; 16/ Middlesex: 'Wire was not well cut and a large body of men would have great difficulty in getting through'; 1/ Lancs Fusiliers : 'Wire was insufficiently cut' and 1/ Border: 'A thick belt of wire was uncut.' According to the records 'Copies were sent to VIII Corps' which, it would appear, ignored them thus helping to explain the failure of the Divisions in VIII Corps

➤ General Staff to 86th Brigade: 'Owing to the heavy rain rendering observation difficult, there appears to be little likelihood of the wire on the enemy's front line being properly cut. Complete cutting by means of Bangalore Torpedoes and parties with wire cutters'

2/ Royal Fusiliers (City of London Regiment):

Casualties: 571   Killed: Officers 6   ORs 161   Nos on Thiepval: 88

- 7.20 a.m. 'rushed forward to occupy the mine crater' (Hawthorn Ridge) but Germans were on far lip

- 'Very few of our men reached as far as the enemy barbed wire'

- CO Lieutenant-Colonel Allen Johnson was half buried in a trench by a British shell and had to be evacuated

1/ Lancashire Fusiliers:

Casualties: 472   Killed: Officers 7   ORs 148   Nos on Thiepval: 103

- 'At 7 a.m. the enemy began to shell the Sunken Road … they had properly spotted the communication trench leading from the end of the tunnel into the road'

- 'B' and 'D' Companies occupied the Sunken Road, which was parallel to the front lines in No Man's Land, in the early hours by going up a tunnel. Ten minutes after the Hawthorn mine exploded, they dashed forward in extended order into NML where they were cut down by machine-gun fire. No men reached the German front line

- Corporal George Ashurst wrote: 'During the day time we played cards in the dug-out, getting quite used to the awful din. It was while having a game of cards one day that we were requested to go out into the trench and be photographed, presumably just fixing bayonets ready to go over the top. It was only a few minutes of a job and we soon obliged, especially as the photographer or war correspondent, or whatever he was, promised us a tot of rum and a packet of cigarettes for our trouble. Anyhow it certainly was the last photo a lot of those gallant lads ever had taken'

- The Battalion was filmed by Malins on the day at 6 a.m. then the explosion of the Hawthorn Ridge mine. A still from the film is of the Fusiliers fixing

Before 1st July ' ...it certainly was the last photo a lot of those gallant lads ever had taken'. Corporal and men in King Street, a communication trench not far from the Sunken Road, with 1/Lancashire Fusiliers 'wearing fighting order' IWM Q 000744

Note the amount of equipment being carried by the Lancashire Fusiliers and the boxes of grenades. The soldiers have tin triangles on their back packs for the purpose of aerial observation

Post attack roll call for 1/ Lancashire Fusiliers IWM Q 000734

bayonets in King Street Trench, the photo probably mentioned by Ashurst taken in late June … later Ashurst 'breathlessly reached the sunken road, practically leaping the last yard or two and almost diving into its shelter. Picking myself up and looking around, my God, what a sight! The whole of the road was strewn with dead and dying men. Some were talking deliriously, others calling for help and asking for water'

- 'The battalion fought nobly but had no chance of success against the enemy machine-gun fire.' However, when some men panicked and tried to retreat into the tunnel, they were brought to order by the threat of their CO Lieutenant-Colonel Meredith Magniac's revolver (he was killed in action in April 1917)

- Official History: 'The Lancashire men were mown down directly they showed above the dip in which the (sunken) lane lies'

- 'Germans sniped at and killed a good many of our wounded whenever they moved'

- Brigadier-General Weir de Lancey Williams: 'I do not think that any troops could have taken the enemy line on that morning.' It had taken him 1 hour and 20 minutes to take in the message from Magniac that machine-gun fire made any further advances out of the question. At 1.05 p.m. Williams cancelled the order … it was too late

16/ Middlesex (Public Schools) (Duke of Cambridge's Own):

Casualties: 522 Killed: Officers 11 ORs 150 Nos on Thiepval: 88

A Staff Sergeant and 16/ Middlesex and a group of 1/ East Lancs, behind their lines before 1st July- note the youthful faces in the foreground IWM Q 000796

- Special orders: 'Our own wounded must be left alone by our men. On no account are men to fall out to attend to them … No looting is allowed. This is a court martial offence for which the punishment is "to be shot"'

Screw picket and barbed wire still in use on the Somme today   *J Kerr*

- A raid on 28th June reported that 'the wire was damaged but there were no clear passages through it.' They were seen by 1/ Lancs Fusiliers at 9.45 a.m. retiring

- 2nd Lieutenant Eric Heaton, studying medicine at the outbreak of war, in a letter to his parents told them that he and his colleagues had read in an English newspaper that 'the guns can be heard in England. I don't doubt it!'

- The Battalion's assault and retirement were filmed by Geoffrey Malins

1/ Royal Dublin Fusiliers:

Casualties: 305   Killed: Officers 3
ORs 55   Nos on Thiepval: 29

- 9.00 a.m. left assembly trenches and followed 2/ Royal Fusiliers. One company attacked in diamond formation

- 'Enemy's wire was very difficult to get through'   … 'A guide led them to a gap cut the previous night but they found there was a further row of wire that had not been touched'

- 'Our own barbed wire was cut at intervals of about 40 yards and by this time the Germans had machine-guns trained on these gaps, the result being that our casualties were very heavy and only a few of our men got through our wire … still fewer of these succeeded in advancing more than 50 or 60 yards before being shot down. Attack abandoned at noon'

88th BRIGADE:

➢ The Brigade was in reserve but sent into action due to the failure of the 87th Brigade to make any headway.

➢ 'Less than half an hour after it began, the Battle of Beaumont Hamel was over.' Huge casualties for the Newfoundlanders. The regulars of 1/ Essex were more experienced and used a communication trench to get to the front line trenches whereas the Newfoundlanders crossed open ground in view of the German machine-gunners.

1/ Essex:

Casualties: 227   🖤   Killed: Officers 2   ORs 33   Nos on Thiepval: 12

- Moved forward to front line at 9.00 a.m. following 1/ King's Own Scottish Borderers- went into attack at 11 a.m. Wire was mostly intact. They did not get much further than their own wire - one platoon got halfway across NML

- Delayed by bodies dead and dying in front trenches and difficulties getting through their own uncut wire

- 'A trying day on the Somme'

1/ Newfoundlanders:

Casualties: 698   🖤   Killed: Officers 12   ORs 221
Nos on Newfoundland Memorial: 134

- The Battalion was the only Empire unit to take part in the 1st July offensive

- 8.45 a.m. moved forward to front line having to cross 250 yards in the open from St. John's Road. At 9.15 a.m. they attacked after 1/ Border

- Problem with four belts of their own barbed wire as there were not enough gaps to go through. They were, therefore sitting ducks, caught in a death trap where, as Colonel Hadow put it, 'they were mown down in heaps'

- A few are believed to have got to the German front line. At 9.45 a.m. CO Colonel Arthur Hadow reported that the attack had failed

- The Battalion sustained the second highest number of casualties on the day

- **Private 'Jim' Stacey** was a runner. For his story see page 58

- The *Evening Telegram* in Newfoundland announced on 6th July that the British casualties had so far been 'comparatively light'

- Four members of the Ayre family died, including two brothers, Captains Eric, 1/ Newfoundlanders (Ancre British Cemetery) and Bernard, 8/ Norfolks (Carnoy Military Cemetery)

- The War Diary of the German RIR 119 recorded that 'the British are lying in front of the first trench and are being shot to pieces … a battalion is gathering there to launch an attack. Sector Order: Destroy them with machine-gun fire'

- In one gap of their own wire, 66 dead Newfoundlanders were found

- 'The sergeant stood there with notebook resting on the end of his rifle, repeatedly putting his pencil through names that were missing'

4/ Worcestershire:

Casualties: 100   🖤   Officers 0   ORs 6   Nos on Thiepval: 5

- In reserve, they moved up from Auchonvillers to attack at 11.30 a.m. Fortunately for them their attack was cancelled, nevertheless they sustained 100 casualties on the way

4th DIVISION
Major-General Hon. William Lambton

➢ Objectives: Serre and the Redan ridge

➢ The Division used various strategies before and at Zero. Some men went into No Man's Land before Zero pushing forward at good pace, some used complicated formations with leading groups of skirmishers and snipers followed by machine-gunners

➢ Wire well cut but dug-outs were unaffected

➢ 'Cat and Rat' tunnels were opened up at 11 p.m. on 30th June with Lewis guns in each. Both were quickly put out of action after Zero

➢ It was hoped the Division's momentum would carry along the 31st Division of Pals Battalions

➢ At 7.42 a.m. it was reported to 4th Division HQ that the entire German front line was in British hands

➢ There was general disarray by lunchtime and there were not enough men to carry out 'mopping up' operations

➢ The only success was the Quadrilateral (Heidenkopf) which, however, was re-taken on 2nd July, described by Sergeant Arthur Cook of 1/ Somerset Light Infantry as 'about the size of Piccadilly Circus'

➢ Four mines were detonated by the Germans in front of the Heidenkopf, intended as a trap but the British had decided to attack its flanks possibly alerted to the danger by one mine which had exploded too early, so overall the effects were limited. 150 men of the German RIR 121 were killed. Their Battalion's History records that the captured prisoners were well equipped and when in the safety of a dug-out started to shave!

➢ The Division was not helped by the failure of the 31st and 29th Divisions on either flank. From 11 a.m. communications from the front were uncertain and information was vague. Exact information about the location of leading battalions was unknown as the signal for 'stopped by uncut wire', one white flare, and that for 'objective gained' three white flares, were too similar to be intelligible. Instructions for leading battalions of 10th and 12th Brigades to wait, came too late

➢ Heavy casualties amongst carriers prevented an adequate supply of bombs or mortars being sent forward

➢ By the end of 2nd July not a man in the Division occupied even a yard of German defences

➢ 'At no time did Divisional HQ have a clue what was going on'- *The Somme* by Robin Prior and Trevor Wilson

- Lieutenant-General Hunter-Weston: 'Well done my comrades of the 4th Division. Your discipline and determination was (sic) magnificent and it was bad luck alone that has temporarily robbed you of success'

- The Division sustained over 5,700 casualties

Pioneers: 21/ West Yorkshire (Prince of Wales's Own) (Wool Textile Pioneers):
Killed: Officers 0   ORs 2   Nos on Thiepval: 1

11th BRIGADE:

- The Brigade was the first to attack with the 10th and 12th to follow through .

- Brigade Diary written by Captain Prideaux MC: 'The result of the whole operation was absolutely nil as we are now in our original front line.'

Redan Ridge Cemetery No. 2 - 1/ East Lancs attacked from the left across No Man's Land which would have looked rather different on 1st July

- 11th Brigade's CO, Brigadier-General Charles 'Bertie' Prowse was the most senior British officer killed on 1st July. He said of the attached Birmingham Pals Battalions, 1/6 and 1/8 Royal Warwicks: 'I did not before think much of the Territorials, but by God they can fight.'

1/ East Lancashire:
Casualties: 491   Killed: Officers 10
ORs 164   Nos on Thiepval: 137

- At 7.26 a.m. 'crept into No Man's Land then advanced in line' in front of 1/ Hants. 'Faced uncut wire'. A few reached the German wire at Redan Ridge and were captured by Germans coming out of their dug-outs. Some held the line of shell-holes in front of the wire until told to retire

- CO Lieutenant-Colonel James.E. Green DSO was wounded in the shoulder

1/ Rifle Brigade:
Casualties: 559   Killed: Officers 12   ORs 153   Nos on Thiepval: 104

- Into NML at 7.29 a.m. followed by 1/ Somerset Light Infantry. Found the wire cut. Few reached the German front line as driven back by counter-attack at the Quadrilateral. Shortage of bombs and a Lewis gun out of action

- Only one man in a platoon was present at roll call

- Among the dead were three buglers, Alfred Atherall and Edward Briggs are remembered on the Thiepval Memorial and Thomas Girling is buried in Serre Road Cemetery No. 2

- 2nd Lieutenant Glover: 'The whole day was hopeless, both flanks in the air, continuous bombardment from the Germans and our guns doing nothing … it was the cruellest slaughter'

- CO Lieutenant-Colonel Donald Wood was killed and is listed on the Thiepval Memorial

1/ Hampshire:

Casualties: 585　　⬛　Killed: Officers 11　ORs 216　Nos on Thiepval: 125

- Followed 1/ East Lancs at 7.40 a.m. onto the Redan Ridge. Hardly a man made it to the German front line. Heavy machine-gun fire from all directions

- 'Our casualties in officers amounted to 100% and was heavy in other ranks.' Among those killed was the CO, 45 year old the Hon. Lawrence C.W. Palk, who 'went calmly forward in front of his men carrying only his stick.' The Regiment's Journal of 1921 included an officer's praise of Palk: 'He was a great character. He used to read Gibbon to his junior officers and spoke French and German fluently. The first time I met him he said, 'There are three things I will never have said to me: "it always 'as been done, Sir"; "never has been done, Sir, and "I thought." It is your business to know and act'. He was often a thorn in the side of the Division and the Senior Staff officers disliked him. He was utterly outspoken and feared nobody. He was a magnificent regimental officer, fresh and amusing, and was revered by the men … the men would have followed him anywhere.' A young officer with the 1/ Hants, E.D. Shearn, remembered Palk addressing his officers 'telling us about this barrage, informed us of the concern he had expressed to High Command lest the barrage should come down on us when we went forward. His exact words were "I told them that there is all the difference in the world between scratching your arse and tearing it" … his epigram to High Command appeared to give him a great amount of pleasure.' Palk is reputed to have quoted from the Bairnsfather cartoon when dying in a shell-hole: 'If you knows of a better 'ole, go to it.' He is buried in Sucrerie Military Cemetery

- Shearn luckily missed death: 'As soon as I got out of the assembly trench I discovered that the story that there would be nothing in the German lines was a myth. We went into literally a hail of machine-gun fire. I got hit in my prismatic compass which I carried on the left front of my belt. I debated briefly whether I needed medical attention but decided that as I felt so unaffected by the bullet wound I had better carry on with the war … I noted with a slight feeling of amusement that Donald Day on my left had his head down as though it were raining…it certainly was, so far as machine-gun fire was concerned.' Shearn was wounded and remembered the regimental padre coming to see him and assuring him that anyone dying that day would go straight to heaven. He concluded that the doctor and padre had written him off. When feeling better he asked the doctor to tell the padre that 'I think I will see Piccadilly before I see heaven'

- The 1921 Regimental History's appraisal of the Hawthorn Ridge Mine: 'This gave away completely the one thing the Germans did not know, the exact time of our attack ...'

1/ Somerset Light Infantry:

Casualties: 498　● Killed: Officers 8　ORs 153　Nos on Thiepval: 103

- State of wire: Report of raid on 28th June by 2nd Lieutenant Winstanley: 'it is completely cut' but on 29th June just before 1.00 a.m. it was reported a raid faced 'great difficulty in getting through the enemy wire'; some got to the Quadrilateral but pushed back by counter-attack and devastating machine-gun fire from there

- On 29th June 2nd Lieutenant Treasure took a fatigue party with 39 buckets to bale out trenches

- At 6 a.m. trench ladders and bridges were put in place, at 7.25 front waves of 'B' and 'C' Companies crawled out following 1/ Rifle Brigade. 'Battalion advanced in magnificent style... at a slow trot'

- **Sergeant Arthur Cook** on the Battalion's assault on Redan Ridge: 'What a sight to watch - advancing in perfect skirmishing order... It was bombs we wanted'. For his story see page 65

- Many were shot in the back due to poor 'mopping up'

- As only 2 officers remained standing, CSM Chappell had to take charge in the Quadrilateral

- 46 year old Lieutenant-Colonel John Thicknesse was killed 'before our trenches were passed'. He is buried in Sucrerie Military Cemetery

- In a last order to the 'Stonewallers Brigade' from Lieutenant-General Hunter-Weston: 'The old Stonewallers have always known how to stand heavy losses and to stick it out ...'

- 'Sergt. Imber and Private Hodges did excellent work in signalling from German trenches for grenades'

1/ 8 Royal Warwickshire: attached from the 143rd Brigade of the 48th (South Midland) Division:

Casualties: 589　● Killed: Officers 8　ORs 207　Nos on Thiepval: 171

- 'Everyone had a good breakfast'

- '7.00 am Very intense artillery on both sides ... 7.25 Enemy machine-guns opened up all along the line'

- Reached German support trench and third line, deeper into German lines than any other unit in VIII Corps but struggled due to shortage of bombs

- 21 out of the 23 officers who went into NML were casualties

- Private Charles Barff was one of the 16 year olds to fight on the day and survive. He served under the name of Charles Dickens possibly because of his German sounding name or because he was under-age when he enlisted

Royal Warwicks at rest - a group of officers with walking sticks are to the right   *Sir Douglas Haig's Great Push*

- 'We did well but none of the support battalions could get to us … No bomb supply'

- An error by German engineers resulted in a mine being blown before the British reached it, one German machine-gun jammed but one at Serre caused huge problems due to the failure of 31st Division

- Private E.C. Stanley: 'Men were falling right and left of me, screaming above the noise of the shell fire and machine-guns we had been assured would have been silenced by our barrage. No man in his right mind would have done what we were doing'

- CO Lieutenant-Colonel Edgar Innes CMG was killed and is commemorated on the Thiepval Memorial

- Colonel Walter Ludlow in a memorial booklet to his 22 year old son Captain Stratford Ludlow, wrote about his trip to the battlefield after the War to see where his son fell: 'I sat on the edge of a shell-hole opposite the German position in No Man's Land and I wondered how it was possible that any troops in the world could attack such a position in broad daylight on a lovely July morning.' Stratford is buried in Serre Road Cemetery No. 2

- Birmingham Pal Corporal Arthur (Archie) Plant of Coldbath Road, King's Heath, Birmingham, was a butcher's carter in 1911 and at the outbreak of war was a tram conductor. His name is on the Thiepval Memorial

1/ 6 Royal Warwickshire: attached from 143rd Brigade of the 48th (South Midland) Division:

Casualties: 472   Killed: Officers 3   ORs 142   Nos on Thiepval: 108   **217**

- Followed 1/ 8 Royal Warwicks in attack on the Quadrilateral. Some reached the third line and a few were reported to have got into Serre. They were back in their own lines by 7 p.m.

- 23 officers were casualties

- The youngest we have found to have been killed on 1st July was Private Henry (Harry) Woodward, 15 years of age, who is remembered on the Thiepval Memorial. Not much older was Private John Perkins from Camp Hill, Birmingham who also fell aged 16 and is buried in Sucrerie Military Cemetery

- 2nd Lieutenant Henry Field, a poet and student at the Birmingham School of Art, reached the Quadrilateral but was killed by machine-gun fire. He is buried in Serre Road Cemetery No.2

- Captain J.M. Mellor at 10.00 a.m. '… such a sight I never saw … only two officers were not hit … I hope I shall never have to go into another, the sight was absolutely indescribable'

- CO Lieutenant-Colonel William H. Franklin was wounded

Royal Warwicks bivouacking before 1st July   *Sir Douglas Haig's Great Push*

10th BRIGADE:

➤ The Brigade was part of the original 1914 British Expeditionary Force

2/ Royal Dublin Fusiliers:

Casualties: 355 ● Killed: Officers 2   ORs 61   Nos on Thiepval: 32

- Many casualties were sustained before they reached their own front line trenches

- Only a few men got to the German front line on the Redan Ridge

- The CO Major Lionel P. Walsh (41) died of wounds on 4th July 1916 and is buried in Beauval Communal Cemetery

2/ Seaforth Highlanders (Ross-shire Buffs, The Duke of Albany's):

Casualties: 395 ● Killed: Officers 7   ORs 118   Nos on Thiepval: 71

- 9.00 a.m. into No Man's Land following 1/ East Lancs and 1/ Hants to Redan Ridge

- Many casualties sustained before their own front line trenches were reached

- VC: Drummer Walter Ritchie (24), an HQ orderly, repeatedly sounded the 'Charge' on his bugle from a shell-hole to rally leaderless men from different units who were wavering and beginning to retire. Throughout the day he carried messages under fire. His gallantry was witnessed by Colonel Hopkinson and Captain John Laurie which was instrumental in the VC award. He survived the War despite having been wounded three times and gassed twice. He died near Edinburgh in March 1965

- 'From 11 a.m. onwards communications from the front were uncertain and information was vague'

- 'At about 9 p.m. two messages were received (from Brigade HQ). The first contained to hold on at all costs and the other contained orders to return to our own lines. These messages were not timed, but both were brought by the same orderly'- a good example of communication problems and general confusion

- Private J.S. Reid: 'I could see that our leading waves had got caught by their kilts. They were killed hanging on the wire, riddled with bullets, like crows shot on a dyke'

- CO Lieutenant-Colonel John O. Hopkinson was wounded

- 5 officers and 20 other ranks were buried side by side in Sucrerie Military Cemetery

1/ Royal Warwickshire:

Casualties: 258   Killed: Officers 1   ORs 13   Nos on Thiepval: 10

- From support position at 9.10 a.m. went in the open in support of 2/ Royal Dublin Fusiliers then ordered to halt

1/ Royal Irish Fusiliers (Princess Victoria's):

Killed: Officers 0   ORs 11   Nos on Thiepval: 3

- 9.10 a.m. advanced from assembly trenches with Royal Warwicks. Some reached the Quadrilateral after dark - troops were withdrawn next morning

12th BRIGADE:

1/ King's Own (Royal Lancaster Regiment):

Killed: Officers 8   ORs 112   Nos on Thiepval: 91

- Attacked between Beaumont Hamel and Serre. Sustained heavy casualties before they reached their own front line, only a few got to the German front line

- Two small mines were fired in No Man's Land

- CO Major John Bromilow, at 28 years of age, was young for a Battalion CO. According to the CWGC, he died of wounds on 2nd July but a diary entry of Lieutenant V. Hawkins, 2/ Lancashire Fusiliers, suggests that Bromilow died on 1st July and his body was not discovered until August 1917. He is buried in Serre Road Cemetery No. 1

- Two officers suffered from shell-shock

2/ Essex:

Casualties: 436   Killed: Officers 8   ORs 134   Nos on Thiepval: 92

- Some men reached Münich Trench but were forced back to the Quadrilateral until 1 a.m. on 2nd July

- At 1.14 p.m. a message was sent to Brigade HQ: 'For heaven's sake send reinforcements'

2/ Duke of Wellington (West Riding Regiment):

Casualties: 323   Killed: Officers 2   ORs 50   Nos on Thiepval: 41

- In support of attack between Beaumont and Serre, a few reached the Quadrilateral

2/ Lancashire Fusiliers:

Casualties: 368   Killed: Officers 5   ORs 67   Nos on Thiepval: 46

- Some reached the German 3rd line then withdrew to the area of the Quadrilateral. Ordered to evacuate at 4 a.m. on 2nd

- Open order advancing in 'artillery formation'

31st DIVISION
Major-General Wanless O'Gowan

➢ Sergeant Jim Myers, Machine-Gun Corps: 'The biggest mistake made on manoeuvres and training was that we were never told what to do in the case of failure'

➢ 31st Division report: 'One dug-out was deep and had about 18 steps and would accommodate about 8 men. The men who saw this, state that there was a notice up with the following in English characters- 'M.G. No. 1 Post'

➢ There were varied reports of the state of the wire

➢ The Division's Battalions went over 10 minutes early…

➢ One machine-gun opposite the Division fired 20,000 rounds. Another, according to Unteroffizier Otto Lais, IR 169, was overheating and as there was a shortage of water to cool it down 'a gunner rushes into the crater with the water container and urinates into it. A second pisses into it too - quick refill!'

➢ Men from the north east in the 31st Division found in a German trench, expressions to be learned by heart on meeting an Englishman: ' "hands up you fool! Arms away." To be pronounced "Hands opp ju fuhl, Arms ewa"'

➢ Division sustained losses of 3,600

Pioneers: 12/ King's Own Yorkshire Light Infantry (Halifax Pals) (Miners):

Casualties: 192   Killed: Officers 1   ORs 38   Nos on Thiepval: 20

- They called themselves T'owd Twelfth

- An hour before the assault, their job was to open up five saps which reached to within 30-40 yards of the German trenches. Two platoons went into attack in NML

- Lieutenant James Welch (20) was killed in No Man's Land and is buried in Queens Cemetery; his CO, Lieutenant-Colonel Ernest Chambers wrote to his family, the Rev. Edward and Mrs. Edith Welch: 'He died instantaneously and could have suffered little pain. His last words to his platoon were: "Never mind me; carry on". I am deeply affected by his death, and we all give you our heartfelt sympathy in your sorrow. He was an excellent officer, and always did his duty, and did it well. I cannot speak of him too highly, and shall never forget him'

93rd BRIGADE:

➢ Colonel C.A. Howard DSO was the Brigade-Major: 'The Corps Commander was extremely optimistic, telling everybody that the wire had been blown away (we could see it standing. strong and well) there were no German trenches and all we had to do was to walk into Serre.'

15/ West Yorkshire (Prince of Wales's Own) (1st Leeds Pals):

Casualties: 528   Killed: Officers 13   ORs 209   Nos on Thiepval: 136

- Reports of state of wire varied … 29th June raiding party: 'At no point was there a clean gap but what was left was low'... 'The enemy front line was thick with men …'

- All 24 officers were casualties 'within minutes' including the wounded CO, Major Redmond B. Neill, and his second-in-command Captain Stanley Neil, aged 27, who begun the war as a private and is commemorated on the Thiepval Memorial

- Private A.V. Pearson: 'Up to this time we had expected the attack would be made just before dawn, which was the usual time for such occasions. But 7.30 a.m. why, that would be in broad daylight!' and one of the most famous quotations that emanated from the Great War: 'We were two years in the making and ten minutes in the destroying'

- 'Not one yard of ground gained'

- Brothers Lance-Corporal Gerald and Private Reginald Wilkinson are both to be found on the Thiepval Memorial

- Lieutenant Morris Bickersteth: 'Here's to a short life and a good one.' He was killed and is buried in Queens Cemetery

- 29 year old 2nd Lieutenant Major William Booth (Major is his Christian name) was one of the finest pre-War cricketers, one of Wisden Almanack's Cricketers of the Year for 1914. He had played for England on their tour of South Africa in the winter preceding the outbreak of hostilities. He died in the arms of an up and coming Yorkshire cricketer, Abraham (Abe) Waddington, 16/ West Yorks in a shell-hole in No Man's Land. It was a tragedy that haunted Waddington for the rest of his life. Booth is buried in Serre Road Cemetery No.1

- Lieutenant Evelyn H. Lintott (33) was one of the first footballers to receive a commission. A teacher, he also played football for Plymouth Argyle, Q.P.R., Bradford City and Leeds City. He is remembered on the Thiepval Memorial

16/ West Yorkshire (Prince of Wales's Own) (1st Bradford Pals) and 'D' Company of 18/ Durham Light Infantry:

Casualties: 515　　Killed: Officers 12　ORs 140　Nos on Thiepval: 121

- Followed 15/ West Yorks and one company of 18/ Durham Light Infantry - '… advanced as if on parade'

- State of wire was reported on 29th June as being 'very thin in places and would not be a serious obstacle'. No advance was made beyond the British front line

- CO Major George Guyon was in a sap when 'struck through the helmet with a bullet before reaching his front line' dying later of his wound. He was referred to as a major in a report by the intelligence officer 2nd Lieutenant C. Laxton but is commemorated on the Thiepval Memorial Royal Fusiliers' panels as a Lieutenant-Colonel

- 'A lot of men never got off the ladders'

- 'D' Company of 18/ Durham Light Infantry were decimated by enemy shelling when in assembly trench. There were only 10 survivors

18/ West Yorkshire (Prince of Wales's Own) (2nd Bradford Pals):

Casualties: 416　　Killed: Officers 7　ORs 92　Nos on Thiepval: 72

- Followed 15 and 16/ West Yorks. Advanced 'as if on parade'. Wire damaged but no clean gaps cut

- 32 year old Lieutenant-Colonel Maurice Kennard MC, three times Mentioned in Despatches: 'When (battalion) came under fire most dropped flat to escape. Kennard, though, stood calm and upright carrying only a walking stick calling out "Come on boys up you get" - which they did but Kennard was killed by a shell.' A regular, he had been wounded earlier in November 1914 when he was a captain in the 6/ Dragoon Guards. Quite a character! He is remembered on the Thiepval Memorial

- Report of Lieutenant R.S. Cross: 'It seemed to me that the artillery played too long on the enemy's front line instead of putting out the Huns guns'

- Report by 2nd Lieutenant A.D. Stephenson: 'The enemy artillery was a great surprise to our troops who had expected to find most of the enemy guns put out of action'

18/ Durham Light Infantry (First County) (Durham Pals) less 'D' Company:

Casualties: 300   🎗   Killed: Officers 1   ORs 67   Nos on Thiepval: 47

- '7.30 a.m. Smoke prevented good observation' and they were heavily shelled on their way to own line

- Sergeant Charles Moss: 'In pre-attack orders there was to be no turning back, every man must advance at a steady pace. The grimmest order to me was that no fighting soldier was to stop to help the wounded … It was like watching heavy seas rolling and roaring onto the Hendon beaches I had seen when last home during winter storms'

94th BRIGADE:

➤ Brigadier-General Hubert C. Rees DSO: 'You are about to fight in one of the greatest battles in the world and in the most just cause' and 'You are about to attack the enemy with far greater numbers than he can oppose to you, supported by a huge number of guns.' At 4.15 p.m. on 1st July he reported that his Brigade 'generally speaking had made no progress.' He also wrote after the event: 'I was looked upon as a bit of a heretic for saying that everything had been arranged for, except the unexpected which usually occurs in war.'

➤ 'Enemy's barrage remarkably well observed, as it was invariably concentrated on trenches where troops were massed.'

➤ 'It appears that considerable numbers of the enemy lay down between the trenches during the bombardment or were hidden in dug-outs. It is certain that the front line filled up with Germans very rapidly.'

11/ East Lancashire (Accrington Pals):

Casualties: 585   🎗   Killed: Officers 8   ORs 143   Nos on Thiepval: 79

- The Battalion was composed of miners, engineers, textile and office workers and shop assistants

- Assembled from Mark Copse to Matthew Copse. At 7.20 a.m. the first wave crawled into NML… following waves advanced according to timetable and 'as if on parade'. Wire was found to be cut

- One company was identified from the air by special markings, metal triangles, as having got into Serre by 9.15 a.m. but were never seen again

- 80% of those who attacked were casualties

- Lieutenant-Colonel Arthur Rickman was laid out by a shell burst in the evening

- Signaller Lance-Corporal Bury: 'We did actually see a flag signalling near the village of Serre but this lasted only a few seconds and the signals were unintelligible'

- One of the wounded officers, 2nd Lieutenant Reginald Battersby was just 16 years of age

- There were 85 deaths on 2nd July, the second highest number for the day

12/ York and Lancaster (Sheffield City) (Sheffield Pals):

Casualties: 510　　Killed: Officers 8　ORs 238　Nos on Thiepval: 161

- 'The wire in front of our lines had been cut away too much and as the gaps were not staggered, our intention to attack must have been quite obvious to the enemy'

- 'Advanced in line'… 'The lines growing ever thinner went on unwavering'

- 'The German front line wire was found to be almost intact. Our wire being cut and tape being laid served as a warning to the enemy'

- A few men got to the German trenches. Some bodies were found in north-west Serre on 13th November 1916

- Operational Order: 'All ranks will start with full water bottles; no water will be drunk until after the assault, and then only on orders from Company Commanders … Mis-use of white flag. All men should be warned against the probable mis-use of white flags and signs of surrender by the enemy. They have also been known to sham death and then shoot into the back of our assault'

- Instructions to COs in relation to the forthcoming advance: 'Every man will carry either a pick or shovel, to the proportion of two shovels to one pick. Two men in each platoon will carry mauls (mallets) and two men per Company will carry Vermorel Sprayers'- an early version of backpack-type weed killer sprayers pressurised by pumping a handle on the side. The French company made this kind of equipment but also cars. They were used to spray neutralising chemicals into places where gas might linger, such as trench bottoms and inside dug-outs

- Wire cutters wore a yellow band on the right arm

- A delay was caused by 'an exceedingly bad condition (in the trenches) owing to the heavy rain and in places the water was well above the knees'

- For the stories of CO Major Plackett and **2nd Lieutenant Kenneth Perkin** see page 69

- Two pairs of brothers were killed - Lance-Corporal Frank and Private William Gunstone, both buried in Luke Copse Cemetery and Adrian and Richard Verner from Chesterfield, recorded on the Thiepval Memorial

- Private Frank Lindley of the 2nd Barnsley Pals described the 'Sheffielders' as the 'élite of Sheffield. We were the ragged arse battalion but they were the coffee and bun boys' as they received numerous parcels full of 'goodies' from home

- Corporal Alexander Robertson (34), lecturer in History at Sheffield University and author of a collection of poems *Comrades* is commemorated on the Thiepval Memorial and Sergeant John William Streets (31) poet and miner is buried in Euston Road Cemetery

- 'The assault should have gone at dawn and in double time and the waves were too far apart'

Will Streets's grave in Euston Road Cemetery

13/ York and Lancaster (1st Barnsley Pals):

Killed: Officers 5   ORs 75 Nos on Thiepval: 46

- 'Advanced as steadily as if on drill parade' in support of 11/ East Lancs. In front of the German trenches were thick belts of unaffected wire

- The Battalion was composed mostly of miners who dug shallow tunnels cut from Matthew, Mark and Luke Copses

- Ernest Walker fell, as did his brothers Charles and Fred, who were on his left with the 14/ York and Lancaster. Ernest and Fred are on the Thiepval Memorial and Charles is buried in Euston Road Cemetery

14/ York and Lancaster (2nd Barnsley Pals):

Casualties: 250   Killed: Officers 5   ORs 87   Nos on Thiepval: 70

- 'Advanced in good dressing'

- Found front line trenches on arrival badly 'levelled' by German shelling. At 8.10 a.m. some got over parapet into NML. 'Barely 20% reached the German wire'

- Charles and Fred Walker were killed as was their brother Ernest in the 13/ Yorks and Lancs. Charles is buried in Euston Road Cemetery. The others are recorded on the Thiepval Memorial

- 16 year old Frank Lindley: 'One bloke must have been climbing out of the trench and it had done him across the middle. It left his feet and bottom half in the trench and all his insides were hanging down the trench wall. I remember thinking "so that's what a human liver and kidneys look like"'

92nd BRIGADE:

➤ Reserve Brigade of 31st Division

10th East Yorkshire (Hull Commercials)   In reserve   Killed: 2 both on Thiepval Memorial

11th East Yorkshire (Hull Tradesmen)   In support trenches one Company fought with 18/ Durham Light Infantry
Killed: 3 (2 on Thiepval)   **225**

| 12th East Yorkshire (Hull Sportsmen) | In reserve | no casualties |
| 13th East Yorkshire (T'Others) | In reserve | no casualties |

48th (SOUTH MIDLAND) DIVISION
Major-General Sir Robert Fanshawe

➤ No attack was planned between Serre and Hébuterne, a distance of over a mile. It was held by 1/ 5 and 1/ 7 Royal Warwicks of 143rd Brigade less 1/ 6 Royal Warwicks and 1/ 8 Royal Warwicks who were attached to 4th Division. The 1/ 5 sustained 3 deaths (1 mentioned on Thiepval Memorial) and the 1/ 7 6 (5 on Thiepval)

➤ On 1st July smoke was discharged to simulate an attack

THIRD ARMY
General Sir Edwin Allenby

VII CORPS
Lieutenant-General Thomas D'Oyly Snow

NPG 81624

IWM Art 01828

➤ Objective: Gommecourt

➤ The attack on Gommecourt was described by General Haig as 'subsidiary', to prevent the Germans there from helping in their defence further south. The aim was to make sure the Germans knew that Gommecourt would be attacked and Lieutenant-General Snow of VII Corps informed Haig that 'they know we are coming all right.' Nonetheless, it was a plan that did not receive the whole hearted support of General Allenby, Commander of Third Army and also Snow. Instructions to the 56th and 46th Divisions were 'to assist in the operations of the Fourth Army by diverting against itself the fire of artillery and infantry, which might otherwise be directed against the left flank of the main attack near Serre'

➤ Third Army General Staff Report: 'Each man had also constantly rehearsed the part that he was to play and it was not possible to alter his role at such a time and teach him a new one' – this exemplifies the inflexibility that could hamper the attacking battalions' chances

- The postponement of the attack by two days: 'No extra allowance of ammunition was made on this account, so on the day before the attack, the bombardment was not as intense as had been originally intended'

- GHQ was unaware of the strength of German defences in the Gommecourt Salient

- The build-up to the attack was not helped by the rain beforehand which left the trenches flooded and muddy

- 'All preparations for the attack were made openly as it was considered that the very fact of showing such intention would tend to carry out the role assigned to the Corps.'

- No Man's Land was 500- 800 yards wide. Communication trenches were dug to create a new 'jumping off trench' referred to in some war diaries as the 'new front line'

- To distract the enemy's attention, carts full of empty biscuit tins were driven up and down in Hébuterne!

- The attack was a fiasco as 6,800 men were casualties for no tangible gains. To those who survived, Snow's message had a hollow ring to it: 'The losses have not been in vain. I can assure you that by your determined effort you managed to keep large forces of the enemy at your front, thereby materially assisting in the operations which were proceeding further south with such marked success.' The *Daily Mail* glorified their efforts: 'They died defeated but won as great a victory in spirit and in fact as English history or any history will chronicle'

- The effect of the week-long British bombardment on the German lines was commented on by British prisoners who saw heaps of German corpses piled six high, rotting whilst awaiting burial

- The German barrage on No Man's Land was worse than in any other sector: the only consolation was that six heavy batteries were moved to Gommecourt from elsewhere

- To Captain Arthur Agius of the 56th Division, the purpose of the Gommecourt attack was unclear: 'We had no idea the attack was a diversion… The whole of the valley was being swept by machine-gun fire and hammered with shells… so many gone… and we'd never even got past our own front line trenches. We were treading on the dead'

- Court of Inquiry re. the Operations on 1st July: Lieutenant-General Snow's conclusion: 'There was no excuse for the uncut state of the wire not being known. The arrangements between the patrols examining the wire and the artillery on the nights preceding the attack was badly arranged by the Division'- a case of Snow ducking responsibility for what happened. He made the following points about 46th Division whose Commander Major-General Montagu-Stuart-Wortley was dismissed:

1. In future more counter battery work was required after the success of the German barrage

2. The Germans had good cover in dug-outs

3. There was a need for 'clearing' or 'mopping up' parties. Limit the first objective to the 1st line trenches and to go further where there were no deep dug-outs

4. One of the chief difficulties experienced by organising officers was that of explaining to the men that they were NOT now to be in their original formations

5. Smoke had been too dense causing men to lose direction

6. Assaulting men should be lightly equipped

7. An element of surprise is essential. Infantry must be taught that they must take risks from their own artillery and that any casualties that may occur will be far less than from hostile machine-gun fire if the artillery lift too soon

8. The attack should be carried out as soon as there is light enough to see gaps in the wire - the earlier the hour for the assault the less time the attacking troops will have to spend in a cramped position in the assembly trenches

56th (1st LONDON) DIVISION
Major-General Charles P.A. Hull

➤ 'A party of 56th Division failed to enter the German trenches owing to the wire not having been cut'

➤ No Man's Land was up to 800 yards wide in places

➤ Mixed reports of state of wire

➤ As part of the decoy a trench was dug in two nights by 500 men …

➤ 'It leaked out that our attack was a subsidiary one to mask the main thrust on the Somme'. The plan was for the Division to go round Gommecourt Wood and meet the 46th Division troops

➤ John Masefield described Gommecourt as being 'heaped with bodies of Londoners'

➤ Smoke let off at 7.20 a.m. 'totally obscured enemy trenches from observation'

➤ The Division suffered 4,300 casualties

Pioneers: 1/5 Cheshire (Earl of Chester's):

Casualties: 178 🌺 Killed: Officers 0   ORs 36   Nos on Thiepval: 29

- Private H. Lancashire: 'Lieutenant Bass gave orders to three of us to make a firestep … as we were digging, some bombers passed along and one accidentally dropped a bomb which exploded. Lieutenant Bass was hit in the eye and Clifford was wounded'

- Lieutenant Philip Bass (21) and Private John Clifford died of their wounds and are remembered on the Thiepval Memorial

168th BRIGADE:

➢ Brigadier-General Loch: 'I deplore the heavy losses among officers and men but am proud to have commanded troops who tried so bravely to carry out their difficult task.'

➢ **Rev. Julian Bickersteth** was chaplain to 1st London Scottish and Rangers. His story is on page 75

1/ 14 London (1st London Scottish):

Casualties: 568 🌺 Killed: Officers 5   ORs 181   Nos on Thiepval: 179

- Wire found uncut at 11 p.m. on 30th June - Bangalore torpedoes used

- 'The smoke was good but it was thicker than in practice. It was hard to keep direction'

- They reached the German front line. Lance-Corporal Aitken: 'It nearly broke my heart to have to retire from those swine. We had held them easily all day'

1/ 12 London (Rangers):

Casualties: 464 🌺 Killed: Officers 4   ORs 94   Nos on Thiepval: 97

- 'All wire cut in front of our line'. Crossed German front line, heavy fighting around 2nd line Nameless Farm but no support from 46th Division

- All in the Battalion who died on 1st July have no known grave apart from one who is buried in Hébuterne Military Cemetery - an extraordinary statistic

- 'At 4.05 p.m. OC 4/ London Regiment informed me by telephone that he was withdrawing his men …'

- 'Rifleman Perkins states that he got into the German trench where he was seized by two Germans but managed to beat them off by striking them in the face with a bomb he was holding in his hand'

1/ 13 London (Kensington):

Casualties: 326 🌺 Killed: Officers 3   ORs 41   Nos on Thiepval: 42

- Followed 1/ 14 London

- 'Shelling on our assembly trenches and No Man's Land'

- The Battalion size was only 549, smaller than average, sustaining 60% casualties

- Major Cedric Dickens (27) CO of 'A' Company was killed later in September and is remembered on the Thiepval Memorial. He was grandson of the novelist Charles Dickens. In his message to Battalion HQ at 2.12 p.m. he wrote: 'I have as far as I can find only 13 left besides myself. Trenches unrecognisable. Quite impossible to hold … I am the only officer left. Please send instructions'

- Command of the Battalion changed mysteriously on 27th June only days before the offensive when William H. Young took over from Lieutenant-Colonel Harry Stafford. His superior, Brigadier-General Granville Loch, was reluctant to explain why he was taking over, other than to say that the men were bad at digging! It is strange that command should have changed so late with an officer who was unacquainted with the details of the operation. It would appear that the commander he was replacing had not been informed and understandably was unimpressed. Young wrote: 'I never heard why this officer was removed from his command.' Young in his Account of Operations on 1st July mentioned that the Commander of 167th Brigade, Brigadier-General Frank Burnell-Nugent (who played once for Hampshire and scored 0 and 0) was also being removed from his post: 'I do not know on what grounds'. Morale amongst the officers of Snow's VII Corps was clearly not all it should have been and on 4th July, the CO of VII Corps' 46th (North Midland) Division was relieved of his command

- CSM A.J. Evans 'I shall always look back on July 1st with pride and sorrow because it was humanly impossible to do more than the Division did, sorrow for the hundreds of gallant Londoners who laid their lives in a desperate attempt to achieve the impossible … Stunned, exhausted and bitter, the survivors at the end of the day straggled back to their own reserve line, too dazed to wonder how they had come through, too tired to care and worst of all with the cruel sense of failure'

1/ 4 London (Royal Fusiliers):

Casualties: 324   Killed: Officers 4   ORs 37   Nos on Thiepval: 34

- '2.45 a.m. the Germans opened an intense bombardment on all assembly trenches' which exemplifies that the British bombardment had failed and that the Germans knew the attack was imminent

- 5 runners were killed

- 19 year old Arthur Wagstaffe: 'Remember, you must remember, do not run, you must walk … You'll run into your own bombardment … Duty is the key word. It was my duty to do this'

169th BRIGADE:

➤ The Brigade dug a new trench in No Man's Land

1/ 9 London (Queen Victoria's Rifles):

Casualties: 545   Killed: Officers 8   ORs 169   Nos on Thiepval: 175

- '23rd - 26th June trench digging and fatigues'

- 'Smoke will be used whatever the direction of the wind'!

- Delayed by own uncut wire. Hit by German barrage at the outset. At 9.50 a.m. shortage of bombs became critical

- Two brothers Riflemen Henry and Philip Bassett were killed and are buried next to each other in Gommecourt British Cemetery No.2

1/ 5 London (1st London Rifle Brigade):

Casualties: 572   Killed: Officers 5   ORs 218   Nos on Thiepval: 216

- 'The lines advanced in excellent order … movements went like clockwork'

- Problems were faced getting an adequate supply of bombs across due to the German barrage: 'At midday the supply of grenades began to run out'

- Rifleman Aubrey Smith wrote that there were no reinforcements, dug-outs had not been destroyed and mopping up had been poor: 'Through the intense artillery barrage and under heavy machine-gun fire, men dropped right and left, until the ground between the trenches was an awful scene of carnage'

- 46th Division's lack of progress meant that German guns could be trained on the 56th Division: 'Undoubtedly the attack failed on account of the lack of success by the Division on our left' (46th North Midland)

- Enemy bombing parties were 'covered by snipers, some of whom were even up trees'

1/ 16 London (Queen's Westminster Rifles):

Casualties: 503   Killed: Officers 6   ORs 127   Nos on Thiepval: 129

- Advanced 'in line and abreast' and reached objective of the Kern Redoubt

- All officers were casualties

1/ 2 London (Royal Fusiliers):

Casualties: 253   Killed: Officers 8   ORs 107   Nos on Thiepval: 112

- 'Wire was well cut. Lines advanced in excellent order.' Retreated at 2.00

- Problems posed by Artillery barrage in NML and shortage of bombs

- 'We were told we were acting as a decoy to draw fire'

- Frank Inglefield: ' … 12 inches of slosh and mud in our assembly trench … 7 a.m. rum ration, a Godsend after spending all those hours in the cold … Queen Victoria's Rifles went over, then us … and what a hearty reception we got too, shells of every description were whistling through the air, machine-guns rattling out, and snipers busy… and what with the aircraft overhead, the roar was something deafening … we were all mixed up, we did not know who was who … it was a hopeless task … nobody was in charge of us and very few remained… made out I was dead when wounded…'

167th Brigade:

1/ 3 London (Royal Fusiliers):

Casualties: 123   Killed: Officers 0   ORs 14   Nos on Thiepval: 13

- Two companies remained in trenches and provided carrying parties - the other two filled the gap between 56th and 46th Division with the 1/ 4 Lincolns to their left

46th (NORTH MIDLAND) DIVISION
Major-General E. Montagu-Stuart-Wortley

➤ Objective: to go round Gommecourt Wood and meet the 56th Division troops

➤ The Division's chances were probably not helped by the interrogation on 27th June of the captured Private Victor Wheat of 5/ North Staffs who indicated the assault would occur within two to three days and would be preceded by four to five days' artillery bombardment. He gave details based on practice in mock trenches at St. Léger. He let on that the attack would be led by 6/ North Staffs as his battalion had gone first at Loos

➤ Wire was mostly uncut

➤ The use of smoke, discharged at 7.27 a.m. proved to be a disaster. It was too dense and troops became disoriented

➤ 'Communications broke down - telephones, flags, lamps, flares, pigeons, discs, rockets failed to work successfully. Runners found it difficult to get through No Man's Land'

➤ **Major-General Montagu-Stuart-Wortley** was dismissed by Haig on 4th July and on 8th July bade farewell to senior officers of the Brigades. For his story see page 80

➤ The Division suffered 2,455 casualties, 850 men were killed and were arguably saved from further losses by Stuart-Wortley who decided not to sacrifice more men and postponed Snow's order to attack at 12.15 and then again at 1.30 and 3.30

Pioneers: 1/ 1 Monmouths:

Killed: Officers 0   ORs 22   Nos on Thiepval: 11

- Moved forward with assaulting troops in order to dig communication trenches and were under constant fire

- 'A' and 'D' Companies were carrying parties and 'B' and 'C' Companies helped with the advance

137th BRIGADE:

➤ The Staffordshire battalions were tasked with digging practice trenches much to the displeasure of the local farmers. Although compensated, they were heard to describe the British as 'les autres Boches' (the other Boches).

➤ Problems were caused by the density of smoke which caused confusion. Isolated parties got to German front line. By 9.00 a.m. Brigadier-General Hugh Williams was sure that the Brigade's assault had failed. He had taken over the Brigade in June after being demoted from Major-General - another example of problems at the top of VII Corps

1/ 6 South Staffs:

Casualties: 219 Killed: Officers 6 ORs 72 Nos on Thiepval: 67

- Crawled out to the 'new front line' within 250 yards of enemy front line. Assault began at 7.30 a.m.

- Men lost their way in the smoke. Some got to German front line but were quickly overcome

1/ 6 North Staffs (Prince of Wales's):

Casualties: 305 Killed: Officers 6 ORs 144 Nos on Thiepval: 127

- 'Owing to the smoke many men lost direction and were unable to see the gaps in the wire … Front trench 2 to 3 feet deep in mud'

- Crawled out to within 250 yards of German front line

- 'Enemy wire found to be very strong in places … well cut for one company but not for 3 companies'

- Attached from 1/ 5 North Staffs, CO Lieutenant-Colonel Charles Boote (41) was killed and is buried in Gommecourt Wood New Cemetery

- Lieutenant G. Ashford: 'The element of surprise was completely lacking … trenches dug, light railway laid in full view of the enemy. This advertisement may have been intentional and calculated to draw troops and guns from further south … if not it is past understanding'

1/ 5 South Staffs:

Casualties: 177 Killed: Officers 5 ORs 35 Nos on Thiepval: 34

- In support of 1/6 South Staffs. Wire uncut

- Problems caused by muddy state of own trenches

- CO Lieutenant-Colonel Robert R. Raymer was wounded

- The 3.30 p.m. advance was cancelled due to chaos in the communication trenches

1/ 5 North Staffs (Prince of Wales's):

🖐 Killed: Officers 2 ORs 28 Nos on Thiepval: 26

- Practice attack on 20th June

- CO Lieutenant-Colonel William Burnett DSO (36) in a speech to his men: 'Well Boys, by sunrise tomorrow I hope to see you on the other side of Gommecourt Wood'

- Followed 1/6 North Staffs

- 'We went over in broad daylight and in full view of the enemy lines ... set off at an easy pace'

- Lance-Corporal R. Tivey: 'Crumps and mortars were bursting all around'

- 4th wave could not be persuaded to go forward. 5th wave went through and were annihilated on the German wire

- Burnett 'on hearing that the attack was not developing as arranged, personally went forward to the advance trench and tried to reorganise and push on.' He was found at 1 a.m. and died of a wound to his abdomen on 3rd July and is buried in Warlincourt Halte British Cemetery

- Description by Thomas James Higgins: 'The trenches were literally running with blood. The dead and dying lay in heaps at the bottom of the trench ... I threw my spade and barbed wire away ... officer Robinson was firing his pistol like mad, then he went down ... Fritz was riddling any poor devil he saw moving with bullets ... I lay still with barbed wire sticking in me, I dared not move ... If the Germans had made a counter-attack they would easily have taken our lines then ... the smell of blood and dead bodies was sickening.' Lieutenant Eli Robinson is commemorated on the Thiepval Memorial

- Narrative of operations on 1st July: 'Things got in utter confusion'

139th BRIGADE:

➤ Smoke discharged at 7.27 a.m.

➤ Brigadier-General Charles Shipley issued orders to discontinue the advance in the afternoon.

1/ 5 Notts and Derby (Sherwood Foresters):

Casualties: 419 🖐 Killed: Officers 9 ORs 156 Nos on Thiepval: 142

- From 8th-17th June the Battalion was training for the attack - bayonet fighting, physical training, rapid firing, live bomb throwing and wood cutting. From 19th -26th cable burying, deepening trenches, making trench mortar emplacements, pumping and carrying

- The first three waves attacked 'with great dash'

- 4th wave were delayed by heavy loads and muddy state of trenches. 'Our men were unable to offer much resistance, their rifles in some cases being muddy… having no supply of bombs those that were left retired and took shelter in shell-holes'

- Private W.B. Stevenson: 'Tea tasting of petrol, rum issue small'

- Two brothers, Privates Allan (Gommecourt Wood New Cemetery) and John Bembridge (Thiepval Memorial) were killed

- CO Lieutenant-Colonel Denis D. Wilson attached from 17th Indian Cavalry fell and is remembered on the Neuve Chapelle Memorial

- VC: 27 year old Captain Leslie Green (27) of the Royal Army Medical Corps, attached to the Battalion, was awarded the VC 'for most conspicuous devotion to duty. Although himself wounded, he went to the assistance of an officer who had been wounded and was hung up on the enemy's wire entanglements, and succeeded in dragging him to a shell-hole, where he dressed his wounds, notwithstanding that bombs and rifle grenades were thrown at him the whole time. Captain Green then endeavoured to bring the wounded officer into safe cover, and had nearly succeeded in doing so when he himself was killed.' The citation was published in the *London Gazette* on 4th August 1916. The officer he rescued was Captain Frank Robinson, 1/6 Notts and Derby (Sherwood Foresters), who was the witness for the commendation for Green's VC but died two days later and is buried at Warlincourt Halte British Cemetery. Green had only been married to Edith Moss, also a doctor, since 1st January 1916. His younger brother was killed in October 1915 at Loos

The grave of Captain Leslie Green VC in Foncquevillers Military Cemetery

- Private W.B. Stevenson wrote in a letter to his mother: 'The battle certainly was a trying experience and I am sorry to say that Nottingham will be plunged into mourning when the casualty lists are published'

1/ 7 Notts and Derby (Sherwood Foresters) (Robin Hoods)
Casualties: 410   Killed: Officers 9   ORs 162   Nos on Thiepval: 145

- On 19th June fatigue parties were sent to deal with trenches in a poor state 'being in many places over the knees in water… 250 men dug a trench 140 yards out into No Man's Land which was described in the BWD as the 'New Front Line'

- The Robin Hoods were said to have attacked their practice trenches 50 times

- Forward British trenches in wretched state - many dead and wounded

Seaforth Highlanders
2nd

Somerset
Light Infantry
1st and 8th

South Lancashire
11th

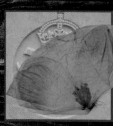

South Staffs
1st, 1/ 5th and 1/ 6th

South Wales
Borderers
2nd

Suffolks
8th and 11th

West Yorks
1/5th, 1/ 6th, 1/ 7th,
1/ 8th, 2nd, 10th, 15th,
16th, 18th and 21st

Wilts
2nd

Yorkshire
(Green Howards)
2nd, 7th and 10th

York and Lancaster
1/5th, 8th, 9th, 10th,
12th, 13th and 14th

Royal
Army Medical Corps

Royal Engineers

Royal Field Artillery

Royal Flying Corps

Machine-Gun Corps

Army Chaplains'
Department

- 'The wire was sufficiently cut to get through.' About 12 men got to 2nd line trenches
- Problems faced: mud in rifles, shortage of bombs, machine-gun fire in NML
- CO Lieutenant-Colonel Laurence Hind MC (38) was killed and is remembered on the Thiepval Memorial

1/ 6 Notts and Derby (Sherwood Foresters):

Casualties: 170   Killed: Officers 0   ORs 19   Nos on Thiepval: 15

- The Battalion practised in front of Lieutenant-General Snow and Major-General Montagu-Stuart-Wortley on 17th June
- In support of 1/5 and 1/7 Notts and Derby. State of wire was strong in many places
- 'Main object achieved of containing enemy forces …'
- Captain Frank Robinson died of wounds on 3rd July. See 1/5 Notts and Derby above

1/ 8 Notts and Derby (Sherwood Foresters):

Killed: Officers 0   ORs 4   Nos on Thiepval: 4

- At 8 a.m. companies began to move towards support lines. Progress hampered by congestion and blown-in trenches. Attack at 3.30 p.m. cancelled
- 2nd Lieutenant Edward Brittain, the brother of Vera Brittain, author of *Testament of Youth*, let her know that 'I was wounded in the action this morning in my left arm and right thigh not seriously. Don't worry, Edward.' She nursed him in J Ward of the First General London Hospital. He wrote: 'I remember noticing what a perfect morning it was, with a cloudless blue sky … In a shell-hole I saw the head of a man who'd been killed only that morning.' Brittain received the MC but was killed in 1918, hit by a sniper on the Italian Front and is buried in Granezza British Cemetery. His MC citation: 'For conspicuous gallantry and leadership during an attack. He was severely wounded, but continued to lead his men with great bravery and coolness until a second wound disabled him'

138th BRIGADE:

1/ 4 Lincolns:

Killed: Officers 0   ORs 4   Nos on Thiepval: 0

- The Battalion was bridging the gap between the 56th and 46th Divisions with 1/ 3 London to their right. A shallow trench was dug facing Gommecourt Park intended to draw the enemy's fire. They were not involved in the assault

1/ 5 Leicesters:

Killed: Officers 0   ORs 9   Nos on Thiepval: 5

- 'A' and 'D' Companies were carrying parties and 'B' and 'C' Companies helped with the advance

IX

Exploring The Front Line

Ten Walks and Drives

BEWARE of the 'metal harvest'

✔   The Ten Walks follow the 1st July front line from Montauban in the south to Gommecourt in the north. Additional sites of interest, for example the 'Grandstand', can be found in the car itineraries. For those wishing to use OS type maps four cover the area: IGN 2408 E, 2408 O 2407 E and 2407 O

✔   Times given for the walks are approximate and include time that might be spent in cemeteries etc.

✔   Maps: show only the battalions which went over the top in the first wave. The route of the walk is highlighted in magenta. The red numbers on the maps refer to information in the text

✔ Battalions: To find out about what happened to battalions in a particular location, use the Index and Chapter VIII

✔ Colour coding in text:

Bold black	Directions
Bold blue	Details of what can be seen or done at a location
Black	Information about cemeteries
Bold green	Satellite navigation coordinates
Bold red numbers	Locations that can be travelled to by car

✔ **CAR ITINERARY** sections:

   o These dots are locations in each of the Walks which can be visited by car. For information about these locations use the red numbers which are in the Walks' text

   • These dots represent sites that can only be accessed by car

✔ Cemeteries: Only 1st July 1916 casualties and figures for unidentified graves (those lost or destroyed) are given

✔ How to find a grave: Every cemetery has a small box with a cross on the outside, in which you will find a register of names and a cemetery plan

✔ N.B. Safety: On tarmac roads keep to the left. Keep to paths and do not cross fields

BEWARE of the 'metal harvest'. Do not touch shells or grenades that you may come across on the edge of fields as 100 years on they can still be dangerous. Remember that 1/3rd of British shells failed to explode!

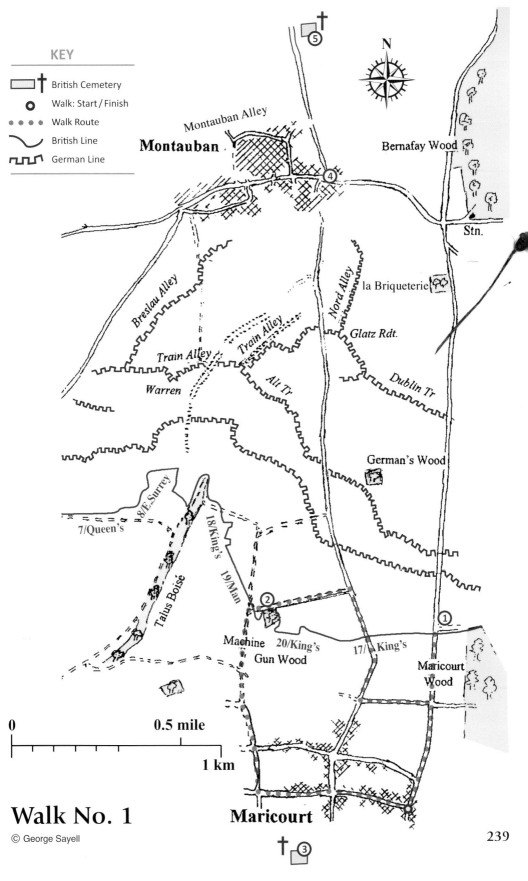

KEY

British Cemetery
Walk: Start / Finish
Walk Route
British Line
German Line

N

Montauban Alley
Montauban
Bernafay Wood

④

Stn.

Breslau Alley
la Briqueterie

Nord Alley
Glatz Rdt.

Train Alley
Train Alley
Warren
Alt Tr.
Dublin Tr

German's Wood

8/E.Surrey
7/Queen's
18/King's
19/Man
②
20/King's
17/ King's

Talus Boisé

Machine
Gun Wood
Maricourt
Wood

①

0   0.5 mile
1 km

Walk No. 1

Maricourt

© George Sayell

③

239

1 Montauban

'The boys got over the top and simply walked across'

Signaller Nelson Mills, 19/ King's (3rd Liverpool Pals)

This walk covers the area attacked by the 30th Division where the British achieved most success on 1st July 1916- all the main features behind the German front line were captured.

Points of interest:

- The British and French commanding officers, Lieutenant-Colonel Bryan Fairfax and Colonel Lepetit linked arms and walked into No Man's Land at 8.00 a.m.

- Private Arthur Seanor went over the top with the 18/ King's (2nd Liverpool Pals) and was killed

Distance:	2.5 miles
Approximate time:	1.5 hours

Park in the layby opposite the café 'Au Chant du Coq' on the D197 in Maricourt. 49.980079, 2.78929 Take the road out of the village leaving the café to your left until you reach two flag poles (1)

The point at which the British and French front lines met. Behind German's Wood is Montauban

The road marks the boundary between the French to the east and the British to the west. It was here that the French and British Commanding Officers linked arms and walked into No Man's Land. Note the church at Montauban in the distance. Montauban Alley and the village were objectives of the 30th Division. The German front line was 275 yards ahead of you and crossed the road

- Retrace your steps ... take the first right at the red and white bollards and the next right - soon after, stop where there is a bend to the left

The British Front line here was occupied to the right and left by the 17/ King's (1st Liverpool Pals). Ahead of you, No Man's Land was 550 yards wide; the copse ahead of you is German's Wood and beyond that, by the road, is La Briqueterie (The Brickyard) where there was heavy fighting: in between were two German fortified positions, Dublin Trench and Glatz Redoubt

• Walk on, take the first track on the left and stop at the small wood

Machine Gun Wood (2) was on the British Front Line from where 20/ King's (4th Liverpool Pals) attacked with the 19/ Manchesters (4th Manchester Pals) to their left. Looking towards Montauban, the British front line went diagonally to the tip of the long stretch of woodland - Talus Boisé, the area where the 18/ King's (2nd Liverpool Pals) and Private Arthur Seanor were entrenched

- Continue to the T junction, turn left and go back to Maricourt village taking the second street on the left. Go over the crossroads and to your car

CAR ITINERARY:

○ **Site of boundary between the British and French Armies - the two flags** (1) 49.987601, 2.791088

○ **Machine Gun Wood** (2) 49.988362, 2.779740

- **Péronne Road Cemetery** (3) 49.978138, 2.782071

Started by: Field Ambulances in 1916

No. of burials: 1348 including 366 unidentified and 53 1st of July casualties (16 from King's (Liverpool) and 14 Manchesters)

Of interest: A 16 year old - Private John Mayhew and an R.F.A. Major John Graham are buried as is 44 year old Lieutenant-Colonel Edward Trotter DSO, CO attached to 18/ King's (2nd Liverpool Pals) from the Grenadier Guards who was killed by a shell in Glatz Redoubt on 8th July 1916

Architect: Sir Herbert Baker

- **Montauban village** (4) 50.006314, 2.783232 Look out for the memorial to the Manchester and Liverpool Pals unveiled on 1st July 1994, the local war memorial and the re-built church where the stone head of the Virgin Mary is the only original piece left. The story goes that a British officer took the head back home and it was eventually returned in 1986

- **Quarry Cemetery** (5) 50.014309,2.782288

Started: After the fall of Montauban when it was used as an ADS

No. of burials: 740 including 157 unidentified and 5 1st July burials

Of interest: Also buried are one French soldier and 15 Germans

Architect: Sir Herbert Baker

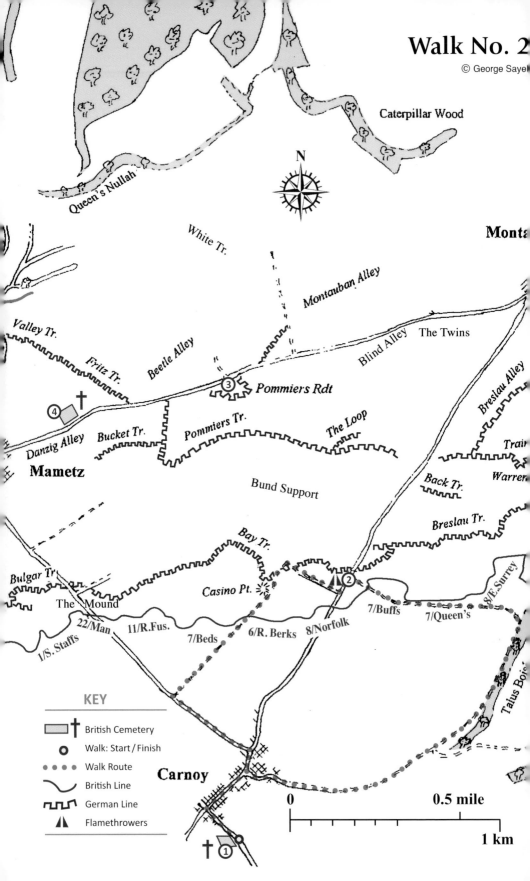

2 Carnoy

'The Great European Cup-Tie Final'
8/ East Surreys

This walk covers the area of the 18th Division's attack

Points of interest:

- Captain Nevill and his Company of 8/ East Surreys kicked two footballs into No Man's Land and his grave at Carnoy Military Cemetery

- One German was found 'chained' to his machine-gun

- Two 'flame projectors' were fired by the British

- Three mines were exploded by the British; one at Casino Point and two due east of it

Distance:	Over 3 miles
Approximate time:	1.5 to 2 hours

Park at Carnoy Military Cemetery 49.982233, 2.754800 **(1) Go into the village, take two right turns. Go past the church and follow the path until you reach the southern end of Talus Boisé. Keep left and go along the western end of the wood and continue until the path (i.e. the divisional boundary between the 18th and 30th Divisions) goes left. Soon after, stop and look to your right towards Montauban church**

The path along Talus Boisé runs parallel to the original local railway line which was used on 1st July to transport supplies and casualties. The 8/ East Surreys assembled about 330 yards ahead of you; look towards Montauban church. Their front line was salient-shaped and opposite two German strong points - the Warren and Train Alley. At Zero Hour Captain Nevill's Company kicked two footballs across No Man's Land towards Montauban

- **Continue along the path**

It was in this area that the 7/ Queen's (Royal West Surreys) attacked Breslau Trench about 400 yards to your right and came across a German chained to his machine-gun. The 7/ Buffs (East Kents) were on their left in a salient 100 yards from the path

- **Stop on reaching the tarmac road (2)**

You are standing in No Man's Land where the 8/ Norfolks went over the top from your left. Look right towards Montauban church - at the brow of the hill the two front lines were at their closest, less than 100 yards apart

- Turn left then immediately right on to a tarmac path. Stop after a further 50 yards

A rare photograph taken on 1st July of soldiers resting on the Montauban Road at 3.30 p.m. before the final advance on Montauban Alley- one of the men is an officer of the 7/ Buffs   *IWM HU 112461*

You are in No Man's Land and near the spot where two 'flame projectors' were fired by the Royal Engineers

- **Continue along the path and stop where it bends sharply to the left**

You have reached the German front line. About 275 yards to your left, trenches were held by the 6/ Royal Berks. Walk on to the site of the Casino Point Mine which is to the right where there is a clear hollow in the field. The original crater was 55 ft in diameter and 12 ft deep. On the left a 'flame projector' was installed but was destroyed by shell fire. After 400 yards you will reach the British front line, held to your right by the 7/ Bedfords

- **Carry on until you reach a tarmac road**

The boundary between the 18th and 7th Divisions was about 450 yards to your right where the front line was held by the 11/ Royal Fusiliers

- **Turn left to Carnoy village, go right at the T junction, then take the second street on your left to your car and**

Carnoy Military Cemetery (1)

Started:	August 1915 on the site of the local light railway station
No of burials:	Over 850 including nearly 30 unidentified and 57 1st July (nine 8/ East Surreys)
Of interest:	Six captains including 'Billie' Nevill and Bernard Ayre, 8/ Norfolks, brother of Eric 1/ Newfoundland also fell. Note the mix of ranks to the left of his grave - a private, lance-corporal, two 2nd lieutenants, a lieutenant and three captains
244 Architect:	W.C von Berg

CAR ITINERARY:

○ **Carnoy Military Cemetery** (1) 49.982233, 2.754800

○ **Casino Point, site of mine and flame projectors off the Montauban to Carnoy road** (a short walk involved here) **(2)** 49.993159, 2.759577

• **Pommiers Redoubt (3) Raised ground signifies where there was a German strong point** 50.001500, 2.754335

• **Dantzig Alley British Cemetery** (4) 49.999498, 2.743703

Started :	Late July 1916 and expanded after the War from 9 small cemeteries
No of burials:	2,053 including 158 unidentified and 714 1st July of which 198 were Manchesters and 81 7/ Queen's (Royal West Surreys)
Of interest:	Note the CWGC spelling of Danzig which they never corrected. 15 Captains are buried here - 7 Manchesters including Alfred Bland and Charles May also Charles Brockbank King's Liverpool, George Scott, Queen's and one RAMC, Douglas Smith. A 16 year old-Private Charles Tempest of the Yorkshire Regiment and 50 year old Private A. Edmonds, South Staffs. Lieutenant-Colonel Henry Lewis (attached 20/ Manchesters)
Architect:	Sir Herbert Baker

Carnoy Military Cemetery

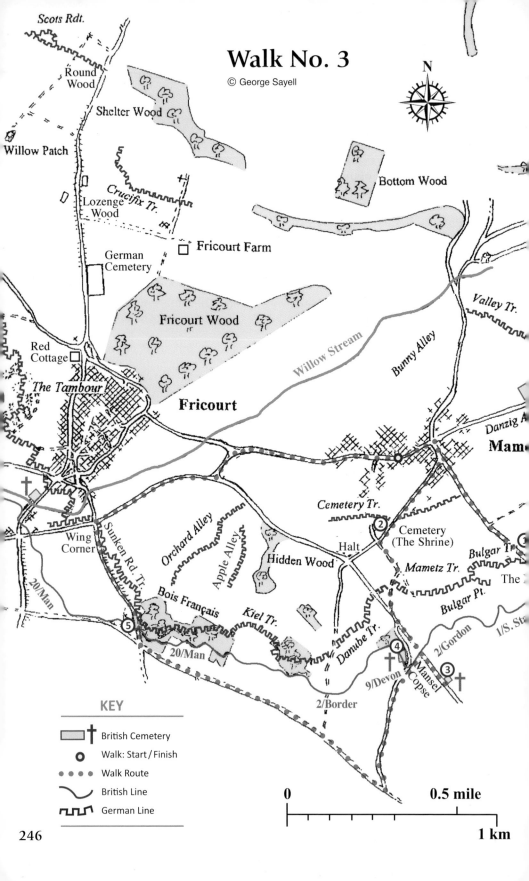

Walk No. 3

© George Sayell

N

Scots Rdt.

Round Wood

Shelter Wood

Willow Patch

Lozenge Wood

Crucifix Tr.

Bottom Wood

German Cemetery

Fricourt Farm

Fricourt Wood

Red Cottage

The Tambour

Fricourt

Willow Stream

Bunny Alley

Valley Tr.

Danzig A

Mam

Cemetery Tr.

Wing Corner

Sunken Rd. Tr.

Orchard Alley

Apple Alley

Hidden Wood

Halt

②

Cemetery (The Shrine)

Mametz Tr.

Bulgar Tr.

The

20/Man

Bois Français

Kiel Tr.

Danube Tr.

Bulgar Pt.

⑤

20/Man

④

9/Devon

Mansel Copse

2/Gordon

③

1/S. St

2/Border

KEY

- ⬛✝ British Cemetery
- ◦ Walk: Start / Finish
- •••• Walk Route
- ∿ British Line
- ⊓⊔⊓ German Line

0   0.5 mile

1 km

3 Mametz

"By all delights that I shall miss
Help me to die, O Lord"

Lieutenant W.N. Hodgson, 9/ Devons

This walk covers the area of the 7th Division's attack

Points of interest:

- Shrine Alley where a particularly destructive German machine-gun was based

- A promising 21 year old chemistry student was killed when attacking with 22/ Manchesters

- The Cemetery where the Devons are buried e.g. Hodgson and Martin

- A very narrow area of No Man's Land

Distance: Over 4 miles

Approximate time: 2 hours

Park in Mametz 49.996906, 2.734838 in front of the Mairie Ecole next to the church. Walk on the main road. Leave the Mairie Ecole on your left. At the crossroads beyond the local war memorial on the left, there is a small red brick wall with a plaque to the Manchester battalions. Turn right following the sign to Carnoy. Keep straight on and stop when you reach the second path on the left

You have reached Bulgar Trench (1) in front of you on the German front line. No Man's Land here was less than 220 yards wide. At a position facing you called The Mound were the 22/ Manchesters and Lieutenant Roy Mellor, the promising 21 year old chemistry student. The 1/ South Staffs were to their left. About 220 yards due right was Bulgar Point where a British mine failed to explode. You and the Germans have a clear view of the British front line. Looking to the right towards the main road, you should see the CWGC cemetery cross which is behind the site of the 2/ Gordons' trenches. To the right by the winding road is Mansel Copse. You can appreciate here the strategic advantage held by the Germans

- Retrace your steps into Mametz and take the first left, Rue de L' Atre, down what was known as Shrine Alley. Stop when you reach the civilian cemetery on the right

You have reached The Shrine (2), a German machine-gun position by the crucifix 275 yards behind the German front line. Look left towards Mansel Copse on the other side of the main road which marks the position of the 9/ Devons. No Man's Land here was 330 yards wide. The 2/ Gordons attacked from the direction of the CWGC cross with the 9/ Devons to the right

- Follow the path on the left and bear right towards the main road. Turn left, ignore the sign to the Devonshire Cemetery and enter Gordon Cemetery (3). Beware of fast moving traffic

Gordon Cemetery

Started by:	2/ Gordon Highlanders in a support trench
No. of burials:	102 including 5 unidentified and 95 1st July
Of interest:	All burials are Gordon Highlanders except for three. There is a piper J. Scott and an interesting row of six 2nd Lieutenants to the right of the entrance
Architect:	A.J.S. Hutton

Exit the cemetery to the right, cross over the road with care, walk up to the embankment and Mansel Copse (4) named after 2nd Lieutenant Spencer Lort Mansel Mansel-Carey (22), 8/ Devons attached to 9/ Devons who was killed in February 1916

Devonshire Cemetery

Started by:	Rev. Ernest C. Crosse chaplain to the 8 and 9/ Devonshires in their old front line
No. of burials:	163 including 10 unidentified and 150 1st July, all Devons
Of interest:	Captain D.L. Martin and the poet Lieutenant W.N. Hodgson and his batman, Private Alfred Weston. Note the famous inscription to the left of the entrance gate: 'The Devonshires held this trench, the Devonshires hold it still'
Architect:	W.H. Cowlishaw

- Turn right out of the cemetery and walk up the hill to a T junction. Turn right, and stop at the first path to the right but do not go down it

  The British front line to your right was held by the 2/ Border. Four mines were detonated near the Germans' Kiel and Danube Trenches where it was also planned to fire a 'flame projector' but when it was being transported to the front line, it was damaged by German shelling

- Continue along the path and before the crossroads you will see several mounds which are 2nd World War anti-aircraft emplacements. Turn right at the crossroads and stop after 100 yards

  You are standing on the British front line. Incredibly the Germans were just 80 yards ahead in Bois Français (5) faced by the 20/ Manchesters who were holding the line. You will see evidence of trenches and shell-holes in the wood

- Follow the path, which is virtually the German front line, down to the road

  This is Wing Corner, the divisional boundary between the 7th and the 21st Divisions where Raymond Asquith met his father, the Prime Minister H.H. Asquith, for the last time before he was killed on 15th September 1916

- Turn right onto the main road- *beware of fast moving traffic* - walk over 800 yards and take the road to the left to Mametz and your car

CAR ITINERARY:

- Bulgar Trench (1) 49.992385, 2.744178

- The Shrine (2) 49.993472, 2.733854

- Gordon Cemetery (3) 49.987577, 2.738479

- Mansel Copse and Devonshire Cemetery (4) 49.988907, 2.735916

- Bois Français (5) 49.989165, 2.718112

Cross of Sacrifice in Devonshire Cemetery - the German front line is in the distance

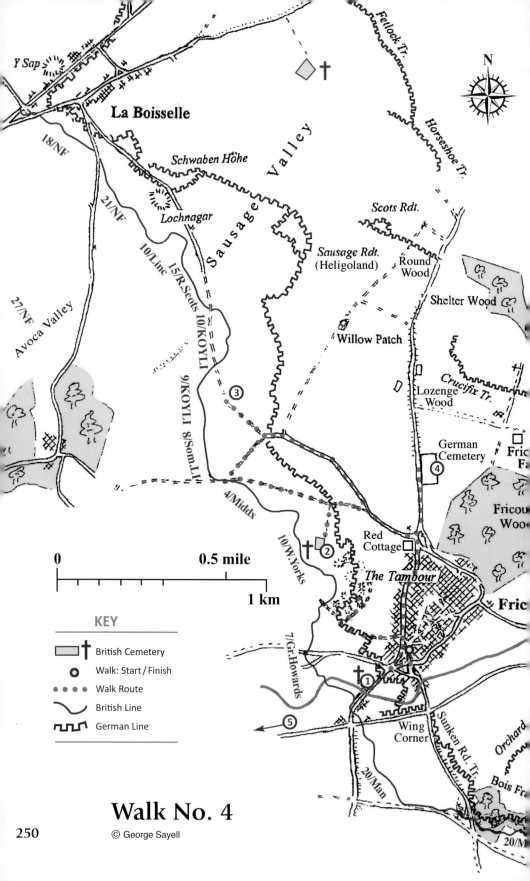

Y Sap

La Boisselle

Schwaben Höhe

Lochnagar

18/NF

21/NF

27/NF

Avoca Valley

10/Linc

15/R.Scots 10/KOYLI

9/KOYLI 8/Som.LI

4/Middx

10/W.Yorks

7/Gr.Howards

Sausage Valley

Fetlock Tr.

Horseshoe Tr.

Scots Rdt.

Sausage Rdt.
(Heligoland)

Round
Wood

Shelter Wood

Willow Patch

Crucifix Tr.

Lozenge
Wood

German
Cemetery

Fric
Fa

Fricou
Woo

Red
Cottage

The Tambour

Fric

③

②

④

①

⑤

Wing
Corner

Sunken Rd. Tr.

Orchard

Bois Fr

20/Man

20/M

N

0   0.5 mile

1 km

KEY

† British Cemetery

○ Walk: Start / Finish

••• Walk Route

〰 British Line

⌐⌐⌐ German Line

Walk No. 4

© George Sayell

4 Fricourt

'When I think of my dear old chums, I could cry'

Private David Sweeney, 1/Lincolns

This walk covers the area of the attack by the 17th (50th Brigade) and 21st Divisions

Points of interest:

- Area where the 7/ Yorkshire (Green Howards) suffered catastrophic losses
- The site of mine craters at the Tambour
- Cemetery with burials of a battalion that suffered the worst casualties on 1st July
- A German cemetery with over 17,000 burials

Distance:	3.5 miles
Approximate time:	2.5 hours

Park in Fricourt opposite L'Auberge'In 49.996559, 2.714027. With your back to the Auberge, go left down to the crossroads. Turn left to

Fricourt (Bray Road) British Cemetery (1)

Started :	By the 7/ East Yorks in July 1916
No. of burials:	133 including one unidentified and 90 1st July
Of interest:	All 90 1st July burials are of the Green Howards (Yorkshire Regiment) except, oddly, for one East Yorks 2nd Lieutenant Arthur Kippax. Note the Celtic Cross to the Yorkshire Regiment
Architect:	W.H. Cowlishaw

The cemetery is in between the German and British front lines i.e. the Germans were at the cross roads you have come from and the British on the other side of Willow Stream by the cemetery. As you face the cemetery, the 7/ Green Howards suffered huge losses attacking from the left

- Retrace your steps and go left opposite the war memorial (which includes a plaque to the memory of those who used to play 'jeu de paume' on the green patch below the Auberge), walk up the path and take the first right alongside woodland. You will come to an opening on the left, enter the clearing and bear left and do a circular walk round the Tambour area where you will see a number of mine craters. N.B. this is private land so exercise discretion!

The cratered area of the Tambour with the cross of Fricourt New Military Cemetery in the background

This is the Triple Tambour area, where 3 mines were laid, two of which exploded

- Return to the main road in Fricourt village, turn left and continue northwards up the road. Follow the CWGC sign to Fricourt New Military Cemetery (2) which is on the left down a grass path. You are in the area where the 10/ West Yorks suffered the worst casualties on 1st July

Fricourt New Military Cemetery

Started by:	10/ West Yorks in July 1916 in four mass graves
No. of burials:	210 including 26 unidentified and 173 1st July (135 West Yorks and 37 East Yorks)
Of interest:	19 year old 2nd Lieutenant Francis Joseph Hicking. A 16 year old - Private A. Barker, East Yorks and Lieutenant-Colonel Arthur Dickson attached to 10/ West Yorks and the poet Lieutenant Alfred Victor Ratcliffe, 10/ West Yorks
Architect:	A.J.S. Hutton

- Go back the way you came and turn left at the end of the grass path. You are on the German front line and about to walk diagonally towards the British front line. Stop when you reach a path to the right

Straight ahead you can see Albert Basilica's Golden Virgin and to the left the white buildings of Méaulte aerodrome beyond which on the horizon was the point from where General Rawlinson watched the early morning action from a position known as 'The Grandstand'

You have reached the trenches held by the 4/ Middlesex with the 8/ Somerset Light Infantry to their left. Following the 4/ Middlesex were the 10/ Yorkshire (Green Howards) one of whom Major Stewart Loudoun-Shand was awarded the VC posthumously

- Take the path to the right and walk through the exact width of No Man's Land until you reach the T junction. Turn left and stop when you can see the village of La Boisselle in the distance (3)

You are now standing in the middle of No Man's Land. The 9/ KOYLI attacked from the left across the path with the 10 / KOYLI on their left. The boundary between the 21st and 34th Divisions is about 500 yards further down the path

Looking from right to left, you can see in the distance Gordon Dump Cemetery where VC winner Donald Bell is buried, Sausage Valley (named after German sausage-shaped observation balloons), the village of La Boisselle, in front of the village the circle of trees which marks the lip of the Lochnagar Crater, beyond the village the top of the Thiepval Memorial, to the left of the crater the Tara and Usna Hills and on the far left the Basilica at Albert

- Return to the main road on the tarmac path ignoring two paths to your right, turn left at the main road and walk up to the German Cemetery (4) an interesting contrast to the British cemeteries where there are several graves of 1st July casualties

Fricourt German Cemetery   *J Kerr*

German Cemetery Fricourt:

The black crosses, darker stone and the lack of flowers evoke a more sombre atmosphere. There are over 17,000 burials. More than 5,000 are in graves of four marked by one cross; 114 of those are unidentified. 12,000 men were buried in four mass graves (Kameradengräber) and of those, 6,500 are unidentified. At least they were afforded a burial unlike many who were unceremoniously burnt in a quarry at Miraumont. Amongst the 1st July casualties there are graves for Leutnant Kurt Seidel RIR 121 opposite the British 4th Division at Beaumont Hamel (Block 1 Grave 54) and Oberleutnant Anton Mühlbeyer RIR 119 opposite British 29th Division on the Hawthorn Ridge (Block 3 Grave 306). In the mass grave is Hauptmann (Captain)

German 1st July casualty: Emil Brose RIR 119 Beaumont Hamel

Friedrich Schorer, 8th Bavarian RIR opposite British 36th Division at Thiepval. You will notice that there are few officers buried here because, unlike the British principle of no repatriation, German families who could afford to, brought their loved ones' bodies home. There are 14 Jewish gravestones - the names had originally been on metal crosses but were removed during the 2nd World War German occupation. Afterwards the gravestones were erected

• **Make your way back into Fricourt and your car**

CAR ITINERARY:

○ **Fricourt (Bray Road) Cemetery** (1) 49.995204, 2.711444

○ **Fricourt New Military Cemetery** (2) 50.002580, 2.711045
This involves a short walk

○ **View of La Boisselle from German front line** (3) 50.005496, 2.704375

○ **Fricourt German Cemetery** (4) 50.004228, 2.714263

• **Dernancourt** (5) 49.987123, 2.622141 **where General Rawlinson watched the start of the Battle and could have seen the front from Thiepval to Montauban**

in the distance

5 La Boisselle and Ovillers

'God, where's the rest of the boys'

Lieutenant, 23/ Northumberland Fusiliers (4th Tyneside Scottish)

This walk covers the area of the attack by the 34th and 8th Divisions

Points of interest to look out for:

- Sausage Valley
- Lochnagar Crater
- The Glory Hole
- Mash Valley
- Area where 2/ Middlesex were cut down as predicted by Lieutenant-Colonel Sandys
- Ovillers Military Cemetery

Distance:	Over 5 miles
Approximate time:	Over 3 hours

Park in the small car park by the church at La Boisselle 50.020680, 2.695382
Walk away from the church down the street, past the local war memorial on your right, and turn left to Bécordel. Keep left at the fork, past the crater to your right and stop after 400 yards at the end of the tarmac road

You are in front of the British line. The 15/ Royal Scots were to your right. Sausage Valley is on your left with Sausage Redoubt, a German stronghold over 500 yards away. The 10/ Lincolns (Grimsby Chums) were located between you and the crater. Following them, Lieutenant Robert Gilson went over the top with the 11/ Suffolks (Cambridgeshire). One man was too drunk to go over the top and one went berserk

- **Return to the crater and walk round one of the most spectacular sights during the walk**

The Lochnagar Crater (1) stands in front of the German line and is probably the largest ever man-made crater. Its aim was to destroy the German Schwaben Höhe fortified stronghold

The 21/ Northumberland Fusiliers (2nd Tyneside Scottish) attacked north of the crater towards the Schwaben Höhe. You should be able to see the Golden Virgin statue on top of the Basilica in Albert and between you and the town, the Tara and Usna hills from where the Tyneside Irish attacked. As you are in front of the German front line, you can appreciate how the Tyneside Irish, who had to cover the greatest distance of any battalions on the day, were easy targets for the German machine-gunners

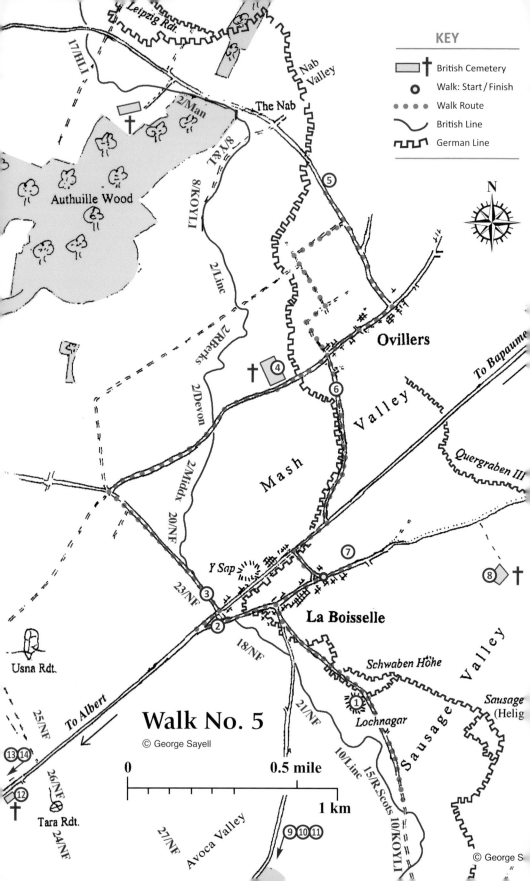

KEY

▭ ✝	British Cemetery
⊙	Walk: Start / Finish
••••	Walk Route
⌒	British Line
⊔⊔⊔	German Line

N

Leipzig Rdt.

17/HLI

12/Man

Nab Valley

The Nab

T8/A8

8/KOYLI

Authuille Wood

2/Line

2/R.Berks

⑤

2/Devon

2/Middx

✝ ④

Ovillers

⑥

Mash Valley

To Bapaume

Quergraben III

20/NF

23/NF

Y Sap

③

⑦

⑧ ✝

②

La Boisselle

Usna Rdt.

18/NF

21/NF

Schwaben Höhe

①

Lochnagar

Sausage (Helig)

Walk No. 5

© George Sayell

Sausage Valley

25/NF

To Albert

10/Linc

15/R.Scots 10/KOYLI

13 14

26/NF

⑫ ✝

Tara Rdt.

24/NF

0   0.5 mile

1 km

27/NF

Avoca Valley

⑨ ⑩ ⑪

© George S

- Go back to La Boisselle - turn left at the T junction to Albert

You will pass the Glory Hole, a much cratered area on your left which was in No Man's Land and faced by the 18/ Northumberland Fusiliers (1st Tyneside Pioneers). When you reach the small wooded park, (2) you are now on the British front line. No Man's Land here was scarcely 100 yards wide. The Tyneside Memorial seat to the Northumberland Fusiliers is to be found at the end of the park

- Cross the main road and follow the sign to Aveluy

The road you are about to take was the British front line (3). The 23/ Northumberland Fusiliers (4th Tyneside Scottish) attacked to your right with the 20/ Northumberland Fusiliers (1st Tyneside Scottish) to their left. It was here that Private Dodd of the 23/ Northumberland Fusiliers was left with only one sergeant and one lieutenant whom he recalled exclaiming: 'God, where's the rest of the boys?'

To the right, half a mile from Lochnagar, Y Sap mine exploded in Mash Valley. The German front line was the road over 800 yards away which made it one of the widest stretches of No Man's Land to attack on 1st July. The British troops attacking along Mash Valley were subjected to lethal machine-gun fire from La Boisselle and also from Ovillers which was defended by 8 machine-guns

- Continue on the road (beware of the traffic) and take the first turn to the right and walk up to Ovillers Military Cemetery (4)

Half way to Ovillers Military Cemetery, you are crossing the British line with the 2/ Middlesex on the right. They were cut down by machine-gun fire as predicted by their CO, Lieutenant-Colonel Sandys. The 2/ Devons were on the left. The divisional boundary was half way to the village of La Boisselle, between the 2/ Middlesex and 20/ Northumberland Fusiliers

Ovillers Military Cemetery

Started:	As a Dressing Station in July 1916
No. of burials:	3,440 including as many as 2,480 unidentified and 290 1st July (104 Northumberland Fusiliers and 31 Middlesex)
Of interest:	5 captains including 19 year old Brian Mullally, 26/ Northumberland Fusiliers; two lieutenant-colonels, Frederick Heneker, CO 21/ Northumberland Fusiliers attached from the Leinster Regiment and Louis Howard, 24/ Northumberland Fusiliers, aged 37 who died of wounds on 2nd July. Two 16 year olds - Private Cecil Davis, Middlesex, and Rifleman R. Power, Royal Irish Rifles. Drummer W. Carr, Devons. Private George Nugent, 22/ Northumberland Fusiliers whose body was found on the lip of Lochnagar Crater in 1998, is buried here. There are 120 French graves
Architect:	Sir Herbert Baker

Y Sap Crater in Mash Valley photographed from the British front line   *Sir Douglas Haig's Great Push*

This photograph is the left hand side of the one above. It shows a great number of British dead bodies in Mash Valley. In order not to offend public sensitivity, it was not used in the publication

- **Turn left out of the cemetery. You soon cross the German front line. In Ovillers take the first path to your left to Calvaire Breton. Stop when the path bears to the right**

  You are just behind the German front line. The undulation in the field to your left marks the German front line. The 2/ Devons attacked from behind the cemetery with the 2/ Royal Berks to their left

- **Follow the path. Turn left when you see the Breton cross, a memorial to soldiers from Brittany who died in the fighting in the area in December 1914. Stop when you reach a path on your left**

  The 2/ Lincolns came towards you from the left led by Lieutenant-Colonel Reginald Bastard

- Continue on the path and turn immediately right and then left onto the tarmac road and walk for 100 yards

From this point (5) you can see the Thiepval monument and, in between, Nab Valley. You are standing behind the German front line. No Man's Land here was about 325 yards wide. The British line was held by the 8/ York and Lancaster and to their right the 8/ KOYLI. Authuille Wood is behind the British front line

- Return to Ovillers on the tarmac road. Turn right at the T junction in the village, go past the war memorial and the church and turn left into Rue Saint-Vincent. Stop when you reach the second house on your left (6)

From here you have a good view of Mash Valley to your right and should just about see the top of the Albert Basilica in the distance. The German machine-gunners had an excellent view of the assaulting troops - the 23 and 20/ Northumberland Fusiliers and the 2/ Middlesex (Lieutenant-Colonel Sandys)

View of German trench from La Boisselle with the ruins of Ovillers in the background - you are about to walk along the trench line shown in the photograph

259

- Continue to La Boisselle, turn right onto the main road and take the first street to your left - Rue de la Place, at the end of which you will find your car by the church. To see the 34th Division Monument, (7) walk beyond the church. Take the grassy path to the left after the last house in the village. You may now be in need of refreshment. The Old Blighty café is down the village street on the right

CAR ITINERARY:

- Lochnagar Crater (1) 50.016249, 2.697232

- La Boisselle, Glory Hole and Tyneside Memorial Seat (2) 50.018512, 2.687237

- Mash Valley (3) 50.019982, 2.687128

- Ovillers Military Cemetery (4) 50.028409, 2.691943

- Nab Valley (5) 50.039203, 2.691465

- View of German front line from Ovillers to La Boisselle (6)
  50.028667, 2.695649

- 34th Division Memorial (7) 50.021293, 2.697303

- **Gordon Dump Cemetery** at the northern end of Sausage Valley (8)
  50.023033, 2.705392

Started:	July 1916 and expanded after the War
No. of burials:	1,676 including 1,053 unidentified and 311 on 1st July (70 KOYLI and 41 Royal Scots)
Of interest:	7 captains including 19 year old Anthony Sapte, Middlesex. An 18 year old 2nd Lieutenant Frank Golding, KOYLI and Brevet-Major Graham Bosanquet MC and Légion d'Honneur, attached 64th Brigade. Donald Bell, a teacher and footballer was awarded the VC for his actions on 5th July and was killed on 10th July
Architect:	Sir Herbert Baker

- **Bécourt Military Cemetery** (9) 50.004123, 2.684294

Started:	August 1915
No. of burials:	713 including 8 unidentified and 16 on 1st July
Of interest:	49 year old Lieutenant-Colonel Arthur Addison, 9/ York and Lancaster and Lieutenant Robert Gilson, 11/ Suffolks
Architect:	Sir Herbert Baker

- **Norfolk Cemetery** (10) 49.999480,2.692640

Started:	August 1915
No. of burials:	549 including 224 unidentified and 27 1st July
Of interest:	CO of 9/ KOYLI Lieutenant-Colonel Colmer Lynch and Major Stuart Loudoun-Shand VC, 10/ Yorkshire (Green Howards)
Architect:	Sir Herbert Baker

- **Dartmoor Cemetery** (11) 49.991690, 2.688130

Started:	August 1915 when it was known as Bécordel-Bécourt Military Cemetery. Its name was changed in May 1916 at the request of the 8 and 9/ Devons
No. of burials	768 including 5 unidentified and 2 1st July
Of interest:	Lieutenant-Colonel Harry Allardice, 36th Jacob's Horse, attached 13/ Northumberland Fusiliers. One of the oldest soldiers to die in the Great War, Lieutenant Harry Webber was killed on 21st July 1916 at the age of 67
Architect:	Sir Edwin Lutyens

- **Bapaume Post Military Cemetery** (12) 50.011824, 2.673913

Started:	July 1916
No. of burials:	410 including 181 unidentified and 40 1st July (27/ Northumberland Fusiliers)
Of interest:	Two CO lieutenant-colonels William Lyle, 23/ Northumberland Fusiliers and Charles Sillery, aged 54, 20/ Northumberland Fusiliers (Indian Army retired- i.e. a 'dug-out')
Architect:	Charles Holden

- **Albert French Military Cemetery** (13) 49.996945, 2.662986. **It was started in the early 1920s. There are 6,290 burials including 2,879 in four ossuaries. There are 1st July burials**

- **Albert-Basilica and Musée des Abris** (14) 50.003542, 2.648010 Albert was a logistical centre for the offensive and was seriously shelled. It is now the main centre for visitors to the battlefields. It was known as the Lourdes of the north of France because in the Middle Ages a shepherd found a statue in a meadow which was reputed to have miraculous properties so the Basilica was built in the 1890s to venerate it and was adorned by a gold-leafed statue of the Virgin Mary. Early in the War the Virgin was dislodged by shelling but did not fall and hanging precariously,

French 1st July casualty

the troops dubbed her 'The Leaning Virgin of Albert'. The British and French believed that the War would end on the day the Virgin fell and the Germans that whoever knocked it down would lose the War. She was eventually brought down by British shelling in 1918 when Albert was in the hands of the Germans. The statue on the re-built Basilica is a gilt replica. Le Musée des Abris is housed in tunnels under the Basilica and square. It features scenes of trench life during battles on the Somme

French Military Cemetery in Albert

6 Thiepval

'Machine-guns bristled like spines on a hedgehog'
Lieutenant-Colonel David Laidlaw, 16/ Highland Light Infantry

This walk covers the area of the attack by the 32nd Division

Points of interest:

- Leipzig Redoubt

- Area where Turnbull won his VC

- Lonsdale Cemetery

- The Memorial to the Missing and the Visitor Centre at Thiepval

- Site of Thiepval Château

Distance: **Over 3 miles**

Approximate time: **2.5 to 3 hours**

Park at the Thiepval Centre. 50.052591, 2.687306 **Go to the Monument and walk past it. Continue on the gravel area until it turns into a path. You will come to a small copse**

> You have reached two formidable German strongholds, the Leipzig Redoubt (1) and further back the Wonder Work (Wundt Werk). Beyond the crossroads, ahead of you is the British front line where the action of Sergeant Turnbull of the 17/ HLI earned him the VC posthumously

- **Turn left at the crossroads and at the Dorsetshire Memorial take the path to the Lonsdale Cemetery (2). Before you reach the cemetery along a line of trees on the left you will see an important communication trench known as 'Tithebarn'**

Lonsdale Cemetery

Started: Spring 1917

No. of burials: 1,542 including 816 unidentified and 228 1st July (83 Highland Light Infantry and 60 Border)

Of interest: A 20 year old captain, Geoffrey Heald, 15/ Lancashire Fusiliers, and posthumous VC Sergeant James Turnbull, 17/ HLI

Architect: Sir Herbert Baker

- **Go back up the path and turn right. Walk 220 yards until you reach a dip which marks the divisional boundary between the 8th and 32nd Divisions**

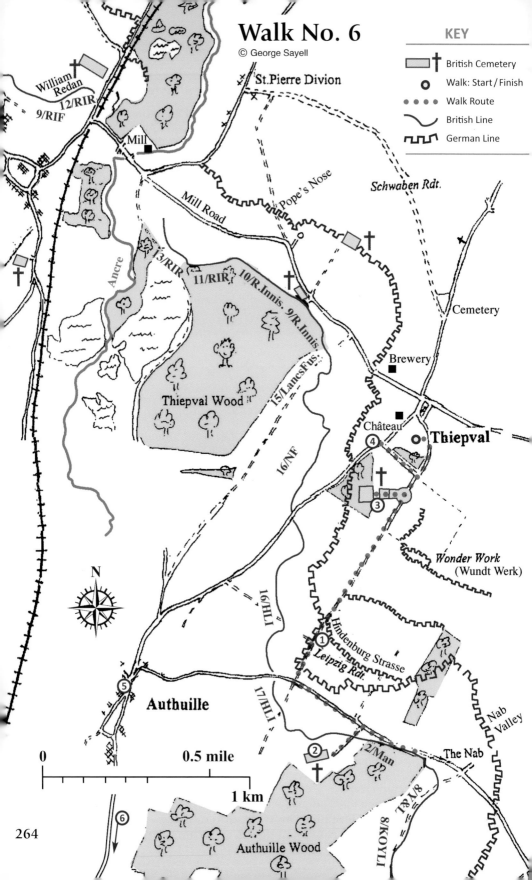

Walk No. 6

© George Sayell

KEY

- ⬜✝ British Cemetery
- ⭕ Walk: Start/Finish
- •••• Walk Route
- ∿ British Line
- ⊓⊓⊓ German Line

William Redan
12/RIR
9/RIF

St.Pierre Divion

Mill

Mill Road

Pope's Nose

Schwaben Rdt.

Ancre

13/RIR

11/RIR

10/R.Innis. 9/R.Innis.

Cemetery

Brewery

15/LancsFus.

Thiepval Wood

16/NF

Château

4

Thiepval

3

Wonder Work
(Wundt Werk)

N

16/HLI

Hindenburg Strasse

1

Leipzig Rdt.

17/HLI

5

Authuille

2

2/Man

Nab Valley

The Nab

8/KOYLI

8/SLI

0   0.5 mile

1 km

6

Authuille Wood

You are on the British front line where the 2/ Manchesters were manning trenches. You can see trenches in the wood on your right. The Germans were 450 yards to your left. The Nab is in front of you

- Retrace your steps towards the Thiepval Memorial

At the turning to the Leipzig Redoubt and the Memorial, the 17/ Highland Light Infantry (Glasgow Commercials) attacked from the left. The 16/ HLI (Glasgow Boys Brigade) were further up to the right of the tarmac road and the enormity of their challenge was highlighted by Private Ramage's description of a wall of German soldiers standing shoulder to shoulder 'waving us to come on'

- View the Thiepval Memorial (3) and Anglo-French Cemetery

Thiepval Anglo-French Cemetery

Started:	Early in the 1930s following a decision to have a small mixed cemetery to represent the two nations' mutual losses
No. of burials:	300 British and 300 French including 492 unidentified and 2 killed on 1st July. Look out for the inscription at the base of the Cross of Sacrifice which commemorates the common sacrifice of the two nations

Thiepval Memorial to the Missing of the Somme

Unveiled:	By the Prince of Wales on 1st August 1932 in the presence of the French President Albert Lebrun
No. commemorated:	72,255 with no known grave who died in the Somme before 20th March 1918. Of those 12,397 died on 1st July amongst whom were:
89 captains	youngest 20 year old Spencer Jeudwine, 2/ Lincolns and oldest 50 year old John Weir, 9/ Royal Inniskilling Fusiliers
10 majors	including 4 in the Northumberland Fusiliers
6 lieutenant-colonels	53 year old Arthur Elphinstone, 22/ Northumberland Fusiliers, George Guyon, 16/ West Yorks (1st Bradford Pals) but listed on the Royal Fusiliers panels, Laurence Hind MC, 1/7 Notts and Derbys (Sherwood Foresters), Edgar Innes CMG, 1/8 Royal Warwicks, Maurice Kennard MC, aged 32, 18/ West Yorks (2nd Bradford Pals) and Donald Wood, 1 / Rifle Brigade

Three of the subjects in Chapter III 'Zero Hour' are also included on the Memorial: 2nd Lieutenant Kenneth Perkin, 12/ Yorks and Lancs (Sheffield City), Lieutenant Roy Mellor, 22/ Manchesters (7th City Pals) and Private Arthur Seanor, 18/ King's (2nd Liverpool Pals). There is one 15 year old, Private Henry (Harry) Woodward, 1/6 Royal Warwicks and seven 16 year olds, all privates - Wilfred Fletcher, York and Lancaster,

George Hart, Northumberland Fusiliers, Thomas Marcus, Royal Inniskilling Fusiliers, Richard Matthew, West Yorks, Charles Osborne, Queen's (Royal West Surreys), Charles Pemberton, Machine-Gun Corps, and Kenneth Reeves, Devons

20 year old Lieutenant Valentine Braithwaite, is remembered on the Somerset Light Infantry panels. His parents erected one of the few private memorials in the Somme next to Serre Road Cemetery No. 2 with the inscription 'God buried him and no man knoweth his sepulchre' (Deuteronomy 34:6)

Three brothers, all in the 9/ Royal Irish Fusiliers, are commemorated: Privates Andrew, David and Sergeant Robert Hobbs. Others of interest include professional footballer Lieutenant Evelyn Lintott, 15/ West Yorks, the poet Corporal Alexander Robertson, 12/ York and Lancaster, and Rifleman William McFadzean VC, 14/ Royal Irish Rifles

Of interest: The Memorial is an Anglo-French Battle Memorial in recognition of the joint nature of the 1916 offensive. It is 150 feet high and space for all the names is created by the design of 16 pillars (piers). It is the largest British War Memorial in the world. Over 90% of those commemorated died between July and November 1916. It was built between 1928 and 1932

Architect: Sir Edwin Lutyens - 'All that is done of structure should be for all and for equality of honour'

- **Exit the Memorial Park, turn immediately left and go down to the**

    18th Division Memorial (4) to the Division, commanded by Major-General Ivor Maxse that captured Thiepval in September 1916. Thiepval Château was across the road immediately to your right - the 15/ Lancs Fusiliers (1st Salford Pals) attacked Thiepval village through its gardens.

    From here five important sites are visible - from right to left: Mill Road Cemetery on top of a ridge, the Ulster Tower, the Sunken Road, Connaught Cemetery and Thiepval Wood (known to the French as Bois d'Authuille) which marks the British front line and the boundary between the 32nd and 36th (Ulster) Divisions. The 16/ Northumberland Fusiliers (Newcastle Commercials) attacked from your left and were cut down by enfilade machine-gun fire, provoking their CO, Lieutenant Colonel Ritson, to exclaim in tears 'My God! My boys! My boys!'

Return to your car

CAR ITINERARY:

- ○ **Thiepval Memorial and Visitor Centre (3)** 50.052591, 2.687306

- ○ **18th Division Memorial, Thiepval (4)** 50.052670, 2.685764

- ○ **Leipzig Redoubt (1)** 50.042883, 2.680204

○ **Lonsdale Cemetery (2)** 50.041252, 2.684790

- **Authuille Memorials:** by the local war memorial is a small brick wall with a plaque to the Salford Pals and on the church wall a black plaque to the 15, 16 and 17/ Highland Light Infantry (5)   50.042876, 2.668966

- **Blighty Valley Cemetery** (6)   50.033124, 2.664705

Started: June 1916

No. of burials: 1,027 including 536 unidentified and 227 1st July (90 York and Lancaster and 56 KOYLI)

Of interest: Four captains including 3 from the York and Lancaster Regiment. Lieutenant-Colonel B. Maddison, 8/ York and Lancaster

Architect: Sir Herbert Baker

View of Thiepval and Ancre Valley
1. *Thiepval Memorial*
2. *Anglo-French Cemetery - to the left was the British front line*
3. *Site of Thiepval Château*
4. *Thiepval Wood (36th Division)*
5. *Connaught Cemetery*
6. *Mill Road Cemetery*
7. *Ulster Tower*
8. *Schwaben Redoubt*
9. *Site of Thiepval Brewery (machine-gun). Notice white markings of trench systems*

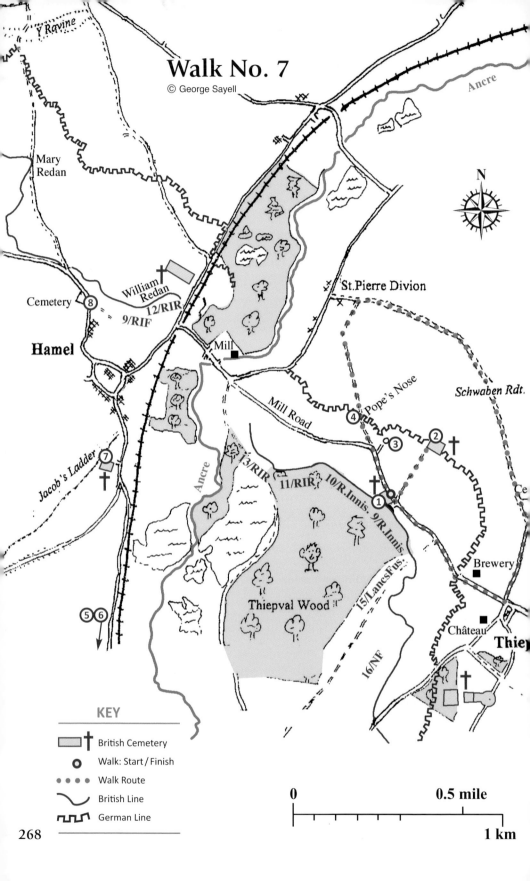

Walk No. 7
© George Sayell

Y Ravine

Ancre

N

Mary
Redan

Cemetery ⑧

William Redan
12/RIR
9/RIF

St.Pierre Divion

Hamel

Mill

Mill Road

Pope's Nose

Schwaben Rdt.

④

③

②

Jacob's Ladder ⑦

13/RIR

11/RIR

10/R.Innis. 9/R.Innis.

①

Ce

Ancre

Brewery

⑤⑥

Thiepval Wood

15/LancsFus.

16/NF

Château

Thie

KEY

British Cemetery

Walk: Start / Finish

Walk Route

British Line

German Line

0   0.5 mile

1 km

7 Ulster Tower and Ancre Valley

'Was there ever such a day?'

Lieutenant-Colonel Frank Crozier, 9/ Royal Irish Rifles

This walk covers the area of the attack by the 36th (Ulster) Division

Points of interest:

- Connaught Cemetery

- Mill Road Cemetery

- Ulster Division's attack, Lieutenant-Colonel Frank Crozier 9/ Royal Irish Rifles

- Ulster Memorial Tower

- The Pope's Nose

Distance:	3 miles
Approximate time:	2.5 hours

Park outside Connaught Cemetery (1) 50.058826, 2.680873 **on what was the Sunken Road which, at the time, was much deeper. On your way from Thiepval you have crossed the boundary between 32nd and 36th Divisions. Visit**

Connaught Cemetery where many in the Ulster Division are buried

Started:	Autumn 1916
No. of burials:	1,268 including 624 unidentified and 193 on 1st July, 83 of the Royal Inniskilling Fusiliers
Of interest:	Two captains and two 17 year olds, Private Robert Wallace, Royal Inniskilling Fusiliers and Private H. Riddell, Lancashire Fusiliers. In November 2013, during roadworks, three bodies were found - Sergeant David Harkness Blakey MM aged 26, 11/ Royal Inniskilling Fusiliers who was posted missing on 1st July, and two unidentified, one Royal Irish Rifles and one Cambridgeshire. They were officially buried in the cemetery in the right hand corner nearest the road in October 2015
Architect:	Sir Reginald Blomfield

The edge of the wood was the British front line. The 9/ Royal Inniskillings (Tyrone) attacked from here with, to their left, the 10/ Royal Inniskillings (Derry). The 9/ Royal Irish Rifles (West Belfast), commanded by Lieutenant-Colonel Crozier were in the third wave of the attack

The first action to result in a VC on 1st July, awarded posthumously, was that of Rifleman W. McFadzean of the 14/ Royal Irish Rifles (Belfast Young Citizens) when they were waiting in the wood

- Take the path opposite to Mill Road Cemetery which is on the German first line 300 yards in front of the Schwaben Redoubt

You are following in the footsteps of the Ulstermen attacking the Schwaben Redoubt, probably the strongest of all the German positions on 1st July

Mill Road Cemetery (2)

Started:	Spring 1917
No. of burials:	1,304 including 115 unidentified and 93 on 1st July of which 8 are Royal Inniskilling Fusiliers
Of interest:	Many of the headstones are lying flat because of subsidence over German dug-outs. Two captains and two majors are buried here
Architect:	Sir Herbert Baker

- Return to the road, turn right and walk to the Ulster Tower. *Note that the site is closed on Mondays.* The custodians of the Ulster Tower organise fascinating and informative tours of Thiepval Wood at 11.00 and 15.00 hours (check beforehand) where trenches, dug-outs and a trench mortar pit have been restored. Afterwards visit the Memorial Room in the Tower and the small museum in the Visitor Centre

The Ulster Tower (3) is in No Man's Land on the site of the attack by the 36th (Ulster) Division's 10/ Royal Inniskillings supported by the 11/ Royal Irish Rifles (South Antrim) on their left. It is a replica of Helen's Tower in the grounds of the Clandeboye Estate near Newtownards, County Down, where the Ulster Division trained. It was unveiled by Field Marshal Sir Henry Wilson, CIGS on 21st November 1921

- Leave the Tower taking the path immediately to your right (don't go down the tarmac road) until you reach a partially destroyed structure in the field to your right, known as

The Pope's Nose (4) which was how the Ulstermen described the shape of the German front line where an Observation Post was located. The 13/ Royal Irish Rifles (County Down) held trenches down to the river Ancre. Hamel village is in the Ancre valley to your left. Beyond the village and slightly to its right is woodland that surrounds the Newfoundland Memorial Park which was the next sector of the two front lines. In early autumn you may be able to see in front of the Park white markings that reveal some of the trench systems. There were no attacks either side of the Ancre due to marshy land

- Continue on the path and then turn right and stop at the highest point of the slope. Look to the right

You are on the Schwaben Redoubt, a heavily fortified underground 'town' with a maze of tunnels and dug-outs. It was sometimes referred to by British troops as the 'Parallelogram'. You can see on your right Mill Road Cemetery which is on the German front line, the British front line on the edge of Thiepval Wood in the distance and the Ulster Tower

Two VCs were awarded, one to Captain Eric Bell, 9/ Royal Inniskilling Fusiliers for actions in the Redoubt and the other to Corporal George Sanders, 1/7 West Yorks (Leeds Rifles), for his 'gallantry' between the Redoubt and Thiepval

- Continue to the end of the path. Turn right at the civilian cemetery onto the road and go to Thiepval. Turn right at the crossroads and stop after about 200 yards when the road bends to the right. You are now in the line of fire from machine-gun Number 9 positioned at the former Thiepval Brewery on your right which also fired towards the Ulster Tower. In total the machine-gun fired 18,000 rounds on the 1st July. Continue down to your car at Connaught Cemetery with care …

CAR ITINERARY:

- ○ **Connaught Cemetery** (1) 50.058826, 2.680873

- ○ **Mill Road Cemetery** (2) 50.058826, 2.680873 This involves a short walk

- ○ **Ulster Tower and Visitor Centre** (3) 50.060932, 2.679461

- ○ **Pope's Nose** (4) 50.060932, 2.679461 This involves a short walk

- **Martinsart British Cemetery** (5) 50.038036, 2.634850

Started:	June 1916
No. of burials:	488 including 155 unidentified and 9 1st July
Of interest:	Colonel Herbert Bernard (50) CO 10/ Royal Irish Rifles. It is the largest CWGC cemetery consisting of experimental graves of red Locharbriggs sandstone which were deemed not to be as satisfactory as white Portland stone
Architect:	Sir Reginald Blomfield

- **Aveluy Wood Cemetery** (6) 50.045311, 2.660154

Started:	June 1916 known as 'Lancashire Dump'
No. of burials:	380 including 172 unidentified and six 1st July, 3 of them sappers
Architect:	Sir Reginald Blomfield

- **Hamel Cemetery and local war memorial** (7) 50.060383, 2.662442

Started: August 1915 by Field Ambulances

No. of burials: 500 including 80 unidentified and 23 1st July of which 17 Royal Irish Fusiliers

Architect: Sir Edwin Lutyens

Note on the wall of Hamel church the plaque to the 1/ Essex who were in the same disastrous wave as the Newfoundland Regiment. Drive up to and park opposite the civilian cemetery

You are at Suicide Corner (8) 50.067011, 2.660597 so-named because of the danger of being targeted by German machine-guns situated in the area of what is now the Ulster Tower. Look across the valley of the Ancre. You can see the Ulster Tower and Thiepval Wood to the right. You are on the British front line. Immediately to your right were the 9/ Royal Irish Fusiliers (County Armagh, Monaghan and Cavan)- to their right towards the river in a small salient known as the William Redan were one company of the 12/ Royal Irish Rifles (Central Antrim)

VCs were awarded for actions in the area to Lieutenant Geoffrey Cather, adjutant of the 9/ Royal Irish Fusiliers and Private Robert Quigg of 12/ Royal Irish Rifles

On your way in the car to the Newfoundland Memorial Park, the British front line is to the right; it twists to the right then to the left in a salient shape known as the Mary Redan, manned by the 1/ Royal Inniskilling Fusiliers. The Mary Redan marks the boundary between the 36th and 29th Divisions

Martinsart British Cemetery
with experimental graves

272

8 Newfoundland Memorial Park and Beaumont

'Dead Men Can Advance No Further'

Major-General Henry de Beauvoir de Lisle, 29th Division

This walk covers the area of the attack by the 29th Division

Points of interest:

- Newfoundland Memorial Park:
  - > *The area where Newfoundlander Jim Stacey was a runner*
  - > *Caribou Monument and Newfoundland Memorial*
  - > *Trench systems*
  - > *The Tree of Danger*

- Beaumont Village

- Hawthorn Ridge Mine Crater

- The 1/ Lancashire Fusiliers and the Sunken Road

- Locations for Geoffrey Malins's filming of the Hawthorn Ridge Mine and troops in the Sunken Road

Distance:	5 miles
Approximate time:	3.5 hours

The zigzag lines on the car park show the position of some British assembly trenches

Park at the Newfoundland Memorial Park. 50.072412, 2.647094 N.B. Check when the car park shuts… Note the zig zag white lines on the car park that signify trenches where troops were waiting to go to the front line. Enter the Park (1). To either side of the path, you will see the British reserve trench. Walk on to the 29th Division Memorial which is between the British reserve and 2nd support trenches. On the right of the path look out for the bronze plaque with the poem by John Oxenham, *Tread Softly Here*

- **Walk to the top of the Caribou Monument**

The Caribou was the emblem of the Newfoundland Regiment. The sculptor was an Englishman, Basil Gotto. It is a memorial to the Newfoundlanders killed on 1st July, pointing in the direction that they attacked. The first support trench is below it and beyond it the front line trench. No Man's Land extended to the line of trees down the slope. Unusually the British trenches were concentrated here on high ground

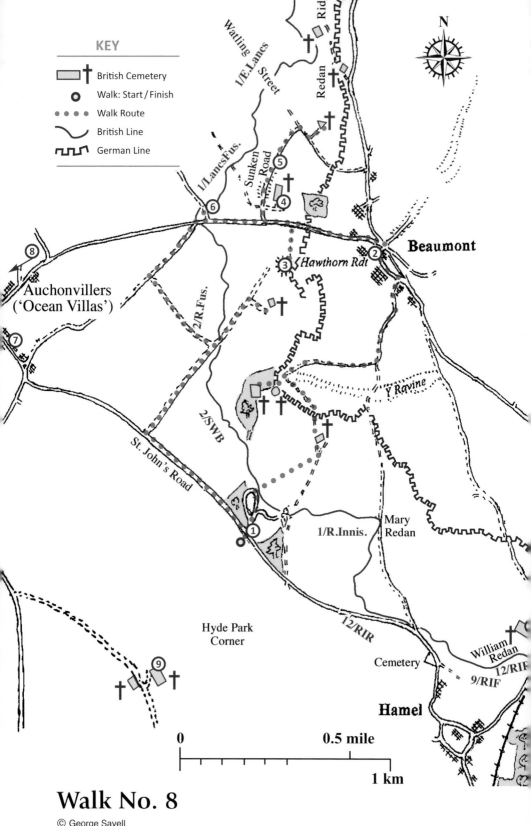

KEY

▭ †	British Cemetery
○	Walk: Start / Finish
••••	Walk Route
∿	British Line
⊓⊔⊓	German Line

N

Redan Ridge

Watling Street

1/E.Lancs

1/LancsFus.

Sunken Road

⑤

④

Beaumont

⑥

②

Hawthorn Rdt

③

2/R.Fus.

⑧

Auchonvillers
('Ocean Villas')

⑦

Y Ravine

2/SWB

St. John's Road

①

Mary
Redan

1/R.Innis.

Hyde Park
Corner

12/RIR

William
Redan

Cemetery

12/RIF

9/RIF

⑨

Hamel

0   0.5 mile

1 km

Walk No. 8

© George Sayell

Newfoundland Memorial Park showing:
1. *The Caribou*
2. *British support trench*
3. *British front line*
4. *Tree of Danger*
5. *Trench for November attack*
6. *Y Ravine Cemetery*
7. *German front line*
8. *Hawthorn Ridge Cem. No.2*
9. *Y Ravine*
J Kerr

- **Walk down to the base of the Caribou mound where you will see the**

Newfoundland Memorial

Unveiled:	7th June 1925 by Earl Haig
No. commemorated:	814 including 134 1st July, the majority in their early twenties. W. Pilgrim is named on the Memorial but he survived the War
Of interest:	2nd Lieutenant Gerald Ayre aged 25, one of four cousins who died on 1st July. One 16 year old, Private William Morgan and two 17 year old privates, Norman Coultas and Stephen Fallon. There are two pairs of brothers - Privates George (21) and Stanley Abbott (22) and 2nd Lieutenant Roy (27) and Sergeant Stewart Ferguson (26)
Architect:	R.H.K. Cochius

- **Now walk into the trench on the right of the path**

It was the first support trench. Those trying to make their way to the front line would have faced large numbers of wounded retreating towards them. Go up the wooden steps to the 1st July British front line trench with a communication trench to the right. No Man's Land is ahead into which the 2/ South Wales Borderers attacked

- Go down the concrete path until you come to a tree stump known as

The Tree of Danger or Danger Tree which marks the spot where many soldiers were killed as they tried to pass through barbed wire and were easy targets for German machine-guns. Further down the path, the trench you see on your left, Wellington Trench was dug for the final action in November

Tree of Danger now

- Go to the bottom of the slope to visit

Y Ravine Cemetery

Started:	Spring 1917
No. of burials:	Over 400 including a third unidentified and 136 1st July of whom 45 Royal Inniskilling Fusiliers and 36 Newfoundlanders
Of interest:	2nd Lieutenant John Karran, 2/ South Wales Borderers is buried here and also in the same battalion CSM Joseph Fairbrass, one of six brothers who served, three of whom were killed during the War
Architect:	Sir Reginald Blomfield

Original Tree of Danger

- **Turn right out of the cemetery until you reach a deep trench on both sides of the path**

The trench marks the German front line - notice how 100 years on it is still deeper than the British one. Take in the German view of No Man's Land up to the Caribou

- **Keep on the path to the 51st (Highland Division) Memorial on the left**

It commemorates the Division's capture of Beaumont village, a 1st July objective not achieved until 13th November. The inscription on the base translates as 'Friends are good on the day of battle.' Opposite, there is a memorial cross to the Division

- **Follow the path to the left, walk over the German trench and take a look at**

Hunter's Cemetery, unusual for its circular shape. Most of the burials are of the Black Watch from November 1916 and then

Hawthorn Ridge Cemetery No. 2

Started: Spring 1917

No. of burials: More than 200 including over 50 unidentified and 137 1st July of which 46 are Border Regiment and 45 Royal Fusiliers

Of interest: An example of a soldier who used an alias: Sergeant W. Cottam who served as D. Kircaldy, Border Regiment. Notice how the bodies were buried in serried ranks at the time

Architect: G.H. Goldsmith

- Go back over the German trench, bear left onto the path and stop at the gate

  Y Ravine to your right is a rare example of Germans not holding higher ground as it was ideal for building their defensive dug-outs. They called it Leiling Schlucht after Hauptmann (Captain) Franz Leiling RIR 99

- Go through the gate to the German held village of Beaumont. Turn left on the tarmac road where there is an unusual local war memorial. Go to the church (2)

  Note the face of an angel or the Virgin Mary in the stained glass window to the left of the main door which was found in the ruins of the original church, taken to Germany and brought back in 1962 by Leutnant Georg Mueller of RIR 99

- Beyond the church turn left at the cross roads noting the white flag pole and plaque to the 51st (Highland) Division. About 350 yards outside the village on the left there is a sign by a fence. Go up to

  The Hawthorn Ridge mine crater (3) created by a charge of 40,600 lbs of ammonal. It was attacked by the 2/ Royal Fusiliers

When at the crater, look back and from right to left, you will see the wood that delineates the German front line where No Man's Land was 550 yards wide, Beaumont Hamel British Cemetery, which is in the middle of No Man's Land and the Sunken Road where some of the 1/ Lancashire Fusiliers hid prior to going over the top. Beyond you can see the Redan Ridge

Lancashire Fusiliers in the Sunken Road before going over the top

From the left end of the long embankment known as Jacob's Ladder, Geoffrey Malins filmed the explosion of the Hawthorn Ridge mine at 7.20 a.m. and the second wave attack of the 16/ Middlesex (the Public Schools Battalion) which took place along the field in front of you

277

View from the German front line at Hawthorn Ridge:
1. Beaumont Hamel British Cemetery
2. The Sunken Road   3. German front line   4. Redan Ridge

As you walk round the crater, bear in mind that many Germans of RIR 119 were killed (8 officers and 93 other ranks) and their bodies never recovered so it is in a sense a war grave. It is about 60 ft deep. What you see is the result of two explosions on 1st July and 13th November

- Return to the road and turn left. Take the path on the right to the

  The Memorial to the 1/ 8 Argyll and Sutherland Highlanders, the largest memorial to a single battalion on the Western Front. It is located near their Battalion HQ from where they attacked on 13th November

- Take the grass path opposite the memorial to the

Beaumont Hamel British Cemetery (4)

Started: November 1916

No. of burials: 179 including 82 unidentified and 38 1st July of which 16 are Lancashire Fusiliers. There is one German grave

Of interest: The cemetery was built in No Man's Land

Architect: W.H. Cowlishaw

- Return to the memorial and turn right and walk up the Sunken Road (5)

  Of the many sunken roads in the Somme, this is the most renowned because of Malins's famous footage of the 1/ Lancashire Fusiliers anxiously waiting to go over the top

- Turn right at the top of the Sunken Road and then left to

Redan Ridge Cemetery No. 2

Started: Spring 1917

No. of burials: Over 250 including 100 unidentified and 107 1st July of which 57 are Hants

Of interest: Three drummers - H. Toomer, 1/ Hants and W. Morgan and A. Lakin both 1/ Lancashire Fusiliers

Architect: Sir Reginald Blomfield

- Return to the Sunken Road and turn right on to the tarmac road. Take the first path on the right and walk up to the small concrete building (6)

  You are standing on the British front line at the spot where Malins was filming. Look towards the mine crater circled by trees which you visited earlier. You can see clearly the slope on the other side of the road along which the Public Schools Battalion were filmed during their assault

- Go back to the road and take the path on the left for 350 yards. Then take the first path on the left and at the end of it, turn left at a T junction and walk up to

Hawthorn Ridge Cemetery No. 1

Started: Spring 1917

No. of burials: Over 150 half of which are unidentified. There are 72 1st July burials - 42 are of 16/ Middlesex (Public Schools)

Of interest: The grave of 2nd Lieutenant Eric Heaton

Architect: W.C. von Berg

- Retrace your steps but keep straight on - do not turn right. When you reach the main road turn left and return to your car

CAR ITINERARY:

o   Newfoundland Memorial Park (1)   50.072412, 2.647094
    A circular walk is involved

o   Beaumont village and church (2)   50.083714, 2.656070

o   Beaumont Hamel British Cemetery (4)   50.085703, 2.648329

o   The Sunken Road (5)   50.085703, 2.648329

o   Hawthorn Ridge Mine Crater (3)   50.084855, 2.650881
    Short walk up to the crater

o   Location from where Geoffrey Malins filmed the Hawthorn Ridge explosion and the Public Schools Battalion's attack (6)   50.085099, 2.644872

- Auchonvillers village (7) 'Ocean Villas' tearooms and museum are well worth visiting   50.080050, 2.631282

- **Auchonvillers Military Cemetery** (8)   50.080769, 2.627056

Started: 1915

No. of burials: 528 including 42 unidentified and 52 1st July of which 13 are 16/ Middlesex (Public Schools)

Architect: Sir Reginald Blomfield

- **Knightsbridge Cemetery** (9) 50.068510, 2.633856   It involves a 10 minute walk taking you past Mesnil Ridge Cemetery (no 1st July casualties here but the graves are of men who died from shelling and raids before July 1916)

Started: July 1916 named after a communication trench

No. of burials: 528 including 141 unidentified and 79 1st July of which 21 are Newfoundlanders and 19 Essex

Of interest:	2nd Lieutenant Wilfrid Ayre (one of four cousins) buried in a row of Newfoundlander casualties. 16 year old Private J. Haston, King's Own Scottish Borderers
Architect:	Sir Reginald Blomfield

- **Ancre British Cemetery** (10) 50.067712, 2.667960

Started:	Spring 1917, expanded after the War from seven small cemeteries
No. of burials:	2,540 including 1,335 unidentified and 167 1st July of which 40 are Royal Irish Fusiliers
Of interest:	CO of 1/ Royal Inniskilling Fusiliers, Lieutenant-Colonel Robert C. Pierce. One major, Thomas Atkinson, Royal Irish Fusiliers, also 3 captains including Eric Ayre, aged 27, Newfoundlander brother of Bernard, 8/ Norfolk, buried in Carnoy Military Cemetery. This cemetery shows how there was little movement north of the Ancre as there are 539 burials from the last action of the Battle of the Somme on 13th November 1916. It is unusual to see unidentified graves dated 1st July 1916 - there are two to be found in Row 8D
Architect:	Sir Reginald Blomfield

Knightsbridge Cemetery was behind the lines -
Newfoundland Memorial Park is in the distance

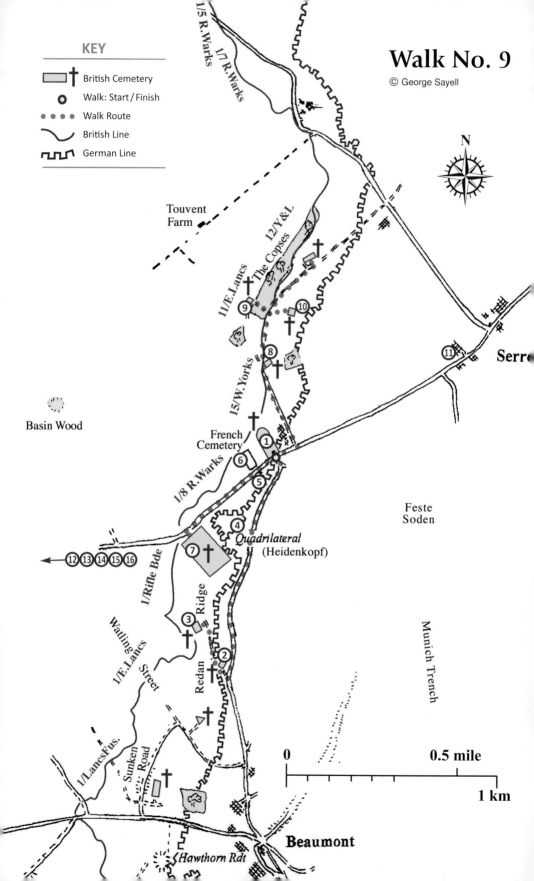

Walk No. 9

© George Sayell

KEY

British Cemetery
Walk: Start / Finish
Walk Route
British Line
German Line

N

1/5 R.Warks

1/7 R.Warks

Touvent Farm

12/Y&L

The Copses

11/E.Lancs

⑨ ⑩

⑧

15/W.Yorks

⑪ Serre

Basin Wood

French Cemetery

① ②

1/8 R.Warks

⑥

⑤

Feste Soden

④

Quadrilateral (Heidenkopf)

⑦

1/Rifle Bde

⑫⑬⑭⑮⑯

Watling Street

Redan Ridge

③

1/E.Lancs

②

Munich Trench

1/LancsFus.

Sunken Road

0   0.5 mile

1 km

Beaumont

Hawthorn Rdt

9 Serre

'If only they had run'

Musketier Karl Blenk, IR 169

This walk covers the area of the attack by the 4th and 31st Divisions and two battalions of the 48th (South Midland) Division

Points of interest:

- Redan Ridge

- A French cemetery

- Six cemeteries in the Serre sector

- Sheffield Memorial Park where Kenneth Perkin attacked

- Pals Memorials

Distance:	4.5 miles
Approximate time:	3 to 4 hours

Park at

Serre Road Cemetery No. 1 (1)   50.099936, 2.657390

Started:	Spring 1917 and extended after the War from six smaller cemeteries
No. of burials:	2,426 including 1,728 unidentified and 134 1st July of which 55 are West Yorks
Of interest:	CO Major J. Bromilow, 1/ Kings Own (Royal Lancaster) died of wounds 2nd July. Sixteen year old Horace Iles 15/ West Yorks (see *Stolen Lives* by Hamilton and Reed), a 17 year old Private Herbert Needham, 18/ Durham Light Infantry, and a Yorkshire cricketer, 2nd Lieutenant Major William Booth (Major is his Christian name). The cemetery is in No Man's Land which was about 200 yards in width with the British line behind the cemetery and the Germans' on the road. The front of the cemetery was the boundary between the 4th and 31st Divisions.
Architect:	N.A. Rew

- Take the small road opposite the cemetery following the CWGC signs up to the Redan Ridge. Stop at the highest point. You should see seven British cemeteries. The German front line runs to your right. Visit

Redan Ridge Cemetery No. 3 (2)

Started:	Spring 1917 in the old German front line

No. of burials:	50 over half unidentified and only one 1st July, a Hampshire, the rest are November 1916
Of interest:	VC: Drummer Walter Ritchie, 2/ Seaforth Highlanders, was awarded the VC for his action here on the Redan Ridge and survived the War
Architect:	W.H. Cowlishaw

- **Turn right out of the cemetery towards**

Redan Ridge Cemetery No. 1 (3) an area of mining and counter-mining before July 1916

Started:	Spring 1917 in No Man's Land which was hardly 100 yards wide
No. of burials:	Over 150 including more than half unidentified and 31 1st July of which 16 are of the 1/ Rifle Brigade
Of interest:	1/ East Lancs attacked south of the cemetery with the 1/ Rifle Brigade to the north
Architect:	W.H. Cowlishaw

- **Retrace your steps until you come to the back of the large Serre Road Cemetery No. 2**

The field to the right of the cemetery marks the site of the Quadrilateral (4) (the Heidenkopf Redoubt). The 1/ 8 Royal Warwicks stormed the Redoubt from the other side of the main road

German view from the Redan Ridge of the Heidenkopf (Quadrilateral) in the foreground which was attacked by 1/ 8 Royal Warwicks, the French Military Chapel and Cemetery and Serre Road Cemetery No. 1 and to the left on the horizon the copses on the British front line

• **Continue until you reach the busy main road and with care turn left**

A French Military chapel (5) is to your left. It was unveiled in 1936 and there is a plaque on the stairs in memory of the French and German soldiers who died in the area. Cross the road and visit the French Military Cemetery - 'Serre-Hébuterne'. (6) It was originally started by the British when clearing the battlefields after the War. All the 834 burials are French soldiers killed in June 1915, 240 in an ossuary. The road is in No Man's Land with Germans to the left and British to the right

- Cross the road and walk up to

Serre Road Cemetery No. 2 (7)

Started: Spring 1917 and greatly enlarged after the War from 16 small cemeteries. It is the largest in the Somme

No. of burials: 7,127 including 4,944 unidentified and 430 1st July of which 64 are of Royal Warwicks

Of interest: 9 captains including Stratford Ludlow, 1/ 8 Royal Warwicks whose father was a brigadier-general who wrote an interesting booklet about his son's last day. Two drummers, Alexander Burr, 1/ 8 Royal Warwicks, aged 18 and Harry Jukes, 1/ Dorsets, aged 48. A 17 year old Private, Albert Wilson, East Lancs and Private Albert Bull, 12/ York and Lancaster (Sheffield City) whose body was found in the Sheffield Memorial Park in 1928. There are two poets, 22 year old 2nd Lieutenant Lionel Field, 1/ 6 Royal Warwicks, and 2nd Lieutenant Gilbert Waterhouse, 2/ Essex

Architect: Sir Edwin Lutyens

- Retrace your steps

  Look out for a cross by the outer wall of the cemetery, a private memorial to 20 year old Lieutenant Valentine Braithwaite, 1/ Somerset L.I. an MC at Mons in 1914 who died on 2nd July and is remembered on the Thiepval Memorial. His father, General Sir Walter Braithwaite, was Chief of the General Staff at Gallipoli in 1915

- Go past Serre Road Cemetery No. 1 and then turn left and go up the path following CWGC signs- *do not attempt to drive*

  You are walking in No Man's Land from the German to the British lines

- When you reach the top of the incline stop and visit

Serre Road Cemetery No. 3 (8)

Started: Spring 1917

No. of burials: Over 80 including over half unidentified and only 22 1st July, 17 of which are West Yorks (Leeds and Bradford Pals)

Of interest: The cemetery lies in front of the British line. Germans shot or bayoneted many wounded here in No Man's Land

Architect: W.H. Cowlishaw

- Continue along the path which is exactly the British front line from which the Leeds Pals attacked. It takes you to a wood which now encompasses the original John, Luke and Mark Copses. Stop at the gate

  The ditch to the left was the 11/ East Lancs (Accrington Pals) front line trench

- Enter

  Sheffield Memorial Park (9). Note the evidence of craters and some trenches. It was opened in 1936. There are several memorials here: to the Accrington, Barnsley and Sheffield Pals and plaques to the Chorley, Bradford and Burnley Pals' Battalions. The Bradford Memorial is a brass plaque on the last tree before you enter

Railway Hollow Cemetery

Started:	Spring 1917 in a British support trench near Mark Copse
Burials:	107 including 44 unidentified and 45 1st July of which 23 are York and Lancaster. There are also two French graves
Of interest:	The cemetery was named after the narrow gauge railway which supplied the front line. A good example of an area where there was no advance in 1916 as there are 14 graves from the last action on 13th November. One interesting inscription can be found on the grave of 23 year old Private Alfred Goodlad, 12/ York and Lancaster (Sheffield Pals). His parents quoted from one of his letters home: 'The French are a grand nation worth fighting for'
Architect:	W.C. von Berg

As you leave the Park, you can see on your left a large cross erected by the parents of Sheffield Pal Private Bull at the site where, according to his comrades, he was last seen alive. His parents had died, however, by the time his body was found in 1928 when it was transferred to Serre Road Cemetery No. 2

- Opposite the gate take the grass path which goes through No Man's Land - over 200 yards wide

  This is where the Accrington Pals attacked. Many of those who fell are to be found in

Queens Cemetery (10)

Started:	Spring 1917 originally known as Queens V Corps Cemetery No.4
Burials:	311 including 131 unidentified and 98 1st July, 45 from the York and Lancaster Regiment
Of interest:	On the grave of Lieutenant Stanley Maurice Bickersteth, 15/ West Yorks (1st Leeds), brother of the Rev. Julian Bickersteth is the inscription 'Fifth son of Dr. Bickersteth, Vicar of Leeds and Ella his wife. Content'. The cemetery is in No Man's Land. Private Willie Dinsdale, 18/ West Yorks (2nd Bradford Pals), served as Metcalfe
Architect:	N.A. Rew

- Retrace your steps turn right and you soon will reach a grass path. On your left is

Luke Copse British Cemetery

The copses (now just one wood) in the background were on the British front line

Started: Spring 1917 on the old front line and named after one of the four Copses - John, Luke, Mark and Matthew

Burials: 72 including 28 unidentified and 14 1st July, all 12/ York and Lancaster (Sheffield City)

Of interest: Two brothers 25 year old Lance Corporal Frank and Private William Gunstone, aged 24, of the York and Lancaster Regiment. Note the double rows indicating mass graves. The cemetery is near the northern extent of the Fourth Army's attack. According to Musketier Karl Blenk, the attacking 12/ York and Lancaster (Sheffield City) 'went down in their hundreds … If only they had run'

Architect: N.A. Rew

- Look back towards the wood and you will see the two crosses of the cemeteries you have visited marking the line of No Man's Land

- Return to your car

CAR ITINERARY:

- Redan Ridge Cemetery No. 3 (2) 50.090758, 2.654298

- Redan Ridge Cemetery No. 1 (3) 50.090758, 2.654298

- The Quadrilateral (Heidenkopf Redoubt) (4) 50.095677, 2.655517

- Serre Road Cemetery No. 2 (7) 50.096502, 2.650992

- Serre Road Cemetery No. 1 (1) 50.099936, 2.657390
  Park here for a short walk to (5), (6), (8), (9) and (10)

- French Military Chapel (5) 50.099936, 2.657390

- French Cemetery (6) 50.099936, 2.657390

- Serre Road Cemetery No. 3 (8) 50.099936, 2.657390

287

○ Sheffield Memorial Park, Pals' Memorials, Railway Hollow Cemetery (9)
50.099936, 2.657390

○ Queens Cemetery (10) 50.099936, 2.657390

• Village of Serre and the

Sheffield Memorial (11) 50.103444, 2.669034

Unveiled: 1923 in the presence of about 150 men who had fought for Serre

Of interest: Serre was adopted by Sheffield after the War

Encouraged in the early 1920s by the British League of Help, many destroyed French villages were adopted by British towns and cities e.g.:

Montauban:	Maidstone	Thiepval:	Tonbridge
Carnoy:	Swansea	Beaumont Hamel:	Winchester
Mametz:	Llandudno	Mailly Maillet:	Winchester
Fricourt:	Ipswich	Hébuterne:	Evesham and Worcester
La Boisselle:	Gloucester	Gommecourt:	Wolverhampton
Ovillers:	Gloucester	Foncquevillers:	Derby
Albert:	Birmingham		

• **Euston Road Cemetery** (12) 50.101870, 2.619745

Started: July 1916

No. of burials: 1,293 including 170 unidentified and 146 1st July of which 41 are York and Lancaster and 41 West York.

Of interest: Unusual grave - Private Stanley Patten (18) 2/ King Edward's Horse. The poet Sergeant Will Streets (31), 12/ York and Lancaster. Two inscriptions of note: 'A boy in years, a man in deeds'- Willie Whitaker (18) 18/ West Yorks (2nd Bradford Pals) and 'The best of sons he nobly did his duty to the last', 2nd Lieutenant Rosser Dean, 4/ Royal Warwicks, attached to Machine-Gun Corps

Architect: Sir Reginald Blomfield

• **Sucrerie Military Cemetery** (13) 50.093383, 2.625611

Started by: The French in summer 1915 and extended by the British

No. of burials: 1,103 including 219 unidentified and 148 1st July 29 of those are Seaforth Highlanders

Of interest: Six captains including J. Young, aged 19, 1/ King's Own (Royal Lancaster), two lieutenant-colonels, John Thicknesse (46) 1/ Somerset Light Infantry and The Hon. Lawrence Palk DSO and Légion d'Honneur (45) 1/ Hants. Note Plot 1 Row H where 19 officers are buried together including 13 1st July. One 16 year old Private John Perkins, 1/6 Royal Warwicks and Rifleman James Crozier, 'Shot at Dawn' 27th February 1916. Spare a thought for Private Alexander McIntyre (50), Cameron Highlanders who died on Christmas Day 1918 and is buried at the end of row HH in plot 1

Architect: Sir Reginald Blomfield

- **Mailly Maillet and church** (14) 50.077009, 2.604190

Mailly Maillet was a billeting village. The 15th Century west façade of its church survived shelling thanks to the foresight of the priest who had it protected by sandbags

- **Mailly Wood Cemetery** (15) 50.075002, 2.598967

Started: June 1916

No. of burials: 702 including 60 unidentified and 17 1st July of which 9 are Lancashire Fusiliers

Architect: Sir Reginald Blomfield

- **Louvencourt Cemetery** (16) 50.089263, 2.503633
  N.B. The cemetery is about a 7 mile drive from Mailly Maillet

Started: July 1915 by Field Ambulances, one of the first three cemeteries to be built by the IWGC

No. of burials: 151 WW1 (including four 1st July), 76 French and three 2nd World War

Of interest: Brigadier-General Charles Bertie Prowse DSO (47) 11th Brigade and 2nd Lieutenant Roland Leighton, 1/ 7 Worcesters, fiancé of Vera Brittain who died on 23rd December 1915 (see *Stolen Lives* by Hamilton and Reed). The French graves were experimental but the design was discarded due to expense and reinforced concrete crosses (béton armé) were used instead

Architect: Sir Reginald Blomfield

The two visible cemeteries Serre Road No. 3 in the foreground and Queens further back stand in No Man's Land. The path to the left was the British front line. In 1916 today's wood was three copses known as Mark, Luke and John. Matthew Copse was to the left   J.Kerr

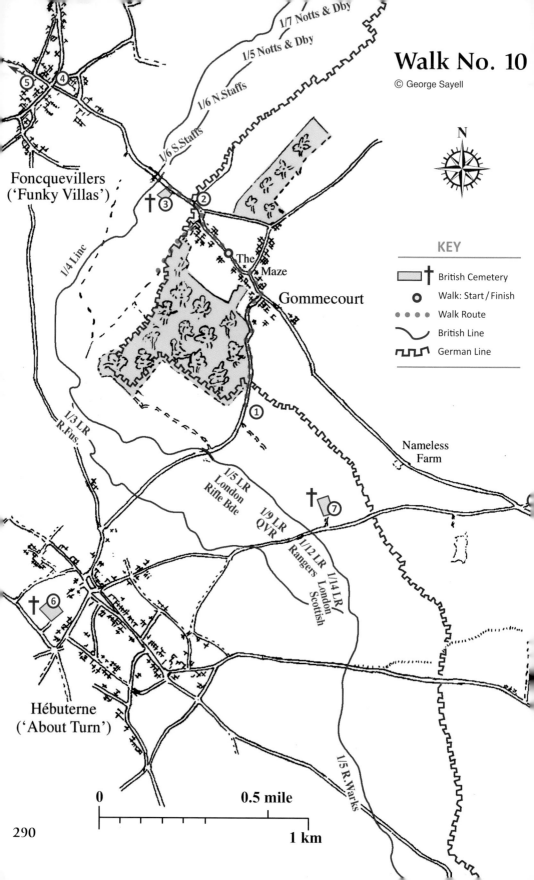

Walk No. 10

© George Sayell

1/7 Notts & Dby

1/5 Notts & Dby

1/6 N Staffs

1/6 S Staffs

1/5 S Staffs

Foncquevillers
('Funky Villas')

1/4 Line

1/3 LR
R.Fus.

The Maze

Gommecourt

Nameless
Farm

1/5 LR
London
Rifle Bde

1/9 LR
QVR

1/12 LR
Rangers

1/14 LR/
London
Scottish

Hébuterne
('About Turn')

1/5 R.Warks

KEY

▭ †	British Cemetery
○	Walk: Start / Finish
•••••	Walk Route
～	British Line
⌐⌐⌐	German Line

0   0.5 mile

1 km

10 Gommecourt

'The whole thing is utterly devilish'

Rev. Julian Bickersteth, Chaplain, London Regiment

This walk covers the area of the attack by the 56th (London) and 46th (North Midland) Divisions

Points of interest:

- Trenches in Gommecourt Wood

- Experiences of a chaplain - Rev. Julian Bickersteth

- Cemetery in No Man's Land

Distance:	2 miles
Approximate time:	Over an hour

Park by the church at Gommecourt. 50.140445, 2.643629 With your back to the church go right, walk past the Mairie where you will see a small plaque in memory of the 1/ 5 North Staffs. Keep on the main road and take the first street on your right (Rue d'Hébuterne). Follow the road and note the evidence of a German trench system on your right in the wood. Stop 200 yards after leaving the edge of the wood (1)

You have crossed the German front line and are now in No Man's Land. The attack on Gommecourt was a diversionary tactic to drag German troops and guns away from the main area of the British offensive. Arguably the British battalions involved were 'cannon fodder' - little was expected of them but the slaughter was as bad as elsewhere on the Somme front

The effect of British shelling on Gommecourt Wood

No Man's Land was over 500 yards wide. The cemetery you can see on the far left is Gommecourt Cemetery No. 2 and stands in No Man's Land with the German line to the left and the British to the right. The 56th (London) Division attacked with four Battalions in the first wave

- **Return to the church and walk past it**

  You are by the 'Maze', the centre of the Kern Redoubt, a fortified position

- Take the farm track on your left beside the house with the Rue de la Chapelle sign. Follow it until you come to the edge of the wood. If possible, enter the meadow on the left and look along the fence into the wood

Gommecourt Wood New Cemetery

You can see clear evidence of German trenches here. The British trenches curved round the wood at an average distance of 330 yards from the Germans

- **Return to the main road, turn left and stop at the village road sign (2)**

You are on the German front line looking about 275 yards ahead to the British trenches. The first wave of the attack here involved four battalions of the 46th (North Midland) Division attacking to the right of the road. In front of the British trenches is

Gommecourt Wood New Cemetery (3)

Started:	After the War from 9 small burial grounds
No. of burials:	750 including nearly two thirds unidentified and 128 1st July of which 55 Sherwood Foresters and 49 North Staffs
Of interest:	The majority of burials are of men from the 46th (North Midland) Division. Lieutenant-Colonel Charles Boote, 5/ North Staffs (41) and 17 year old Private Clarence Armstrong, Sherwood Foresters, were killed. Note the plaque to the 46th Division on the right hand wall
Architect:	Sir Reginald Blomfield

Return to your car

CAR ITINERARY:

- Area south of Gommecourt Wood (1) 50.134192, 2.644361
- View of No Man's Land north of the wood (2) 50.142438, 2.641609
- Gommecourt Wood New Cemetery (3) 50.143394, 2.639473
- **Foncquevillers - plaque by the war memorial to officers and men of the 1/ 5 North Staffs (4) and the inscription 'One day we will understand'** 50.147770, 2.631820
- **Foncquevillers Military Cemetery (5)** 50.149239, 2.626079

Started by:	The French in 1915
No. of burials:	648 including 53 unidentified and 24 1st July of those 51 are 1/ 5 Notts and Derby (Sherwood Foresters). Also 5 2nd World War airmen, 4 Germans, 2 Chinese Labour Corps and one French civilian
Of interest:	5 captains including John Green VC, RAMC, attached 1/ 5 Notts and Derby (Sherwood Foresters); three 17 year olds, Privates Frank Blake and Charlie Tilley, Leicesters, and Thomas Riley, MGC. Bugler Arthur Morris, Notts and Derby (Sherwood Foresters). Note Plot 1 Row L is a mass grave of over 120

Architect: Sir Reginald Blomfield

- **Hébuterne village - plaque on church wall to the Bradford Pals** 50.124483, 2.637642

- **Hébuterne Military Cemetery** (6) 50.125155, 2.630478

Started: August 1915

No. of burials: Over 750 including nearly 50 unidentified and 92 1st July of those 72 are London Regiment. Also one German 1st July burial Wehrmann (Private) Paul Schuster

Of interest: One 17 year old private, Frank Corbell, London Regiment (Royal Fusiliers). Note mass grave Plot 4 Row M with over 60 burials

Architect: Sir Reginald Blomfield

- **Gommecourt British Cemetery No. 2** (7)   50.129388, 2.650054

Started: 1917 and expanded after the War from 3 cemeteries (Number 1, 3 and 4 but Number 2 was kept and expanded)

No. of burials: 1,357 including 682 unidentified and 253 1st July of which 239 are London Regiment

Of interest: It was the area from which the London Rangers attacked from newly dug trenches. Two brothers of the Queen Victoria's Rifles, Henry (25) and Philip (20) Bassett are buried next to each other. Drummer Herbert Sutcliffe, 1/ 5 Cheshire, and a 17 year old Private J. Sheldrick, London Regiment (Royal Fusiliers) are also to be found here

Architect: Sir Reginald Blomfield

- **Rossignol (Nightingale) Wood Cemetery** (8) 50.129629, 2.665503

Started: March 1917 west of the wood. German graves were added after the War

No. of burials: 111 of which 70 are German including 42 unidentified. There are 41 British of which two are unidentified. All six 1st July graves are Germans

Of interest: Unusual in that there are more German than British graves. The cemetery stands in the area of the German 2nd line

Architect: N.A. Rew

- **Owl Trench Cemetery** (9) 50.128646, 2.669313

There are no 1st July burials as the cemetery was started in a July 1916 German trench and was designed by N.A. Rew

1st July German grave in Rossignol Wood Cemetery

293

X Abbreviations and Glossary

- Administration — Name given at the time for logistics
- ADS — Advanced Dressing Station
- Artillery formation — Four units attacking in a diamond formation
- ASC — Army Service Corps: responsible for provision of ammunition, food and equipment, disparagingly known by the troops as 'Ally Sloper's Cavalry'. Ally Sloper was a lazy and scheming comic-book character
- Bangalore torpedoes — Sections of pipe with an explosive charge at the end
- BEF — British Expeditionary Force

Ranks in BEF:

Field Marshal	Commander-in-chief
General	i/c of an army of approximately 200,000
Lieutenant-General	Corps between 30,000 and 75,000
Major-General	Division of 20,000
Brigadier-General	Brigade of 4,000
Lieutenant-Colonel	Battalion of 1,000
Major	Second i/c a battalion
Captain	Company of 250
Lieutenant	Platoon of 60
2nd Lieutenant	Platoon of 60
Other ranks	Sergeants and corporals
No rank	Privates

Units:

Army	Consisting of three to five corps
Corps	Two to five divisions
Division	Three brigades
Brigade	Four battalions
Battalion	Four companies
Company	Four platoons
Platoon	Four sections of 15

- Bivouac — Temporary encampment
- Blighty — From the Hindustani word 'belati' originally used by British troops posted to India to mean 'home', hence to 'catch a blighty one' was soldiers' slang for being wounded badly enough to be sent home for further treatment
- Bombs (Mills) — British hand grenades
- Brevet rank — Reward for an officer's exceptional service. If there was a full complement of officers in his unit it would not be possible for him to be promoted so he could be given a brevet rank, i.e. one higher than his current rank but he would not be entitled to any extra pay
- BWD — Battalion War Diary
- CIGS — Chief of the Imperial Staff
- Close order — Infantry attack in a line
- Coy — Company

- C-in-C — Commander-in-Chief
- CO — Commanding Officer
- Creeping barrage — Curtain of shelling in front of advancing infantry, lifting at pre-arranged intervals
- CSM — Company Sergeant Major
- CWGC — See IWGC
- **Decorations:**
  CB — Companion of the Order of the Bath
  CMG — Companion of the Order of St. Michael and St. George awarded at the monarch's pleasure since 1818
  GCB — Knight Grand Cross of the Order of the Bath
  GCVO — Knight Grand Cross of the Royal Victorian Order
  CGSI — Knight Grand Commander of the Order of the Star of India
  KCB — Knight Commander of the Order of the Bath, it has been awarded 'at the Monarch's pleasure' since 1725
  KCMG — Knight Commander of the Order of St. Michael and St. George
- Dixies — Iron cooking utensils of Hindustani derivation 'degchi' for making tea or stew
- DLI — Durham Light Infantry
- 'Dug-out' — Retired officer who was recalled or volunteered for Great War action
- Enfilade fire — Machine-gun fire from the flanks along the line of attacking troops
- Extended order — Infantry attack in a line with 5 pace gaps between troops
- Fatigues — Chores, mostly heavy ones
- Fire and movement — Troops attack in open order in a dispersed formation
- German ranks:
Gefreiter	Equivalent to lance corporal/ corporal
Leutnant	2nd lieutenant
Oberleutnant	Lieutenant
Unteroffizier	Sergeant
- GHQ — General Headquarters
- GOC — General Officer Commanding a brigade, division, corps or army
- HLI — Highland Light Infantry
- HQ — Headquarters
- IR — German Infantry Regiment
- HE shells — High explosive shells
- IWGC — Imperial War Graves Commission established by Royal Charter in 1917. It was renamed the Commonwealth War Graves Commission on 1st April 1960
- IWM — Imperial War Museum
- Kite Balloon — Sausage-shaped balloons used by both sides for observation
- KOSB — King's Own Scottish Borderers
- KOYLI — King's Own Yorkshire Light Infantry
- Lewis Gun — Portable British machine-gun

- Maxim Gun   German machine-gun
- MCC   Marylebone Cricket Club founded in 1787
- MGC   Machine-Gun Corps

- **Medals:**

  DCM   Distinguished Conduct Medal awarded for 'gallantry in the field' to NCOs and privates

  DSO   Distinguished Service Order awarded to officers for 'distinguished service during active operations against the enemy'

  French: Croix de Guerre was created in 1915, it was awarded to French and Allied troops for cited acts of gallantry

                        Médaille Militaire awarded to all ranks for 'valour in combat or long service'

                        Légion d'Honneur was awarded for 'excellent civil or military conduct delivered upon official investigation'

  MC   Military Cross awarded for the first time in December 1914 to commissioned officers for 'gallantry during active operations against the enemy'

  MM   Military Medal awarded for 'acts of gallantry and devotion to duty under fire' to other ranks i.e. NCOs and privates. Instituted in 1916 but backdated to 1914

  VC   Victoria Cross was instituted in 1856 and was the highest award for 'most conspicuous bravery, or some daring or pre-eminent act of valour or self-sacrifice, or extreme devotion to duty in the presence of the enemy'

  VC and Bar   The second award of a medal i.e. VC and Bar means two VCs

- Mention in Despatches   When a soldier's gallantry is mentioned in an official report by a superior officer
- MO   Medical Officer
- Mopping up   Clearing the enemy out of captured trenches and dug-outs
- NAM   National Army Museum
- NCO   Non-Commissioned Officer e.g. corporals and sergeants
- NML   No Man's Land
- NPG   National Portrait Gallery
- OC   Officer Commanding companies and platoons
- Open order   Troops attack in a dispersed formation - also known as fire and movement
- OR   Other ranks: private soldiers or NCOs
- OTC   Officers' Training Corps established mostly in universities and Public Schools
- Parados   Mound/ sandbags on back wall of a trench
- Parapet   Top part of the front wall of a trench built up with sandbags
- Pickelhaube   German spiked helmet
- Pioneers   Manual labourers near front line- mostly trench digging
- Puttee   Long strip of cloth wound round lower leg for protection (from Hindustani word for bandage)

- RAMC — Royal Army Medical Corps: it numbered over 110,000 personnel by 1918- in soldiers' slang - 'Rats After Mouldy Cheese'
- RE — Royal Engineers
- Redan — Small salient on the front line
- Redoubt — Defensive position fortified by bunkers e.g. Schwaben Redoubt
- Regulars — Professional soldiers
- RFA — Royal Field Artillery
- RGA — Royal Garrison Artillery
- RHA — Royal Horse Artillery
- RFC — Royal Flying Corps which became the Royal Air Force on 1st April 1918
- RIR — German Reserve Infantry Regiment
- RSM — Regimental Sergeant-Major
- Runner — Soldier who acted as a messenger
- Russian sap — Tunnels dug under No Man's Land for various uses
- SAA — Small Arms Ammunition
- Screw picket — Corkscrew-like metal bar screwed into the ground with three or four loops through which barbed wire was pulled to establish a defensive wall in No Man's Land. The French called it a 'queue de cochon' (pigtail).
- Serjeant — This was the spelling used by the British Army until November 1953. During the War, British and New Zealander soldiers of this rank were spelled 'serjeant'. Canadian units, from 1 to 7/Canadian Infantry were spelled with a 'j' but with a 'g' for the others. The Rifles Regiment in the British Army still spell it with a 'j'. However, in personal diaries, war diaries and letters, 'sergeant' was the commonly used spelling
- SLI — Somerset Light Infantry
- Stand to — 'Stand to your arms'- a time in the trenches when soldiers had to be on alert e.g. at dawn or dusk
- Strafing/Strafe — To give the British a hard time from shelling (German: to punish)
- Tambour — Construction attached to a wall that projected outwards to enable enfilade defensive fire
- Territorials — Volunteer part-time soldiers
- Tommy/ Tommies — Slang for British soldiers
- Trench Mortar — Propels shells from a trench at high angles
- Very Pistol — Fired coloured flares for signalling and illumination
- Vigilant periscope — Small mirror placed at the end of a bayonet - of French design
- WFA — The Western Front Association
- 'Z' Day — Planned day of attack
- Zero Hour — Time given for the start of an attack

XI   Acknowledgements and Thanks

We have tried to acknowledge those who have assisted us and the authors and publications to which we have referred. We have been struck by the generosity of authors and owners of photographs and documents who have been most generous in allowing us to use their material. We have attempted to trace copyright holders with the occasional lack of success. If we have overlooked anyone, we offer our sincerest apologies and promise to include your name in the next edition.

- Maurice Bott for proof-reading and textual advice
- James Kerr for kind permission to include his excellent photographs
- Tom Morgan for his wholehearted support of the venture, providing us with information, answering our many questions and for offering many apposite comments on the text
- Monica Ory for proof-reading
- George Sayell for the huge amount of time spent in meticulously producing a superb set of maps
- Ruth Smith for another beautifully designed book (www.damsoncreative.co.uk)
- Mark Sykes for lending us his extensive World War 1 library and for spending four days trialling the 10 Walks and Drives

***

o   Ron Alpe - permission to use the diaries of Cyril José
o   Beryl Bone and Jill Slora - permission to use the diary and photograph of Arthur Seanor
o   Teddy Colligan for his help and advice on the 36th (Ulster) Division
o   Dahlia and Terry Harrison for help with the Royal Warwicks and nurses
o   David Hill who first brought to public attention the life history of Roy Mellor and for help with the Manchester Regiment
o   Helen Lenygon - research into soldiers' ancestry
o   Julia Margretts - kind permission to use Robert Gilson's drawing and the photograph of him from the Gilson Archive
o   Edwina Rees, Moseley History Society, for her work on the Birmingham Pals - 2nd Lieutenant William Furse and Corporal Arthur Plant
o   Karin Sheldon for allowing us to use the letters of her great uncle Roy Mellor and photographs of him
o   Catherine Smith, Charterhouse School Archives - details of Old Carthusians killed on 1st July 1916
o   Jean Edwards Stacey permission to use her *Memoirs of a Blue Puttee*
o   Mark Warby for providing Bruce Bairnsfather's sketch 'A Matter of Moment' and permission for its use from the Estate of Barbara Bruce Littlejohn
o   Peter Wilkinson of Bramcote School, Scarborough for help with the Francis Hicking story
o   The Great War Society and Trevor Poole for allowing us to disrupt a re-enactment day to take photographs for the front cover

We should like to thank the following for their kind permission to use documentary and photographic material:

➤ *Churchill Archives Centre, Churchill College, Cambridge*:   The Diaries of Sir Henry Rawlinson- thanks also to Andrew Rawlinson and the Rawlinson family.
The Bickersteth Diaries and Letters

➤ *Crowood Press and Sue and Phillip Simm:*   *My Bit* by George Ashurst

➤ *Durham County Record Office:* Reproduced by permission of the Trustees of the former DLI and Durham County Record Office:
Private William Roberts 18/ DLI   D/DLI 7/ 577 /2
Sergeant Charles Moss 18/ DLI   D/ DLI/ 7/ 478/ 4

➤ *Harper Collins Publishers Limited:*
Reprinted by permission- *To Fight Alongside Friends: The Great War Diaries of Charlie May*

➢ *Imperial War Museum:*
Bland, Captain A.E., 22/ Manchesters
Bloor, Captain W.H., RFA
Cousins, Private Jack 7/ Bedfords
Boswell, 2nd Lieutenant Percy, 8/ KOYLI
Crosse, Rev. E.D. Chaplain to 8 and 9/ Devons
Gavin-Jones, Lieutenant-Colonel A.N. 2/ Middlesex
Gosling, A.J., 6/ Royal Berks
Heaton, 2nd Lieutenant Eric, 16/ Middlesex
Hurst, Private Albert, 17/ Manchesters
Inglefield, F.L. 1/ 2 London
Kennedy, Private Pat, 18/ Manchesters
Miller, Private Ralph, 1/8 Royal Warwicks
Monckton, Lieutenant J.F.E. 1/ 2 London
Nevill, Captain 'Billie', 8/ East Surreys
Russell-Jones, Lieutenant E., 30th Trench Mortar Battery
Seneseall, Private W.J. 11/ Suffolks
Shearn, Captain E.D., 1/ Hants
Walton, Private James, 11/ Suffolks

➢ *Martin Middlebrook* for kindly allowing us to quote from *The First Day on the Somme*, the
    best reference book on the First Day of the Battle of the Somme:
Blenk, Musketier Karl IR169
Bury, Lance-Corporal, Accrington Pals
Cameron, Private F., 1/ King's Own Scottish Borderers
Dodd, Private, Tyneside Scottish
Essex Regimental History 'A trying day on the Somme'
Gathercole, Private, 11/ Suffolks
Gordon, Brigadier-General J.R., 70th Brigade
Lloyd, Corporal G.A., West Belfast Volunteers
Pearson, Private A.V., 15/ West Yorks
Pilcher, Lieutenant-General 17th (Northern) Division
Reid, Private J.S., 2/ Seaforths
Ritson, Colonel, Newcastle Commercials
Scheytt, Paul RIR 109
Stanley, Private E.C., 1/8 Royal Warwicks
Ulster Commander re. the address by Major-General Nugent to divisional troops
Waller, Private G.E., Glasgow Boys' Brigade
Wide, Private H.L., 9/ Devons

➢ *National Archives:* N.B. Document references for units can be found in the Index

Director, Medical Services IV Army   WO95/ 447
McCarthy, Emma Maude, War Diary of Matron-in-Chief, BEF, France and Flanders
    WO95/ 3989
Papers of Major-General E.J.M. Stuart-Wortley   WO138/ 29
1/8 Royal Warwicks- Colonel Ludlow's booklet about his son Stratford's death WO95/ 2365

➢ *National Library of Scotland:*
The Diaries of Earl Haig

➢ *Northumberland Fusiliers Museum:*
Letters of Alfred Kettle ALN FM 2006 6/5
Letters of J. Scollen   ALN   FM 2006 6/5
The Journal   ALN   FM 1123/2 re. Arthur Rutherford and Lieutenant Ritson

➢ *Orion Books:*
A Machine-Gun to Cambrai George Coppard (Macmillan 1986)
General Jack's Diary ed. John Terraine (Cassell   2000)

➢ *Rotherham Archives and Local Studies Service, York and Lancaster Regimental Collection:*
Kenneth Perkin Scrapbook : 578-K/8/2/750
Leonard Duke: 578/ K/812/880:
2nd Lieutenant Sam Oakes: 78/K/812/322
Major Alfred Plackett: 578-K/7/7/3/3/6
Reference to use of pigeons as message carriers
Sheffield Telegraph: 30.6.1917

➢ *Royal Highland Fusiliers Museum:*
History of 16/ Highland Light Infantry and The Outpost

➢ *Jack Sheldon:* for kind permission to use material from *The German Army on the Somme 1914-1916 re:*

Frick, Leutnant Alfred
Gerster, Leutnant
Hensel, Hauptmann
Hinkel , Unteroffizier, RIR 99
Lais, Unteroffizier Otto, RIR 169
Lipmann, Josef, 2/ Royal Fusiliers
RIR 119 War Diary
Stadelbacher and Schusele
Wheat, Private, interrogation of, 5/ N Staffs

and references: a) to British soldiers beginning to shave after capture
                b) charcoal burners being employed in the trenches
                c) MG 9 in the Brewery position firing 18,000 rounds

➢ *Somerset Archives:*

The Diaries of Arthur Cook: DD/ SLI/ 17/ 1/ 40 and DD/ SLI/ 17/ 1/40
Photograph of Arthur Cook MG 3727a
Diary of Captain Prideaux DD/ SLI/ 16/2/11 and 17/ 1/45

➢ *Surrey History Centre:*

'The Surreys Play the Game"' by R. Caton Woodville, published in the Illustrated London News, 27th July 1916 (Incorrectly captioned as occurring at Contalmaison) ESR/25/NEVI/3
Colonel Treeby, displaying the football to the assembled ranks ESR/1/12/12
Captain W.P. 'Billie' Nevill in the trenches ESR/25/NEVI/1

➢ *Websites*:

www.cwgc.org (Commonwealth War Graves Commission)
www.hellfirecorner.co.uk   (Tom Morgan)
www.longlongtrail.co.uk   (Chris Baker)
www.pals.org

Bibliography

Ackerley, J.R. *My Father and Myself   The Bodley Head*   1968
Aggett, W.J.P.   *The Bloody Eleventh*   The Devon and Dorset Regiment   1995
An der Somme   R. Piper and Co. Verlag   Munich   1917
Appleton, Edith   *A Nurse at the Front*   Simon and Schuster   2012
Ashurst, George   *My Bit*   Crowood Press   1987
Bailey, Sergeant O.F. and Hollier, Sergeant H.M.   *The Kensingtons 13th London Regiment*   Regimental Old Comrades' Association   1935

Ball, Tony *Over the Top* Stand To! No. 103 The Western Front Association

Barton, Peter *The Somme* Constable 2011

Bickersteth Diaries 1914-1918 Leo Cooper 1998

Billie The Nevill Letters 1914-1916 Ruth Elwin Harris The Naval and Military Press 2003

Brown, Malcolm *Somme* Sidgwick & Jackson 1996

Carter, Terry *The Birmingham Pals* Pen and Sword 1997

Carton de Wiart, Sir Adrian *Happy Odyssey* Jonathan Cape 1950

Cave, Joy B. *What Became of Corporal Pittman* Breakwater Books Ltd. Newfoundland 1976

Cave, Nigel *Beaumont Hamel* Leo Cooper 1994

Cave, Nigel *Gommecourt* Leo Cooper 1998

Cave, Nigel and Horsfall, Jack *Serre* Leo Cooper 1999

Chapman, Guy (Ed.) *Vain Glory* Cassell 1968

Chasseaud, Peter *Mapping the First World War* Collins 2013

Clark, David *The Seventeenth Highland Light Infantry* Glasgow 1920

Congreve, Billy *Armageddon Road (A VC's Diary)* William Kimber 1982

Coppard, George *With a Machine Gun to Cambrai* Macmillan 1986

Crozier, Brigadier-General Frank *A Brass Hat in No Man's Land* Gliddon Books 1989 (First published 1930)

Crozier, Brigadier-General Frank *The Men I Killed* Michael Joseph 1937

Devereux, Joe *A Singular Day on the Somme The Casualties of the Liverpool Pals on 1 July, 1916* Printsat 2013

Donovan, Tom *The Hazy Red Hell Fighting Experiences on the Western Front 1914-18* BCA 1999

Dorset Echo The Kaisers pre-war Dorset residency 1st August 2014

Douglas Haig's Great Push Hutchinson and Co. 1916/1917

Douie, Charles *The Weary Road* John Murray 1929

Duffy, Christopher *Through German Eyes: The British and the Somme 1916* Weidenfeld and Nicolson 2006

Dugmore, Captain A. Radclyffe *When the Somme Ran Red* George H. Doran 1918

Dunn, J.C. *The War the Infantry Knew 1914-1919* Abacus 1994

Edmonds, Brigadier-General J.E. *Official History of the Great War Vol 1 1916* 1931

Elwin Harris, Ruth *Billie The Nevill Letters 1914-1916* Naval and Military 2003

Farrar-Hockley, Colonel A.H. *The Somme* Batsford 1964

Fraser-Tytler, Lieutenant-Colonel Neil *Field Guns in France* 1929

Garth, John *Tolkien and the Great War* Harper Collins 2003

Gilbert, Martin *Somme Heroism and Horror of War* John Murray 2006

Glasgow Herald 28th November 1916

Gliddon, Gerald *VCs of the First World War The Somme* Sutton 1994

Goodwin, Albert *Diary 1883-1927* Privately published

Haig, Douglas *War Diaries and Letters 1914-1918* Edited Gary Sheffield and John Bourne Weidenfeld and Nicolson 2005

Hamilton, Andrew and Reed, Alan *Meet at Dawn, Unarmed* Dene House 2009

Hamilton, Andrew and Reed, Alan *Stolen Lives Individual Tragedies of the Great War* Dene House 2014

Herwig, Holger *The First World War- Germany and Austria-Hungary* Arnold 1997

Higgins, Thomas James *Tommy at Gommecourt* ed. Alan Henry Higgins

Hill, David *For King's and Country* Chameleon Press 2003

Holmes, Richard *Tommy* Harper Collins 2004

Holt, Major and Mrs. *Battlefield Guide to the Somme* Leo Cooper 2000

Jack, James *General Jack's Diary* ed. John Terraine Cassell 2000

Jackson, Andrew C. *The Accrington Pals- re. Reginald St. John Battersby*

Jesuan News Spring 2014

Le Miroir no. 138 July 1916

Levine, Joshua *Forgotten Voices of the Somme* Ebury Press 2008

Lewis, Cecil *Sagittarius Rising* Greenhill Books 1993 (first published 1936)

Lewis-Stempel, Lewis *Six Weeks* Weidenfeld and Nicolson 2010

Lincolnshire Echo Thursday 13th August 2015 Dr. Andrew Jackson *Lincolnshire Co-op at War*

Luard, Kate *Unknown Warriors* Chatto and Windus 1930

Macdonald, Lyn *Somme* Macmillan 1983

Mace, Martin and Grehan, John *Slaughter on the Somme 1 July 1916* Pen and Sword Military 2013

Maddocks, Graham *Montauban* Leo Cooper 1999

Masefield, John *The Old Front Line* Pen and Sword 2006

Maurice, Major-General Sir Frederick (ed.) *Soldier, Artist, Sportsman The Life of Lord Rawlinson of Trent* Houghton Mifflin 1928

May, Charles *To Fight Alongside Friends First World War Diary of Charles May* Ed. David Crane William Collins 2014

Mayhew, Emily *Wounded* Vintage 2014

McCarthy, Chris *The Somme: The day-by-day account* Brockhampton Press 1993

Meeres, Charles *I survived the Somme* Amberley 2013

Messenger, Charles *Broken Sword The Tumultuous Life of General Frank Crozier* Pen and Sword 2013

Middlebrook, Martin *The First Day on the Somme* Allen Lane 1971

Middlebrook, Martin and Mary *The Middlebrook Guide to the Somme Battlefields* Viking 1991

Moynihan, Michael (Ed.) *People at War 1914-18* David and Charles 1988

Neillands, Robin *The Great War Generals on the Western Front* Robinson Publishing 1999

Passingham, Ian *All the Kaiser's Men* Sutton 2003

Philpott, William *Bloody Victory The Sacrifice of the Somme* Little, Brown 2009

Pope, Stephen and Wheal, Elizabeth-Anne *Dictionary of the First World War* Pen and Sword 2003

Prior, Robin and Wilson, Trevor *The Somme* University of South Wales Press 2006

Read, I.L. *Of Those We Loved* Pentland Press 1994

Reed, Paul *Walking the Somme* Leo Cooper 1997

Richardson, Neil *A Coward if I Return Stories of Irishmen in World War 1* O'Brien 2010

Robertson, Sir William *The Military Correspondence of Field Marshal C.I.G.S. 1915 - 1918* ed. David Woodward The Army Records Society 1989

Royal Hampshire Trust *Regimental Journal* 1921

Seldon, Anthony and Walsh, David *Public Schools and the Great War* Pen and Sword 2013

Sheffield, Gary *The Chief Douglas Haig and The British Army* Aurum Press 2011

Sheffield, Gary *The Somme* Cassell 2003

Sheldon, Jack *The German Army on the Somme 1914-1916* Pen and Sword 2005

Sheldon, Jack *The Germans at Beaumont Hamel* Pen and Sword 2006

Sheldon, Jack *The Germans at Thiepval* Pen and Sword 2006

Shephard, Ernest *A Sergeant-Major's War* Crowood Press 1987

Simkins, Peter *The First World War: The Western Front 1914-1916* Osprey 2002

Slowe, Peter and Woods, Richard *Fields of Death Battle Scenes of the First World War* Robert Hale 1986

Smith, Aubrey (A. Rifleman) *Four Years on the Western Front* Odhams Press 1922

Smither, R. (Ed.) *The Battles of the Somme and Ancre* DD Video 1993

Stacey, A.J. and Stacey, Jean Edwards *Memoirs of a Blue Puttee* D.R.C. Publishers, St. John's Newfoundland 2002

Stedman, Michael *Thiepval* Leo Cooper 1995

Stedman, Michael *La Boisselle-Ovillers* Leo Cooper 1997

Stedman, Michael *Fricourt-Mametz* Leo Cooper 1997

Storer, Jackie *Hidden Stories of the First World War* The British Library 2014

Terraine, John *White Heat: The New Warfare 1914-18* Book Club Associates 1982

Times, The *History of the War* Volume IX 1916

Turner, William *Accrington Pals* Leo Cooper 1998

Turner, P.W. and Haigh, R.H. *Not for Glory The Story of Gilbert Hall of 13/ Yorks &Lancs* Pergamon 1969

Van Emden, Richard *Boy Soldiers of the Great War* Headline 2005

War Studies, University of Birmingham *Lions led by Donkeys* 2015

Westlake, Ray *British Battalions on the Somme* Leo Cooper 1994

Whitehead, Ian *Doctors in the Great War* Leo Cooper 1999

Wilkinson, Ronie *Pals on the Somme 1916* Pen and Sword Military 1994

World War I Document Archive *The Daily Telegraph Affair* 2009

www.pals.org.uk/battersby 2013

Zeepvat, Charlotte *Before Action* Pen and Sword 2015

XII   Index

There are main headings for:

- Architects of Cemeteries and Memorials
- Battles
- Cemeteries and Memorials
- Medals/ Orders
- Newspapers/ Periodicals/ Memorial books
- Places in Belgium, France, Somme, U.K. and elsewhere
- Units/ Regiments
- Schools
- Soldiers
- Universities and Colleges

Names highlighted below are featured in Chapter III 'Zero Hour'

Thiepval Memorial to the Missing of the Somme

Lochnagar Crater – note the white markings on the other side of the road which were the German trenches   J Kerr

Railway Hollow Cemetery then and now   *J Kerr* *(colour photo)*